This *Book*

was

Donated By

the estate of
Fred Zinnemann

Date July 2001

Guts & Glory

★ ★ ★ GREAT AMERICAN WAR MOVIES

If you glorify war
you create a climate for more wars.

—Arthur Hiller,
director of
The Americanization of Emily

Guts & Glory

★ ★ ★ **GREAT AMERICAN WAR MOVIES**

Lawrence H. Suid

▲
▼▼

Addison-Wesley Publishing Company

Reading, Massachusetts · Menlo Park, California
London · Amsterdam · Don Mills, Ontario · Sydney

Library of Congress Cataloging in Publication Data
Suid, Lawrence H
    Guts and glory.

    Includes index.
    1. War films—History and criticism. 2. Moving-pic-
tures—United States. I. Title.
PN1995.9.W3S9   791.43'0909'3   77-92162
ISBN 0-201-07488-5
ISBN 0-201-07489-3 pbk.

ISBN 0-201-07488-5-H
ISBN 0-201-07489-3-P
ABCDEFGHIJK-HA-798

To my parents,

the best patrons
an author ever had

CONTENTS

★

ACKNOWLEDGEMENTS

★

It would take a whole chapter, if not a second volume to thank everyone who has made this book possible. However, the dedication, though brief, contains my largest thanks. Without my parents' support in all ways for the last two-and-a-half years, the book would not have been written.

My thanks to Donald Baruch may confirm the feelings of some readers that he influenced my views of the Pentagon and its relationship with the film industry and so gave the book a pro-military bias. If Mr. Baruch or Norm Hatch, chief of the Audio/Visual Division of the Defense Department's Public Affairs office, had once attempted to impose their ideas on my work, there would be no acknowledgement. In fact, the book would have been difficult if not impossible to write without Mr. Baruch's information, suggestions, and continuing patience. He knows more about the subject of military assistance to the film industry than any other person. But this acknowledgement and thanks is given less for his information than for his scrupulous refusal to tell me how to write the book. His advice was always of a factual nature; his suggestions for improving the manuscript always dealt with style and detail rather than interpretation or conclusion.

My initial interview with Mr. Baruch was the first of more than 300 separate interviews with people in the film industry, the media, and the military. These interviews make up the basic source material for this book. To thank each person would be impossible. To thank even those whose interviews were used in the book or those who went out of their way to talk to me would also be impossible. Nor can I explain in a few words why so many people now or formerly connected with the film industry were so willing to be interviewed. Perhaps they recognized that their information should be preserved, and I showed up at the right time and place. Seldom did I have to push people for interviews. To those very few I did impose upon—Mervyn LeRoy, General Curtis LeMay, General Lauris Norstad—I can only say that the interviews were extremely helpful to me and I appreciate their assistance.

While I cannot thank everyone, I must single out one person not only for direct thanks, but perhaps to represent all the others who helped make the

Acknowledgements book possible. Fred Zinnemann was in the process of moving from Los Angeles to England when I first approached him, but he found time to provide me with one of my key interviews. More than that, he has continued to respond to my letters with additional help despite his involvement in making *Julia*. His interest in my project provided encouragement at times when the work went slowly. There is probably no way to adequately thank him.

It is easy to sound like a broken record trying to thank Mr. Zinnemann, Edmund North, Frank McCarthy, Daniel Taradash, George C. Scott, James Harris, and others for responding to requests for information and for commenting on the manuscript. But how does one thank someone like Andrew Marton for two interviews, comments on the manuscript, and lending his personal photographs to help illustrate the book?

People in the film industry are accustomed to interviews and requests for information. But the military people to whom I talked, the technical advisors in particular, were often retired and had nothing to be gained from talking to a researcher. Yet, with few exceptions, men and women from all branches of the armed forces willingly told me about their film experiences. In most cases, since it was their only involvement with Hollywood, their stories remained vivid, complete, and accurate. Like the film people, military people have gone far beyond the call of duty in providing information, photographs, and reviews of parts of the manuscript to insure accuracy, but without imposing their own interpretations. Admiral Lewis Parks called long distance to correct errors, Admiral James Shaw allowed me into the privacy of his island home in Maine, Captain Slade Cutter provided hospitality for a tired traveler, John Eisenhower talked about his "dad" over lunch in Valley Forge—these and many, many others have all helped make the book possible.

I am also indebted to the American Council of Learned Societies for the grant that made my second research trip to California possible.

Later on came those who read the manuscript for style and clarity. My brother Murray was perhaps my severest critic; his suggestions were not only appreciated but improved every chapter. And his encouragement was ever constant. The staff of Addison-Wesley deserve special thanks not only for their fine editing but also for tolerating many delays in the interest of a more complete and accurate presentation. And, given the way the book was put together, Constance Bourke, my copy editor, deserves a medal.

Two other people must be thanked even though their contribution was less direct. Dr. Cramer, who has followed my development as a writer and scholar for more years than either of us probably care to remember, has served as a model in my research and writing. More than that, he has been a friend, some-

Acknowledgements

one I could turn to when I needed to talk. Also I must thank Gertrude Weiner for giving me a home away from home during the time I spent in Boston completing the book. She made me feel welcome, and by listening to my problems, literary and otherwise, helped immeasurably to get the words on paper.

Finally, without Dent, there would have been no book.

PREFACE

★

Until the early 1960s, most Americans perceived the nation's military as an all-conquering and infallible force for good in the world. Conveyed in history books, popular literature, and the mass media, this image originated in Washington's victory over the British in the Revolution and received its highest expression in the military's overwhelming success in World War II. If Korea did not prove to be another smashing conquest, most people believed the fault lay with the politicians in Washington rather than the armed forces in combat. Consequently, the military retained its positive image throughout the 1950s.

During the 1960s, however, the nation's perception of its armed forces underwent a profound transformation. As the victories of the Second World War receded from memory and the 1962 Cuban missile crisis threatened the American people with nuclear holocaust, disenchantment with things military began to develop. The escalation of the Vietnam War and the concurrent rise of the antiwar movement after 1965 accelerated the criticism of the armed forces in the print and visual media.

Tet, the My Lai massacre, and the ultimate realization that the nation had in fact been defeated in Vietnam left the old military image in disrepair. Since the end of that war, the Pentagon has launched a massive public relations campaign to reestablish a positive perception of the armed forces as part of the nation's effort to build an all-volunteer military. The form this image will take remains to be seen.

Guts & Glory focuses on the creation of the American military image in one medium—the Hollywood feature film. The book is not a definitive history of the relationship between the film industry and the armed forces. Nevertheless, that relationship forms a framework in which to study the vision of an all-powerful, all-conquering armed force and of the heroic men who fought and won America's battles.

The book does not question the legitimacy of the military's public relations efforts—Congress has legislated such a function. The book does not deal with the cost of military assistance to filmmakers. Government regulations state that assistance must be at no cost to the taxpayer. The degree to which the military adheres to this regulation is probably not measurable. In any event, it is clear that cooperating on commercial films is less expensive for the military than producing its own "message" movies. More important, commercial films are far more effective in reaching large audiences than service-produced documentaries, which have a relatively limited distribution.

The book does not deal in any significant manner with military comedies or musicals with a military background, films which seldom contain even an illusion of military reality. Instead, *Guts & Glory* concentrates on war movies, or movies about noncombat military situations. For the purposes of this study, a war movie is defined as one in which men are portrayed in battle in a recognizable military action or in which they are directly or indirectly influenced by actual combat. A military movie is defined as one in which military men are portrayed in training situations during peacetime or performing duties intended to preserve the peace.

Most films discussed in this book received armed forces assistance during their production. But the book also examines movies that did not receive cooperation. In considering these films, the book analyzes the reasons why the armed forces did not extend assistance and looks at the images of the military they present in comparison to the images of the armed forces in assisted movies.

Essentially, the book examines the development of the military image in Hollywood films. In doing so, it necessarily considers how the American people perceived that image, since research for the book makes it clear that sixty years of war movies have profoundly influenced the nation's ideas about the military and the American combat experience.

These perceptions of an always-victorious armed force may have prevented people from asking, during the period of U.S. escalation in Vietnam, whether the military could in fact succeed there. Such a hypothesis does not provide a complete explanation of how the American people came to find themselves trapped in the quagmire that Vietnam became. Nevertheless, the research on which this book is based suggests that without the consistently positive image of the American military on movie screens, the nation would probably have been more skeptical of General Westmoreland's claim that the light was at the end of the tunnel in Vietnam.

Guts & Glory may thus provide some insights into the impact war movies have had on the nation. It also examines the paradox of Hollywood's efforts to make antiwar statements in the context of combat and military films. At the same time, the book can be read simply as a story about war movies, how they are made, and what they are about. Hopefully, it also makes observations about Hollywood as an industry and about movies as art and as entertainment.

A good movie, whatever the genre, should make a comment on the human condition by telling a story with a beginning, middle, and end. Further, a great film should be able to stand by itself as a complete entity—independent of its original source. To succeed as art and as entertainment, a movie should tell a story about people with whom the audience can empathize.

Most war films, in contrast, attempt to create their dramatic impact through noise, spectacular combat scenes, and violence. Since most Americans like escapist entertainment in the form of action and adventure more than social commentary, the war film has remained, along with the Western, the most enduring of Hollywood genres. But few war films have become works of art.

Consequently, *Guts & Glory* does not consider the dramatic quality of the movies under discussion except as that quality may affect the image of the military. Instead, it describes how the nation perceived the military establishment until the early 1960s, how filmmakers began to present a new image of the armed forces even before the Vietnam War became a national concern, and how that war and subsequent peace have combined, in Hollywood films of the 1970s, to change the old image of the American military.

Washington, D.C.
March 1978

L.H.S.

INTRODUCTION

★

by Charles Champlin

Film Critic of the *Los Angeles Times*

Every day during the summer and early fall of 1977 I looked at the movies made during and about World War II. I was writing the brief narration for a two-hour television special, awkwardly titled "Oscar Presents the War Movies and John Wayne," with that pre-eminent warrior as the principal host. The brilliant and indefatigable film editors had chosen significant moments from more than 350 movies (104 of them were represented in the program as it was finally assembled), reflecting everything from pre-war innocence to wartime zeal to postwar disillusion.

Through the magic of video cassettes I ran those dozens of hours of excerpts in my living room in the peaceful quiet of those warm and sunstruck mornings. The accidents of compilation made for some almost surrealistic sequences: Abbott and Costello, signing up for the Army instead of (as they thought) a raffle, yielded to John Huston's footsoldiers fighting and dying at San Pietro, and then Lucille Ball lifted a welder's mask at her shipyard job, and Irene Dunne sang "I'll Get By" to Spencer Tracy to a wistful harmonica accompaniment (watch that one dry-eyed if you can; I couldn't), and James Whitmore led his battered but proud platoon, counting cadence, back for a rest as fresh troops marched in to carry on the struggle.

It became an extraordinary cram course in a special segment of film history. And for all the jumbled presentation, the excerpts sorted themselves out, as the special ultimately did, into a chronicle, not only of the progress of the war from Pearl Harbor to VJ Day but also of the evolution of our ideas about the war, about all war, about the world.

Guts & Glory examines a selection of war movies from 1915 to the present—how they came to be made, who made them, and what the movies said (or didn't say) about war and battle and those who fought and those who stood and waited. It is a book that needed to be done, and Suid has done it fully and well, with scrupulous fairness. Indeed, the book illuminates a part of the social history of our times, and it documents not only the growing freedom and sophistication of the movies as a telling medium but also the changing attitudes of the movies toward war (mirroring national attitudes, though with some delay and some reticence). It is a book that evokes both memory and thought. It brings back the past, and, equally, gives it a fresh and useful perspective.

Of course, there is always more mediocre art and bad art than great art in any form at any time, and the worst of the war movies were really awful, technically and creatively. The backlot jungles and the miniature planes and the sea battles in the studio tank rippling with manmade waves looked all too exactly like what they were. But the shabbier deceptions had to do with human beings—the phony heroics, the upper lips stiff as petrified wood, the happy endings, with the bestial enemy mowed down in glee. It was patriotic gore at its least imaginative, and no wonder the troops in the field hooted it off the portable screens and demanded dancing girls and romance.

A lot of *that* rated its own hoots. In fact, Hollywood at its most self-congratulatory had a way of patronizing our boys in service that brings on toothache if you watch it now.

But that was the worst of it, and the heaviest, corniest war films came and went early. Even now the best of the wartime movies are deeply affecting to watch: *Cry Havoc*, about the nurses trapped on Bataan, John Garfield blinded in *Pride of the Marines*, Humphrey Bogart saying goodbye to dead comrades in *Action in the North Atlantic*, William Wellman's tribute to Ernie Pyle and the infantryman in *The Story of GI Joe*.

By the end of World War II, movies about the war already had a deeper resonance, were giving a truer account of the fear, the loneliness (including the loneliness of command), the confusion, the misery, and the sobering realization that the enemy who shot at you was not so much a beast as another man who marched to a different rhetoric.

The harsher cynicism came still later, and a retrospective realism that discovered bigotry in the ranks (*Home of the Brave*) and incompetence in the leadership (*Catch-22*). Some of these later films found as much profiteering and opportunism as patriotism and saw war as an exercise in folly and futility, a spectacle both lethal and absurd.

Now, more than 30 years afterward, World War II has become an object of memory, its crueller truths softened by time and by nostalgia for a conflict whose issues and dangers were sharp and clear (and have stayed so, despite the cynicism and the reconsiderations).

World War II is now a safe source of derring-do adventures (*Where Eagles Dare*, or Robert Aldrich's cynical *The Dirty Dozen*), almost as remote from present reality as the western. *Midway*, with a mixture of its own footage, historical footage, and borrowings from *Tora! Tora! Tora!*, translated the past into a deafening (and commercially successful) comic strip.

Yet films like *Patton* and *MacArthur* and even Joseph Levine's splashy *A Bridge Too Far*, with its star cameos, proved that a balance could be struck between gaudy fireworks and the bloody truth that war is hellish and ugly. They explored the complexity of complex leaders, avoiding both hero worship and ruthless demythologizing—even leaving open the question whether the film was pro-war or anti-war, hawkish or dovelike.

And now, once more, Hollywood is met on the battlegrounds, this time of Vietnam, a divisive struggle the studios had assiduously avoided, save for *The Green Berets*, because there seemed no way to do a film about the war that did not take a stand for or against the American presence, and either stand bound to be controversial. The industry wisdom generally is that a little controversy is good for the box office and a lot is not.

Already Francis Ford Coppola's *Apocalypse Now* brings new attention to the peculiar, edgy, and—until Lawrence Suid—little-studied relationship between the Hollywood establishment and the American defense establishment.

Most books on war movies have concentrated on casts and story lines, with much less attention to the problems of production, especially those of military cooperation. Yet the matter of assistance to the movies—granted or withheld—grows steadily more significant instead of less.

As Suid points out, the question of cooperation did not arise during World War II: Hollywood was conspicuously on the team, a vital force in the recruiting effort as well as in homefront and warfront morale. Through the 1950s, Hollywood was rarely in an adversary relationship to the services. That has changed, and movies like Stanley Kubrick's *Dr. Strangelove* (not that there are many remotely like it) are calculated to raise blood pressure rather than morale in the Pentagon.

But the consequence is that the Department of Defense sits uneasily but powerfully as a censoring force, giving or withholding its support on the basis of scripts that do or don't display a proper enthusiasm for the armed services. The influence may also be more subtle than a flat yes or no on cooperation. In one recent film, it was clear to me that one implicit message—that technology can fail, devastatingly—was significantly muted because it might have been embarrassing to the service that had cooperated so generously.

Much film history has been divided between the fan and the scholar, and while Larry Suid is undeniably a scholar, he writes with a lively appreciation of movies as movies as well as historical documents.

CHAPTER ONE

HOLLYWOOD AND THE MILITARY IMAGE: AN OVERVIEW

★

Why war movies? Why military movies? Why the attraction of war to the American people? General George Patton, through his film reincarnation George C. Scott, provided perhaps the quintessential explanation of the nation's continuing fascination with things military. Standing beneath a huge United States flag, Patton-Scott addressed his unpictured audience, the troops and, implicitly, the nation: "Men, all this stuff you've heard about America not wanting to fight, wanting to stay out of the war, is a lot of horsedung. Americans traditionally love to fight. All real Americans love the sting of battle. When you were kids you all admired the champion marble shooter, the fastest runner, the big league ballplayers, the toughest boxers. Americans love a winner and will not tolerate a loser. Americans play to win all the time. I wouldn't give a hoot in hell for a man who lost and laughed. That's why Americans have never lost, and will never lose a war, because the very thought of losing is hateful to Americans."[1]

Scott's monologue re-created in somewhat revised form Patton's exhortation to his officers and NCOs on the eve of the Normandy invasion. In classic terms, he glorified combat as the highest form of manliness: "You know, by God, I actually pity those poor bastards we're going up against—by God, I do. We're not just going to shoot the bastards. We're going to cut out their living

---

George C. Scott opens Patton *(1970) with a salute to his men and a monologue to the audience.*

1

guts and use them to grease the treads of our tanks. We're going to murder those lousy Hun bastards by the bushel." Urging his men not to worry about chickening out under fire, he assured them that they would all do their duty: "The Nazis are the enemy. Wade into them. Spill their blood. Shoot them in the belly. When you put your hand into a bunch of goo that a moment before was your best friend's face . . . you'll know what to do."

Patton then reminded his men that they were never to merely hold their positions: "We are advancing constantly and we're not interested in holding on to anything except the enemy. We're going to hold onto him by the nose and we're going to kick him in the ass. We're going to kick the hell out of him all the time, and we're going to go through him like crap through a goose." To Patton, these actions would not only assure victory, but would allow his men to return home with a sense of pride: "Thirty years from now, when you are sitting around your fireplace with your grandson on your knee and he asks you what did you do in the great World War II, you won't have to say, 'Well, I shoveled shit in Louisiana.' "

If Patton's espousal of combat had appeared on movie screens any time before the mid-1960s, few people would have raised dissenting voices. *Patton* would have undoubtedly been viewed as simply another Hollywood film glorifying America's success in battle. Only after the antiwar movement caused people to question the morality of combat could a film like *Patton* be interpreted by at least a portion of the populace as critical of the martial spirit of the American people.

Until the mid-1960s, most Americans saw their nation as peaceloving, involving itself in war only in self-defense and to uphold democratic ideals. To preach peace, however, has never committed the nation to a philosophy of nonviolence. The United States won its independence violently and has continued to exist and expand through selective but regular use of its military power, not always justified but usually approved by its people. Ultimately, and ironically, a government dedicated to returning the world to peace following two World Wars attempted to achieve that goal by unleashing the most terrible weapon mankind had ever seen. As a result, there remains an apparent contradiction between the great emphasis the United States has put on peace and the means it has used to preserve itself.

As long as the nation remained unvanquished on the battlefield, this ambiguity in its national character could be safely ignored. Into the 1960s, Hollywood did its part to show war in terms that Patton would have appreciated. Virtually all American films about war and the military followed the pattern established from the earliest days of the industry, showing only the glamorous side of combat—the excitement, the adventure, the camaraderie.

Lieutenant Hap Arnold at controls of the Army biplane he flew in The Military Scout *(1911), one of the first films in which an active duty serviceman participated.*

Henry B. Walthall as "The Little Colonel" in Birth of a Nation *(1915) prepares to lead a Confederate charge on Yankee fortifications.*

Battle was not always shown as pleasant, but the films made it clear that pain was necessary for ultimate victory. Not until the growing disenchantment with the Vietnam conflict did Americans begin to explore their long-standing love of the martial spirit and their previously unquestioned respect for the military establishment. In this new atmosphere, Patton's justification of war and the virtues of combat became subject to a new interpretation.

As the antiwar movement grew and television brought the realities of the Vietnam conflict into American homes during the dinner hour night after night, the film industry backed away from military subjects. Following the release of *Patton, M*A*S*H, Catch-22,* and *Tora! Tora! Tora!* during 1970, the production of war films virtually ceased. With few exceptions, the industry avoided even films that portrayed the armed forces unfavorably.

Not until 1976, after a six-year hiatus, did Hollywood again begin to release movies about war and the military. The United States was no longer waging a war that might require morale-boosting, patriotic films. Vietnam was finally fading from the American conscience, though the wounds from that divisive conflict had not yet completely healed. Supposedly, the trauma of the

King Vidor's army marches in the hills above Hollywood during the filming of **The Big Parade** (1925), the first major American film of the 1920s about World War I.

war experience had eroded Americans' interest in things military. Nevertheless, *Midway* became the sixth largest grossing film that year and the first of a growing number of movies that once again began exploring the American military experience.

Walter Mirisch, the producer of *Midway*, offered two reasons for making his film. He felt young people had a nostalgic interest in seeing the old planes shown in the movie. In addition, he wanted to give the American people a Bicentennial gift. In portraying the victory of the badly outnumbered American task force over the Japanese Armada, Mirisch believed he was reminding the nation of a glorious day. The comparison to the American experience in the

(Above) Lon Chaney, as the archetypal Marine sergeant, along with actors and U.S. Marines, film Tell It to the Marines (1927) at the Marine barracks in San Diego.

(Right) Swirling fighters grace the cover of a 1927 program for Wings, the first Hollywood movie about aerial combat.

Revolution was implicit. Americans had, at least in the past, emerged victorious from battle whatever the odds.

Like *Midway*, the films that soon followed it focused on World War II, both in Europe and in the Pacific. By the end of 1977, *The Eagle Has Landed, Cross of Iron, A Bridge Too Far,* and *MacArthur* had all appeared. Even a film depicting other worlds, *Star Wars*, which immediately began to challenge box-office records, contained many elements from the old World War II movies about air battles. George Lucas, the director, viewed combat footage from films such as *Twelve O'Clock High* and *The Memphis Belle* to help him create a sense of authenticity in the dogfight and bombing sequences in outer space.

Hollywood and the Military Image: An Overview

On television, old Hollywood war movies remained a staple item on the late show, while documentary series such as "The World At War" and the venerable "Victory At Sea" found regular time slots. At the same time, the networks turned out new productions portraying the military at work and play. "Baa, Baa Blacksheep" tried to combine elements of "Sergeant Bilko," *The Dirty Dozen*, and "M*A*S*H" into a glorification of the World War II flying exploits of Marine hero Pappy Boyington. "M*A*S*H" itself continued to be a ratings leader. In a more serious vein, NBC broadcast the miniseries "Once An Eagle," based on Anton Myrer's best-selling novel. Focusing on the "necessary" wars, the series followed American participation in both World Wars through the eyes of its major characters. Although the novel concluded with the early years of American involvement in Vietnam, the television version chose to ignore the less accepted wars in Korea and Vietnam.

By the middle of the decade, however, Vietnam and its aftermath had become the inspiration for a growing number of Hollywood productions. Francis Ford Coppola, the director of the two *Godfather* films, turned from violence in America to violence in Southeast Asia when he began work on *Apocalypse Now* in 1975. Originally expected to be released in 1977, it became the first major Hollywood film about Vietnam to go before the cameras since the release of John Wayne's *Green Berets* in 1968. While suffering through many difficul-

Gregory Peck, as General Frank Savage, in the cockpit of a B-17 bomber during the filming of Twelve O'Clock High *(1950).*

ties that delayed its release until 1978, *Apocalypse Now* was joined in production by *Rolling Thunder, Dog Soldiers, Tracks, Coming Home, The Deer Hunter, Heroes, The Boys in Company C,* and *Go Tell the Spartans*—all films about Vietnam and its returning veterans.

The renewed production of films with a military background again focused attention on one of Hollywood's most enduring genres. Like the western, war movies offer escapist entertainment that appeals to the viewer's most basic, most primitive instincts. According to Otto Preminger, "Whether it is a western or a war film, there's lots of action. You have undoubtedly some scenes where people fight and kill each other, where people run or drive fast tanks, ships. . . . It's the basic motion picture thing that one man runs after the other and whoever can run faster kills the other."[2] Films such as *Wings, Air Force, Bataan, Sands of Iwo Jima,* and *The Longest Day* have created the image of combat as exciting, as a place to prove masculinity, as a place to challenge death in a socially acceptable manner.

Probably the only significant difference between westerns and war films is that victory is more compelling in the latter, because the future of the nation is at stake rather than a mere wagon train, stagecoach, or town. So at least until the early 1960s, Hollywood combat pictures always ended in an American victory, with the American fighting man running faster than his enemy—whether German or Italian or Japanese. These screen victories reinforced the image of the American military as all-conquering, all-powerful, always right. Hollywood war films have, therefore, helped justify war and the use of violence to achieve national goals.

John Wayne discussing his portrayal of Sergeant Stryker with Leonard Fribourg, the Marine technical advisor for Sands of Iwo Jima (1949).

The contradiction between this justification and the existence of an idealized, peaceloving nation may help to explain the difficulty some Americans had in recognizing that the United States had embarked on a disastrous policy in Vietnam. Moreover, the paradox of glorifying war while opposing conflict finds no better expression than in Hollywood itself. Virtually all filmmakers claim to be against war and militarism. They maintain that their war movies portray antiwar messages, usually through the "war is hell" theme.

In many respects, *Patton* is the ultimate example of the filmmakers' efforts to convey an antiwar message. The movie contains a multiplicity of scenes of the horrors of war—the dead bodies, their mourning friends. Patton himself comments about the waste of lives of so many young men, yet he adds, "I love it. God help me, I do love it so,—more than my life!" For the most part, the film does portray war as exciting and romantic, as an escape from the mundane world and a chance to attempt great feats in the companionship of one's fellow man. Most important, the film ends on a note of victory and a scene of the living Patton.

In *Patton* there are no women to soothe the soldiers during their time away from battle. But in most war movies women exist as objects of men's pursuit, to provide calm moments during lulls in the high-risk adventure. Women may satisfy men's sexual needs but, in the end, cannot compete with the thrill, the challenge of facing possible death in combat. For the soldiers the excitement of war itself replaces their need for a woman's body. Recalling his wartime flying experience, which served as the basis for *Catch-22*, Joseph Heller recalled, "There's something sexual about being in a big plane, with a *big* gun and having *big* bombs to drop."[3] Pete Hammill, in commenting on the connection between violence and sex, recalled that while reporting on the war in Vietnam, he observed a sexual-like "euphoria" on soldiers' faces as they came out of combat.[4] Planes, bombs, guns, the destruction they cause, the very elements that filmmakers believe show the evil of war ultimately provide the attraction that makes war films so popular.

War films do more than serve as a means for vicariously experiencing the proximity of death, the romance, and the adventure of war. They offer the same appeal that war itself offers those who are involved in combat. In his autobiography, Leon Trotsky gives a classic explanation of this appeal in describing the celebrations in Vienna at the outbreak of World War I. He observes: "The people whose lives, day in and day out, pass in a monotony of hopelessness are many: they are the mainstay of modern society. The alarm of mobilization breaks into their lives like a promise: the familiar and long-hated is overthown, and the new and unusual reigns in its place. Changes still more incredible are in store for them in the future. For better or worse? For the better, of course—what can seem worse to [the ordinary person] than 'normal' conditions?"[5]

These "normal" conditions include wives and children. Men may love their families and their women but still feel tied down by the responsibilities of marriage. More than that, in psychosexual terms, women's greater capacities for sex can threaten men's security and ego. Military life and war offer a legitimate alternative to this threat. A soldier can do his duty to his family by being away from them, protecting them from outside danger. He then has the best of both worlds—a women when he wants her, masculine friendships, and the sexual release of combat.

David Halberstam, who observed military life firsthand in Vietnam, explained that "there are a lot of men in the military who are very good at what they do because they prefer it to the normality of life." According to the author of *The Best and the Brightest*, "They prefer danger and threat, dislocation, to what we would call normality. They don't really want to be at home." Halberstam concludes that war is liberating to these men. While they are heterosexual, they really don't like women; they replace sex with war.[6]

At least while attending war films, viewers experience the same escape that combat itself provides the participants. John Wayne and the military image he created in his many war movies offered and continue to offer viewers an alternative to their rather dull lives. In his films Wayne is seldom married, although he may have been and may even have a son whom he misses. Marriage, however, only interferes with his more important job of fighting to protect the nation. Often, as in *Sands of Iwo Jima*, Wayne has been rejected by a woman because of his commitment to the military. But he retains the memory of his one-time family. By identifying with this Wayne image, men can feel heroic, can have their home life, but can vicariously free themselves from home and responsibility.

Since half the movie-going population is female, filmmakers have, of course, included ingredients designed to appeal to women. The uniforms are colorful, the men are strong and attractive, the wait for their men is noble and patriotic. With very few exceptions, women in war films, apart from being convenient sex objects, have been willing martyrs waiting for the return of their husbands and boyfriends, ready to nurse them back to health if need be, but in all cases standing by them whatever injuries they have suffered. By clothing war in noble terms, filmmakers have given women a commitment to the successful outcome of the battle.

Combat has always been a relatively small part of military life—however much attention filmmakers have given it. Hollywood has regularly recognized the general appeal of the military by producing noncombat films about life in

Hollywood and the Military Image: An Overview

the service. Especially in the 1930s, as an escape from problems of the Depression, but also during other periods of peace as well as war itself, Hollywood has used the armed forces as the setting for musicals, comedies, and romances. For women, these films were little different from similar movies set in other milieus. For men, they showed the lighter side of military life, the fun of travel, the pursuit of women, the humor inherent in good fellowship. For filmmakers, military settings provided alternative locales in which to tell their stories, locales not experienced by the average person, and so offering added appeal.

Whether the setting has been peace or the most desperate combat, Hollywood has always believed that for military movies to succeed, they must have an authentic atmosphere. Over the years filmmakers have regularly sought assistance from the armed forces in the form of technical advice, men, and hardware. In turn, the military has seen the films as a superb public relations medium. Consequently, the services have always been careful to assist only on those movies that would benefit them by informing the public and the Congress of their activities, by aiding recruitment, and by boosting the morale of the officers and men who actually participated in the filming. Apart from saving Hollywood thousands of dollars and insuring visual accuracy, cooperation has enabled filmmakers to create the illusion of the proximity to death, dramatic action, exotic vistas, and romance, characteristics which contribute to the continued popularity of war films.

In addition to adding to the films' success, these combat sequences have offered Hollywood a socially acceptable means of bringing violence to the screen. Undoubtedly more people have died in war movies than in all the conflicts in which American servicemen have ever fought. While the Motion Picture Production Code Office has opposed mass slaughter on the screen, officials have always had a difficult time refusing to approve films in which violence was directed against the enemies of the United States. To be sure, requests to play down scenes of violence and death in war movies have been made over the years by both the military and the Code Office. The Navy Department, for example, asked MGM to delete repetitive scenes showing a sailor trapped in a flooding submarine in *Hell Below* (1933) because the sequence was "unduly oppressive."[7] For its part, the Code Office requested that Darryl Zanuck eliminate some of the blood from *The Longest Day* (1962). While recognizing that many men had died on D-Day, the Office felt that this aspect of the story should be minimized rather than stressed.[8]

Hollywood's special effects men have worked hard to make the violence as realistic as possible. For example, not satisfied with the way actors were "dying" during the filming of *Bataan* (1943), they tied ropes to the intended casualties and, on cue, jerked the men into the air to create the illusion of being

(Above) Darryl Zanuck re-creates Omaha Beach during the making of The Longest Day (1962).

(Left) German soldiers fighting off a combined French/American assault on the fortified Ouistreham Casino in The Longest Day.

The mock-up of the U.S.S. Arizona that Twentieth Century Fox built in Hawaii for Tora! Tora! Tora! It cost more than $1,000,000 and also represented the other battleships during the sneak attack on Pearl Harbor.

(Above) Director Franklin Schaffner and technical advisor Paul Harkins discussing the filming of the Battle of the Bulge sequence in Patton.

hit by bullets.[9] The greatest special effects achievements in creating violence on the screen have come not in "killing" individual soldiers, however, but in combat spectaculars ranging from *Birth of a Nation*, the first great war film, through the 1920s classics *The Big Parade* and *Wings* to the more recent *Tora! Tora! Tora!*, *Midway*, and *A Bridge Too Far*. In these films, meagre plots serve only to move the viewer towards the climactic scenes of death and destruction.

Hollywood's renewed production of war films in the mid-1970s may derive in part from its desire to portray violence on the screen without criticism. In recent years, excessive mayhem in movies and on television has come under increasing attack. Nevertheless, if surveys are any indication, bloodshed continues to be popular with audiences. Only in the war genre can filmmakers justify their use of violence in the name of patriotism and historical reality.

How closely the Hollywood image of war has ever approximated the reality of battle is another matter. Military men have always been divided as to the authenticity of combat scenes in war movies. General Maxwell Taylor has written that he stopped going to military films after a few early exposures because he found "little reality in the portrayal of war and military life, either in Hollywood or on TV."[10] On the other hand, General David Shoup, who won the Congressional Medal of Honor for action on Tarawa, thought the re-creation of the Tarawa landing in *Sands of Iwo Jima* was the Tarawa he remembered.[11] And General Paul Tibbets, for another, said that *Above and Beyond* (1952) accurately portrayed his experiences in training for and dropping the first atomic bomb on Hiroshima.[12]

Irrespective of whether the new wave of war films matches the authenticity of these earlier pictures, the post-Vietnam films contain for the most part a less worshipful attitude toward the military. From *Birth of a Nation* (1915) through *Patton* (1970), Hollywood films created an image of the American fighting man as brave, determined, and successful. Vietnam changed most people's perception of the military establishment. The recent Hollywood spectaculars about World War II may in some ways resemble the old-fashioned combat movies of the 1950s and early 1960s. But even *MacArthur* (1977), a respectful homage to the general's career, portrays his shortcomings—though in the end, he is depicted as successful in battle and respected by his country and peers.

Vietnam, in contrast, presents filmmakers no happy climaxes, no opportunity for military men to rhapsodize about their victories. The films about the Vietnam experience may show Americans winning a particular engagement, or they may even portray an individual fighting man doing his job in a professional manner. Nevertheless, Hollywood cannot interpret the war in Southeast Asia as another in a long line of glorious American victories in the name of freedom and the democratic way of life. Whether audiences will see films lacking this positive image as the continuation of the antiwar sentiment of the late 1960s or simply consider them an extension of the action-adventure war movies of the pre-Vietnam era remains to be determined.

In any event, war films will remain popular as long as men still love war itself above their own lives as Patton did, as long as men still find in war a unique confrontation with death, and as long as it reflects a pervasive sexuality. In his much-praised book *Dispatches*, based on his journalistic experiences in Vietnam, Michael Herr captures these twin emotions as well as any recent writer: " . . . . your senses working like strobes, free-falling all the way down to the essences and then flying out again in a rush to focus, like the first strong twinge of tripping after an infusion of psilocybin, reaching in at the point of calm and springing all the joy and all the dread ever known, *ever known by everyone who ever lived,* unutterable in its speeding brilliance, touching all the edges and then passing, as though it had all been controlled from the outside, by a god or by the moon. And every time you were so weary afterward, so empty of everything but being alive that you couldn't recall any of it, except to know it was like something else you had felt once before. It remained obscure for a long time, but after enough times the memory took shape and substance and finally revealed itself one afternoon during the breaking off of a firefight. It was the feeling you'd had when you were much, much younger and undressing a girl for the first time."[13]

War films can only create the illusion of such emotions. Nevertheless, their continued popularity over the years attests to the degree Hollywood has successfully captured the atmosphere of combat.

229-119

CHAPTER TWO

A STANDARD FOR THE FUTURE

Only in the few years following a major war has the film industry avoided combat and the military as subjects for its cameras. During World War I, movies such as *The Unbeliever* (1918), a story of Marines in training and combat, had found large, appreciative audiences. But with the cessation of hostilities, most Americans preferred not to dwell on the nation's participation in the Great War. As disillusionment with the peace settlement increased during the early 1920s, the isolationist impulse developed, and the armed services shrank in size. Nevertheless, war remained one of the subjects worthy of a major screen effort, waiting only for a good story and the proper moment to give the impetus for renewed production of combat movies.

The Big Parade

King Vidor, a young and promising director during the mid-twenties, originally thought it "would take ten years to evolve a true War Picture. Propaganda and the passions of the struggle blind the participants from seeing it sanely; then satiety and a cynical reaction follow, no less blinding or distorting." Because war was "a very human thing," he believed it would be a long time before its

Army troops, equipment and planes move to the "front" during the filming in Texas of The Big Parade.

human values became dominant and the rest sank into insignificance. By 1924, however, Vidor was seeking a worthy subject for his first major film, one that "comes to town and stays longer than a week." He suggested to Irving Thalberg, head of MGM, that "war, wheat, or steel" would provide a suitable subject.[1]

Thalberg dismissed steel and wheat, but asked if Vidor had a particular war story in mind. At the time Vidor had no clear concept but later recalled that he "wanted to make an honest war picture. Until then, they'd been all phoney, glorifying officers and warfare. There hadn't been a single picture showing the war from the viewpoint of ordinary soldiers and privates, not one that was really antiwar." He told Thalberg that he wanted to show the reactions of a typical young American who goes to war and reacts normally to all the things that happen to him.[2]

This approach interested the studio head, and he immediately directed MGM's Story Department to send Vidor all the synopses it could find of stories about World War I. According to Vidor, "they all looked the same after a while," and he told Thalberg that the stories had an "unreal, almost musical-comedy flavor about them" and so lacked any sense of the realism he envisioned for his film. He wanted the audience to "share the heart beats of the doughboy and his girl and mother and folks." Though Vidor did not want to ignore "the huge surrounding spectacle" of war, he did hope to show it through the eyes of the common soldier. In this kind of film, the viewer would see how the "human comedy emerges alongside the terrific tragedy. Poetry and romance, atmosphere, rhythm and tempo, take their due place."[3]

While Vidor continued to read story ideas at MGM, Thalberg went to New York, where he was impressed by *What Price Glory?*, which had just opened to "some of the wildest applause" Broadway had ever seen. He immediately hired Laurence Stallings, one of the co-authors, to work on a story with Vidor. The ex-Marine captain, who had lost a leg at Belleau Wood, arrived in Hollywood with a five-page story entitled "The Big Parade." His scenario focused on three young men—a millionaire's son, a riveter, and a bartender—who join the Army and become friends despite their divergent backgrounds. In France the rich doughboy falls in love with a French girl and loses a leg in battle; his two friends die in combat. Unlike most war stories, "The Big Parade" portrayed the lives of ordinary soldiers trying to survive in a situation not of their own making. Stallings had no glory-seeking heroes and no strutting officers winning the war by themselves. This was the sort of story Vidor had wanted, and the studio purchased it immediately.[4]

While providing additional material to fill out the screenplay, Stallings moved into Vidor's house. Vidor later recalled that Stallings "had more knowl-

edge to communicate—more knowledge for my purpose—than the Committee on Public Information's 750,000 feet of stored films through which my agent pored in Washington." Despite his obvious help to Vidor, the playwright had no desire to remain in Hollywood writing the screenplay. He soon headed back to New York accompanied by Vidor and a young studio writer, Harry Behn. After reminiscing with him on the trip across the country, and when they could catch up with him during the following week in New York, Vidor and Behn returned to Hollywood. Writing all the way back, they turned in a completed script three days after their arrival.[5]

Lieutenant Hap Arnold at controls of the Army biplane he flew in The Military Scout.

Vidor's next task was to re-create the authentic flavor of wartime Army life. Like virtually every maker of war movies over the years, he believed each detail had to be accurate, because so many men had taken part in the events he was portraying and could be harsh critics. Since he hadn't been in the war himself, Vidor spent hours viewing combat footage that the War Department provided. He also hired two ex-soldiers as technical advisors. In addition, during the course of shooting the film, Vidor often got firsthand information from unexpected sources. In trying to construct a number of German gun emplacements, for instance, he discovered that his technical advisors had only seen blown-up gun nests. A laborer listening to the discussion offered to describe the proper alignment. He had been a German noncom during the war and ended up commanding the German machine gun position in the film.[6]

When it came to shooting large-scale scenes of whole units of men advancing to the front, Vidor turned to the United States Army for assistance. Since the earliest days of the industry, the military had participated in movie making with advice, personnel, and equipment. As early as 1911, Hap Arnold, who later commanded the Air Force in Europe during World War II, picked up "a few extra dollars" by performing in a movie shot on Long Island. For *Birth of a Nation* (1915), D. W. Griffith asked West Point engineers for technical advice in preparing his Civil War battle sequences. The Military Academy even supplied some Civil War artillery pieces for close-up shots.[7]

D.W. Griffith stages the Battle of Antietam for The Birth of a Nation.

Griffith subsequently turned to the Army for more extensive assistance in filming *America*, his 1924 re-creation of the Revolutionary War. In response to his request, Secretary of War Weeks ordered the military to provide the director with every reasonable help. The Army loaned Griffith more than 1,000 cavalrymen and a military band to help stage the crucial battles of the War of Independence. Reportedly, the cavalry units loaned to him constituted the largest number ever assembled outside actual war maneuvers. The War Department justified its assistance by saying that the combat sequences gave Army observers the opportunity to study the Revolutionary War battles with a precision never before possible. According to Griffith, he received thousands of dollars worth of help because President Coolidge and Secretary Weeks believed the film would have a "wholesome and quieting effect" on the American people.[8]

Knowing about the military's earlier assistance, Vidor asked the Army for two hundred trucks, three to four thousand men, a hundred planes, and other equipment to help portray a large-scale troop movement to the front. When the War Department agreed, Vidor sent a film crew to Fort Sam Houston near San Antonio to shoot the needed scenes. Vidor had wanted the men and trucks to move in a straight line away from the camera and into the horizon with the planes flying over at a specific moment. Unfortunately, the assistant director got caught up in the Army's bureaucracy and, accepting the generals' claim that there were no long, straight roads in France, allowed the commanders to stage the maneuver on a curved road. While Vidor found the performance "magnificent," none of the twenty-five reels of film contained the effect he was seeking.[9]

To get the right shots, Vidor told Thalberg he wanted to go to Texas himself, find a straight road, and stage the march again. With permission from the studio head, the director went to Fort Sam Houston, found an appropriate road about twenty-five miles from the base, and told the commanding general he wanted to reshoot the maneuver there. Vidor naturally met with strong opposition because of the Army's original assistance and because of the distance the soldiers and equipment would have to travel to the new site. The director finally persuaded the commander to provide the additional assistance through sheer persistence, recalling, "I was firm about my request." By combining footage from both trips to Fort Sam Houston, Vidor was able to create the impression that he had received more assistance than the Army actually provided. In fact, the camera crew shot only one day on each trip to Texas and used several cameras in capturing the troop movements.[10]

While relatively limited in scope, the Army's assistance proved essential in enabling Vidor to give his film a feeling of openness and size. In acknowledging the importance of this cooperation, the director said the military "cannot be overpraised." Except for the scenes shot in Texas, however, Army help consisted only of a small amount of Signal Corps training and combat footage used to create a few battle sequences. Vidor filmed the remaining combat scenes in and around Los Angeles with most of the shooting taking place on a tract of land about as large as a city block.

All the "soldiers" in these scenes were extras, most of whom had served in the Army though not necessarily overseas. Their military experience saved the director the expense of training them to act like soldiers, something future filmmakers often had to do when using extras in their war movies. At the same time, Vidor had only a limited number of men and trucks at his disposal in Los Angeles. Consequently, to create the illusion of large troop movements, he had the men and trucks move in circles (out of camera range) to sustain the action for the desired length of time. More important, Vidor's immersion in the Signal Corps combat footage, his long discussions with Laurence Stallings, and the advice of his military advisors enabled him to produce the authentic atmosphere of combat in *The Big Parade*.[11]

On occasion, Vidor actually came closer to re-creating reality by ignoring the advice of his technical advisors. In one instance, he chose to photograph soldiers going into battle in columns of two and then had them fan out as they deployed for battle. The advisors argued that these maneuvers had never occurred in France, but Vidor used the scenes anyway. He "just figured that nobody could have seen the whole front." His feeling was later confirmed when he found several sequences in Signal Corps footage showing troops actually advancing in columns of twos. In another instance, Vidor ignored expert opinion and filmed the soldiers opening their ranks as they advanced into battle. In the titles, the director labeled the maneuver "Attack Formation." The War Department itself confirmed the accuracy of the action when it wrote to Vidor that everything in the completed movie was technically accurate.[12]

Although *The Big Parade* contained an essentially antiwar theme, Vidor said that the military never objected to the film's content. He personally thought the film had "an antiwar feeling, definitely. . . . But I don't know if you can call the whole film an antiwar film." Before it opened, he had "anticipated an attack from militarist factions. But there were none." The reverse proved to be the case. When one of the Du Ponts, the manufacturers of large amounts of war materials, visited the set during shooting, he liked what he saw so much that he told Vidor he would supply a tent in which to show the picture if exhibitors refused to handle it. The offer proved unnecessary. The film met with instant acclaim and box-office success.[13]

Even though Vidor wouldn't label his movie "antiwar" in its totality, he did create a feeling within the audience that war has few socially redeeming qualities. Because Vidor believed "war has always been a very human thing," he did not feel the Great War had been different from earlier conflicts. He saw it as the result of "a mixed-up sentiment," the culmination of a "long series of human misunderstandings." As a result, he observed: "When a nation or a people go to war, the people go and do not ask why. But in this last war they asked one question at all times. It was, 'Why do we have war?' " In developing that theme in his film, the director said he did not wish to appear as having taken a stand one way or another: "I certainly do not favor [war], but I would not set up a preachment against it. You might as well try to sweep Niagara backward as stop war when people start it. It bursts upon them, and must then be taken as a matter of consequence and a job that requires immediate attention and no argument."[14]

Vidor captured this feeling by focusing on the common soldiers to show "that all people concerned are affected alike, that they are just the same in habit and living, with similar hopes, loves, and ambitions." Moreover, none of his characters are heroes, not even the film's star, John Gilbert, who plays the millionaire's son. To Vidor the big message was that he "lost his leg instead of coming home a hero. . . . He laughed at anything heroic, overly patriotic." The director saw Gilbert as the common man, "neither a pacifist nor an over-patriot. He just went in and experienced what he experienced and then reacted. You couldn't call him an activist."[15]

Similarly, Vidor did not attempt to create an antiwar feeling by strewing
the screen with blood and gore to show that war is hell, as many filmmakers
have done over the years. By using violence in this manner, directors have
usually produced movies which suggest that war is an exciting adventure filled
with romance and good times. In contrast, Vidor pictured the unglamorous side
of combat. Gilbert's buddies die; he comes home with only one leg; and the girl
he left behind falls in love with another man. In itself, this plot twist is almost
unique in the history of war films. Even though Gilbert returns to France to
claim the girl he had fallen in love with, the audience comes away with the
impression that war offers few rewards. According to Vidor, in all Gilbert's
"war actions, all of the praise and the hospital bit and the killings of his
buddies, he is cynical about the war thing. It was a great adventure as far as
the girl goes, but not as far as the war goes."[16]

*D.W. Griffith talks to Jonathan Wainwright, mounted, who is about to lead a charge
during the filming at Fort Myer, Virginia, of* America *(1942).*

At night, American soldiers reach a German gun emplacement in The Big Parade.

Whatever effect the story had on the martial spirit of the audience, *The Big Parade* did attract record-breaking crowds because of Vidor's direction, the quality of the acting, and the authenticity of the combat sequences. According to the film critic of the *Boston Transcript*, *The Big Parade* gains "sweep and pathos and a certain boisterous humor through the directorial acumen of King Vidor. To watch it unroll is to realize anew all the shallow bombast, all the flatulency and all the saccharinity with which previous picture-makers have encumbered the trade of war." The writer noted that Stallings and Vidor "are not content with spectacle. They must have interludes of gusty and sentimental humor." He observed that scenes of the soldiers at rest, doing mundane tasks interspersed with moments of romance, followed by the "intense confusion of the moving up into the line," make the actual attack stand out "the more vividly."[17]

Not all critics found *The Big Parade* totally realistic, especially when compared to *What Price Glory?* One writer argued that Vidor's film was not the cinematic equivalent to Maxwell Anderson and Stallings' play: "There is in the picture none of the matter-of-fact bitterness, none of the professional disillusionment, little of the humdrum sordidness that characterizes the spoken play." Despite Vidor's intent to make a realistic movie, the critic further said that audiences would find "sentiment" in *The Big Parade* because filmmakers are "distrustful of too much realism." Nevertheless, he conceded that the film "goes farther toward honest naturalism than any preceding film of the German war. It indulges in a minimum of affect flagwaving and makes no bones about allowing the unpleasant to intrude."[18]

How close *The Big Parade* or any war movie can ever come to capturing the feel of combat has remained an area of dispute throughout the history of film-making. The *New York Times* critic felt Vidor's treatment of war was "so compelling and realistic that one feels impelled to approach a review of it with all

King Vidor talks to John Gilbert as the director prepares to film a scene from The Big Parade.

the respect it deserves, for as a motion picture it is something beyond the fondest dreams of most people. . . . The battle scenes excel anything that has been pictured on the screen and Mr. Vidor and his assistants have even seen fit to have the atmospheric effects as true as possible."[19]

The actors' commitment to the film greatly contributed to this feel of authenticity. In particular, John Gilbert changed his characterization from the "dandyisms" of his earlier roles to a down-to-earth doughboy. He refused to use make up and wore an ill-fitting uniform. Dirty fingernails and a sweaty, grimy face replaced the perfectly made-up character of his "great lover" roles. Although Gilbert at first had resisted this change, he became sold on this common man portrayal after seeing a few of the rushes. As a result, he became willing to work day and night on the film. Vidor recalled that after "rolling around in the French farmhouse mud in the daytime, he would crawl on his belly across No Man's Land by night." The director said the actors got their make up from the "muck. It was laid on with the trowel, not the paint brush."[20]

King Vidor in 1975.

These efforts by Vidor, his crew, and the actors produced a film that may not have been a literal reproduction of combat, but at least it created a superb illusion of war. The ultimate judges of authenticity, of course, were soldiers who were there, who rolled in the real mud and were maimed by the real bullets, the two million men Vidor intended to satisfy when he said, "I did all that was humanly possible to insure accuracy on this picture." An ex-sergeant who had been in the trenches agreed after seeing the movie: " . . . it is all there, good people—incredibly real, incredibly tragic, and therefore true to nature." Watching a scene in which the soldiers were eating, this veteran said he "could actually smell those beans and that amazing coffee, so useful in getting gravy or grease off your mess kit." To him, *The Big Parade* was "a war film. And when I say 'war' I do not mean a sham battle in the suburbs of Peekskill either. This means that some folk, and particularly our women folk, won't like it, but it will 'get' them just the same." It was war "with all its horror and its comedy, its agony and its gayety, its ruthlessness and its infinite love and sacrifice."[21]

A man who watched the movie with the ex-sergeant agreed, "This is no picture. This is the real thing." Both men thought the actual war scenes "were so obviously true that if you forgot for an instant you were only looking at a picture you caught your breath and wondered how the Signal Corps ever did it, and how King Vidor ever got these films released for his picture."[22] That soldiers believed they were viewing actual combat footage instead of a re-creation is perhaps the ultimate compliment to the filmmaker. Nevertheless, for the studio, the ultimate compliment was its box-office success. Released in 1925, *The Big Parade* ran at the Astor Theater on Broadway for two years, taking in a million and a half dollars. It played for six months at Grauman's Egyptian Theater in Hollywood. And in a few years, it had grossed over 15 million dollars on an investment of only $245,000.[23] Clearly people were ready to have Hollywood re-create the Great War for them.

What Price Glory?

With the stage set for a cycle of war films, *What Price Glory?* became the obvious choice to be the next major Hollywood production. Its long-running success on Broadway meant the movie version would have a presold audience. Moreover, the story offered the opportunity for a filmmaker to focus on the Marines rather than do another Army feature so soon after *The Big Parade*.

In bringing *What Price Glory?* to the screen, Raoul Walsh turned an essentially pacifistic play into "the archetypal celebration of war as a game played by roistering comrades." In making use of the visual possibilities that film offered, the director's "characteristically sweeping battle scenes" became a model for all future major war films. Although the movie paid lip service to "war is hell" sentiments, Walsh diluted their potential effect on the audience by having them spoken by "weaklings and hysterics who get killed while military careerists lament 'civilians' being in war at all."[24]

True, the hero of the film, Captain Flagg, says, "There's something rotten about a world that's got to be wet down every thirty years with the blood of boys like those." But his antiwar expression doesn't seem genuine, because in the film it is set in a comic context that denies the irony and bitterness of the stage version. As a result of this new focus on romance and excitement, the Marines loved the way they appeared in the film. According to Walsh he always stood well with them after the release of *What Price Glory?* He said the Marines "had more recruits after that picture than they'd had since World War I. It showed the boys having fun, getting broads. Young fellers saw it, they said, 'Jesus, the Army [sic] is great.' " Years later, when Walsh was making *Battle Cry* (1955), the World War II Marine spectacular, a general came up to him during the shooting and told him he had joined the Marines after seeing *What Price Glory?*[25] More important to Hollywood, the success of the film confirmed the fact that audiences would pay to see war films. It also demonstrated that moviegoers wanted to see them not because of any antiwar sentiment they might contain, but simply to watch great battle scenes, scenes of men fighting and dying, of planes flying, and of men loving on their time away from combat.

★

Wings

Wings (1927), Hollywood's next major production, therefore dispensed with all pretensions of a serious plot. With the Army and the Marines already covered, the Army Air Corps became the logical subject for the next war film. Moreover, the prospect of filling the air with planes locked in mortal combat offered filmmakers the opportunity to outdo the battle scenes in *The Big Parade* and *What Price Glory?* To help William Wellman achieve a breakthrough in filming the spectacular "flying" and battle scenes, the War Department provided him with more assistance for a longer period of time than any subsequent war movie was ever to receive. As a result of this cooperation, *Wings* stands out as the standard against which all future combat films and all military assistance to Hollywood must be measured.

Despite the military's commitment to the film's production, the idea for *Wings* did not originate in Washington. As with virtually all war movies, the concept came from within the film industry and, more specifically, from a writer trying to sell one of his stories. In February 1926, John Monk Saunders brought his idea for a movie about World War I fliers to Paramount producer Jesse Lasky in New York. The writer argued that the war-in-the-air had never been filmed, the sky was a "virgin-province" for the motion picture camera, and that the battlefield of the fliers offered the opportunity for spectacular combat scenes. Aerial combat, planes falling in flames, balloons being shot down could not be presented on a stage or "imprisoned" within the covers of a book, according to Saunders. To him, the air war "was a subject whose proper medium of presentation was—the screen."[26]

Lasky liked the picture Saunders described but was concerned about the cost. Saunders conceded that it would be expensive: "If it were attempted at all, it must be done on a grand scale. The very magnitude of the subject demanded heroic treatment." Lasky also wanted to know where a filmmaker could obtain the quantity of planes and men needed to stage the action. Since Saunders knew about the military assistance extended to *The Big Parade* and *What Price Glory?*, he felt that the War Department would also provide men and equipment to make an Air Corps picture: "We all take pride in our Army, our Navy, our Air Force. Suppose we present a really fine war picture, a picture of historical significance, of national interest, of military importance. Suppose the picture reflects the practice, spirit, and tradition of American aims. Why shouldn't the War Department go hand-in-hand with us?" Lasky agreed that if the military saw *Wings* in that context and would assist in its production, he would commit the full resources of the Paramount-Famous-Lasky Corporation to the production of the movie.

Saunders immediately left for Washington to discuss the project with Secretary of War Dwight Davis. According to the writer, the merits of the proposed film, the help of Will Hays (head of the Motion Picture Producers Association), and the interest of several high-ranking military officers rather than his own presentation resulted in the War Department's approval. In agreeing to assist, the Army suggested that the action sequences be filmed in the vicinity of San Antonio, Texas, since both flying facilities and Army bases were located close by. Even with cooperation assured, however, the studio required six months to develop a script based on Saunders' story, plan the production, and assemble the film crew in San Antonio.[27]

As it turned out, the screenplay was a relatively insignificant aspect of *Wings*. It portrayed the friendship of two young men, Buddy Rogers and Richard Arlen, who join the Air Corps at the beginning of America's participation in the Great War, become friends while learning to fly, and go off to France to win the war. The dramatic high point of the weakly built story occurs when Rogers shoots down his friend who is attempting to return to his own lines in a stolen German plane after having crashed in enemy territory. The accidental killing stretches credibility since Arlen should easily have been able to identify himself to his friend, given the open cockpits and slowness of the World War I planes. Few people noticed such incongruities in the plot, however, since it served primarily to ensure that the true stars of the film, the fighter planes, would be on the screen as much as possible.

To put them there, Paramount hired William Wellman, a young and relatively inexperienced director who, by his own admission, had made one "stinker" as well as one successful film for the studio. Wellman was later to

Director, film editor, and original author as pictured in program for Wings.

achieve renown not as a creator of great visual compositions, but as a director of action films such as *Public Enemy* (1931), *Beau Geste* (1939), and *The Oxbow Incident* (1942) as well as two of Hollywood's great war movies, *The Story of G.I. Joe* (1945) and *Battleground* (1949). While he brought to *Wings* little in the way of pictorial style, he did introduce Hollywood to the big boom shot in the movie. The sequence in which the camera sweeps through a Paris nightclub to locate the featured players started a trend; other filmmakers also began using a boom to get inside a scene without interrupting the take to move actors or to get furniture out of the way.

Wellman did offer the production two attributes without which *Wings* would have undoubtedly failed. He was the only director in Hollywood who had had flying experience in World War I. This knowledge enabled him to know exactly what he wanted to do with his planes and pilots on the screen, even to the extent of actually flying one of the planes to demonstrate the maneuver he wanted. Perhaps even more important, Wellman brought a no-nonsense attitude to the project and, once on the job, he ran the production completely whether in dealing with the military or with studio executives.

Wellman's assignment to direct *Wings* undoubtedly influenced the War Department's agreement to support the project to the degree it ultimately did. Until regulations were changed during the early 1960s, however, the final decision on the amount of assistance actually provided rested with the local commanders. They could give whatever help they saw fit as long as it did not interfere with normal operations. In essence, this procedure allowed a commander to label any assistance a regular training maneuver if he liked the filmmaker and the project. On the other hand, if a base commander didn't want to be bothered with a film company, he could permit the shooting only of scheduled exercises and provide only a minimum of other assistance.

Given Wellman's attitude toward his work, he took the War Department's initial agreement to provide assistance to *Wings* as a blank check. According to him, the local commanders were there "to help *me*. Nobody else!" He said he "went down to Texas and told the commanders what I needed."[28] Predictably,

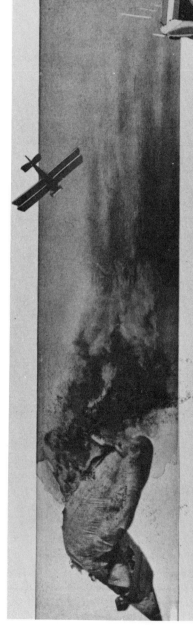

"WINGS"
~ the story

WITH the great adventure of the sky as its background, "Wings" is the story of two boys,—Charles Rogers and Richard Arlen—and a girl—Clara Bow. The two boys are American aviators, first enemies, then buddies. The girl is "the girl next door" who, like so many other American girls, answered when the country needed her.

The story opens in a small town of the middle west, introducing Charles Rogers as a boy born with the whir of wings in his ears. It is in 1917 when War, to this country, and especially to this small town, is remote. Rogers is a happy, care-free, lovable chap who is adored by Clara Bow, just "the girl next door," to him, for there is another girl.

There is another boy, Richard Arlen, fine youth of the aristocratic family of the town. The boys are rivals for the affections of the other girl, played by Jobyna Ralston, and because of this there is little fondness on the part of either Rogers or Arlen for the other. The maelstrom of War devours them both and both enlist in the air corps. Rogers leaves thinking Jobyna loves him and takes by mistake a locket meant for Arlen, who understands the situation.

The boys are plunged into training school. Marvelous scenes show every stop necessary in the making of a flier. The first days in the air. The first thrill of the "ship" leaving the ground.

It is here that the two boys are bound together in inseparable companionship. Their enmity is buried forever. Their commissions arrive. They are in France as members of the 39th Aero Squadron. Clara Bow, in the meantime, has volunteered and is also at the front as an ambulance driver.

(Continued on Page 12)

Wellman had no problems with this approach to the commanders of the flying facilities. The Air Corps not only saw the film as a way to boost its branch of the service, but most of the officers knew Wellman from his flying days.

Arranging use of the infantry for the ground scenes proved far more difficult. Wellman later claimed that the infantry commander "had two monumental hatreds: Fliers and movie people." He recalled that he was in the general's doghouse before he "hardly drew a breath." Being only twenty-nine didn't help him either. When the two men had "a hell of an argument" almost immediately, Wellman said he "gently" reminded the general of the War Department's orders and told him, "Look. You're just being a goddamn fool because the government has told me you have to give me all your men and do just exactly what I want you to do." Pointing out that the general knew how to obey orders, Wellman said that the officer "straightened himself out" even though "he hated to do it."[29]

With the matter of cooperation settled, Wellman could devote his full attention to using the military assistance to the best advantage. His first two months in Texas produced little usable footage, because he had not yet developed techniques for taking close-ups of fliers in the air or for capturing a sense of an airplane's motion and speed on film. In addition, Wellman discovered that the training facility at Kelly Field did not have sufficient fighter planes or skilled pilots to perform the dogfights and other aerial maneuvers that formed the heart of the film. Consequently, while shooting early sequences depicting pilot training, Wellman sent an SOS to Washington for technical help and experienced pilots.

In response, the Air Corps detached six fliers and their planes from the First Pursuit Group stationed at Selfridge Field near Detroit and sent them to Texas. According to one of the pilots, General Clarence "Bill" Irvine, then a young lieutenant and flight engineer, then-Major Hap Arnold told him to "make sure it's a first class job" so that it would not only make money for the producer, but also be good for the Air Corps. Irvine served as Wellman's advisor and engineered an airborne camera system that enabled the director to get close-ups of fliers aloft. In addition to helping plan and flying in dogfight scenes, Irvine performed one of the major crashes in the film when the chief stunt pilot botched the crackup and broke his neck.[30]

Even with all the flying and technical aspects of the project going smoothly, the filming of the aerial sequences dragged on for most of the company's stay in Texas. The early flying footage shot on cloudless days had lacked any visual excitement because the scenes had had no background that would emphasize the plane's movement. Wellman later explained that "motion on the screen is a relative thing. A horse runs on the ground or leaps over fences or streams. We know he is going rapidly because of his relation to the immobile ground." In contrast, it was difficult to show a plane that was high in the sky and in motion relative to the ground or even to another plane. Ultimately, Wellman obtained the proper sense of height and speed by shooting the planes in front of or above cloud banks. He said, "They furnished a background that was exactly what we needed for the dogfight, or battle sequences. Against the clouds we could see the planes dart at each other. We could see them swoop down and disappear in the clouds. We could sense the plummet-like drop of a disabled plane."[31]

These new techniques, of course, put the filmmaker at the mercy of the elements. Wellman admitted, "We waited—while costs surmounted budgets—for the right kind of clouds, heavy banks of them that would show on the screen correctly." This budget-be-damned approach to making *Wings* insured spectacular shots but the unhappiness of the studio. At one point Paramount sent an executive to Texas to insist that Wellman shoot the big dogfight scene regardless of the clouds. Wellman treated him as he had treated the infantry general. He recalled that he gave the executive two choices, a trip home or a trip to the hospital.[32]

Although the wait was to extend to more than a month, Wellman did not remain idle. He was also preparing for the climactic ground engagement of the film, the Battle of Saint-Michel. For its great cinematic moment, the infantry had re-created the battlefield down to the last barbedwire obstacle and trench. In looking over the site, Wellman recalled, "It seemed a shame that we couldn't transplant some of our enemy here and fight out our differences." To guarantee the split-second timing needed to coordinate the planes, special effects explosions, and troop movements, the director rehearsed the 3,500 infantrymen and five dozen planes for ten days. Seventeen manual and twenty-eight remote-controlled cameras were positioned around the prepared set so that no angle would be uncovered in this one-time performance. Wellman also decided that he himself would operate the control panel which detonated the explosions in front of the advancing men.

In scheduling the shooting date, Wellman was master of everything—including the weather! Instead of the clouds he had needed for the dogfight sequence, he now required bright sunlight for the ground sequences because of the slow film stock available then. Wellman faced two additional burdens as the shooting date approached. The Air Corps had served the company with an ultimatum after two military planes crashed, with minor injuries to the pilots and major ones to the planes: One more damaged plane and Air Corps participation would be withdrawn. With the major aerial dogfights still awaiting proper clouds, Wellman said that the loss of the planes would mean that "the whole damned picture would go down the drain." In addition, the three major

A typical scene from the program for Wings.

financial backers of Paramount Pictures were coming to Texas to see where all their money had been going and, appropriately, they were supposed to arrive the day of the big battle.

The appointed day dawned cloudy and apparently unsuitable for filming. Describing it as "just as dark as hell," Wellman surveyed the sky with a "hunch" he could get sunshine for the five minutes he needed to complete the shot. As soon as the sun started to break through the clouds, he ordered the planes into the air and told the soldiers to stand by. When the film's production manager yelled that there wasn't any sun, Wellman responded, "You get your big ass back and get ready!" With everyone in place, the sun appeared, as if on cue, Wellman shouted "Camera," and he began pressing buttons. According to the director, the first explosion nearly blew him off his platform and "all hell broke loose, advancing infantry, diving planes, falling men." Concentrating on hitting the buttons in the right sequence, Wellman could only see what was happening directly in front of him, but what he saw "was majestic."

The "war" continued until Wellman got to button thirteen, with only six more to go and one more minute of sunshine needed. At that point, he recalled,

Army plane strafes German train in Wings.

"Some son of a bitch spoke to me. I pushed the wrong button, and a couple of bodies flew through the air. They weren't dummies." Worse, as Wellman continued to push the buttons, he saw one of the pursuit pilots deviate from his assignment, swoop down almost on top of the soldiers, and threaten to foul up the rest of the advance. When the plane suddenly crashed, Wellman felt "almost glad." Nevertheless, he hit the remaining buttons, and, again on cue, the sun went behind a cloud.

Despite the accidents, the film crew exploded in excitement and relief. The cameramen yelled that they had gotten "sensational" shots. Wellman's only reaction was to head toward the accident sites. He found the "infantry" had not been killed, though it was seriously hurt in the mistimed explosion. The plane was demolished, but its pilot had somehow survived. He was in a dazed condition—but not because of the crash. Wellman suddenly realized that in all his planning, he "had forgotten one terribly important factor, the human element. This pilot had flown at the front. He had been decorated. He had flown missions just like this one. For five minutes it was not 1926 to him; it was 1918. He just stuck out his hand and said, 'I'm sorry.' *C'est la guerre.*"[33]

Wellman captured this feeling of realism on film so well that audiences found themselves caught up in the movie despite its superficial plot. Once the early romantic antics of the lead characters have played themselves out, the story of men learning to fly and then fighting in the air provides viewers with visual excitement seldom found on the screen—even fifty years later. So successfully did Wellman do his job that subsequent filmmakers have regularly imitated shots such as a plane spinning to earth trailing a cloud of smoke or an aircraft strafing a bridge from which enemy soldiers fall or dive frantically into the water to escape. **Wings**

These actions moved one early reviewer to write, "Nothing in the line of war pictures ever has packed a greater proportion of real thrills into an equal footage. As a spectacle, *Wings* is a technical triumph. It piles punch upon punch until the spectator is almost nervously exhausted." Another critic observed, "The exceptional quality of *Wings* lies in its appeal as a spectacle and as a picture of at least some of the actualities of flying under wartime conditions." Wellman's re-creation of the dogfights seemed so realistic that a writer looking at the movie forty-five years after its release thought the director had "made use of authentic war pictures in which machines crash to the earth in flames."[34]

Wellman was primarily concerned with the technical accuracy of the combat scenes, not with the literal reproduction of the World War I period. Unlike Vidor's careful adherence to detail, Wellman used 1927 clothes and cars in the picture. When asked about this incongruity much later, Wellman admitted he never had thought about it before. Despite such lapses, the movie ran for a year and a half in New York and six months in Los Angeles, made a fortune for Paramount, and won the first Academy Award for best picture of the year.[35]

For its part, the Air Corps found the product of its assistance eminently satisfactory. Wellman dedicated the film "To those young warriors of the sky, whose wings are folded about them forever." General Irvine, looking back on *Wings*, said that the film showed the public the kind of people and kind of equipment the Air Corps had and communicated the military's message that "if you are second best, you are dead." He also thought that as a recruiting instrument, the film had an immediate and continuing effect. "Beginning about that time," Irvine noted, "the Air Corps never had problems getting enough people."[36]

While the Air Corps was to help on only a few other movies before 1940, the other services began to cooperate regularly with filmmakers following the release of *Wings*. But no Hollywood film has ever received as much military assistance for so long a time as Wellman received in Texas in 1926. And very few other films have ever managed to re-create aerial battles as well as *Wings*. As a result, Wellman's movie became the yardstick against which all future combat spectaculars have had to be measured in terms of authenticity of combat and scope of production.

CHAPTER THREE

WORLD WAR II: FANTASY

★

Although *Wings* set the standard for future combat movies, few filmmakers chose to challenge its supremacy during the 1930s. While the armed services remained willing to assist on suitable scripts, their own limited appropriations and reduced manpower prevented cooperation on the scale extended to Wellman. At the same time, *The Big Parade, What Price Glory?,* and *Wings* had, to a large extent, satisfied the need to portray the serious, combat side of World War I, especially since the American people's isolationist impulse reduced their interest in refighting the Great War on motion picture screens. Perhaps most important, with the advent of the Depression, people lost their taste for mass carnage in their escape entertainment. Nevertheless, throughout the decade the military, and particularly the Navy, remained fertile sources of potential screen stories.

★

Creating an Image

Unlike the Army, Marines, and Air Corps, the Navy had participated in few major battles during World War I and so had little in the way of combat stories to offer Hollywood. Ships, the sea, and sailors did, however, provide opportunities for romance, comedy, and drama of a noncombat nature. Moreover, because so many Americans lived far from oceans, movies about the sea provided

---

Army stages opening battle for Sahara *(1943) in California desert.*

audiences with new vistas of a previously unseen and often mysterious world. These Navy films proved to be good box office for Hollywood and a powerful recruiting tool, as a significant proportion of the Navy's recruits during the 1930s came from the nation's midlands, inspired at least in part by these films.

Since the Navy appreciated the value of movies for recruiting as well as for informing the American people about its activities, it worked diligently to create a positive screen image. At least until the 1960s, the Navy regarded itself as an elite organization, particularly in its officer cadre. Throughout the thirties, most of its officers attended Annapolis, which helped ensure familiarity, common values, and the sense of being part of a unique society. Regular Navy officers usually served a tour of duty in the Public Relations Office, which functioned under the direct supervision of the chief of naval operations. This helped ensure that films receiving Navy cooperation were accurate as well as complimentary.

A serious drama such as John Ford's 1930 submarine movie, *Men Without Women*, was assigned a technical advisor experienced in undersea operations who supervised the military aspects of the production: he had the authority to correct errors that might slip into the script, he secured needed equipment for the sound stage, and he arranged for ships during location shooting. This assistance guaranteed that the finished movie would depict authentically life aboard a submarine.

During the shooting of *Men Without Women*, the technical advisor succeeded almost too well. In the film's dramatic highlight, a destroyer runs over the submerged submarine, damaging the sub's hull and loosing an avalanche of water into the control room. Watching the scene as it was filmed, the technical advisor was so startled by the realism of the action he had helped create that he shouted, "Jesus Christ!" even though the cameras and recording equipment were still running. This spontaneous reaction forced Ford to reshoot the whole sequence since the sound recordings then used couldn't be edited for extraneous noise.[1]

With the exception of a few realistic dramas like *Men Without Women*, however, Hollywood used the Navy and the other services as background for conventional love stories, musicals, and comedies. Among others, *Shipmates* (1931) and *Shipmates Forever* (1935) portrayed the romantic and colorful side of the Naval Academy in the same way that *Flirtation Walk* (1934) featured life at West Point. Still, whatever the subject, the Navy maintained strict control over films on which it assisted. Occasionally it even requested deletions in the completed films, such as with *Hell Below* (1933).[2]

The Navy also refused to cooperate on the making of films it did not find in its best interest. RKO's request for help on *King Kong* (1933) met with disapproval because the Navy said the script did "not fulfill the department's requirements . . . in that there is nothing pertaining to the Navy, and the use of planes as requested would compete with [the] civilian airplane industry." In this instance, the producer thwarted the Navy's rejection by approaching the local commanding officer at Floyd Bennett Field on Long Island when he went East for the film's location shooting. In return for $100 to the Officers' Mess Fund and $10 to each pilot, he had four Navy biplanes fly over New York City in formation, first peeling off, then diving at an imaginary target, then looping and attacking from the other direction. Ultimately, twenty-eight scenes of real aircraft were intercut with process shots and miniatures to create the attack on Kong atop the Empire State Building.[3]

By the end of the decade, as Nazi Germany began to pose a threat to the United States, Hollywood returned to serious movies about the military, portraying the services defending the nation against possible attack. Such films as *Flight Command* (1940), *I Wanted Wings* (1941), and *Dive Bomber* (1941) showed the American people how the Navy and Army Air Corps trained for their anticipated missions. From the film industry's point of view, these essentially documentary movies enabled studios to put popular actors like Errol Flynn and William Holden in military settings where they could combine flying sequences with the obligatory romantic interludes. Filmmakers also drew on the World War I exploits of heroes like Sergeant York to create within the American people a patriotic feeling that would unite the nation against its potential enemies.

Whether these films succeeded in their mission is another matter. One viewer wrote to Secretary of the Navy Frank Knox on December 1, 1941 saying, "If there ever was a picture shown to discourage anyone from joining the Air Corps it is the picture *Dive Bomber*." The writer thought it would lead every "potential draftee to stay clear of aviation" because the film showed that "every aviator loses his health due to flying. Perhaps this is so, but it seems a queer time to advertise this throughout the country. If this picture was made in Germany and sent here I could see the point." The man could see that the film was intended to educate the public, but observed that it "sure won't get any recruits in the air service."[4] In response to a similar letter, the Navy's Public Relations Office said that the general reaction to the film had been favorable and suggested that if the movie had shown only the positive side of the aviation story, "it would not ring true and would be declared propaganda by the public."

★

Senate Investigations

Propaganda was exactly the label applied by the leading isolationists in the Senate, Champ Clark and Gerald Nye, to *Dive Bomber, I Wanted Wings, Sergeant York* and several other "preparedness" films released in 1940 and 1941. Claiming these movies were drawing the United States into World War II, the senators convened a hearing of the subcommittee of the Committee on Interstate Commerce in September 1941 to investigate the making of these films. They summoned Hollywood's leading filmmakers to Washington to answer charges that they were making propaganda films. With the defeated 1940 presidential candidate, Wendell Wilkie, as the industry's counsel, Harry Warner, Darryl Zanuck, and Barney Balaban among others argued that they made movies purely for entertainment and profit. In denying the charges against the industry, Harry Warner, president of Warner Brothers, acknowledged he was "opposed to Nazism" and told the subcommittee, "I abhor and detest every principle and practice of the Nazi movement. To me, Nazism typifies the very opposite of the kind of life every decent man, woman, and child wants to live." He denied that the pictures produced by his company were "propaganda" as the senators had alleged.

Rejecting Senator Nye's claim that *Sergeant York* was designed to create war hysteria, Warner maintained that the film "is a factual portrait of the life of one of the great heroes of the last war. If that is propaganda, we plead guilty." Likewise, he said that *Confessions of a Nazi Spy* (1939) was a "factual portrayal of a Nazi spy ring that actually operated in New York City. If that is propaganda, we plead guilty." In fact, Warner argued, these films were "carefully prepared on the basis of factual happenings and they were not twisted to serve any ulterior purpose." Most important, he said that "millions of average citizens have paid to see these pictures. They have enjoyed wide popularity and have been profitable to our company. In short, these pictures have been judged by the public and the judgment has been favorable."

Warner acknowledged that his company had during the past eight years made feature films about the armed forces. But he stressed that the studio "needed no urging from the government and we would be ashamed if the government would have had to make such requests of us. We have produced these pictures voluntarily and proudly."

In fact, the reasons why the Warner brothers made such films were not hard to understand. The three brothers, sons of a Polish immigrant, were strongly committed to the country that had given them the opportunity to become rich and successful. They saw their films that glorified the military and

William Bendix and Robert Preston prepare for a scene in Wake Island (1942) filmed on the shore of the Salton Sea in California.

their documentaries made at cost for the services as ways of repaying the country.[5] In any case, the testimony of Warner and other industry leaders did little but produce acrimonious exchanges with the subcommittee, and the hearings were soon temporarily adjourned.

Before they could reconvene, Pearl Harbor rendered the debate moot and ended any caution within the industry about making military pictures. Even with the congressional criticism, however, filmmakers had continued to draw on the war in Europe and Asia for films such as *To the Shores of Tripoli, Flying Tigers,* and *Across the Pacific,* which were in production before December 7 and were released the next year with the appropriate tag lines to update history.

The United States' entry into the war and the events of the first months of the conflict provided new material for Hollywood. While these early movies were, as always, intended to make money, they were also consciously designed to lift the morale of the nation and stimulate the war effort.

Hollywood had no problem finding suitable subjects for these films. Pearl Harbor, the fall of Wake Island, and the fall of the Philippines all provided inspirational stories to stimulate America's patriotic impulse. Nevertheless, the time required to transform an idea into a completed movie meant that the films did not begin to reach theater screens until almost a year after Pearl Harbor. Because the armed forces had more important things to do with their men and equipment than give them to filmmakers, the early movies about American war activities were of necessity small scale, fictionalized stories that were only loosely based on historical fact.

Wake Island, for example, the first attempt to dramatize American servicemen in combat, was not released until the end of August 1942. Portraying the Japanese capture of Wake Island as envisioned by the screenwriter, the film was shot on the shore of the Salton Sea in California, with the battle scenes re-created by special effects, miniatures, and some stock footage. Despite these limitations, the *New York Times* reviewer though that the story of Marines fighting to the last man should "surely bring a surge of pride to every patriot's breast."[6] The film's box-office success proved that Hollywood could combine wartime propaganda with exciting entertainment.

Air Force

Focusing on a small group of besieged Marines, *Wake Island* needed little, if any, military assistance. *Air Force*, on the other hand, did receive a limited amount of help from the Army Air Corps because General Hap Arnold saw the need for a movie that would show the American people the Air Force in action. Jack Warner, executive producer of Warner Brothers, had accepted Arnold's suggestion for this kind of film and initiated the project almost immediately after Pearl Harbor. In writing the script, Dudley Nichols had at his disposal battle reports supplied by the War Department and the technical advice of Captain Samuel Triffy, an Air Corps pilot who had worked on a couple of "March of Times" reports about the service. The plot, which grew out of the collaboration of Nichols, Triffy, and the director, Howard Hawks, proved to be little more than a vehicle for portraying the Air Force winning the war almost single-handed.[7]

Starting with the historical fact that a squadron of B-17s arrived in Hawaii during the Japanese attack on Pearl Harbor, *Air Force* traced the adventures of one bomber crew across the Pacific to the Philippines, to the Battle of the Coral Sea, to a crash landing on an Australian beach. While the movie contained the usual mixture of human emotions and comic relief among the crew members of the "Mary Ann," the lack of any real dramatic conflicts and the loose attention to history contributed to a pseudodocumentary quality in the **Air Force** movie.

Air Force provided its message of hope for ultimate victory through a number of rather obvious devices. After the plane's crew briefly expresses its horror at the disastrous results of the sneak attack at Pearl Harbor, the bomber is ordered on to the Philippines to help stem the Japanese tide. While in the air, the crew listens to President Roosevelt's war message to Congress, with his call for an "absolute victory" over the "treacherous enemy." When the Philippines are overrun, the "Mary Ann" manages to take off just ahead of advancing Japanese soldiers and heads for Australia. On the way, the plane comes across a huge Japanese fleet also heading toward the subcontinent and radios the flotilla's position. The "Mary Ann" then circles overhead—endlessly it seems—until the Air Force arrives like the cavalry, even though the B-17 had not been completely fueled before leaving the Philippines. What happens next, in its own way, resembles the end of Samuel Peckinpah's The Wild Bunch: wave upon wave of American planes slaughter the Japanese fleet, thereby turning the tide in the Pacific. As the "Mary Ann" reaches the Australian coast, it finally runs out of gas and makes a crash landing in the surf. At the film's close, the surviving crew members are looking ahead to making the first large-scale raid on Tokyo to begin the final push to victory.

Air Force in fact anticipated history, sometimes by months, sometimes by years. The climactic air-sea battle, created with miniatures and special effects, might have borne a vague resemblance to the Battles of the Coral Sea and Midway. But it had been staged and filmed before the actual battles had taken place. B-17s did participate in both actions, although not in the manner portrayed in the film. At Coral Sea, three B-17s actually attacked part of the American fleet accidentally, but fortunately without inflicting damage. At Midway, Navy carrier-based planes carried the brunt of the attack to the Japanese fleet. The Air Corps did bomb Tokyo in April 1942, but the mission was a hit-and-run operation carried out with B-25 bombers launched from the U.S.S. Hornet. Regular bombing raids on Japan did not begin until 1944, carried out exclusively by B-29 Super Fortresses.

Despite its mythical cum-historical narrative, however, Air Force did more than entertain the American people. The movie slaughter of the Japanese fleet provided a catharsis for the setbacks suffered at Pearl Harbor, Wake Island, and the Philippines. Tied into the plot were continuous overt and subtle propaganda messages, conveyed in terms that were becoming familiar to wartime moviegoers. The crew of the "Mary Ann" consisted of a heterogeneous cross section of the nation, except for a black, of course. The plane's crew chief, a crusty old sergeant, provided a father figure to the younger men. The pilot's wife and copilot's girlfriend served as the faithful women, waiting loyally at home. And the mascot, an all-American mutt who raged at the mention of Tojo, provided some comic relief. While one of the gunners, a washed-out pilot, becomes a temporary malcontent, the "crew takes care of each other" and everyone does his assigned job for the good of the plane. The final didactic message is related through a fighter pilot. Along for the ride to the Philippines, he learns how important bombers are for the war effort, and by the time he reaches Australia, he is ready to fly a B-17 for the duration.

In contrast, the Japanese are all characterized as sneaky and treacherous and throughout the film are referred to in derogatory terms. This message is constantly reinforced beginning with the opening scenes. On the way to Hawaii, the crew hears a news broadcast that a Japanese peace envoy was planning to meet with Secretary of State Hull on the morning of December 7. When the plane lands at Pearl Harbor, the crew is immediately told of Japanese sabotage of American planes before the attack (historically untrue). The Japanese are portrayed as fighting unfairly, attacking without warning, and shooting at a helpless flier as he parachutes from his disabled plane. Not only were the Japanese evil, but they were shown as inferior in fair combat. The "Mary Ann" shoots down Japanese plane after plane, and the Air Force sinks the entire enemy fleet.

The message stands out clearly: the United States will win the war, we may have lost the first round through deceit, but victory will be ours. This ideal is expressed most forcefully when the crew's father-figure arrives in the Philippines and discovers that his pilot-son had been killed in the first attack while trying to take off. He receives his son's personal effects in a handkerchief, asks if this is all that is left, sheds perhaps a single tear, and returns to his job as the American people all must do. Whether the audience left the theater with this same commitment is, of course, another matter. Given the quality of the production, the first-rate acting, the taut script, the fine photography and special effects, many viewers may well have simply enjoyed the film as escapist entertainment, irrespective of any messages it offered. Nevertheless, the movie's prophesy of victory, repeated enough times, would inevitably have a positive influence on the war effort.

The sense of urgency in presenting this message to the nation manifested itself in the speed with which production of *Air Force* got under way. Even before Nichols completed his script, Warner Brothers' special effects department constructed a Japanese fleet in miniature and then began bombing it in Santa Monica Bay. As a result, before photography of the principals ever began, the company had spent a half million dollars and filmed the climactic battle of the movie.[8] For its part, the War Department acted with all appropriate speed when it finally received a script from Jack Warner in mid-May of 1942. In requesting an "analysis as to military detail and advisability of giving full War Department cooperation," the chief of the Pictorial Branch (a section of the Bureau of Public Relations) asked the Special Service Branch to return the script with comments in twenty-four hours because the film was "a special Air Corps recruiting job." All Department offices approved cooperation within this time limit, requesting only minor script changes that related to security matters. The Review Branch, for one, informed the Pictorial Branch that "Mention of any blind spots of any aircraft or other indications of vulnerability is restricted. Also no reference may be made to position of turrets, cannon, and machine guns of Flying Fortresses."[9]

The War Department notified Jack Warner of its decision to cooperate on May 22, and reminded him that all regulations governing assistance would be strictly adhered to, including the need to have the film reviewed prior to any screening. The Air Corps formally assigned Captain Triffy and another officer to be technical advisors on the project. When notifying the commander of Drew Field near Tampa that Warner Brothers would be shooting the film on his base, the War Department said it "desired that you extend such assistance as, in your judgment is deemed necessary to insure the success of the sequences planned." The Department placed only one restriction on its cooperation: "It is the policy of the War Department not to allow soldiers or military equipment to be disguised and photographed as representing the personnel or equipment of foreign countries."[10]

Despite this directive, the local commanders ignored the policy when the film crew arrived at Drew Field. Warner Brothers had in fact selected the site partially because they could not photograph "Japanese fighters" along the West Coast due to the continuing fear of enemy attack. At Drew Field, Triffy obtained fighters, had them painted with the Rising Sun insignia, and then flew them in the sequences portraying Japanese attacks on American planes and positions. His ability to arrange this assistance had little to do with Washington's help, however. According to Triffy, there was "not a hell of a lot of support for the film because everyone was concerned with the war."[11]

The technical advisor was able to accomplish his assignment because he knew most of the officers in charge of planes and equipment around the Tampa area. Also, he had a card on which General Arnold had written "Good idea" after he had seen the original script of *Air Force*. With this tacit approval of the film and his friendships, the technical advisor could usually obtain the planes Hawks needed to film either solo or formation flights. Also, the commanding officer of the bomber facility at Siebring, Florida provided the B-17 bomber to play the "Mary Ann."[12]

As with the pursuit planes in *Wings*, the "Mary Ann," rather than the actors, was the star of *Air Force*, flying from one crisis to the next like any Hollywood heroine. Like most actresses, the bomber played a composite character, representing several planes and their crews' actions including Colin Kelly's heroic, if mythical, sinking of a Japanese battleship off the Philippines in the first days of the war.

To create a proper sense of men in battle, Hawks and the film crew showed little concern for the safety of military equipment. After one flight in a disguised fighter, Triffy was almost forced to crash-land because of a balky landing gear. When the director found out, he suggested that Triffy should have made a belly landing—after making sure the cameras were rolling. According to Triffy, the filmmakers were *"ruthless, absolutely ruthless! If they could have damaged a plane in flight so I would have had an accident, they would have done it! Really, I couldn't trust them!"*[13]

But Hawks' single-minded pursuit of authenticity did make the career of the "Mary Ann" and her crew seem almost real. A *New York Times* reviewer felt the director's "boundless enthusiasm and awe" for the American fliers had enabled him to make a "picture which tingles with the passion of spirits aglow. . . . Mr. Hawks has directed the action for tremendous impact. . . . Maybe the story is high-flown, maybe it overdraws a recorded fact a bit. [But I would] hate to think it couldn't happen—or didn't—because it certainly leaves you feeling awfully good."[14]

This "feeling awfully good" about something represents the goal of all effective propaganda. As a result, *Air Force* became one of Hollywood's highest achievements in World War II morale-building, a film to rival the dramatic quality of *Wings*, and one that became a major box-office success. As with the best propaganda, *Air Force* blended some truth with much fiction to create a sense of reality. Hawks made a first-rate adventure movie filled with action, a careful build-up of tensions, and human interest. With the exception of an occasional cliché, the screenplay was sparse and authentic, giving the viewer a sense of the war as it was actually fought in the air. The camera work, acting, and editing were of uniformly high quality. The special effects, particularly important because of the limited military help and the lack of combat footage, equalled such recent spectaculars as *Tora! Tora! Tora!* and *Midway* in believability, if not in scope.

★

Bataan

In contrast to the Air Corps, the Army did relatively little in the first year and a half of the war to help Hollywood represent patriotism and a brighter future. On its own, however, MGM portrayed the Army defending the flag to the last man. *Bataan* told the story of a rear guard action by thirteen doomed Americans in the days just before the Japanese overran the Philippines. Like most war films, the idea for the movie came from a studio screenwriter, Robert Andrews, who suggested to Dore Schary, MGM's production chief, a story set in the Philippines along the lines of *The Lost Patrol,* a film about a British unit lost in the desert and wiped out by the Arabs. Schary "jumped at the idea.... because I wanted to tell the people they were in for a tough fight." As pure propaganda, he saw the film preparing Americans for a long struggle and giving the audience a morale boost.[15]

Bataan accomplished this by showing the strength and success of the Japanese military while at the same time creating a feeling of pride in the gallantry of the American soldiers as they faced certain death. Andrews wrote a script in which all of the characters had individual identities and traits with which people could empathize. As in *Air Force* and most war films made during the conflict, the unit included representatives of all ethnic groups. In *Bataan,* Schary went one step further. He told Andrews to include one character in the script without describing him. Then, in casting the film, he assigned a black to play the unidentified role. Schary later admitted that "it really was inaccurate, because there were no combat soldiers who were black." Given his political liberalism, Schary did what he felt was right and didn't worry about the many critical letters he later received.[16] More important, because the men had identities, even if they were stereotyped ones, their ultimate deaths (including that of superstar Robert Taylor) were more powerfully felt than in the average war film. The losses became almost personal and helped make the fall of the Philippines more meaningful to the audience.

Focusing on a small group of men interacting within a limited area, *Bataan* duplicated the intimacy of a stage play. Given the film's modest production demands in terms of men and equipment, MGM did not require military assistance. Nevertheless, the studio submitted the script to the Army in October 1942 "for the record." The Public Relations Office found it "a good story" which "could make a good picture—but not a great picture." The chief of the service's Feature Film Division didn't think the script justified cooperation, nor did he think it was necessary, "as the equipment of the personnel involved can all be assembled at the studio; all of the men in the patrol would have to be actors; the Japs, extras. The whole picture could probably be made on the back lot, or on location very nearby."[17]

Even though it didn't intend to provide assistance, the Army, as usual, informed the studio it "desired that where officers or soldiers appear in uniform, they be correctly attired, and conduct themselves in a manner consistent with the customs and courtesies of the Service." The Pictorial Branch therefore suggested that the producer hire a retired officer to serve as technical advisor and asked to review the film for military accuracy prior to its release.[18]

Given the wartime restrictions on travel and the film's small-scale combat scenes, MGM decided to shoot *Bataan* entirely on its Sound Stage 16. According to the director, Tay Garnett, the studio's set designers constructed "a real-as-hell jungle" which had "everything except sixteen foot snakes."[19] Moviegoers who are used to the feel of reality created in recent years by filming on actual location may be put off by the "made-on-a-set" quality of *Bataan*. Audiences in 1943, however, were conditioned to accept studio jungles and special effects that helped provide the illusion of reality, and the artificiality of the set did not interfere with the action to any great extent.

To increase the dramatic impact of this action, Garnett used all the tricks of the filmmaking art. When he became unhappy with the way his actors were reacting when shot, the Special Effects Department tied ropes around the men selected to be killed and, on cue, the lines were jerked to provide the desired visual effect.

The feel of reality in the film's climactic scene was heightened through the use of "ground fog," which often occurred in jungle settings. To create the fog through which the Japanese soldiers had to advance, the special effects men dumped dry ice into tubs of water and blew the resulting vapor across the set. In addition to creating the proper appearance of a misty terrain, the fumes nearly killed two extras who ignored warnings not to breathe as they crawled through the fog.[20] Despite the near tragedy, the visual effect of the vapor added greatly to the power of the closing sequence.

At the film's climax, Robert Taylor, playing the sergeant, is the only survivor of his patrol. Having buried his men, Taylor digs his own grave, mounts a machine gun in front of it, and prepares to stall the enemy for as long as his ammunition lasts. As the Japanese emerge from the fog, Taylor mows them down, firing nonstop and yelling wildly, "Come on, you bastards, I'm here. I'll *always* be here." The camera moves forward so that the firing machine gun fills the screen. Suddenly, it falls silent with only a wisp of smoke slowly curling up from its barrel.

As message, the closing sequence had the proper effect. While noting that *Bataan* had "melodramatic flaws" and technical mistakes, the *New York*

Times reviewer thought the film "still gives a shocking conception of the defense of that bloody point of land. And it doesn't insult the honor of dead soldiers, which is something to say for a Hollywood film these days." *Time* magazine thought that the film's drama was "constantly loud and overemphatic. But there are a few stretches when the military situation calls for silence; the noisy sound track quiets down and, for a moment, incredibly enough, Hollywood's war takes on the tense, classic values of understatement."[21]

Like most directors, Garnett undertook the project because it was a good current story with excellent dramatic possibilities. The movie also had an excellent cast: Robert Taylor, Lloyd Nolan, Desi Arnez, George Murphy, Barry Nelson, and Lee Bowman. Garnett also recognized that the film would "arouse a great deal of admiration for the courage of these boys and pride in the American man."[22] This patriotic feeling was reinforced by characters who represented traditional American stereotypes, enabling audiences to more readily identify with the men, empathize with their bravery, and mourn their deaths. In doing this, *Bataan* contributed to the war effort when victory remained a hope, not yet a certainty.

Hollywood's stereotypes were not limited to Americans, of course. If anything, the characterizations of the enemy in films made during the war were even more sharply delineated. In movies such as *Wake Island, Air Force,* and *Bataan,* the Japanese were portrayed as an enemy who machine-gunned fliers dangling in parachutes as easily as it had attacked Pearl Harbor on a peaceful Sunday morning. The Germans, on the other hand, fared better in American films, possibly because their skin color and cultural heritage were closer to those of most Americans. As soldiers, they always appeared efficient, disciplined, and patriotic, and they seldom delighted in cruelty, although they were determined to win the war at all costs.

Sahara

The clash between this Nazi aspiration for world domination and the American determination to stop Hitler's conquests had one of its best expressions in *Sahara* (1943). The film carried stereotyping to its logical conclusion by having actors represent whole nations. The hero, Humphrey Bogart, plays a typical American sergeant—tough, resourceful, determined, "probably the best screen notion of the American soldier to date."[23] As commander of an American tank, the "Lulubelle," which has been fighting alongside the British in

Libya, Bogart and his crew battle the desert as well as the enemy in an attempt to reach Allied lines. The three tankmen first pick up four Britishers, all stereotypes of their respective social classes and their nation. The passenger list grows with the addition of a South African, a Frenchman, and a Sudanese and his Italian prisoner. While the Sudanese character provides a legitimate role for a black man, he is only a corporal, and so occupies the inferior position which blacks typically played in Hollywood films until the mid-1960s. The final addition to the multinational caravan, a German pilot shot down and captured after strafing the tank, plays the typical film Nazi—unrepentant, proud, and determined to get the best of his captors.

Bogart and his traveling companions (minus one of his crew who has died of wounds) finally reach a water hole and defend it against attack from a 500-man German patrol desperately searching for water. After a fierce battle in which all the Allies except Bogart, the Italian, the German pilot, and seemingly hundreds of German soldiers die, Bogart captures the surviving Nazi force and convoys them to his own lines. Apart from the liberties taken with history —American tanks did not fight alongside the British in the desert in early 1942—the soldiers' test of endurance against the desert environment and their fight against a vastly superior German force make the film a "laudable conception of soldier fortitude in this war and it is also a bang-up action picture cut out to hold one enthralled."[24]

In contrast to their disinterest in *Wake Island* and *Bataan*, the Army helped create the brutal action in *Sahara*, giving Columbia Pictures its full cooperation. In preparing for production, the director, writer, and production staff visited the Army's desert training facilities in desert areas of California, Arizona, and Nevada. The Army provided briefings and demonstrations of tank operations, agreed to allow the company to shoot the film in an area near Eagle Pass, 100 miles east of Palm Springs, and donated a tank to the filmmakers for the two months the crew and actors were on location.

As part of the technical advice during preproduction, the Army had a plane strafe a tank to demonstrate for the special effects man what bullets

(Opposite, top) Humphrey Bogart with British soldiers and the Lulubelle during the making of Sahara.

(Opposite, bottom) The Lulubelle under attack by "German" plane during the making of Sahara *(note German markings on P-40 despite War Department regulations against American equipment portraying enemy materiel).*

looked like kicking up the dirt. The officer in charge offered to repeat the attack for the cameras during filming, pointing out that the tank could take a direct hit without damage. The director graciously rejected the offer and had the special effects man simulate the bullets hitting the ground by using compressed air forced through buried hoses. Disregarding the regulation against disguising American equipment to represent foreign materiel, the Army allowed one of its planes to masquerade as a German one to play the attacking fighter in the sequence. Likewise, for the German attack on the water hole, the Army allowed 500 soldiers to be dressed in German uniforms for the two days it took to rehearse and film the battle.[25]

This assistance enabled Columbia to take the production out of the sound stage and back lot where most of the early war films had been made, and lent *Sahara* a new feeling of authenticity. The movie worked as drama however not because of the assistance, but because the contrasts between the stereotyped Allies and their stereotyped enemies mirrored the tensions and differences between the warring nations themselves.

Bogart for example, at first refuses to include the captured Italian soldier on the "Lulubelle" because of the scarcity of food and water. American ideals would not of course permit such an inhumane act so Bogart quickly changes his mind. The Italian soldier has all the mannerisms and background that audiences associated with Italians: he has a relative in the United States; he loves his large family; he is apolitical and has no love of war; he likes Americans. At the same time, the soldier is not a traitor to his country; he does not reveal to Bogart that his fellow prisoner, the German pilot, understands English and so knows the American's plans. And to point up his essentially peaceful nature, the Italian is ultimately killed by the German when he tries to prevent the pilot's escape. Such a stereotype enables the viewer to infer that one man, Mussolini, not the Italian people, wanted war. This kind of presentation had obvious value given the number of Italians in the United States.

Although *Sahara* worked as action, drama, and message, it still did not recreate World War II as it was actually being fought. The British could point out that the Americans had had no part in defeating the Germans at El Alamein in 1942, Humphrey Bogart and "Lulubelle" notwithstanding. Likewise, the British felt they had a right to be furious over the film *Operation Burma* (1945), where Errol Flynn single-handedly appears to defeat the Japanese—even though no Americans fought in Burma at that time. Nevertheless, in the early days of the war, the United States had few successes to which it could point. The fantasies the filmmakers created within a broad historical framework could not provide victories. But they could impress the American people with some of the reali-

ties of war. In doing so, Hollywood helped stimulate patriotism and the war ef- **Sahara**
fort on the home front, and it offered the message of ultimate victory for the
Allies.

CHAPTER FOUR

WORLD WAR II: REALITY

★

By the end of 1943, Allied victory was not yet in sight. Nevertheless, the tide had turned. The Doolittle Raid on Japan in April 1942, had done relatively little damage, but it had demonstrated that the enemy's homeland was not inviolate. The combined Navy/Air Force operation showed both the Japanese military and the American people that the United States fleet had rebounded from its losses at Pearl Harbor and could carry the war to all parts of the Pacific. The American defeat of a vastly superior Japanese armada at Midway, Allied successes in North Africa, the invasion of Italy, and the regular bombings of Occupied Europe and the German homeland all contributed to a growing feeling of optimism in the United States.

The improved military situation enabled the armed services to again assist filmmakers, thus allowing them to turn out more authentic-looking combat movies than had been possible during the first year of the war. The military's successes also provided sources for a series of movies that portrayed war with greater historical accuracy, either depicting actual events or a synthesis of several actions that were combined for heightened dramatic impact. Of all the military operations in the first two years of the war probably nothing so stimulated the imagination of the American people as Doolittle's mission against Japan. Planned and carried out in absolute secrecy, revealed to the American people with mystery still shrouding most of the mission, the attack on the Japanese mainland spawned two major Hollywood productions.

Marines advance through typical Hollywood jungle in Marine Raiders *(1944).*

★

Destination Tokyo

Released at the very end of 1943, *Destination Tokyo* attempted "to tell a factual kind of story" about submarine warfare drawing on incidents from several submarine cruises in enemy waters. In the script submitted to the Navy, the writers said the movie would show the public that submarines "are of much greater value to the Navy and the nation than simply sinkers of ships. We want them to know the high caliber of submarine officers and men, that they are skilled, well-trained, and that they can take it as well as 'dish it out.' " Unlike earlier characterizations of the Japanese, the filmmakers told the Navy that *Destination Tokyo* intended "to show the Japanese as a tough adversary, an intelligent one." Furthermore, the scriptwriters said that the submarine in their film would not be going "into mythical waters" and would not "sink the whole damned Jap fleet." Instead, they explained that the "Copperfin" would perform its mission "quietly and well," the action would show that both the men and their ship "can take it, that a submarine can take a terrific depth-charging and still come home." Finally, and *"most* of all," the writers said they wanted "to show the public that the submarine service is doing a great and varied, though silent, job in this war!"[1]

To accomplish their goals, the writers produced a relatively simple plot. The "Copperfin" is detailed to the Aleutians to pick up a Navy meteorologist and then deliver him to the shore of Tokyo Bay to gather weather data for Doolittle's raid. While waiting for the officer to accomplish his mission, the submarine itself gathers intelligence data to radio to the attackers. Within this slim framework, the "Copperfin" and her crew experience several adventures that heighten the dramatic impact of the film.

In Alaskan waters, the submarine undergoes an attack by a Japanese plane, which scores a direct hit. The bomb does not explode and must be disarmed in a tense scene. Once the "Copperfin" arrives in Tokyo Bay and dispatches the meteorologist, one of her crewmen suffers an appendicitis attack and is operated on successfully by the ship's pharmacist's mate, although he is inexperienced and lacks proper medical equipment. Following the recovery of the weather expert and the bombing of Tokyo, viewed through the ship's periscope, the "Copperfin" sinks a Japanese carrier. Enemy destroyers retaliate with an archetypal depth-charge attack that became the model for all subsequent submarine movies about World War II. Having survived the barrage, the "Copperfin" returns to San Francisco.

While not the true story of a single submarine or even a completely accurate historical re-creation, most of the fictionalized incidents in *Destination*

Tokyo either happened during the war or were in the realm of the possible. Bombs did strike United States submarines without exploding; a submarine did radio back weather information to Doolittle's raiders, but from off the Japanese coast; American submarines did venture into Tokyo Bay, though not in the manner portrayed in the film; several appendectomies were performed in submarines during the war; and an American undersea craft did sink a Japanese carrier before the end of hostilities. But even more than the authentic-like situations, the filmmakers' adherence to detail and concern for accuracy of procedures created a sense of reality and believability not found in many later submarine films.

Run Silent, Run Deep (1958), for example, a highly praised adaptation of Edward Beach's popular novel, received substantially more material assistance from the Navy than Destination Tokyo. This cooperation and a highly detailed studio mock-up of a submarine's interior gave the film a better visual sense of what life was like aboard a World War II submarine. Nevertheless, many of the incidents depicted leave the audience confused or incredulous. In the film's opening sequence, a submarine is attacked and sunk apparently by depth charges. Yet the sub's captain somehow finds his way onto a life raft, avoids capture in Japanese waters, and makes his way in short order back to Pearl Harbor. The story itself is built on the premise that a Japanese submarine torpedoes an American craft while both are submerged. Actual battle experience, however, showed that an attacked ship was always cruising on the surface. While not denying the possibility of a successful attack on a submerged sub, former submarine commanders suggest it would be a remote occurrence. Likewise, while conceding that a submarine could torpedo an attacking destroyer with a straight-on bow shot as shown in the movie, submariners say it was done only rarely. (In fact, the commander who perfected the technique later disappeared on a cruise.)[2]

In contrast, Destination Tokyo did not force audiences to stretch their credibility to any great extent, thanks to the care writer-director Delmer Daves lavished on the film. While working on the script, Daves went to the Mare Island Submarine Base in San Francisco Bay, lived with the submariners for a week and returned to the studio to incorporate the material into a meaningful story. One result of this attention to detail was an almost too realistic reproduction of still-secret radar equipment. When the Navy saw the "radar" set, it demanded to know the source of Daves' information. He was finally able to mollify the service's Security Branch by explaining that he had conceived the prop from his own research. The Navy was further satisfied to discover that the "Copperfin's" device operated on the principle of an oscilloscope, while actual radar scopes project images by means of an electronic sweep. As a result, the

Navy was more than willing to allow the Japanese to "learn" from Daves' invention.[3]

The American people learned from the film how men exist aboard submarines during wartime. The "Copperfin" was manned by the typical mixture of ethnic backgrounds, commanded by Cary Grant cast "as a crisp, cool and kind-hearted gent who is every bit as resourceful as he is handsome and slyly debonair." Unlike later submarine tales in which conflicts among the crew help create the dramatic tensions, *Destination Tokyo* depicts a crew that is united in its effort to win the war as quickly as possible, a goal still in the distance when *Destination Tokyo* was released at the end of December 1943. The successful mission of the fictionalized "Copperfin," juxtaposed with the success of the historical Doolittle raid, undoubtedly helped maintain the morale of the American people as their war entered its third year. This purpose aside, the movie made "a pippin of a picture from a purely melodramatic point of view."[4]

Thirty Seconds Over Tokyo

In contrast to *Destination Tokyo*, *Thirty Seconds Over Tokyo*, released in 1944, was forced to avoid melodrama. Based on Ted Lawson's book of the same name, which recounted his experiences as a pilot on Doolittle's raid, the film stuck with the facts and created its dramatic impact solely through the events it portrayed. As with any historical movie, the filmmakers faced the difficulty of bringing suspense to a historical event whose ending the audience already knew. Recent films such as *Tora! Tora! Tora!* (1970), *Midway* (1976), and *A Bridge Too Far* (1977) have demonstrated that relatively good history without three-dimensional characterizations and dramatic tensions fail as creative art. In contrast, *Thirty Seconds Over Tokyo* offered the audience living heroes in Ted Lawson, played with boyish good humor by Van Johnson, in Jimmy Doolittle, portrayed with appropriate reserve by Spencer Tracy, and the rest of the men who volunteered for the mission. Yet the fliers were more than heroes. The producers explained to the Army that they wanted "to make a picture in which there are no individual heroes because all are heroes; a picture in which the leading characters are the living symbols of millions of service men and their wives who quietly and gallantly offer to the American people the greatest sacrifice within their power to give." Likewise, the War Department hoped that the "picture will result not in the glorification of one officer, but the heroic

Lieutenant Col. James Doolittle wires a bunch of prewar Japanese medals to the fin of one of the 500-pound bombs he and his volunteer fliers were to drop on Japan in April, 1942. Spencer Tracy was to re-create Doolittle's pre-launching ceremony in Thirty Seconds Over Tokyo *(1944), and the raid was also to figure in the stories of* Destination Tokyo *(1944),* Purple Heart *(1944), and* Midway *(1976).*

exploits of the [whole] Army Air Force" in the raid. The Pictorial Branch further noted that the Army "has been reluctant to glorify any single individual. As Captain Lawson was one of a great number of men on this particular mission, it is expected that this picture will result in giving equal credit to all, rather than any single member."[5]

The producers indicated in the first script sent to the War Department that they felt "a heavy responsibility" in approaching Lawson's book. They believed a picture based on it would contribute "constructively and dynamically to the public morale. The best propaganda, of course, is the truth; and in Captain Lawson's book the truth is presented simply, decently, and dramatically." Also, by dramatizing the close cooperation between the Army and the Navy that made the Tokyo raid possible, the filmmakers sought "to destroy the malingering whisper that a harmful rivalry exists between these two branches of the service." Finally, they expected that the scenes showing "the devotion and courage of the Chinese people as they smuggled scores of American airmen to safety [would] constitute a genuine contribution to the relations between the American people and their courageous Chinese allies."[6]

Thirty Seconds Over Tokyo was supposed to show all these things factually. But in putting across its message, the film did not tell the entire story of the mission. Intended more as a public relations event than a military maneuver designed to inflict heavy damage, the raid did bring the war to the Japanese homeland for the first time. While the government now had to devote some of its resources to homefront defense, the actual bombing did little damage to military or industrial targets at a cost of every one of Doolittle's planes. As a propaganda document, the film stressed the public relations aspects of the raid while it ignored the lack of military success. Likewise, while it showed Chinese civilians helping the fliers to safety, it did not indicate that the rescuers were Communist guerrillas, not citizens loyal to Chiang Kai Shek. According to screenwriter Dalton Trumbo, everyone knew the truth "but there was no point in emphasizing this. The object of this film was to establish in the American minds that we had a powerful ally in the Chinese people, and that made the war effort more hopeful."[7]

To transfer Lawson's first-person account to the screen as accurately as possible, Trumbo interviewed the pilot and others involved in the raid. The conversations also enabled Trumbo to describe details of the training and flight as thoroughly as security would allow. Among other things, he was not permitted to identify the aircraft carrier used to launch the mission, nor could he reveal that one of the planes had landed in Siberia and the crew interned there. Within the limits of security and the demands of the war effort, the military cooperated fully with MGM. Trumbo recalled that he flew on a B-25 until "I knew every position on the plane and every job on the plane."[8]

Unlike director-oriented filmmaking of the 1960s and 70s, Trumbo worked closely with producer Sam Zimbalist in developing the script and preparing for the film. MGM did not select Mervyn LeRoy to direct the movie until shortly before it went into actual production, and he spent only two weeks working on the script before shooting began. According to Trumbo, very few changes were made on the script during this period, "nothing fundamental."[9]

The movie traces the events leading up to and including the raid through Ted Lawson's eyes. From their training camp at Eglin Air Force Base near Pensacola, the men fly their planes to San Francisco for loading on the aircraft carrier. Although their training has included takeoffs that are consistent with the length of a carrier flight deck, the fliers are kept in the dark about their mission until they are actually on their way to the western Pacific. After unexpectedly encountering a Japanese patrol boat, the bombers are forced to take off when they are more than 650 miles from the Japanese coast instead of the

400 miles originally planned. Led by Doolittle, all sixteen planes make it off the pitching carrier deck and successfully bomb their targets. Afterward, they must attempt to reach friendly territory in darkness with their fuel rapidly being exhausted. With the exception of the crew that lands safely in Russia, the rest of the fliers either bail out or crash-land once they reach the China coast.

Until the takeoff, Lawson shares the film with Doolittle and his fellow fliers as they train for the mission. However, once in the air, Lawson and his crew become the focus of the story. Once in China, their odyssey through enemy territory assumes heroic dimensions, with the crew suffering various injuries. Lawson himself perseveres despite a painfully shattered leg that must ultimately be amputated. Lawson's homecoming and reunion with his wife re-created the nation's welcome to the fliers for their courageous achievement in bringing the war to the Japanese homeland in the first dark months of the war.

The War Department found Trumbo's version of the raid acceptable for cooperation subject to certain changes that had to do mainly with military procedures and security matters. In a letter to the studio, the Pictorial Board told them not to show an enlisted man in an Officers Club scene; to delete the words "Singapore itself will fall" because it had "a defeatist implication"; to eliminate all references to the speed of the B-25s; to disguise the names of several characters who might be in Japanese-held territory.* The Army noted that the accuracy of many points "must be the responsibility of Captain Ted Lawson, particularly regarding his personal affairs. If he vouches for the correctness of the scenes involving matters of his own personal knowledge, then there is no War Department objection." The Army suggested, however, that Lawson's operation should be "toned down" or photographed so that "pictorially it will not exhilarate the emotions through these unfortunate situations." The service acknowledged "that there is a certain amount of dramatic value in Captain

---

* The crews of three downed planes were captured by the Japanese, and three men were subsequently beheaded. From this historical foundation, Darryl Zanuck wrote a fictional story and then produced *The Purple Heart* (1944), the third film to have its origins in Doolittle's raid. Although the movie itself had no basis in fact, Lewis Milestone's direction produced a flim which seemed so real that people thought Twentieth Century Fox had been provided secret information about the captured fliers. Unlike *Destination Tokyo* and *Thirty Seconds Over Tokyo*, however, *The Purple Heart* was not made to tell a "true" story of American men in war. By showing American men being tortured and hauled into Japanese courts as murderers, the film presented an image of American courage and steadfastness in the face of enemy brutality and thus inspired the nation to continue the struggle against its cruel and bloodthirsty foe.

Shot of actual takeoff of B-25 from the U.S.S. Hornet, *used in* Thirty Seconds Over Tokyo *and* Midway.

Lawson's experience, but this action should be handled most carefully and with dignity." Finally, because of the possible repercussions of emphasizing Chinese assistance in getting the fliers out of enemy-occupied territory, the Army suggested that this aspect of the story "should be reduced to a minimum, and only utilized where it is necessary to carry the thread of the story and where assistance by individuals is important to the picture."[10]

In agreeing to provide assistance on *Thirty Seconds Over Tokyo,* the War Department explained that cooperation might present a "problem" because of normal demands on training facilities. By the time the film went into production in early 1944, however, Mervyn LeRoy was allowed to do his location shooting at Eglin Air Force Base, the same site Doolittle's men had used for their training. During the month in Florida, with a crew of ninety-three people including the cast, LeRoy received technical advice from Ted Lawson and two other officers. He also had the use of as many as eighteen B-25 bombers when the script called for scenes of the entire squadron preparing for its mission.[11]

The location shooting was only the first step in the film's production. The War Department and the Navy could not provide the planes and a carrier for MGM to photograph scenes of the bombers and crew aboard ship or to actually restage the launching of Doolittle's raiders. The studio was therefore forced to build a section of the U.S.S. *Hornet's* flight deck on its Stage 15 and managed to squeeze four B-25s onto it. To recreate the takeoffs themselves, Buddy Gillespie, head of MGM's special effects department, built about four-fifths of the deck of the *Hornet* on a scale of one inch to the foot. The sixty-foot miniature was then set in the studio's 300-square-foot water tank. Because of its size in relationship to the tank, the miniature was kept stationary. Gillespie made the carrier rise, pitch, and roll hydraulically as water was moved past the ship with pumps and wave machines. He then photographed miniature bombers, attached to an overhead trolley with piano wire. The planes' "takeoffs" were controlled by means of little synchronous motors. These sequences were then combined with a limited amount of the newsreel footage taken during the actual takeoffs. Gillespie did his job so well that only someone familiar with the newsreel film can pick out the recreated takeoffs from the actual launchings. To reproduce the raiders' approach to the Japanese mainland, the Air Force flew several B-25s carrying cameras mounted on their noses inland over Los Angeles from the Pacific. The technique worked so well that later the producer of *Midway* resurrected the footage to open his film, even though the original montage is in black and white and the 1976 re-creation of the Battle of Midway is in color.[12]

This care in detail and visual reproduction resulted in a film that had "the tough and literal quality of an Air Force documentary."[13] In fact, the production may have succeeded too well in this regard. According to Trumbo, when he later did a brief stint as an Air Force correspondent in the Pacific, he discovered that B-25 pilots, after seeing the film, felt challenged to imitate the quick, short-distance takeoffs whenever they had the chance. Commanding officers told him that the result was an increased number of accidents that might have been avoided if the film hadn't shown the short takeoffs.[14]

Trumbo himself was critical of the movie from a dramatic point of view. In dealing with a historical subject, he explained that a film's climax often came at the end of the second act rather than the third. In *Thirty Seconds Over Tokyo*, Trumbo said the raid itself was the climax, yet, "We had to go on for another hour." As a screenwriter he explained he had "to go to so many tricks to cover it up . . . , you have to dance." Under the circumstances, Trumbo thought that the success of the picture "depends more or less on the ability, principally of the writer, because he constructs the picture, to fake it and to conceal that enormous defect in the structure."[15]

While the film may have had this dramatic flaw, as war propaganda, each act of *Thirty Seconds Over Tokyo* worked well. According to Mervyn LeRoy, "It showed the Air Force in a great light which they should be shown in.[16] Volunteering for a secret, implicitly dangerous mission and quickly learning new flying techniques illustrated the spirit of taking chances, of challenging the unknown that is inherent in American tradition and in the growth of the nation. Flying the almost suicidal mission because it might shorten the war illustrated the courage of the American fighting man for the nation better than any headlines could do. While the journey to safety may have been anticlimactic dramatically, to Trumbo it demonstrated the determination of the the armed forces to persevere despite adversity and physical pain. The movie was "a fitting tribute" to all the participants in Doolittle's raid and, according to Bosley Crowther of the *New York Times*, "It is certainly a most stimulating and emotionally satisfying film."[17]

Thirty Seconds Over Tokyo satisfied critics and audiences, and it provided a reasonable re-creation of history. However, it portrayed only a limited kind of war. The film showed little combat and no dead bodies. It presented the conflict in the detached way most fliers participate in it—at a distance, whether over Tokyo, Berlin, or the jungles of Southeast Asia. Even the struggle of Lawson and his comrades to reach friendly territory had little to do with combat as most American participants saw the war. The "real" war between 1942 and 1945, the one that finally made a difference, was fought not on the sea or in the air, but on the ground, infantry against infantry, man against man, struggling for every foot of territory. Airplanes and ships may have had more glamor. But only the foot soldier experienced all the grime, discomfort, and blood.

The Story of G.I. Joe

Wake Island, Bataan, and *Sahara* had only hinted at the true nature of this struggle because they sprang from screenwriters' imaginations. In contrast, *The Story of G.I. Joe*, which did not appear until 1945, showed the American people the stark reality of World War II ground combat. It did so because it was based on the reporting of Ernie Pyle, who had experienced combat firsthand was able to put what he had seen into words. It did so because 150 or so combat veterans served as extras and, in some cases, as speaking actors, recreating before the camera what they had done in actual combat. Most important, it did so because an old World War I flier, William Wellman, agreed to direct the film despite his inherent dislike for the infantry; he brought his directing skills to what he felt was a "beautifully written" story.[18]

As the director, Wellman served as a catalyst in bringing together Ernie Pyle, his stories, the actors, and the military to create a uniquely realistic movie. Nevertheless, *The Story of G.I. Joe* illustrates the extent to which film-making has been a collective process, not an author's medium. Unlike most World War II films initiated by the major studios, the concept for *G.I. Joe* originated with an independent producer, Lester Cowan. As Wellman later recalled, when Cowan started talking, all you could do was "just sit and listen."[19] He started talking with the War Department about an idea for a major Army film as early as September 1943. Though he had no clear concept in mind, he wanted to make a film in the class of *Air Force,* a prospect the service found of "particular interest."[20]

By October 1943, Cowan had reached an arrangement with United Artists for financial backing and distribution and had a scriptwriter talking to Ernie Pyle. As a result of these conversations, Cowan sent the War Department an outline of a story based on a collection of Pyle's columns in *Here Is Your War*. He proposed to feature the infantry, its training, and its actions at the front. The Army Ground Forces Headquarters approved the outline on November 27, but noted, "It must be realized that many modifications will occur before this picture is completed."[21]

The film did not go before the cameras for more than another year, since Cowan had problems in developing a suitable script. In a letter to the Army's Bureau of Public Relations in June 1944, the producer explained the delay:"In our script we are undertaking something quite without precedent. It is a challenge to undertake the writing of a dramatic story about the war and the soldier *during* the war. As you know, in the past, the best war stories evolved during the ten-year period following the war, when issues and events had become resolved and could be viewed with some perspective." Cowan claimed that the picture would represent the first attempt at a screen autobiography, in the sense that it would use the words of Ernie Pyle. Translating Pyle's words into visual drama had caused for the writers a problem that Cowan said they had solved by approaching Pyle's reporting "as a love story, figuratively speaking, of Pyle and the soldier."[22]

Cowan admitted that it was "an ambitious claim" to now say he had licked the story, since the script seemed to be bogged down in the mud of Corsica along with the war. But the recent D-Day landings had provided the solution. Victory was in sight and Pyle would be shown moving toward victory. As a result of this breakthrough in the evolution of the script, he felt prepared to commence photographing on August 1, since he would have enough of the script written in two weeks to cover the first four weeks of shooting. Cowan was in fact being wildly optimistic, since the writing continued throughout July. More important, he did not have a director for the film yet.[23]

In early July, he sent a telegram to the Pictorial Branch of the War Department to inquire about the possibility of securing John Huston as the director for his film. While Huston had made only two films before entering the Army, since enlisting he had directed *Report from the Aleutians* and was then completing *The Battle of San Pietro,* a documentary about the Italian campaign. Cowan felt this gave him "irreplaceable experience of living with soldiers under frontline conditions, so that he knows and feels the difference between the real thing and any Hollywood version." Cowan also felt he had the "rare opportunity to make Hollywood's first honest and authentic picture about the infantry soldier," and so wanted to work "with people who know from actual first-hand experience." Unfortunately, although Huston read a draft of the screenplay and made "very constructive and helpful criticisms," Cowan was not able to secure his services.[24]

Turning to another unsolved question, whom to cast as Ernie Pyle, the producer learned that Pyle wanted Burgess Meredith to play the role. Meredith, however, was on active duty in the Army, and the service presented Cowan with a choice: Either turn over all profits of the film to the Army Emergency Relief Fund (as had been done in other films) or Meredith would have to resign his commission.[25] Eventually, when Meredith accepted the role, he went on inactive status and seemingly became Pyle, "because his impersonation [was] so consummate." According to Dudley Nichols, who had written *Air Force,* it didn't matter "whether Pyle looked like himself or like Meredith; the feeling that Meredith projects into the whole film, illuminating the lifting scenes into high significance, is the feeling that Pyle projected through all his writing. Out of all this ugliness, it seemed to say, out of all this horror, this filth and misery and butchery and waste, comes this—this wonderful thing, man!"[26]

By the beginning of August 1944, Cowan had still not found a director, and he decided to approach William Wellman. Walking into his house uninvited, Cowan proceeded to tell the director all about the film. Before running out of breath, Cowan said that both he and Pyle had decided Wellman was the man to direct the picture. Wellman "politely declined the great honor that they would bestow on me," but Cowan refused to accept the rejection. He continued to argue until Wellman told him bluntly: "I was not interested in working my ass off for the infantry." He explained why he "hated the infantry with such a fury. . . . that I frightened him into getting the hell out of my house. That was that, I thought."[27]

Not for Cowan, who returned a few days later with a letter from Pyle. Wellman knew Pyle by reputation but "had not bothered to read any of his writings because they touched on but one subject—the infantry—and to me, that was like waving a red flag in front of a bull, so I slammed the door in [Cowan's] face." Again Wellman believed the subject was closed. Cowen, however, was not to be denied, and he returned a few days later with presents for his five children. "The son of a bitch even knew their names," Wellman recalled. After telling Cowan off in "well-chosen four-letter words," he told him to stay away or he would put him in the hospital.[28]

Wellman soon discovered that Cowan was "a persistent bastard." The same night, Pyle himself called Wellman from his home in Albuquerque, inviting him to visit and listen to his story first-hand. He was sure the director would change his mind after he realized the great need for such a picture and "what it would mean to the thousands of kids that were fighting for his and my country." Wellman later said that Pyle almost had him crying on the phone. He went to New Mexico two days later. After another two days of talks, with Cowan in attendance part of the time, Wellman finally agreed to direct the film. Pyle returned with him to Los Angeles to work with Wellman on polishing the script, which had finally been completed. According to the director, he and Pyle worked together to create "a great shooting script. Cruel, factual, unaffected, genuine, and with a heart as big as Ernie's. This was *the* story of G.I. Joe."[29]

William Wellman, director of Wings *(1927),* The Story of G.I. Joe *(1945), and* Battleground *(1949), in a 1975 photo.*

In the conventional sense of Hollywood's dramatic films, *G.I. Joe* had no plot, no story that built up to a grand climax. It simply followed an infantry unit in battle and at rest as it slogged up the Italian penninsula. In documentary style, the film recorded the interactions of the men, their foibles, and their longings to be home or anywhere but in war. *G.I. Joe* succeeded in visualizing Ernie Pyle's newspaper columns. The men's names may have been changed but their experiences were real. There were no Hollywood theatrics. The usual formula—single-handed heroics, dramatic firefights, and a little romance on the side—was avoided. There were no women in the film. *G.I. Joe* showed men at war, trying to survive—no more, no less.

The rewriting and polishing of the script ended in mid-November 1944, when shooting was about to begin. Although the Army had promised full cooperation, Wellman required only a limited amount of military hardware. His primary need was for experienced soldiers, and the War Department provided 150 veterans of the Italian campaign who were then in transit to the Pacific theatre. Although their stay in California was a respite from combat, during the six weeks of filming, the officers and men carried on their regular training when not before the cameras.

The Army stressed that since "it is the plan of everyone concerned to have the troops make the best possible appearance in the film, both in physical condition and in military techniques, the training program will be rigorously pursued." The Army expected the men to show "exemplary conduct" and warned that any trouble in public places would be dealt with sternly. The men were allowed to let their beards grow, but only "for purposes of realism in combat scenes." At the same time, the soldiers had been through some of the worst fighting in Europe and were about to go to the Pacific, and the film company tried to make their stay in Hollywood enjoyable by providing them with spending money and entertainment.[30]

Wellman had his own instructions for the soldiers. When they had settled in their quarters, Wellman asked the officer in charge to assemble them so he could "straighten them out." He wanted to be sure that the soldiers knew what the film meant to them, to him, and to Pyle. Although Pyle had told the G.I.s about Wellman's change in attitude toward the infantry, Wellman wanted to make his feelings clear. He told them, "Look, you have a goddamn broken down old flier who is going to be your boss. Now you have to make up your mind that I'm a tough son of a bitch. I want you to do just exactly what I want you to do. But I'll never double-cross you. I'll never ask you to do something you don't want to do." He told them that *G.I. Joe* wasn't going to be just another war picture, "but something that you, Ernie, and I will be proud of. That's a big expensive job, that's why you are here, that's why actors have been training with you, so they will look like you, handle themselves the way you do. That's also why a lot of you fellas will be playing scenes, speaking lines. I want to make this the goddamndest most honest picture that has ever been made about the doughfoot." [31]

To prepare the actors ("as few as possible") for their roles, Wellman insisted that they go through regular training with the soldiers and live with them. He wanted them to act and smell like soldiers, and he made this requirement very clear when he cast them: "Look, you are going to live with the group or you don't get the job." Wellman also selected several of the soldiers themselves for speaking roles. He told them: "All through the picture, when a G.I. has something to say, I want a G.I. to say it, not some bastard G.I. You know the story is good, and it's real, and it's beautifully written by a man whose very life is you." He assured them that the camera wouldn't "bite," but it would "pick up everything, and what I want it to pick up is honesty and sincerity." With a little luck, he said, "when it's all over, you'll see something up there that will be more than a picture of the infantry; it might just be a monument, and I am going to make it that if it breaks my ass." [32]

Wellman recalled that the men responded by learning their lines and carrying out their orders: ". . . all those kids that were in it were great, and they all went to the South Pacific, and none of them came home." Nor did Ernie Pyle, who died covering one of the island landings. The director wondered, "How does that make you feel? You, the man that directed the picture, that got to know all of them and liked most of them. How do you feel? [I] felt lousy, . . . but at least we had some fun together. We were shooting, but [with] blanks, and nobody was getting hurt. We had a lot of laughs together, a lot of work, a lot of drinks. . . . It all seems so futile now. It's the one picture of mine that I refuse to look at." [33]

Even without the personal involvement of Wellman, looking at *The Story of G.I. Joe* provides an image of men in combat that few other American films have created. General Eisenhower called it "the greatest war picture I've ever seen." When the men of the Fifth Army in Italy, some of whom had fought in the campaigns portrayed, saw the film they reacted with: "This is it!" [34] Lewis Milestone's *A Walk in the Sun*, released in early 1946, created a similar impact by focusing on even fewer men during a single action. But *The Story of G.I. Joe*, of all the films made during the war period, best visualized the nature of the infantrymen in combat, the day-to-day struggles with the elements and a formidable enemy.

Wellman succeeded in doing this by making the faces of his actors and the combat veterans the symbols of all the young men the American people had been reading about since December 7, 1941. Approaching Ernie Pyle's experi-

World War II: Reality

ences and writings with a starkly documentary style, Wellman concentrated on the lives of average soldiers, not on the false heroics usually portrayed in Hollywood war movies. Having committed himself to telling the story of Ernie Pyle and his relationship with the infantrymen, Wellman created a film containing an "extreme sensitivity and deep tenderness for manly human beings."[35]

To screenwriter-reviewer Dudley Nichols, the inclusion of Pyle as a character in the film was responsible for raising the film above the level of "an almost monotonous story of a company of foot soldiers." He explained that using Pyle was a beautiful "device," one that is "used as pure film, what I would call screen-film, and not the kind of stage-film we frequently are given because it is easier to write words than to imagine pure film." Nichols observed that Pyle seldom talked in the movie and when he did, "there is no eloquence. But in his silences, in his contained compassion, his profound sense of tragedy and waste, there is a continued eloquence that soars beyond the scope of words."[36]

The only other movie made during the war that contains an equally eloquent statement about the American experience in World War II is John Huston's documentary *The Battle of San Pietro* (1945). Huston's film creates its feeling of war through the use of combat footage taken by the director and his Signal Corps cameramen during and after the Battle of San Pietro. He does not dwell on individuals, does not develop characters with whom viewers identify as in a dramatic film. Using the camera to report rather than tell the story, Huston captures the sense of the war's impersonality, the individual's insignificance, the impermanence of life itself. Even though *San Pietro* is a documentary and the men real, the film presents no less an illusion of war than the fictionalized *Story of G.I. Joe*.

All film creates an *illusion* of reality. The camera sees and captures only what the filmmaker allows it to record. Reality, in contrast, is the continuity of unbroken images. Once a camera stops, once an editor cuts the strip of celluloid, the image projected on the screen becomes the vision the filmmaker chooses to present. So whether in a documentary or in a dramatic film, the audience sees an illusion of love, hate, peace, or war. How close any of these images approximates reality depends on the skills of the filmmakers, their scripts, the resources available to them. Even in the best of circumstances, as in the making of *The Story of G.I. Joe*, it is not possible to recreate all the realities of war.

Wellman, in reminiscing about his film, touches on the problem of communicating this sense of authenticity, of being there: "The writing, poetry of the doughfoot, cruel poetry but so honest, so tragic, so miserable, so lonely, and so many wonderful kids gone. You can't replace them, ever, but maybe you can stop wars so we don't keep adding to that castigated list. Castigate—'to punish in order to correct.' It's a hell of a punishment, and we haven't corrected a thing. . . .''[37]   **The Story of G.I. Joe**

CHAPTER FIVE

WORLD WAR II REFOUGHT

★

By the time *G.I. Joe* appeared in the summer of 1945, the film industry was beginning to fear that as entertainment, war films were losing their popularity. After V-E Day, the end of the war could be measured in months rather than years. Studios believed that the war films market would dry up with the Japanese surrender, and they began to cut back their production of combat movies so that most of them would be finished whenever the war ended. Two that were in the final stages of completion on V-J Day, *They Were Expendable* and *Walk in the Sun* were subsequently released to highly favorable reviews. But neither film enjoyed much box-office success during the first blush of peace, even though their direction by John Ford and Lewis Milestone produced the same authenticity seen in *Thirty Seconds Over Tokyo* and *The Story of G.I. Joe*. *Task Force*, which was about to go into production, was suspended soon after the Japanese surrender. For the time being, Hollywood limited itself to films like *Best Years of Our Lives* and *Till the End of Time*, which dealt with the transition of servicemen from war to peace.

The abrupt cessation of combat films by the close of 1945 did not, of course, signify the end of Hollywood's interest in war stories. As after the First World War, filmmakers faced the question of how soon the public would again be ready to spend money to see World War II fought on a screen. During 1947, several studios began discussing possible military projects, and by early 1948 two small-scale films were in production. Warner Brothers' *Fighter Squadron* portrayed a P-51 fighter group stationed in England in 1944 and included a

---

Director Henry King rehearses a scene with Gregory Peck in B-17 mock-up for Twelve O'Clock High *(1950).*

young Rock Hudson as one of the fliers. Made up largely of combat footage, the film received a limited amount of Air National Guard assistance and was released in the fall of 1948. MGM's *Command Decision*, based on the 1947 play of the same name, dealt with the strategic bombing of Germany during the buildup of American air strength. This picture was filmed mostly on the studio's sound stages, with some combat footage to open the movie up, and it also was released by the end of 1948.

In the meantime, work had begun on the four major projects that were to re-create the market for war movies and start the cycle of World War II films that would run into the 1960s. *Battleground* usually receives credit for initiating the cycle because of its critical acclaim and box-office success. In fact, it appeared almost simultaneously with *Task Force, Sands of Iwo Jima,* and *Twelve O'Clock High.* However, *Task Force* had its origins more than two years before the other three films.

Task Force

When Warner Brothers initiated the project in early 1944, the company anticipated the war might end before it could complete the film. So it conceived of *Task Force* as both a dramatized history of Naval aviation and an account of World War II carrier warfare. Despite this broadened approach, after V-J Day the studio shelved the project, but allowed producer Jerry Wald and writer-director Delmer Daves to continue developing a script and collecting combat footage.

Having written scripts for *Shipmates* and *Shipmates Forever,* and written and directed *Destination Tokyo,* Daves had established close contacts with the Navy by early 1944 when he first discussed with Navy officials the possibility of making a major movie about the development of aircraft carriers. By April 1945, he, Wald, and writer Ranald MacDougall had researched the history of Naval aviation and compiled an extensive set of story notes. Daves had also begun looking at Navy documentaries and newsreel footage that traced the story pictorially. The Navy helped by tracking down and selecting the best combat footage sent back from the Pacific. In formally assigning junior officers to the task in mid-May, the secretary and under secretary of the Navy indicated they were "interested in the successful production" of the Warner Brothers' film.[1]

MacDougall turned in a preliminary script at the end of June, a revised script in July, a completed script at the end of August, and a final script in

October. All of these 1945 versions, as well as the final script written by Daves in 1948, tell basically the same story of the struggle of Navy officers committed to the development of aircraft carriers and Naval aviation. As the representative officer, Gary Cooper flies off the first Navy carrier, the U.S.S. *Langley* during the 1920s. He so strongly advocates the need for a carrier fleet that his career is sidetracked in the 1930s. During the war, he commands a carrier and soon after retires as an admiral, saluted as he departs by Navy jets flying over one of the new 60,000-ton floating airfields. The fictional story serves primarily as a framework around which the historical development of Naval airpower is portrayed. As a result, *Task Force* lacks the dramatic impact of other military films that focus on individuals and their efforts to survive during battle. Still, the combat footage, carefully selected and superbly integrated into the second half of the film, effectively provides the audience with a real sense of carrier warfare.

The theme of *Task Force*, the struggle of a small group of Naval aviators for planes and carriers, is summed up in one line from an early script: "You might as well know appropriations for aviation are hard to get—that our planes were not designed for carrier operations. We do our best with what we have."[2] In addition, the film also contains a strong implicit Navy message: that aircraft carriers won the war in the Pacific and can protect the nation against any future aggression. In fact, the film's release date was advanced several months so that it appeared at the height of the Air Force-Navy battle waged in Congress over appropriations for bombers versus aircraft carriers. Anticipating the contemporary debate, the film's characters debate senators, Army officers, and battleship admirals about the efficacy of carriers over other military hardware. In one scene, a senator observes that four carriers were lost in the first six months of the war, and a Navy flier asks, "Is it your contention, Senator, that we should abandon *airplanes*—because they've been shot down? *Tanks*—because they've been knocked out of action? We need to out-produce the enemy in planes, tanks, *and* aircraft carriers! The only thing wrong with carriers is that we don't have enough of them!" Later in the meeting, Gary Cooper responds to a general's argument in favor of land-based bombers: "The General is right—*if* we have to take every Pacific Island enroute to Japan. But two dozen carriers are worth more than 200 enemy-held islands, anchored in one spot! Our carriers *won't* be anchored—they'll be fast moving islands from which we can launch fighters and bombers against the enemy wherever we choose!"[3]

These arguments clearly represented the Navy's position. When *Task Force* appeared, the advocates of Naval aviation had been vindicated, and the film was a monument to their victory as well as a tribute to the contribution carriers had made in winning the war. Warner Brothers admitted that the decision to advance the release date sprang from a desire to take advantage of public interest aroused by the congressional hearings over the bomber-versus-aircraft-carrier issue. The Navy denied that it had asked the studio to move up the film's release date. In fact, the Navy did not construct the arguments in favor of carriers for the script, however much it later approved of them. The scripts of August and October 1945, written four years before the Army-Navy confrontation, contain virtually the same dialogue as the final screenplay.[4]

This is not to say that the Navy played no role in the film's pitch for aircraft carriers. The friendships both Daves and Wald had built up with Navy men while working on earlier films undoubtedly influenced their perceptions of the service. Moreover, during their five years of research, they worked with officers who had a pro-carrier bias. Finally, the actual history of the war in the Pacific, from Midway onward, clearly demonstrated the importance of carriers in defeating the Japanese.

Message aside, *Task Force* became the first major postwar film made with large-scale military assistance to bring World War II to American theatres. Using extensive Navy combat footage, the movie portrayed the reality of war in ways no special effects men could ever hope to. In the dramatic highlight of the movie, a kamikaze attack on Cooper's carrier turns the ship into a flaming wreck. Using color footage taken aboard the U.S.S. *Franklin*, the most extensively damaged ship in World War II to return to port, the filmmakers gave the audience a sense of the horror of combat: the flaming ship is real, not a set or a miniature; the dead men will not get up and walk away; and the burns cannot be washed away as they are when a scene is completed. So despite its pseudo-documentary style and lack of a dramatic story line, *Task Force* created an emotional impact unequaled in most war films.

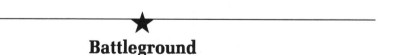

Battleground

In contrast to the epic dimensions and great sweep of time portrayed in *Task Force*, the next major postwar film, *Battleground*, focused on the actions of a small group of men caught up in a single major battle. This film created its version of war not by using combat footage and great numbers of soldiers, but by developing the characters of individuals and their reactions to unexpected adversity. Most of the action took place within the controlled environment of a sound stage, not on an outdoor location.

The struggle to make *Battleground* provides enough material for its own movie. When Dore Schary first conceived the project in early 1947 at RKO, he was strongly opposed by those who felt that audiences were not ready for more war movies. Schary himself feared that Americans might experience the same sort of disillusionment that swept the country after World War I. To him, therefore, "it was imperative to do a film about World War II that would say the war was worth fighting despite the terrible losses. . . The men who fought this war were not suckers. They had not been used. There was something at stake. It was the first time, in a long, long time, hundreds of years, that there had been a real danger of a takeover by a very evil and strong force."[5]

To symbolize this threat, Schary looked for a specific situation in World War II where the Allied cause was in jeopardy. Believing that the Pacific had been well-visualized, he turned to the European Theatre, which had been portrayed during the war by only "a couple of very good pictures." Schary considered the rest to have been "kind of bang-bang pictures" with virtually none dealing with the period after Normandy. He decided that a portrayal of the crucial siege of Bastogne during the Battle of the Bulge would represent the threat to freedom he was seeking. Then, in his capacity as RKO's production head, Schary called in Bob Pirosh, a writer who had been in the war, and asked him what he knew about Bastogne. "Know anything?" he responded, "I was there!"[6]

William Wellman talks to screenwriter Bob Pirosh (center left) and producer Dore Schary on outdoor lot used for opening drill scenes in Battleground *(1949).*

Pirosh had come out of the war with notes on his experiences and a desire to do a movie about the Battle of the Bulge. As a result of his meeting with Schary, he began work on the project, but under the title *Prelude to Love* to disguise its subject, because Schary "did not want anyone in the industry to know I was making a war film." In April 1947, Pirosh, as an initial step in his work, returned to the battlefields where he had fought. He quickly decided to content himself "with an attempt to portray the activities of one squad of riflemen —without heroics, without fancy speeches, without a phony romance." He wanted to write "a picture which would ring true to the men [who had fought there] and which would not be an insult to the memory of those we left there." Pirosh felt that the story of one squad "was, in a sense, the story of all squads. I happened to be sent to Europe, you happened to wind up in the Pacific, somebody else sweated it out in the Aleutians. The important thing is, what did it do to us? How did we feel?"[7]

Although Pirosh had fought in the Battle of the Bulge, he had not been in the 101st Division, which had been surrounded at Bastogne for eight days. Consequently, he was worried that he might not be able to develop a true-to-life script. He approached General Anthony McAuliffe, who had commanded the 101st Division during the siege and asked if his not having been at Bastogne would hamper him in producing an accurate script. McAuliffe, whose succinct "Nuts!" to the German demand for surrender had become the symbol of American determination during the war, responded with another "Nuts!" He told Pirosh, "You were fighting under the same kind of conditions. You were just as cold, the fog was just as thick, the suspense was just as great. Go ahead and write it the way you feel it."[8]

Meanwhile, Schary was testing the market for a war film by broaching the subject to sales representatives who visited the West Coast. Disagreeing with their negative evaluations, he polled movie exhibitors across the country by phone and by letter. When they indicated that a good war film would draw audiences, Schary formally announced the project, now titled *Battleground*.[9]

Pirosh finished his first draft of the screenplay in mid-January 1948, and by early spring, Schary, who was personally producing the picture, had begun to cast the main roles. At that point, Howard Hughes suddenly bought RKO. Initially, he allowed Schary to continue running the studio, but when he told the producer to take *Battleground* off the studio's production schedule, Schary resigned. He told Hughes that he was "too tough" and "too rich" to fight. Schary's only request was that Hughes agree to sell him the script of *Battleground*. Hughes agreed.[10]

When Schary became production head at MGM a few weeks later, he indicated that he wanted *Battleground* to be his first film. Louis B. Mayer, head of

A helmeted William Wellman rehearses his actors (including James Whitmore to the director's left) and soldiers from the 101st Airborne Division on soundstage with writer Pirosh (center, also in helmet) listening intently.

Snow-covered Bastogne recreated outdoors in Culver City, one of the few exterior locales for Battleground.

the studio, expressed the same reservations about a war film that Schary had already encountered at RKO. Nevertheless, neither he nor Nicholas Schenck, president of Loew's Inc., the distributing branch of MGM, wanted to oppose Schary too strongly so soon after his return to the studio, especially since they knew how strongly he felt about *Battleground*. Consequently, Mayer suggested that they allow Schary to make the movie, and if it were a failure, they would be better able to keep him under control. Although Schenck agreed, the project quickly became known as "Schary's folly."[11]

With studio approval in hand, Schary asked Hughes how much he wanted for the screenplay of *Battleground*. Hughes said he wanted only what had been spent to write the script, about $20,000, which Schary considered a "bargain." He then brought Pirosh to MGM to complete the script and arranged with

Denise Darcel provides the only respite from combat in Battleground.

General McAuliffe and the Army to provide some veterans of the 101st Division's struggle at Bastogne as extras on the film. Schary also supervised the casting of the principal roles including Van Johnson, James Whitmore, and George Murphy, all veterans of earlier war films.[12]

While the picture remained essentially an all-male production, the script did include one woman, a French farm girl who feeds some of the soldiers during a lull in the battle. For the part, Schary hired Denise Darcel, "a buxom, juicy French girl" who, he said, "sashayed into the office with ample, rounded buttocks and breasts that, as she walked, presented a movable feast." An MGM public relations man later went so far as to suggest that the success of *Battleground* could be attributed to an ad that showed Darcel in a tight black sweater. She was cutting a loaf of bread—with the knife coming perilously close to her breasts. William Wellman, who directed the film, didn't think "that kind of stuff" should have been in a war film. He said he wouldn't have put a girl in *The Story of G.I. Joe* "for all the money in the world." Actually, given the quality of the picture and the critical acclaim it received, the public relations man undoubtedly gave his ad too much credit for the success of *Battleground*.[13]

Wellman was an obvious choice as director for *Battleground* given his successful portrayal of infantrymen in *G.I. Joe*. While he claimed to dislike Schary and did not agree with his desire to put messages in films, Wellman's animosity was naturally directed toward anyone who might interfere with his work. He recalled, "I hate all producers, frankly, if you want to know the truth!" He did,

"Was this trip necessary?" asks the chaplain on MGM's winterized sound stage as he verbalizes Dore Schary's rationale for making Battleground.

however, like Pirosh's script for *Battleground*, and when the studio offered him "an awful lot of money to do it," he agreed to direct the film. Nevertheless, he told Schary, "Look, I can't make a G.I. *Joe* out of this thing. I'll make a film about a very tired group of guys."[14]

Both the studio and the military went all out to help the director make the film as realistic as possible. Since the Battle of the Bulge had taken place over snow-covered terrain, the major problem for the studio was to provide a winter-like atmosphere. To do this, Schary took out a wall between two sound stages and built a huge indoor battlefield, giving Wellman a completely controlled environment to work in. Apart from the obvious benefit of not having to worry about melting snow, he had a set that facilitated lighting and camerawork. For scenes in which G.I.s moved across open spaces, Wellman used rear view projection of actual long shots. For large movements of men and trucks, the film editor matched staged action with combat footage. Only the opening and closing sequences took place outdoors. Unlike *Battle of the Bulge*, made in Spain in 1964, in which palm trees are visible in the background and dust replaces snow as the tanks roar into combat, *Battleground* has carefully dressed exteriors that match both the interior shots and the combat footage.[15]

General McAuliffe and the Army liked the project from its inception. McAuliffe's interest stemmed from his original discussion with Pirosh about the story, and he served as a technical advisor for the writing of the script. He also recommended Lieutenant Colonel Harry W. O. Kinnard, who had served under him at Bastogne, to be technical advisor during the shooting. McAuliffe helped arrange for twenty members of the 101st Division to be sent from Fort Bragg to serve as extras during the production. Wellman had his actors train with the soldiers, as he had during the making of *G.I. Joe*, so that they would perform in military fashion. The Army provided Wellman with a couple of tanks, trucks, and other needed equipment.[16]

"Was the trip necessary?" A chaplain asks the question at the end of the film, after the seige of Bastogne has been broken. The rhetorical query served as the instrument for inserting Schary's rationale for making *Battleground*. His message, conveyed through Pirosh's script, was a response to the Nazi threat: "Nobody wanted this war except the Nazis. A great many people tried to deal with them, and a lot of them are dead. Millions have died for no other reason except that the Nazis wanted them dead." Their actions gave the Americans no choice but to fight. The chaplain-Schary saw in this a great lesson, and "those of us who are learning it the hard way are not going to forget. . . . We must never again let any kind of force dedicated to a super race or a super idea or a super anything get strong enough to impose itself on a free world. We have to be smart enough and tough enough in the beginning to put out the fire before it starts spreading."[17]

Message aside, *Battleground* justified the efforts put into its production. Wellman thought it was "very movie-picture like" in contrast to *G.I. Joe* which was "real." While the incidents in *Battleground* actually occurred, they were distilled through a screenwriter, and the film was essentially a motion picture story while *G.I. Joe* was a documentary. Underlying *G.I. Joe* was the knowledge of a war in progress and the reality of soldiers returning to battle when the film was finished. This sense of impending doom gave *G.I. Joe* a quality that *Battleground*, made during peacetime, could not attain. Nevertheless, Wellman conceded that a lot of people liked the new film better: "I don't know why. I guess because there was a lot of humor, a dirty kind of humor."[18]

This humor helped make *Battleground* a box-office success. A nation at peace could laugh at a big-breasted girl's efforts to cut a loaf of bread without doing herself bodily harm; people could laugh at jokes about a soldier's lost teeth; audiences could enjoy the well-staged combat sequences without having to worry about boys at the front who might be dying. Schary may have made the movie to remind the nation of the reasons men did die in the war. But both he and Wellman knew that in peacetime, a war film had to do more than create a patriotic feeling in its audience. *Battleground* also had to entertain, and so the filmmakers had to accept the compromises which separated it from *The Story of G.I. Joe*, the compromises that made it a war movie instead of a pseudo-documentary.

At the same time, *Battleground* offered audiences much more than most Hollywood war movies. Thanks to the skill of the studio technicians and the military assistance, Wellman captured the feel of battle, the loneliness of being surrounded by a superior enemy force, the struggle against the elements and against a German force making its last effort to win the war. These feelings were the result of top-notch performances by the actors and soldier-actors working with a taut, powerful script that only a survivor of the Battle of the Bulge could have written. To Pirosh, the commitment to the project by all those involved had made the film a "dream come true."[19] To the audience it was a grim, authentic war drama, one the nation was ready to see, however close in time it might be to the war itself.

★

Twelve O'Clock High

Unlike *Battleground*, in which men are under fire almost continuously, *Twelve O'Clock High* contains only a short combat sequence at the very end of the movie. The film pictures men at war in a different context, by studying leadership and the terrible effect of responsibility on a commander. As General Frank Savage, Gregory Peck prepares his men for aerial combat by pushing them to their limit and beyond, setting an example by pushing himself even harder. In wanting his men to be survivors of the air war over Europe, not dead heroes, Savage initially alienates his officers by his hard-driving methods and cold exterior. Ultimately, his men come to realize that his teaching offers them the tools to survive and win the war.

Novels and movies have seldom dealt with the command-level decisions that commit men to battle and often to death. In actual combat, military officers must think of their men as numbers and impersonal units before thay can consider them as human beings, as sons, brothers, husbands, or fathers. To think of them as individuals would produce too great a psychological burden on leadership. So in war, fighting men are reduced to symbols that are moved on maps and committed to lists—whether of numbers of battle-ready soldiers or of casualties.

Most war literature, print or visual, has not concentrated on this level of reality or on the burden of command leadership. The portrayals deal instead with the relationships among officers in the field, among officers and their men, or among the men themselves. Whatever their rank, theses men receive orders from commanders that must be carried out without question, because soldiers, sailors, or fliers must act, not think. The dramatic conflict develops from interpersonal tensions between men or between two combatting forces. Death, always close at hand, usually is a traumatic, individual loss. In contrast, *Twelve O'Clock High* shows the effect of the command decisions on the leaders themselves. (So well does it do so that over the years the film has been used in leadership training seminars to illustrate the problems of decision-making for the commander in war, business, or education.)

Even though *Twelve O'Clock High* dealt with a seldom-portrayed subject, the film followed the usual complicated path from its inception as a project in the spring of 1947 to its completion in 1949. Twentieth Century Fox's original interest had been William Wister Haines' play *Command*, based on his novel *Command Decision*. Its plot represented "a constant and powerful undertone of the inevitable friction between staff and command," the doers versus the planners. Even so, Lyman Munson, a Fox executive, thought Haines was "either off the track or frankly overboard when he touches on the relationships between soldiers and congressmen, officers and men, and so forth." But Munson stressed that with easily made revisions the story "should make a great picture, and someone will certainly make it when the deluge of war films gets underway." Nevertheless, he advised "against touching" it unless Haines modified his financial demands, which the executive termed "utterly ridiculous."[20]

Becoming interested in another Air Force story, an as-yet unpublished novel by Sy Bartlett and Beirne Lay titled *Twelve O'Clock High*, Fox did not pursue *Command*, the rights to which MGM quickly bought. Just as quickly, Munson now found *Command Decision* "synthetic and artificial," saying it "does not ring true. Its characters and its situations are almost hysterically overwritten. It has no love story. . . . And unless it is drastically changed, the Air Forces will give neither cooperation nor assistance." In contrast, Munson found *Twelve O'Clock High* "practically photographic in its accuracy. Its characters and its situations are plausible and believable. It has an unusual love story. And the Air Forces obviously will give to the limit with assistance, stock footage, and publicity." He noted also that "the story is jammed with incidents which are generally dramatic but also occasionally delightfully humorous." He hoped the studio would buy it.[21]

Such praise and suggestion notwithstanding, Darryl Zanuck, head of production at Twentieth Century Fox, took his time about deciding to buy the rights to the novel. He had a number of problems to face, including possible charges by MGM of plagiarism of *Command Decision*, the authors' high price for the rights to their novel, the cost of the film's production, and the feeling of Joe Schenck, Fox's president, that people were not yet ready for films about

B-17 at rest following Paul Mantz's spectacular crash that was one of the visual high-lights of Twelve O'Clock High.

World War II. Harper & Brothers settled the plagiarism issue to Zanuck's satisfaction in September, when the company decided that *Twelve O'Clock High* told a different story from Haines' work and so accepted the novel for publication. Since Bartlett was a writer for Fox and wanted the studio to do the film, he and Lay were flexible in their negotiations, particularly when presented with the possibility of doing the screenplay. Studio executives advised Zanuck that production costs, apart from the salaries of the director and actors, could be kept relatively low since the film would require little set construction and material, assuming that planes and military equipment could come from the Air Force. Finally, while no one knew in 1947 how soon people would be willing to pay to see war movies, Munson told Zanuck that he disagreed with Schenck's feelings. More to the point, he saw the story not as a war movie, but "primarily as a clash of personalities, as a highly dramatic, personal story of people."[22]

With these inputs before him, Zanuck decided in early October to buy *Twelve O'Clock High,* indicating to Munson that he felt it "imperative that we be prepared to go into production in late spring or early summer" of 1948. He said he had already decided Gregory Peck was "the absolutely perfect choice" to play General Savage because he "has the guts, the age and the deep quality."[23] Despite Zanuck's eagerness, it was eighteen months before cameras began rolling. The studio first had to arrange to obtain combat footage from the Air Force not only to be used in the film, but also to help guide the scriptwriters and production department. The script itself had to be written and submitted to the Air Force as the first step in obtaining cooperation. After the military agreed to assist, equipment had to be located and shooting sites found. And a director and cast had to be selected.

By November of 1947 the Air Force had read a synopsis of the novel and had expressed a willingness to provide assistance. The studio had selected Bartlett and Lay to do the screenplay, albeit with some hesitation, since Zanuck thought that the authors may "have shot their wad on the [novel]." Knowing that they would be replaced if "they did not pan out early in the game," the writers worked "pretty slowly" throughout the spring and early summer. In July of 1948, Bud Lighton, the film's producer, noted that their slowness was to be expected. "They have lived together on the material long enough, between the book and the script, that I begin to gather that the marriage is wearing a bit thin." At the same time, he thought the script was beginning "to fall fairly solidly into place."[24]

Even before the writers completed the script, however, Zanuck began to worry about the Air Force's initial commitment to assist on the film. Ignoring normal channels, as was his manner, the filmmaker went right to the top, writing on a personal, first-name basis to Air Force Chief of Staff Hoyt Vandenberg in an attempt to ascertain the service's current position. He reminded the general that *Gentleman's Agreement* had won him an Oscar as best picture of 1947 and that he had the film rights to *Twelve O'Clock High,* a best-seller that had impressed all the Air Force men he had met.

Getting down to business, Zanuck explained he was hesitant to invest the $2,000,000 needed to turn the book into a movie given the current situation in the film industry and the need for "so-called sure-fire entertainment." He noted that *Twelve O'Clock High* could not be "classed as orthodox entertainment. It is a powerful, sincere, and dramatic story and a glorification of the officers and men of the Eighth Air Force. There is no doubt in my mind that unquestionably it can serve as tremendous propaganda to stimulate interest in the Air Force." To further his case, Zanuck said he had temporarily assigned William Wellman to direct the film. But before proceeding, he wanted to know if the Air Force wanted the film made and if so, whether he could expect their assistance.[25]

Despite Zanuck's request for an answer within a week, an invitation to the general to visit him in Palm Springs, and some high powered name-dropping (General Mark Clark, Harry Luce, Averell Harriman, and "Ike"), the Air Force took two weeks to prepare a response for General Vandenberg. Saying he found Zanuck's letter "most interesting," the general indicated that his Director of Public Relations, Stephen Leo, would give the request for assistance his personal attention. In his own letter two weeks later, Leo agreed with Zanuck that *Twelve O'Clock High* would "make a most interesting picture. Its effect on the public should be quite favorable to the Air Force." He indicated that the service would "be glad to extend cooperation within the limits of regulations and present restrictions. However, he warned Zanuck that there might be a problem finding a sufficient number of now-obsolete B-17 bombers, although he expected the Air Force could come up with eight or ten planes. He also explained that a script would have to be approved for security and policy before cooperation could be formally extended and said the Air Force looked forward to reading the completed screenplay.[26]

The script, which finally reached the Pentagon the next week, told the story of General Frank Savage's efforts to rebuild the hapless 918th Bomb Group during the years of American daylight bombing over occupied Europe and Germany. He is forced to take the place of his friend, Keith Davenport, who has looked after his fliers like a brother and so suffered the strain of identifying with them on their near-impossible missions. Savage subjects the depressed fliers to merciless discipline and training to bring them back to fighting peak. In doing so, however, he is caught between his own developing friendships with the men and the inherent inhumanity of ordering them to face death. Gradually earning the respect of his men, Savage comes to know them as comrades, and when they are shot down, he loses not combat crews but friends. Ultimately he breaks down under the same pressure of leadership that Davenport had previously experienced.

In dramatizing this breakdown, Bartlett and Lay portray Savage as becoming irrational and bursting out hysterically. As might be expected, the Air Force had problems accepting this behavior. In commenting on the script, the Air Force suggested to Fox that it would "prefer not to indicate to the public that a commanding general like General Savage became as irrational as indicated. . . . We do not believe that a man with the strength of character as indicated and of his moral fiber would burst out hysterically or have a complete

The Leper Colony, designated as the home for the incompetents and misfits of General Savage's bomb group, became one of his best planes until it was shot down, thereby contributing to Savage's breakdown.

General Savage is helped from the field after being unable to board his plane for a crucial mission.

mental collapse. It seems that he would be more likely to break down with physical ailments, nervousness, short temper or just plain fatigue."[27]

In the script Bartlett had tried to explain the burdens of leadership as he observed them during his wartime experiences in the Air Force. He recalled that "there was so much abuse heaped on anybody who was a commander. They were looked upon as people who just waved the wand and sent boys off to die." He explained that few people "understood what a dreadful experience it was for a man to have the responsibility" to order men into combat. To him, Savage's breakdown showed what such responsibility "can do to a man who carries that load, that a man made of pigiron can break down under this kind of stress."[28] Nevertheless, the original portrayal of Savage's collapse was transformed into a quieter, more subtle breakdown in the completed film. The climactic scene, one of the most powerful in any war film, if not in any Hollywood film, shows Savage incapable of pulling himself into his bomber to lead the crucial mission and then sinking into a comatose state until the group returns.

While the portrayal of a command officer failing to fulfill his responsibility was unique in a Hollywood film to that time, the Air Force accepted the sequence because the situation was plausible in the context of the story.[29] The service did ask for other changes in the script, however, in particular the seemingly excessive use of alcohol by the officers of the group. The Office of Information told the studio, "We have no desire to portray all Air Force personnel as being teetotalers. However, the use of liquor in innumerable scenes might create an unfavorable public reaction by fostering a belief that the Air Force drank its way through combat, and important decisions were made by officers while under the influence of liquor."[30]

The Office of Information also objected to another scene in the original script that showed a plane being wrecked deliberately so that its parts could be used to repair battle-damaged planes. While acknowledging the accuracy of the scene, the service requested a change. Instead of the dialogue, "Run a tractor into one so you can report it a total loss," which "might cause unfavorable public reaction," the Air Force wanted the film to suggest that only inoperative planes were cannibalized for their parts. Similarly, the service said it "would prefer not to show the Chaplain actually playing poker. . . . We believe the idea that the Chaplain is one of the boys could be achieved if he is standing watching the game just as well as showing him participating in it." With these exceptions, the requested changes related to technical matters and inconsistencies in the script itself.[31]

Revisions proved to be no problem, and the Air Force quickly began the process of locating the required planes and equipment. Ultimately two southern bases were selected as shooting locations. For the exterior scenes of the base and its Quonset huts, the studio chose Eglin Field outside Pensacola, Florida. However, its white concrete runways couldn't be used for shooting takeoffs and landings since wartime fields in England were black to make them less visible to possible enemy bombers. Consequently, the studio went to Ozark Field, an inactive training base in Alabama to film the flying sequences.[32]

Ozark offered not only the right landing strip, but also surrounding countryside that appeared properly English. The waist high grass at the edges of the runway hid the airstrip as required for the opening and closing scenes that took place several years after the war. Once these sequences were shot, mowers cut the grass for the flying shots. Since the film company re-created battle scenes with actual combat footage, it had to shoot only landings and takeoffs and a few close formation "training" maneuvers for the film. In these sequences the director used twelve B-17s, which the Air Force had collected from the Air-Sea Rescue Service and refitted to their combat configurations. However, for the spectacular crash early in the film of a battle-damaged plane returning from its mission, the studio had to buy a new B-17 and stage the landing using its own stunt pilot.[33]

For this Fox hired Paul Mantz, Hollywood's premiere stunt flyer, a man who had performed at least ninety crashes in films. The script called for Mantz to belly-land the 38,000-pound plane and skid it off the runway through a row of tents before it came to a stop. Since he didn't want to risk additional lives, Mantz arranged the controls so that he could take off, fly, and crash the four-engine plane by himself, normally a two-man operation. The pilot could not anticipate every eventuality, however. The night before the crash, the first tent in the row Mantz was to hit blew down. To prevent a recurrence, the prop man replaced the wooden support pole with an iron one. Fortunately, Mantz had a premonition as he landed the plane, and instead of hitting the tent directly, he aimed the plane so that the tent struck it between the fusilage and the inboard engine. The smashup of the bomber remains one of the most spectacular in Hollywood stunt flying, and the sequence was resurrected for use in *Midway* (1976).[34]

Twelve O'Clock High does not derive its power from these spectacular sequences, however. Even the use of rare combat footage, which gains added impact from being used only once as the keystone of the film's build-up to its climactic moments, is not its primary attraction. Of the four major films that initiated the cycle of postwar combat movies, *Twelve O'Clock High* tells the best dramatic story. The film's power is also a tribute to excellent acting by Peck, Gary Merrill, and Dean Jagger and to Henry King's taut directing. Few side issues distract from the plot's primary focus, the rise and fall of General Savage. What little humor the movie has occurs in Savage's relationship with his driver and in the scene in which the general discovers that his over-age ground executive, the base doctor, and even the chaplain have flown on a crucial mission. After the bombing raid, the executive tries to defend himself by saying he thinks he hit a plane. Savage dryly asks whether it was one of ours or one of theirs. Even here, however, the general reinforces the grim reality of his responsibility, pointing out that he would have had to write to the stowaways' families had their planes been shot down.

The weight of this responsibility in the end destroys Savage, even though his strength and determination transformed the 918th Bomb Group from its

Savage sits comatose, waiting for his group to return from its mission. Meanwhile his friends try to explain his breakdown.

Davenport: It's screwy. I would never think it could happen to him.
Stovall: I did. I watched him sweep his feelings under the carpet long enough. It had to spill out someday.
Davenport: But I never saw him more full of fight than at briefing.
Doctor: Did you ever see a lightbulb burn out? How bright the filament is just before it burns out. I think they call it maximum effort!

deep state of depression into an effective instrument of war. The focus on one man's psychological as well as physical struggle to survive lifted *Twelve O'Clock High* out of the category of war films to the level of those few movies that make a significant comment on the human condition. Most war pictures have tried to attract audiences with their scenes of battle, men in mass attacks, ships churning through the oceans, planes filling the skies. They give the illusion of authenticity by the use of military hardware, not by delving into the psychological states of men in conflict. In contrast, *Twelve O'Clock High* created its dramatic impact by focusing on an individual with whom the audience can empathize.

In the end, General Savage has broken down, but he has accomplished his goal. As the group's doctor explains, Savage gave his "maximum effort." His men have become well-trained and are prepared to carry the battle in the air to German soil. The 1950 audience left the theatre enjoying the fruits of victory that men like Savage helped bring about. As *Battleground* had done, *Twelve O'Clock High* reminded the American people that the trip was necessary, that the losses were necessary so that America could again live in peace.

CHAPTER SIX

THE IMAGE OF THE MARINES AND JOHN WAYNE

★

The men who helped remind the American people that the trip was necessary—actors such as Gary Cooper, Van Johnson, George Murphy, James Whitmore, and Gregory Peck—portrayed traditional Hollywood servicemen, who were synthesized by the screenwriters from their research and experiences and given life by the directors. However well they performed their roles, the actors remained only actors, soon moving on to other characterizations. Throughout the history of Hollywood war movies, few actors have created a military presence that carried beyond the immediate film in which they appeared.

Victor McLaglen developed his role of Captain Flagg in *What Price Glory?* into a stereotypical image of the professional soldier in a series of films culminating in *The Professional Soldier* (1936). Lon Chaney became recognized as the hard-bitten sergeant after his starring role in *Tell It to the Marines* (1927). Wallace Beery created the image of a crusty old military man in films such as *West Point of the Air* (1935), *Salute to the Marines* (1943), and *This Man's Navy* (1945). And Randolph Scott, as the star of the early World War II film *To the Shores of Tripoli* (1942), developed a portrait of the wartime Marine, the lean-jawed servicemen doing his duty in the face of adversity. But none of these

---

Felix W. De Weldon, sculptor of the Iwo Jima Monument, advises the actors representing the three survivors of the flag raising, Ira Hayes, John Bradley, and Rene Gagnon, on the proper position to take during the shooting of this climactic scene.

images remained permanently etched in the American mind. None of these actors became *the* symbolic American fighting man.

Not until John Wayne created the role of Sergeant Stryker in *Sands of Iwo Jima* and then merged his own personality with the character did Americans find a man who personified the ideal soldier, sailor, or Marine. More than twenty-five years after he appeared in *Sands of Iwo Jima,* Wayne and his military image continue to pervade American society and culture. References to Wayne and his film-made image appear in virtually every book about Vietnam. His name and cinematic characterizations are regularly bandied about in television dramas and newspaper and magazine articles. In the twilight of an almost fifty-year Hollywood career, more than ever Wayne has become a living legend, a member of the "loyal opposition, accent on the loyal," a narrator of television programs, an author of *America, Why I Love Her.*[1]

Wayne has been a part of the American culture for so long that occasionally even people in the television film industry forget when his impact actually began. For example, in an episode of "Baa, Baa Blacksheep," while fleeing from Japanese captors, one of Pappy Boyington's rescuers volunteers to hold off the group's pursuers. A fellow rescuer asks, "Who do you think you are, John Wayne?" In fact, Wayne did not begin to develop his movie image as a military man until at least seven years after Boyington's wartime heroics.[2]

To be sure, Wayne had played military roles for many years before the release of *Sands of Iwo Jima* at the end of 1949. He had been a submariner in *Men Without Women* (1930), a pilot in *Flying Tigers* (1942), a Seabee in *The Fighting Seabees* (1944), and a PT-boat commander in *They Were Expendable* (1945). Nevertheless, until his Sergeant Stryker portrayal, most audiences thought of Wayne primarily as a western hero in countless horse operas, some of distinction, but most less than memorable. Only with his success in *Red River* (1948) and *She Wore a Yellow Ribbon* (1949) and the great acclaim (including an Academy Award nomination) for his Stryker role did Wayne emerge as Hollywood's all-time leading star.[3]

Sands of Iwo Jima did more than propel Wayne to his unique position and help launch the post-war cycle of movies about World War II. It was a classic portrayal of the Marines' military achievements in the recent war, and it was the best movie to result from the Corps' long relationship with the film industry. Of all the armed forces, the Marine Corps has been the one branch that over the years best publicized its role in the nation's martial history. Recognizing the potential of the film medium from its earliest days, the Corps made appearances in motion pictures as a major part of its public relations operations.

Beginning with *Star Spangled Banner* (1917) and *The Unbeliever* (1918), the Marines had used dramatic films to help create the image of the Corps as an

"The Star Spangled Banner"

Edison Studios

Herbert Evans, as Colonel Barron, stands before Marines lined up in front of their barracks at the Bremerton, Washington, Navy Yard during filming of Star Bangled Banner (1917).

Raymond McKee and Darwin Karr portray Marines in The Unbeliever (1918) filmed in part at the Quantico Marine Base.

Lon Chaney, as the tough drill sergeant, forces the raw recruit to grow up quickly in Tell It to the Marines (1927).

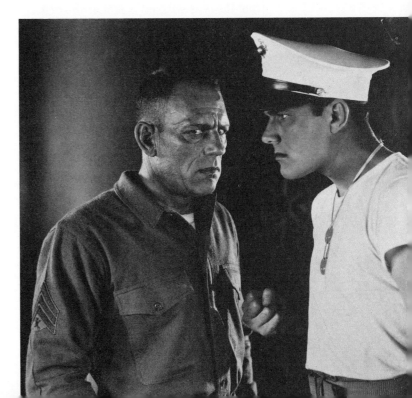

elite organization, one prepared for any eventuality. *Star Spangled Banner*, shot in part at the Bremerton, Washington Marine Barracks, portrayed peacetime training maneuvers. Released shortly after the United States' entry into World War I, the film contained the added message that the nation and the Marines must devote their entire energy to victory. *The Unbeliever*, filmed mostly on the Quantico Marine Base in Virginia, showed Marines training for combat and then fighting in France. Many of the Marines who served as extras during the shooting went to France shortly afterward, a fact that both the Marine Corps and the film company publicized.[4]

Except for the post-war *What Price Glory?*, most films about the Marines made during the 1920s and 1930s focused on the peacetime exploits of the Corps including its actions in Latin America and China. Of these, only *Flight* (1929), a Frank Capra movie about the development of Marine aviation rose above the level of the average Hollywood adventure story or musical comedy set in a military environment. Even during World War II, despite the spectacular successes of the Corps, only two films about the Marines were more than run-of-the-mill combat stories. *Wake Island*, although a fictional re-creation of the fall of Wake Island, did capture the spirit of the Corps and encourage the nation during the first dark year of the war. *Guadalcanal Diary* (1943), a semi-documentary account of the bloody Marine battles on Guadalcanal, also portrayed the Corps in one of its finest hours. Nevertheless, the Marines emerged from the war without a film of the critical stature of *Air Force*, *Thirty Seconds Over Tokyo*, or *The Story of G.I. Joe*. Nor did filmmakers immediately look to the Marines as a subject when Hollywood renewed its interest in war movies.

★

Sands of Iwo Jima

By the time Edmund Grainger, a producer at Republic Pictures, began developing his story in 1948, work was already underway on *Task Force*, *Battleground*, and *Twelve O'Clock High*. Grainger came up with the title for his proposed film after seeing the line "sands of Iwo Jima" in a newspaper, and Joe Rosenthal's picture of the flag raising on Mount Suribachi suggested the movie's climax. With these two ideas in mind, Grainger wrote a forty-page treatment that told the story of a tough drill sergeant and the men he leads into battle.

To write the screenplay he hired Harry Brown, a veteran Broadway playwright, who had previously done the screenplay for Lewis Milestone's *A Walk in the Sun* (1946). According to Grainger, Brown did "a brilliant job" of translating his outline into a shooting script.[5]

Sands of Iwo Jima focuses on a small group of men commanded by Sergeant Stryker, a tough, outwardly emotionless leader. Just as General Savage beats his men into fighting shape, Stryker molds his unit into a first-rate fighting force despite personality conflicts much like those portrayed in *Twelve O'Clock High.* Beneath his stoic exterior, Stryker bears the pain of a wife who, with their son, has left him because of his single-minded commitment to the Marines.

Stryker transfers his feelings of love and loneliness for his son to his men and becomes a father and teacher whom they come to respect, if not love. *Sands of Iwo Jima* follows the sergeant and his men through the invasions of Tarawa and Iwo Jima to the successful capture of Suribachi. As Stryker's unit relaxes there, he is shot by a sniper, and dies instantly. His death, of course, inspires the men to further action, and they carry on the battle as they had been taught by their father-teacher.

Edmund Grainger, like Dore Schary, felt his film told the story of a crucial battle, because Iwo Jima proved to the Japanese that they could not hold their island outposts: "If they had won there, they would have felt that they could have stood off the assault on the mainland of Japan." The defeat on Iwo Jima, in Grainger's opinion, made the Japanese realize they had lost the war and could only fight defensively until peace was negotiated. Ironically, his film portrayed the battle of Tarawa in much more graphic detail. General David Shoup, who received the Congressional Medal of Honor for his actions at Tarawa and later became commandant of the Marine Corps, noted this discrepancy: "It was sort of a screwed up thing, really. The sands of Iwo Jima really didn't have anything to do with most of the film."[6]

Correct titles aside, Grainger and his film received the most extensive assistance of any of the four films that began the cycle of movies about World War II. The producer's only significant obstacle to obtaining cooperation from the Marines was the small size of Republic Pictures and its limited financial and technical resources. But after Grainger spent a week in Washington talking to top Marine officers, he convinced the Corps that the studio could complete a project of the magnitude of *Sands of Iwo Jima.*[7]

As the first step in the cooperation process, the Marines assigned Captain Leonard Fribourg to serve as the film's technical advisor. His only instruction from the Marine Corps commandant was to ensure technical veracity on the film and provide complete cooperation to the studio. Marine Headquarters did recognize that the exigencies of filmmaking might require occasional bending of military procedures. In pursuance of these instructions, Fribourg worked at the studio during preproduction helping to polish the script and selecting combat footage to match with the company's own battle sequences. Fribourg also made arrangements with Camp Pendleton for Republic to do all its external

Preparing to film a scene of Sands of Iwo Jima *(1949) at Camp Pendleton, left to right: Captain Leonard Fribourg, the technical advisor; director Allan Dwan; John Wayne; and Lieutenant Col. Andy Geer, a Marine consultant.*

Marines restage the landing on Tarawa and their struggle to move inland from the seawall for Sands of Iwo Jima.

shooting on the base, where the necessary men and equipment would be available for the action scenes.[8]

This assistance enabled Grainger to carry out his intention of making *Sands of Iwo Jima* "very realistic" rather than simply turning out another "Hollywood version of the Marine Corps." His commitment to accuracy of detail and procedure notwithstanding, the film succeeded primarily because of John Wayne's presence. Grainger originally had envisioned Kirk Douglas as Sergeant Stryker. But in the middle of negotiations with Douglas' agent, Wayne approached the producer requesting the role. He later told Captain Fribourg that he had wanted the part so badly "he could taste it."[9]

Wayne saw *Sands of Iwo Jima* as a "beautiful personal story," one that "made it a different type of war picture." He felt that Stryker's relationship with his men was "the story of Mr. Chips put in the military. A man takes eight boys and has to make men out of them. Instead of four years in college, he's given eighteen weeks before they go into battle." Unlike *Battle Cry* (1955), which tries to tell its story of Marines in World War II in broad strokes, Wayne thought that *Sands of Iwo Jima* showed it was possible "to paint a picture of the whole [war]" from the vantage point of a small unit.[10]

Responding to Wayne's belief that he would make the perfect Stryker and to problems in securing Douglas for the role, Grainger went to Herbert Yates, head of Republic Pictures, to suggest that the studio cast Wayne in the film. According to Grainger, Yates rejected the proposal—he considered Wayne's career to be on "the downgrade." Although he had just completed *Red River* and *She Wore a Yellow Ribbon*, these films only reinforced Wayne's image as a western hero. Consequently, only after Wayne's personal visit to Yates and Grainger's continued urging did the studio chief finally allow Wayne to play Sergeant Stryker.[11]

With the casting thus settled, the script completed, and arrangements made for assistance at Camp Pendleton, the film went into production during the summer of 1949. At the Marine base, the director, Allan Dwan, used a company of Marines as background for the principal actors. For the large assault sequences, Captain Fribourg arranged to have the equivalent of a battalion of Marines as well as various types of equipment and vehicles perform for the cameras. He also ran a modified boot camp for the actors to teach them to act like Marines. Fribourg recalled that he never had any problems with the cast: "They wanted to do it, wanted to cooperate. They wanted to wear the uniform right, the emblems, wanted to know what the stripes meant, wanted to know Marine Corps lingo, and put the right words in the right places." Dwan himself paid a great deal of attention to detail, and he never rolled the cameras on a scene in which the military was involved without asking "Does that look okay?"[12]

The director's concern with accuracy and the Marine Corps' own recognition of the need for some dramatic license facilitated Fribourg's relationship with the film company. In the combat sequences, for example, he permitted Dwan to keep the men bunched closer together than they would have been in actual battle because the small-screen era cameras could capture only a limited area on film.

Rarely did Fribourg object to a sequence. His major problem came in a scene calling for Wayne to teach bayonet fighting to a member of his squad who is having difficulty. The script required Wayne to hit the man with a horizontal butt stroke. When he did this in rehearsal, the technical advisor remembered, "I almost fell off my chair." He told Dwan that he couldn't "have your sergeant hit this guy with a rifle butt."[13] Although Dwan argued that the sequence was excellent drama, Fribourg refused to budge, and the matter was sent to Marine Headquarters to resolve. In this instance, Washington overruled the technical advisor. The final version was not as extreme as the sequence to which Fribourg had objected, however. According to Wayne, the Marines allowed the "jaw smashing" to take place because it was immediately followed by a humorous scene that ameliorated the severity of Stryker's actions. The final scene showed Stryker and the awkward Marine doing the Mexican hat dance, which Wayne described as "being the most humorous scene in the script." Nevertheless, he recalled that Grainger still was "evidently afraid of the scene" and tried to have it left out of the film. Wayne said, however, that he interceded by going directly to Herbert Yates, who ordered Dwan to shoot the sequence.[14]

By his own admission, Wayne became a "sort of 'Richelieu' of Republic" in the behind-the-scenes "struggle and conniving" that took place during the production of *Sands of Iwo Jima*. His main concern, though, was to become a Marine sergeant. He questioned Fribourg and other Marines about all aspects of their work and combat experiences and spent a great deal of time with a warrant officer who seemed to typify Stryker. From all this on-the-spot research, Wayne discovered that the Marines didn't train men to die for their country. They were trained "to live for their country and to live to fight again. It was survival training. We learned that you didn't get to the bottom of the barrel toward the end of the war. You got to the young fellow who was so damn good that the older fellows couldn't hardly keep up with him."[15]

To realistically portray the Marines in this historical context, Wayne and Grainger received not only military assistance, but also help from several Marine heroes. David Shoup and Jim Crowe re-created their actions at the Tarawa seawall, but not until the script was rewritten—at Shoup's insistence—to portray events as they had actually occurred. Originally, some of Shoup's dialogue with Crowe over a field telephone and some of his actions weren't accurate according to the later commandant of the Corps. Because of his advice, the sequence included the actual words spoken on Tarawa. In addition, his and Crowe's advice along with the use of combat photos and newsreel footage made the Tarawa beachhead re-creation so realistic that Shoup recalled, "it was a fearsome thing to look at because having experienced the battle, goddamn, I didn't want to go through it again."[16]

For the Mount Suribachi sequence that climaxed the film, Grainger had Captain George Schrier play his own part leading the patrol that raised the flag. The producer also brought to Pendleton the three surviving members of the flag-raising detail to re-create their actions. (One of them, Ira Hayes, later became the subject of *The Outsider* (1961), which detailed the Puma Indian's

Marines land on "Iwo Jima," this time for the camera.

life following Iwo Jima.) This concern for detail produced a film that Shoup said reminded him of the actual battles. Other Marines later told Grainger that the film "was the finest Marine Corps picture ever made by the motion picture industry." According to Grainger, this "was because it told the truth about the Marine Corps."[17]

While noting that the film "contained the standardized movie conniptions back in the staging area," critics generally agreed with Grainger's appraisal. The *New York Times* reviewer felt that it contained "so much savage realism . . . so much that reflects the true glory of the Marine Corps' contribution to victory in the Pacific that the film has undeniable moments of greatness." In addition, the critic noted that Dwan brought "to the shipboard sequences as the convoys stand off the beaches an overpowering sense of the dread which gripped the men immediately before going over the side into the landing craft." Likewise, the *New Yorker* thought it was a "worthwhile film. . . . The invasions are represented here in a frighteningly authentic manner, and no attempt has been made to gloss over the squalor and horror that go with war." Despite objecting that the dialogue "gets a trifle lofty, and now and then love makes an unlikely appearance," the reviewer thought that "by and large the picture is a whole lot better than many highly touted war films that have gone before it."[18]

While critics found much to praise, and General Shoup called *Sands of Iwo Jima* "the finest military film I've ever seen," moviegoers remained the ultimate judges of the picture. Viewers make it the eighth largest-grossing movie of 1950 and still regard *Sands of Iwo Jima* as the film that best portrays the

Sergeant Stryker's men turn from his body to watch the flag-raising on Mount Suribachi during rehearsal for film's climax.

Marines in action. Nearly thirty years after its release, Marine recruiters claim volunteers still increase whenever the movie appears on television.[19]

Apart from the realistic combat sequences, John Wayne's embodiment of the tough Marine sergeant gave the film its unique staying power. Nonetheless, Marines themselves seem divided in their loyalties between *Sands of Iwo Jima* and *Battle Cry*. Many consider the later film more representative of their service experiences. To them, *Sands of Iwo Jima* tells the story of one Marine, Sergeant Stryker. In contrast, *Battle Cry* tells of the varied experiences of many men, both in military situations and off-duty.

As the Marines had done on Grainger's movie, they fully cooperated in filming the screen adaptation of Leon Uris' bestselling novel. While shooting the battle scenes at Viequas, a small island off Puerto Rico, director Raoul Walsh had use of the men and equipment then taking part in regularly scheduled Marine amphibious exercises and the expertise of Colonel Jim Crowe of Tarawa fame who served as the movie's technical advisor. Since Uris' book did not identify actual historical battles, Walsh and Crowe were free to create military action for the best visual and dramatic effect and were bound only by the limits of terrain and military authenticity. While the scenes do gain impact from being shot in color for the wide screen, some Marines have found the battle sequences overdrawn and unrealistic in contrast to the historical accuracy of *Sands of Iwo Jima.*

Thanks to the Corps' subsequent assistance at the Marine Recruit Depot at San Diego and at Camp Pendleton, where the story's New Zealand sequences were filmed, *Battle Cry* does have the same authenticity of Marines in training that distinguished *Sands of Iwo Jima.* At the same time, *Battle Cry* also shows a side of Marine life lacking in Wayne's film, the drinking and masculine camaraderie, the search for love, and the pain of rejection. Since these aspects of life occupy their thoughts and time as much as training and combat, Marines suggest that Walsh's film presents a fuller portrayal of their lives in the Corps than the singular focus on Sergeant Stryker and his small group of men in *Sands of Iwo Jima.*[20]

Once these feelings are acknowledged, however, these same Marines concede that they have never considered any of the stars of *Battle Cry* (Van Heflin, James Whitmore, Tab Hunter, or Aldo Ray) as the typical Marine, the man who personified the Corps, stimulated young men to enlist, or served as a model for military skill or courage. To them, as to most Americans, John Wayne remains the symbolic Marine even today as he did when *Sands of Iwo Jima* first appeared. According to *Newsweek*, John Wayne gave "one of his best performances as the rugged top sergeant who bullies and beats his men into a fighting unit." The *New York Times* reviewer thought Wayne was "especially honest and convincing for he manages to dominate a screen play which is crowded with exciting, sweeping battle scenes. . . . His performance holds the picture together." Wayne received an Oscar nomination for his role and felt he was "worthy of the honor. I know the Marines and all the American Armed Forces were quite proud of my portrayal of Stryker."[21]

Edmund Grainger agreed with the reviewers that Wayne's Stryker "dominated the screen." He thought the actor's "innate character, his thinking about life, his philosophy of life" helped create the role. While conceding that Kirk Douglas would have given a professional performance if he had accepted the part, the producer said Wayne "was a more typical Marine sergeant because he believed in the role. . . . He was so immersed emotionally in this part that it came out. I think it is the best thing he's ever done." Most moviegoers probably think of Wayne as a cowboy first, but to the Corps he was one of them. Speaking for most Marines, General Shoup said Wayne symbolized the "hell for leather, go and get'em attitude [of the Corps] . . . When we went into combat, we went after the enemy."[22]

★

The John Wayne Image

By the time he played Stryker, Wayne had been going after the enemy in films for almost twenty years. But only with *Sands of Iwo Jima* did he become the symbol of the American fighting man, the defender of the nation. As with all images, Wayne's action-hero did not emerge full-blown. His career has spanned almost half a century and more than 200 films. While appearing in more westerns than any other genre, his military characterizations ultimately established him as America's quintessential fighting man. While this image has come to pervade American society to the extent of becoming a cliché, it remains a powerful influence on the nation's youth. Wayne in fact became the model of action for several generations of young males, representing the traditional American ideal of the anti-intellectual doer in contrast to the thinker.

Admittedly, Wayne created his fighting man image on the motion picture screen rather than through real conflict. For most Americans in recent years, however, the reality of life and the illusion of the screen are tightly intertwined. Americans may now find their heroes in cops and robbers adventures, James Bond-type exploits, or even in sports. Nevertheless, the image of the action hero remains the same as it was in the days of the Alamo, the cowboy and Indian, the charge up San Juan Hill, or the flaming beachhead. While Wayne has perpetuated his action image through the guise of fictionalized or historical characters, he has become just as much a military hero, a frontier hero, and a supporter of God, country, and motherhood as the Andrew Jacksons, Davy Crocketts, Buffalo Bills, and Teddy Roosevelts of the past.

In creating this symbolic, mythical American hero, Wayne has incorporated elements of Sergeant Stryker into his characterizations, whatever the role or the locale. He has been at once the fighter and the teacher, instructing the next generation how to survive in combat as he has taught his men to fight on Tarawa and Iwo Jima. The oilwell firefighter in *Hellfighters* (1969), Colonel Kirby in *The Green Berets* (1968), the old rancher in *The Cowboys* (1973), all pass along to younger men the knowledge accumulated from Wayne's experiences fighting the elements or human enemies. With the possible exception of Rooster Cogburn in *True Grit* (1970), this Stryker-Wayne characterization will be the one people remember, the one that forever established Wayne as the fighting man who remains ever ready to fight for and defend his country.

Wayne's portrayal has often been cited by Marines as the reason for their attraction to the Corps. Ron Kovic, a Vietnam veteran, recalled in *Born on the Fourth of July*, "The Marine Corps hymn was playing in the background as we sat glued to our seats, humming the hymn together and watching Sergeant Stryker, played by John Wayne, charge up the hill and get killed just before he reached the top. And then they showed the men raising the flag on Iwo Jima with the marines' hymn still playing. . . . I loved the song so much, and every time I heard it I would think of John Wayne and the brave men who raised the flag on Iwo Jima that day. I would think of them and cry. Like Mickey Mantle and the fabulous New York Yankees, John Wayne in *Sands of Iwo Jima* became one of my heroes."[23]

The appeal of Wayne's heroics has spread wherever his films have appeared. Richard Pryor recalled, "My heroes at the movies were the same as everyone else's. I wanted to be John Wayne too . . . I didn't know John Wayne hated my guts." The man who grabbed the arm of President Ford's would-be assassin in San Francisco said that when he signed up for the Marines, "I didn't really know what war was, but I wanted to fight for my country." Only after a tour in Vietnam did he learn that it "is no John Wayne movie." Wayne's image as a successful fighter has even impressed his long-time foes. Despite his slaughter of thousands of Japanese, or perhaps because of his film victories over the Emperor's subjects, Hirohito specifically asked to meet John Wayne while visiting the United States in 1975.[24]

In countless films, Wayne has extolled the simple virtues of doing right and feeling useful. The "Duke" and the roles he has played have become fused in the opinion of the public. Playing Davy Crockett in *The Alamo*, for example, Wayne sermonized: "Republic! I like the sound of the word. It means people can live free, talk free. . . . Republic is one of those words which makes me tight in the throat."[25] To Wayne, as to the character he was playing, republic is a word that makes a heart feel warm, something worth fighting for, dying for. It is also a place to be supported—right or wrong. The Colonel Kirby who advocates the virtues of American policy in *The Green Berets* differed little from the John Wayne who told Jimmy Carter and the American people on Inauguration Eve: "I am considered a member of the opposition—the loyal opposition, accent on the loyal. I'd have it no other way."

Wayne's portrayal and advocacy of patriotism and action enjoy instant recognition in the United States as well as throughout the world. When asked who their favorite actor was, the first response from a class of black fourth graders was John Wayne, not Jim Brown or O. J. Simpson. When he was told he was "perishable" by his doctor, a heart attack victim suddenly realized he just couldn't picture himself as "a brown-edged, sagging sponge of leaves" or "a rotting piece of fruit." His fantasized self-image was always of "John Wayne in any number of westerns . . . a man with inexplicable charm who overcomes psychological confusion and winds up, in the end, with the girl."[26]

In person, perhaps even more than on the screen, Wayne's character and charisma are all-enveloping, even to those who may disagree with his philosophy and politics. Because of this presence, his son Michael believes Wayne "would have been an outstanding anything because he has that drive. He has a particular personality. He has charisma. It is just something that differentiates people. He has it. So no matter what field of endeavor he went into, he would have been a star or one of the most important people in that field." That characterizes him more than anything else."[27]

That something has caused presidents, politicians, and even an emperor to court Wayne as if he were a political figure. His political views are known and debated by his constituency as if he were in politics, and he is welcomed in the gatherings not only of those whose views he shares, but of the "opposition" as well. He reached that position by visualizing in movies a mythic quality inherent in the American character. According to Dore Schary, Wayne "was a representation of the American image of the soldier, of the frontiersman, of the American who doesn't knuckle down and the American who when things get tough is willing to pick up the gun and fight."[28]

While shooting *The Outsider* at Camp Pendleton in 1960, Delbert Mann asked a group of Marine recruits why they had joined the Corps in light of the strenuous training they had to undergo. Half of them answered that it was because of the John Wayne movies they had seen. On an "Owen Marshall" television episode, the mother of a deserter asks him why he thought war was right before he joined the Army, but not after he had fought in Vietnam. He responds, "I was eighteen and war was something John Wayne fought or we watched on our new color TV."[29]

Why did the screenwriter draw on the Wayne military image? His answer: "Because in the predominantly liberal community that makes up the film industry, Wayne, though not disliked for it, is outspokenly gung ho. He supported the war vocally and his professional image repeatedly made heroic those men who fought wars or used guns and violence to achieve their goals. Wayne . . . is larger than the man himself. An 18-year-old boy saw Wayne fight endless battles on the big screen and the boob tube . . . from *Sands of Iwo Jima* to *The Alamo.*[30]

Countless references in fiction and non-fiction to Wayne and his military roles illustrate his influence in creating an image of life in the armed forces and of combat to young men. In *The Lionheads,* a novel about Vietnam, one of the characters recalls his drill instructor describing how the Japanese attacked in World War II "like in the John Wayne movies: 'Marine, you die.' "[31] In non-military novels as well, the Wayne image appears. Hawk, the freaked-out lover of the heroine in Lisa Alther's *Kinflicks* is described as going to Vietnam "in the grip of the basic male thing: Here was this rite that would either make a man of you or destroy you. If you returned alive, you'd somehow conquered Death." Once in Vietnam, however, Hawk finds his only concerns are

Director Delbert Mann discusses with Tony Curtis his portrayal of Ira Hayes during the filming of The Outsider *(1961) at Camp Pendleton.*

to endure the incredible boredom, stay alive, and get home, all of which require him to do as he is told. While on a patrol, he and four other men abduct a Vietnamese girl. He protests and is told to shut up. His immediate reaction is to speculate "on pulling a John Wayne and rescuing her." He then pictures the probable result of his effort—being shot in the head: "It was one of those jarring moments when a person realizes that he's stepped out of the familiar everyday world into a realm of primal lawlessness in which anything goes." So Hawk joins in raping the girl, indulges in the reality instead of the movie-made image.[32]

The body of personal literature growing out of the American experience in Vietnam and the first-hand accounts of journalists document both the pervasiveness of the Wayne image and the dichotomy between the Wayne model of masculine behavior and the reality the war itself imposed. In *365 Days*, a doctor's recollection of stories he heard while treating wounded men from the battlefields, an officer describes his training "with the crazies, the tough, role-playing enlisted kids right off the streets of Chicago, Gary, and back roads of Georgia who had gone airborne because of all the John Wayne movies they'd seen."[33]

Ron Kovic recalled that after listening to the Marine recruiters at a high school assembly, he couldn't wait to run down and meet them: "And as I shook their hands and stared up into their eyes, I couldn't help but feel I was shaking hands with John Wayne and Audie Murphy." Ron Caputo, in *A Rumor of War,* recalled that even before he talked to recruiters, he saw himself "charging up some distant beachhead, like John Wayne in *Sands of Iwo Jima,* and then coming home a suntanned warrior with medals on my chest. The recruiters started giving me the usual sales pitch, but I hardly needed to be persuaded."[34]

Knowledgeable journalists who covered the Vietnam War including Bob Schieffer, Ward Just, and David Halberstam have all attested that the Wayne image profoundly influenced the men who fought in the war. Each has reported seeing men fight and talk about fighting as they had seen John Wayne fight the Japanese in his World War II films—without regard to the efficacy of the techniques. As a result, an exasperated old sergeant was once reported as having told some careless troops: "There are two ways to do anything—the right way and the John Wayne way." Soldiers' imitations of Wayne even assumed mythic dimensions. David Halberstam recounts the story, perhaps apocryphal, that made the rounds in Vietnam of a soldier throwing a grenade into a hut as he had seen John Wayne do only to have "his ass blown off" because the hut was made of grass rather than the more solid material of a Japanese bunker.[35]

Wayne's influence reached not only enlisted men, but also the decision-makers and officers in the field. One high-ranking officer who was in Vietnam during the build-up of American forces in the mid-1960s thought the escalation of American efforts to win the war was at least "in a simplistic sense" the response of people "racing around trying to be John Wayne, applying force to a problem which required something else." On a more basic level, Josiah Bunting, author of *The Lionheads* and an officer in Vietnam, confirms the journalists' reports. Based on his own military experiences, Bunting observed: "There is no question that the officers in Vietnam, combat infantry officers, especially in the grade of lieutenant colonel, which was *the* rank in Vietnam [were influenced by] this whole aura of machissmo. . . . The influence of John Waynism, if you want to call it that, on these people was terribly profound."[36]

To Wayne, this influence had its basis in his characterizations, which always appealed to the same emotions: "You can call it primitive instinct or you can call it folklore. It has no nuance. It's straight emotions, basic emotions. They laugh hardy and hate lustily. There is a similarity in that. I wouldn't call it primitive as much as I would call it man's basic fight for survival." In response to critics who suggest that these portrayals primarily appeal to adolescents, Wayne answers that he hopes his attraction is "to the more carefree times in a person's life rather than to his reasoning adulthood. I'd just like to be an image that reminds someone of joy rather than of the problems of the world."[37]

Wayne's hope notwithstanding, the problems of the world, the bullies and the bad guys, provide the challenge he has confronted in virtually all his films. To solve these problems, the characters he plays use action and violence in the most direct manner. Action not only speaks louder, but violence leaves a more lasting impression on a majority of viewers. Josiah Bunting visualizes Wayne as "a guy constantly kicking over cans, kicking over lamps" as he did in *The Horse Soldiers*. Such men cut through the Gordian knot to get to the heart of the problem. To Bunting, this manner of solving problems has "a fundamentally anti-intellectual kind of appeal" that becomes as attractive to an educated, thinking person as to the "anti-intellectual Archie Bunker temperament. . . . In other words, after three or four hours of trying to solve a problem, here comes this great big strong guy who kicks over a lamp, gets on a horse, and kills a bunch of people. It's so simple. It's fulfilling. It's finite."[38]

Wayne and his roles both reflect and help to create the desire in Americans to solve problems simply and directly. One screenwriter who used the Wayne image as the instrument to convey the idea of war to his male character suggested that this reflection/creation process is "probably symbiotic." To him, the John Wayne fan "is a relatively simple person who is very independent, believes you get out of life what you put into it, . . . that force is the great solver of problems. Certainly, he believes in America and believes in it simplistically. . . . He enjoys the father image. Wayne represents all of this."[39]

Most of all, Wayne represents the use of violence rather than reason to solve problems. In the early days of American involvement in Vietnam, this part of his image was widely admired by the men in the field. Covering the war for the *New York Times* during this period, David Halberstam observed this appeal at close range: "It influenced the officers and men, everyone. The Wayne image of the guy cleaning up the town, the good guy standing alone was there." He saw it in the imitation of Wayne's "swagger, the tough guy walk. . . . there were a lot of guys out there playing John Wayne."[40]

Wayne himself acknowledges the appeal of his "swagger," but considers it a part of his sexuality: "There's evidently a virility in it. Otherwise, why do they keep mentioning it?" William Wellman, on the other hand, attributes Wayne's military appeal directly to his "swagger": "He walks like a fairy. He's the only man in the world who can do it." While sex and combat violence seem to be closely related, Wayne nevertheless denies that his screen violence has had a particularly profound impact, pointing out that "Children's stories have always included knights and dragons with blood, fire and everything." At the same time, he admits, "I've shot as many people on screen as anybody." However, he differentiates between his killings and other screen violence: "I haven't shot them—like they do today—with snot running out of my nose, sweating, and with my pants torn open."[41]

To Wayne, his violence has always been somehow cleaner, neater, more pristine than other people's: "When I came into this business, it was a medium where we used illusion to set off reality. The bad guy always wore a black hat, the good guy always wore a white hat and gloves and he wouldn't hit first. Someone would always break a chair over his back. When someone threw a vase at me, I always hit right back. That started a different kind of western. But it was illusion. I never used things like animal livers to show someone getting shot. That's just bad taste." Wayne complains, "Today they're trying to make 'em real either by concentrating on turning your stomach with violence or running everyone by nude. Well, I'm too old to play in-the-nude stuff. And I really like the illusion of violence more than putting a squib in a cow's liver and a bunch of catsup on it and blowing it up in slow motion."[42]

Wayne's death in *Sands of Iwo Jima* was the type of clean violence he approved of. A shot rings out and Sergeant Stryker lies dead. No blood trickles from his mouth or streams down his shirt.

Wayne's brand of violence can only be directed against the bad guys. Because of his concern for correctness, Wayne turned down the lead in *Patton*. He told the producer the military characters he portrays don't go around slapping American soldiers. He felt that he had always tried "to portray an officer . . . or a non-commissioned officer or a man in the service in a manner that benefits the service and also gives a proper break for the man to react in a human manner."[43]

In spite of their admiration for John Wayne and his image, young men in Vietnam quickly discovered that their war bore little resemblance to the conflicts he had fought on the movie screens. Survival rather than giving a man the opportunity to react in a human manner was all that mattered. As the war dragged on into the late 1960s, it became less and less clear to the American people and more particularly, to the men in Vietnam, that we were in fact the good guys fighting the bad guys. But most disillusioning to the men in Vietnam was their discovery of the falseness of the visual model Wayne had provided them of war as clean and bloodless with little suffering. Instead, they saw their buddies torn apart and mutilated for a cause that ultimately seemed to have no socially redeeming features.

In *Home From the War*, Robert Lifton details the anger returning veterans felt at being betrayed by these screen models. Where Wayne had once provided them with their images of war, he now became a scapegoat for their frustrations and bitterness. Likewise, in *Born on the Fourth of July*, Ron Kovic speaks for all those who came to see that the reality of war bore little resemblance to the antiseptic battles he had watched Wayne fight in the name of patriotism and justice. His bitterness and anger most clearly illustrate the betrayal he came to perceive in the Wayne image. Paralyzed from the chest down, Kovic rages over his lost manliness: "Now I can't even roll on top of a basketball, I can't do it in the bathtub or against the tree in the yard. It is over with. Gone. And it is gone for America. I have given it for democracy. . . . I have given my dead swinging dick for America. I have given my numb young dick for democracy. . . . Oh God oh God I want it back! I gave it for the whole country, I gave it for every one of them. Yes, I gave my dead dick for John Wayne. . . . Nobody ever told me I was going to come back from this war without a penis. But I am back and my head is screaming now and I don't know what to do."[44]

To Wayne, of course, death or loss of manhood has always been as important as life. Death gave life more meaning: it gave the new generation the opportunity to assert itself. *The Cowboys* (1972) contains the explicit manifestation of Wayne's symbolic role as the the transmitter of cultural values from one generation to the next. Playing an aging rancher whose men have deserted him to take part in a gold rush, Wayne gathers a bunch of schoolboys to help drive his herd to market. During the trip, Wayne passes on to them his skills and values. When he is murdered by an outlaw, his boys kill the killer. The ultimate expression of manhood has been passed from one generation to the next.

During the making of the film, the studio suggested to Wayne that he didn't have to die. He responded that the movie would be "no good if I live. The whole idea of it is what this Mr. Chips teaches the kids. If I'm alive and they recapture the herd of cattle from the rustlers, it doesn't mean as much."[45] Nor does his death matter any more than Sergeant Stryker's death matters. In each case, his men will carry on the skills and values he has imparted to them.

Thus while Wayne's image of war proved deficient during the Vietnam experience, his model of courage and patriotism remained viable to the men who fought in the conflict.[46] The majority of men obeyed their orders, did their jobs, and returned home still loving their country. If most people ultimately rejected Wayne's hawkish view of the war, the message of national preparedness explicit in his movies remains the goal of virtually every citizen. Nevertheless, Wayne denies that his military movies had an undue influence on the American people.[47]

He claims that his movies were made primarily for "entertainment" and that people are interested primarily in the personal or provocative parts of the story. To him, the military served only as a device to attract attention to the picture and to its subject matter.[48] From *Sands of Iwo Jima* onward, however, John Wayne rather than an actual military hero has served as the symbol of America's fighting men for a significant number of American movie-goers.

CHAPTER SEVEN

A DIFFERENT IMAGE

★

If none of the successors to *Sands of Iwo Jima* produced a hero figure to equal John Wayne, the failure did not result from lack of effort. Following the lead of the successful filmmakers, every Hollywood studio began cranking out its own versions of the war. Films like *Halls of Montezuma* (1951), *Above and Beyond* (1952), and *Take the High Ground* (1953), all attempted to duplicate the box-office appeal of the cycle-initiating movies. As often happens, however, the imitators lacked the clarity and insights into war and men in combat that distinguished the original films. Instead, they relied on spectacular battle scenes, women, and romance to attract audiences. As escapist entertainment, they were popular, but as drama, they lacked the power of *Twelve O'Clock High*, *Battleground*, or *Sands of Iwo Jima*.

For the armed forces, however, the primary consideration was not dramatic quality, but their appearance in as many films as possible. Recognizing the value of the visual medium as both an informational and recruiting tool, the individual services began to compete for time on the motion picture screen as soon as it became clear that Hollywood was again regularly making war movies. In particular, the Navy and Air Force saw films as ideal vehicles in which to carry on their interservice debate over the relative merits of aircraft carriers versus intercontinental bombers. Made with the full cooperation of the services, films such as *Flat Top* (1952), *Men of the Fighting Lady* (1954), *Bridges at Toko-Ri* (1954), *Above and Beyond* (1952), and *Strategic Air Com-*

Director Fred Zinnemann discusses scene in From Here to Eternity *(1953) with Montgomery Clift and Frank Sinatra at Schofield Barracks in Hawaii.*

Donald Baruch in his Pentagon office. Beginning in 1949, he helped arrange cooperation between the military and the film industry in his position as Chief, Motion Picture Production, in the Department of Defense Public Affairs Office.

mand (1955) attempted to convey the messages of their sponsors to the American people.

Ironically, this screen rivalry began when the individual services were being unified into the Department of Defense under the direction of James Forrestal. As part of the unification process, Forrestal consolidated all public affairs operations into one office, leaving each service with a limited staff that would act only in an advisory capacity and as a line of communication to the field for the Defense Department's director of public information. Included in this reorganization was the creation in 1949 of the Motion Picture Production Office. Under the direction of Donald Baruch, its first and only chief, the office was intended to take over the cooperation process from the individual services and supervise the details of assistance, thereby regulating the armed forces' zealous pursuit of film roles.

After Forrestal's resignation as secretary of defense in March 1949, however, the individual services began to regain control over their public affairs operations, a process further accelerated by the outbreak of the Korean War. As a result, Baruch's office failed to function as originally planned, and until the early 1960s it served essentially as a conduit for requests from Hollywood to the individual services. In this capacity, the office could recommend that a service provide assistance, could help with negotiations between a filmmaker and a service, or could refuse to approve cooperation on a film that was not in the best interests of the military. But it could not require a service to assist on a movie, and once the office had approved a project, it had no involvement in the cooperation process. Consequently, throughout the 1950s, the services had virtually a blank check to provide assistance, much as they had from the earliest days of their relationship with the film industry. Filmmakers received as much help on any movie as a service's public affairs office in Washington and its commanders in the field decided was in its best interest.[1]

★

The Korean Conflict

Though the Korean War helped abort Forrestal's plans to regulate assistance, the war itself never became a popular subject for filmmakers, most likely because of the nature of the conflict. In contrast to World War II, which was a struggle between good and evil that would be fought until victory was achieved, Korea was a "police action." While the fighting still pitted good against a well-perceived evil, the goal was not victory, but a negotiated settlement. If Americans had a difficult time understanding the conflict as the stalemate dragged on, Hollywood had as difficult a time portraying a conflict shaded in gray instead of painted in the easily defined black and white of World War II.

To capitalize on the initial wave of interest, filmmakers did immediately seize the war as a new subject. In much the manner of *Wake Island* and *Bataan*, Samuel Fuller's *The Steel Helmet* (1951) was rushed into production and hastily completed with the resulting backlot appearance of the early World War II films. While Fuller incorporated some anecdotes gleaned from early accounts of the fighting, the combat he portrayed could just as easily have taken place during World War II.[2]

Following the pattern of World War II moviemaking, the armed forces showed an interest in assisting on films about the Korean conflict as soon as the military situation stabilized. In fact, in one of the rare instances of the military's solicitation of Hollywood during the entire history of their relationship, the Air Force approached Howard Hughes and RKO Pictures about making a movie showing the close air support its fighter planes were supplying troops on the ground. The resulting film, *One Minute to Zero* (1952) received full cooperation from both the Air Force and the Army during its production at Camp Carson in Colorado. However, despite its origins in the Pentagon and the large-scale assistance it received, the Army refused to approve the completed film because it contained a scene not in the original script in which artillery fire is directed against a group of Korean refugees that has been infiltrated by

Communist troops. Once Hughes ascertained that the Pentagon would not revoke his extensive military contracts, he refused to delete the scene—the film's dramatic high point—and released it without the traditional acknowledgement of armed forces assistance.[3] Although the controversial scene had basis in fact, the Army felt it did not want to be associated with a film that showed its men killing innocent civilians.

On the other hand, the Marines fully assisted on a film that showed the beginning of the end of American military dominance in the world. Shot at Camp Pendleton among hills painted white to simulate snow, *Retreat, Hell!* (1952) recreated the Marine withdrawal from the Changjin Reservoir in December 1950 in the face of the massive Chinese attack across the Yalu River. The movie shows the Marines courageously "advancing in a different direction" under the most adverse conditions, finally reaching the sea unbowed. Nevertheless, the withdrawal from the Yalu represented the first important failure of American military power, and so the film became the first Hollywood production to visualize a major defeat.[4] Released during the war, audiences may have missed the significance of the film's content because of the Marines' successful escape from Communist encirclement and the as-yet unresolved conflict.

By 1954, however, even a film intending to justify American involvement in Korea could not avoid a pessimistic ending. Based on James Michener's best-selling novel of the same name, *Bridges at Toko-Ri* attempted to explain why the war had to be fought in series of dialogues between William Holden, playing a lawyer called back to Navy duty as a jet pilot, and Fredric March, as an admiral aboard the carrier. Despite full Navy cooperation, which helped create spectacular flying scenes, and superb special effects work, which used miniatures to produce a realistic bridge-blowing sequence, the film succeeded only in emphasizing the futility of the war.[5]

Trying to justify the need for American action in Korea, March explains: "All through history men have had to fight the wrong war at the wrong place. But that's the one thing they're stuck with. People back home behave as they do [indifferently] because they are there. A jet pilot does his job with all he's got because he is here. It's as simple as that. Militarily this war is a tragedy. But if we pulled out they'd take Japan, Indo-China, the Philippines. Where would you have us take our stand? At the Mississippi?" But in the end, having helped knock out the bridges at Toko-Ri, Holden is forced to crash-land his damaged plane behind enemy lines and is shot in a muddy ditch where he has sought cover. Even though he has done his job in a war that was tragic, but perhaps necessary, his death offers no spiritual uplift as Sergeant Stryker's had, only the feeling that the war was worse than tragic: it had no redeeming feature.[6]

Bridges at Toko-Ri made perhaps the first true antiwar statement in a post-World War II film by showing the futility of combat. But it did so without dis-

William Holden discusses crash scene in Bridges at Toko-Ri (1954) with Captain Marshall Beebe, the film's technical advisor who had arranged to transport the wrecked jet to Thousand Oaks, California, for the location shooting.

tracting from the image of the American fighting man. Like General Savage and Sergeant Stryker and the other heroes of Hollywood's war films, William Holden was brave and, if he questioned the conflict in which he was participating, he nevertheless did his job to the best of his ability. Whatever their doubts about the outcome of the Korean War, filmmakers, like the population as a whole, blamed the politicians rather than the military for our failures. Consequently, the American experience in World War II, the all-conquering Army, Navy, Air Force, and Marines, continued to be the model on which most directors, producers, and screenwriters based their military portrayals during the 1950s.

To be sure, practical considerations contributed to Hollywood's positive image of the armed services during the decade. Given the high cost of filmmaking, few studios cared to gamble large sums of money on unconventional or controversial films, whatever the subject. Moreover, because of the unique requirements of large-scale movies dealing with military subjects and the expense in trying to fulfull them through civilian channels, filmmakers preferred traditional stories about men in war, ones that would guarantee Pentagon cooperation. At the same time, the political climate of the early 1950s discouraged the production of any movie that might call a filmmaker's loyalty into question. For these reasons, Hollywood seldom had problems with the military during the first few years of the war-film boom.

★
New Interpretations of World War II

In contrast to the generally positive visual re-creations of the military, the first major literary works about the war to appear following the end of hostilities reflected their authors' personal and often unflattering perceptions of their own participation in the events they wrote about. Unlike the collective artistic and financial compromises inherent in filmmaking, writing requires an individual effort, with the author answering only to himself. Moreover, while publishing manuscripts represents some financial gamble, one or two failures do not bankrupt a company. A publisher can usually take a risk on a potentially controversial work, while a film studio can only rarely do so. In any case, unlike the film image of the armed forces, the early post-war novels exposed facets of life and command in the military that the services either rejected as inaccurate or preferred to keep out of sight.

Still, the novels did capture the atmosphere of military life, and their authenticity helped make instant critical and popular successes of Norman Mailer's *The Naked and the Dead* (1948), James Jones' *From Here to Eternity* (1951), and Herman Wouk's *The Caine Mutiny* (1951). As a result, Hollywood expressed immediate interest in transferring the books to the screen. The studios were cautious, though. Because of the novels' essentially unflattering portrayals of the military, studios approached the armed forces about possible assistance before actually committing themselves to any of the novels. As one of the would-be producers of both *From Here to Eternity* and *The Caine Mutiny* pointed out, companies are willing to risk all kinds of money on scripts they think they can ultimately turn into finished films. But *they* want to make the final decision on whether they make a film. Where these novels were concerned, the studios feared the decision would be made by the Defense Department or the individual services, not their own production staffs.[7]

With this consideration in mind, Warner Brothers, for one, asked its Washington representative to submit a synopsis of *The Caine Mutiny* to the Defense Department in April 1951, for an official reaction as to possible Navy assistance on a film. In response, Lieutenant Colonel Clair Towne of the Public Information Office wrote that "the development of a screenplay which could be considered acceptable for official cooperation would be a difficult, if not impossible, task for any writer to achieve." Towne explained that the consensus of military officials was that the plot was a "combination of extremes, both as to characterizations and situations." The Navy, he said, would not have "tolerated" these extremes for long. Towne pointed out that the "resolution of conflicts is accomplished after such a lapse of time as to be of no value in redeeming the service, or in offsetting the derogatory and very harmful sequences through which one must wade during the major part of the story." Towne also noted that although the story itself was "full of errors," the Department of Defense would make no attempt to "offer constructive criticism in the interests of accuracy and authenticity . . . in view of the nonacceptability of the overall story line." In sum, the military did not want to offer any hope of its cooperating on the project.[8]

Despite the armed forces' opposition to the contents of the novels, their great success with the public ensured that some filmmakers would ultimately adapt them for the screen. Given Hollywood's long-standing reliance on military men, equipment, and locales in providing a proper atmosphere, there were continued efforts to win approval for screenplays based on the novels. As it turned out, each production received assistance only after the filmmaker agreed to significantly modify crucial elements in the plots of the novels. These changes illustrate again the manner in which the armed forces have worked to create what they have considered the proper image of themselves through commercial films.

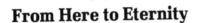

From Here to Eternity

Given the Defense Departments' requirement that its cooperation must be in the best interest of or provide benefit to the service being portrayed, a script faithful to *From Here to Eternity* would clearly not qualify for assistance. Picturing Army life in the days immediately before Pearl Harbor, James Jones' novel focused on the stories of First Sergeant Milton Warden, Pfc. Robert Prewitt, and the women they loved. Warden, who runs a company at Schofield Barracks for his weak and pompous commander, Captain Dana Holmes, knows the Army system and willingly works within its limits. Prewitt is a struggling nonconformist whose determination to maintain his individuality undermines his basic love of the Army. When Prewitt refuses the captain's request to box on the company's team, Holmes initiates his destruction through "the treatment." Despite this abuse of power, the captain is ultimately promoted. Around these stories, Jones interweaves subplots of love and infidelity, camaraderie, and the brutality of soldier against soldier that culminate in violence in the stockade of Schofield Barracks.

While the Defense Department and Army did not deny the accuracy of the narrative, they did argue against the novel's depiction of negative aspects of Army life that they claimed were no longer tolerated. They felt that the portrayal of a situation that no longer existed would mislead the millions of mothers, wives, and sweethearts of men currently in the service. They maintained that no film based directly on the novel could benefit the Army, and so it did not qualify for assistance under the Department's regulations.

Although aware of Pentagon stipulations, Warner Brothers did take an option on the book and asked its Washington representative to approach the Pentagon about assistance. When the Army told him it would never assist on the film, the studio dropped its rights to the novel. Twentieth Century Fox met the same reception and likewise backed off. Finally, Henry Cohn, president of Columbia Pictures, simply bought the book—without inquiring about the possibility of military assistance.[9]

Daniel Taradash, who wrote the screenplay for the film, said that Cohn bought it "because he was a man with a lot of guts." Taradash believed that the studio head thought he would have a great movie if he could develop a script acceptable to both the military and the Motion Picture Code Office. At the same time, Taradash noted that Cohn bought the book despite "immense protests" from Columbia's New York office.[10]

Aware of the problems he faced in transforming the novel into a movie, Cohn asked Raymond Bell, Columbia's Washington representative, for his assessment of problems Columbia would face from the Defense Department, from the Motion Picture Code Office, and from state censorship boards and religious organizations. After reading the book, Bell told Cohn, "I feel like I spent the weekend in a whore house." He wrote Cohn a long letter detailing the difficulties he foresaw. His first objection was that the book contained "a lot of apparent Communist doctrine" that would cause problems with the American Legion and other organizations."[11] Taradash strongly disagreed with this analysis, arguing that Jones had written "an honest book" into which no "political doctrine entered."[12] In any event, Bell was sensitive to the Red Scare in Hollywood in the early 1950s, and he felt it was necessary to warn Cohn that the studio might have problems with organizations that would label Jones "either a sympathizer or a dupe" of the Communist party. Moreover, Bell felt the book was anti-Catholic and anti-Jewish.[13]

To Bell, however, the most significant problems centered on Jones' portrayal of life in the pre-Pearl Harbor Army. He noted that the subplot of the "gold-bricking captain" whose top sergeant was carrying on an affair with his wife would not be looked on favorably in the military. Far more serious was the explicit brutality directed against both Prewitt and Maggio throughout the book. Bell recognized that Jones was describing life in an army where tough discipline may have had a place. Nevertheless, he noted in his letter to Cohn that potential recruits or parents would probably not understand that conditions in the Army had changed since 1941.[14]

With all these potential obstacles in mind, Cohn and his producer S. Sylvan Simon faced what most people in Hollywood believed were impossible odds in developing an acceptable screenplay. As a first step, Simon went to Washington at the end of March 1951 with a preliminary treatment and discussed Columbia's proposed movie with Department of Defense officials. On April 3, Clair Towne, writing for the Pictorial Branch of the Department's Office of

Public Information, informed Bell that the reaction was unfavorable: "The basic ingredients of accuracy and authenticity, [of] value to the public information programs of the Department of Defense and Army, and overall benefit to National Defense, are not apparent in the Columbia proposal. The treatment portrays situations which, even if they ever did exist, were certainly not typical of the Army that most of us know, and could serve only to reflect discredit on the entire service." According to Towne, the Defense Department concurred with the Army's comments that had been forwarded separately. As a result, he concluded that it was "very difficult to conceive of any revisions to the current treatment which would justify reconsideration of this project."[15]

At this point, Columbia hired James Jones to a attempt a draft. The novelist (who received $85,000 for the rights to his book), did little serious work during his stay in Hollywood. By his own admission, he ran around, met a lot of starlets, and went to a lot of parties. He said he actually "knew so little about screenplay writing at the time" that he was "helpless," and he described his treatment, written in May 1951, as "very bad." Apart from his lack of experience, Jones explained that he could never lick the problem of "how to have whore houses without having whore houses" in the film. They were an integral part of the novel but could not be mentioned in the movie because of censorship restrictions.[16]

Taradash, who eventually solved the problem by calling a brothel a "social club," said of Jones' effort that he had "never read a worse treatment based on a first-rate novel." He explained that Jones had virtually gutted his own novel of any vitality. Instead of Karen being Holmes' wife, as in the novel, Jones made her Holmes' sister; he had Holmes tell Warden to "take it easy" with Prewitt, the reverse of his orders in the novel; instead of having Holmes initiate the brutality against Prewitt for refusing to box, Jones made the noncoms the villains and Holmes a nice, fair man. Taradash observed, "This is absurd. This isn't *From Here to Eternity*."[17]

While Jones was struggling with his treatment, the producer, Simon died. When the novelist's effort ended in failure, the project entered a period of limbo. Finally, in fall of 1951, Taradash approached Cohn through studio channels with his own concept of how the book could be transferred to the screen. When he had first read *From Here to Eternity* shortly after publication, he "thought it was great" but "they'd never be able to make it into a movie." But the story stuck with him, and he ultimately came up with two notions "which suddenly made me see the whole thing."[18]

In his meeting with Cohn, Buddy Adler (who had taken over as producer), and other studio executives, Taradash explained that the brutality in the stockade could be suggested rather than literally depicted. In the novel, Maggio, a cocky enlisted man from the streets of New York, fades from view after he is released from the stockade. In the movie Taradash suggested having him escape and die in Prewitt's arms as the result of the bludgeoning he received from Fatso, the brutal sergeant in charge of the jail. This would give Prewitt the opportunity to play taps as the climax to the second act of the screenplay. Taradash's second idea was that the two love stories should be intercut from one pair of lovers to the other throughout the film, even though their paths never cross in the novel until the very end. The writer explained that this cutting "solved a major dramatic problem, the structure of how you do this immense story."[19]

Cohn and Adler immediately recognized the merit of Taradash's proposal and gave him the assignment to write the script. Even so, it took more than a year, until February 1953, to complete the final draft of the screenplay, obtain military approval and promises of cooperation, select a director, and cast the roles. In beginning the task, Taradash reread the book, took notes, and spent two months writing a 135 page detailed outline. The first draft of the actual script took another three months. To satisfy industry censors, Taradash turned the New Congress Hotel into the New Congress Club, and he described it as "a sort of primitive U.S.O., a place of well-worn merriment. It is not a house of prostitution." He handled the novel's many four-letter words by simply eliminating them rather than replacing them with recognizable substitutes. Nudity, as in the famous beach scene, was not even considered. And Karen's sterility, caused by gonorrhea in the book, is explained as the result of a miscarriage.[20]

By anticipating what the Army would object to and changing the offensive material himself, Taradash opened the door to military approval of the script and cooperation. The key change was the elimination of the explicit brutality of the stockade, which was central to Jones' novel. To pacify the Army, Taradash had the dying Maggio (played by Frank Sinatra) explain to Prewitt that he had fallen from the truck during his escape from the stockade: ". . . shoulda seen me bounce . . . musta broke something." Nevertheless, Maggio continues, in two long speeches, to tell of Fatso hitting him repeatedly "in the gut with a billy . . . hit me ten times runnin. . . ." He also vividly describes what it was like "in the Hole." Consequently, without showing actual brutality and despite the implication that some of Maggio's injuries came after escape, Taradash felt "that the last impression received by the audience is that Fatso and the stockade beatings are what really killed Maggio."[21]

Columbia sent the revised script to the Department of Defense on February 11, 1952. Hoping to smooth its entry, Taradash included in a preface excerpts from several reviews of *From Here to Eternity* to remind the Army that it "was a damn fine novel, not just an anti-Army novel." From the *New York Times*, for example, he quoted, ". . . it will be apparent that in James Jones an original and utterly honest talent has restored American realism to a pre-eminent place in world literature." From the *Saturday Review of Literature* he cited, ". . . this is the best picture of Army life ever written by an American, a book of beauty and power despite its unevenness, a book full of the promise of things to come."[22]

Despite Taradash's efforts, no one in the Pentagon thought the new script would produce a picture that could benefit the military in any way. Within the Public Information Office, some officials felt that while the script was "less objectionable" than earlier versions, it still did "not qualify for cooperation." They argued that the Defense Department "should keep hands off completely. It contains no informational value nor can it be of benefit to the defense effort." Don Baruch, on the other hand, felt that by working with the studio, it

From Here to Eternity

Fred Zinnemann rehearses Montgomery Clift and Frank Sinatra for scene in From Here to Eternity.

would be possible to remove some of the worst features of the script. General Frank Dorn, the Army's deputy chief of information agreed with this tactic since Columbia Pictures had committed itself to make the picture even without cooperation. By assisting, Dorn thought any improvements in the finished film would justify cooperation as being in the best interest of the Army.[23]

Reacting to the debate with the Pentagon, Clayton Fritchey, director of the Office of Public Information, wrote to General Floyd Parks, the Army's chief of information, on February 19: "It has always seemed to me that our purpose in cooperating with commercial film companies has been to portray the armed services, their personnel, officers, training, ideals, aims and goals with the general intent of informing the public, of increasing morale among military personnel, and perhaps indirectly to aid recruiting." According to Fritchey, the consensus in his Office and in the Army was that *From Here to Eternity* would "obtain none of the above-mentioned results." Rejecting the belief that providing Columbia with assistance could "mitigate in some way the unfavorable impact of the filmed story," Fritchey said "it would be difficult if not impossible to explain" any cooperation. Moreover, Defense Department assistance "would be linked to a commercial enterprise upon which it could never look with favor" and so would be setting "an ill-advised precedent." Therefore, he said that neither the Army nor the Office of Public Information should "in any way" cooperate in the production of the film.[24]

Despite this stricture, Fritchey did not cancel a meeting Baruch had scheduled for the next day with Taradash and Adler. He thought General Parks might want to protest his decision and that as long as the filmmakers had come to Washington, they should have their day in "court." He also felt that the session would give all parties the opportunity to present their cases and then decide how they should proceed.[25]

In the meeting, Baruch explained that any definite commitments about cooperation would have to come from the "front office." He pointed out that the military's objections to the screenplay were "personal recommendations," and even if the filmmakers acted on the suggestions, "they would help the script but might not qualify the picture" for cooperation. He stressed that the changes "are the intangible ones of making the picture positive rather than filled with negative values." Taradash and Adler were told that the Defense Department would read the script after it had been further revised and would judge it on its own merits apart from the book. He also arranged for the Army to provide research in Hawaii at Pearl Harbor and Schofield Barracks.[26]

At this point, the studio selected Fred Zinnemann to direct the film. Taradash had recommended him after watching Zinnemann's *Teresa* (1951), which he found the most "realistic depiction" of soldiers he had ever seen. Zinnemann had also direced two other movies having a military environment, *The Search* (1948) and *The Men* (1950) and had received two Oscars for his direction of short films. He and Taradash spent "five months of intensive work" on the second draft of the script with additional inputs from Harry Cohn and Buddy Adler. While the collaboration produced many changes, "some of them quite fundamental" according to the director, the new script maintained the structure Taradash had created in his initial treatment.[27]

When the revised screenplay reached the Pentagon in early September, Don Baruch found it did "nothing" for the Army's image, but he felt that it would "not be anti-Army with a few additional changes." To effect these revisions and discuss cooperation, Baruch, General Dorn, and other Defense Department officials met with Ray Bell and Adler on September 11. Among other requests, the Pentagon asked the producer to revise the portrayal of the stockade treatment "to eliminate the impression that the treatment was universal"; they also wanted the studio to delete Karen Holmes' admission of previous affairs. If these changes were made, the Pentagon told Adler, he could again submit the script with a request for cooperation. Whether the Army's help would be acknowledged in the screen credits would be held in abeyance until the military saw the completed film.[28]

Although the Army had tentatively agreed to cooperate as a result of this meeting, it did so with more resignation than enthusiasm. Baruch still felt *From Here to Eternity* was "never going to be a good story for the military." The advantage of agreeing to assist, he explained, was that the Pentagon would be able to exert some leverage to get the screenplay revised and so "make it less objectionable or more presentable. We didn't destroy any of the dramatic impact on the story values" but modified "the way it was being presented."[29]

Modifications occurred not only in the manner in which the film dealt with the brutality in the stockade, but also in the way Taradash portrayed the Army's treatment of Captain Holmes, Prewitt's tormentor. In the novel, the officer is promoted despite his brutality and abuse of authority. From his initial treatment onward, Taradash has Holmes returned to the United States after he is severely condemned by the officer who discovers his brutal treatment of Prewitt: "You have no capacity for leadership. What you did was shameful. The sooner you get demoted in rank to a spot where you won't be in command of troops, the better for everyone, especially the Army." After his discussions in the Pentagon, Taradash added, "You have your choice of a court martial or resignation."[30]

The military's image clearly benefited from the removal of Holmes rather than simply his humiliation. Taradash conceded that dramatically it was "not as good as the book; it's much more ironic that Holmes be promoted. I like that

"Japanese" fighter strafes Schofield Barracks on December 7, 1941, in From Here to Eternity. *Alvin Sargent, the "machine-gunned soldier," years later wrote the screenplay for Zinnemann's* Julia *(1977).*

infinitely more." Nevertheless, he felt he had to make concessions to the Pentagon: "We had to show that we were not out to attack the Army." According to Taradash, the military was "delighted" with the change, with the "idea that the Army had found its rotten apple itself and gotten rid of it rather than this horror, to them, of promoting Holmes."[31]

Fred Zinnemann, who won an Academy Award for his direction of *From Here to Eternity*, agreed that he "would have liked to see the captain being promoted because it was a fine sardonic touch." But he also accepted the change "as a sacrifice that had to be made" to obtain cooperation. Also, Zinnemann's contract limited his creative control of the film, and as he pointed out, Harry Cohn ran the show: "It was his pet project."[32]

Cohn often sat in on script conferences, offering suggestions and attempting to play Taradash off against Zinnemann and Adler, a ploy the writer thought was "part of his game." Ultimately, Taradash and Zinnemann were able to squelch most of Cohn's ideas, which Taradash described as "really dreadful." Wanting the end to be "real sentimental," Cohn first proposed that Prew die in Warden's arms. Later, he even suggested that Prew didn't have to die at all. Cohn also adamantly insisted that Aldo Ray should play Prewitt. Zinnemann felt the character needed "spirit, particularly strong, indomitable spirit, a kind of nobility. And Monty had that beyond a question of a doubt, more than anybody I knew." He finally told Cohn that he could not make the film without Clift. After additional objections, the studio head ultimately agreed to Zinnemann's selection.[33]

What Cohn would not agree to was allowing *From Here to Eternity* to run more than two hours. He told Taradash, "I don't give a goddamn how good it is. I don't care if it's the greatest picture ever made. I don't care if it will gross a fortune. It's not going to run more than two hours." Taradash at first thought the restriction was "madness." While both he and Zinnemann thought the film could have used a few more minutes, Taradash did concede Cohn's restriction "wasn't madness," and Zinnemann admitted, "Harry made it move."[34]

To Taradash, Cohn's time restriction was simply one example of the kind of limitations a writer works under when he does a script. Consequently, he did not consider the Army's requested changes a form of censorship but simply another restriction he had to accept, "just as I accepted that I couldn't use the word 'whore' or 'fuck' at that point even if I had wanted to."[35]

In fact, the Code Office proved far more intransigent than either Harry Cohn or the Pentagon. In addition to putting absolute restrictions on language, industry censorship forced the filmmakers to eliminate themes and change situations in developing their script. Apart from changing the brothel to a social club and not mentioning gonorrhea, Taradash was forced to make Lorene into a club hostess rather than the prostitute she was in the novel, ignore the book's homosexuality, and punish Warden and Karen for their illicit affair through the expediency of adding a line about the "scheming, sneaking and hiding" their relationship required. Even when the film was completed, the Code Office required changes, insisting that the famous beach scene be cut about six feet, even though the deleted footage contained nothing different from what remained.[36]

In contrast, except for the time restriction and a budget limitation of $2 million, Cohn had little influence on the structure and content of the film. Likewise, apart from Taradash's pragmatic elimination of the stockade violence in anticipation of military objections and the subsequent decision to have Holmes removed from the Army rather than simply transferred, the Pentagon had little direct impact on the final form of *From Here to Eternity*. Nevertheless, the Army continued to suggest revisions almost up to the beginning of actual shooting.

Despite Taradash's firmness in ignoring their earlier requests, as late as January 19 Ray Bell forwarded a list of changes the Army wanted incorporated into the final shooting script. To four of them, Taradash simply said no. He agreed to insignificant changes on two other requests. To the last request, he agreed with the Army's observation that the script still failed to provide proper motivation for Prewitt's failure to halt for the MPs as he tries to return to his unit after the attack on Pearl Harbor. To resolve this problem, the writer inserted several lines to clearly establish the reasons for Prewitt's desperate desire to get back to Schofield Barracks after he had been AWOL while recovering from wounds suffered when he killed Fatso.

In his cover letter attached to Taradash's responses, Buddy Adler told Bell, "I do hope that both Defense and Army understand we have made every effort to be cooperative so that we could justify their cooperation." He said the suggestions had been studied "with great care and with much thought." As a result, the producer explained that the studio's responses represent "firm conclusions that to proceed in any manner other than indicated would work harm to the dramatic effect of our picture."[37]

Despite the changes made as a result of the Pentagon's decision to work with Columbia Pictures, the Defense Department still did not consider the completed film a "representative portrayal of the Army or of the typical men and officers who make up its ranks today, or who comprised the pre-Pearl Harbor Army." After looking at the rough cut of *From Here to Eternity*, however, the Pentagon made only one objection to the movie. It wanted one scene trimmed in which Sergeant Warden is shown as acting excessively drunk, staggering around, and stumbling off a porch. In discussing the sequence with Buddy Adler, the Pentagon pointed out that Warden had been presented as an outstanding representative of the Army up to that time and that emphasizing his drunken condition would shock audiences. Nevertheless, the Army did not put its request very strongly ("as much as is possible should be trimmed") and Columbia left the scene as it was since Warden's condition was dramatically necessary to subsequent events.[38]

Whatever the changes needed to satisfy the military, Zinnemann believed their cooperation was essential to his success in capturing the atmosphere of the story. He said he would have resigned from the project had Columbia not obtained Army assistance. The service allowed the film company access to Schofield Barracks and the use of training planes made up to look like Zeroes to recreate the attack on Pearl Harbor. The Army also assigned a top sergeant to supervise military details, particularly for the leading actors, some of whom had not been in the armed forces. While actual soldiers appeared in only a few scenes, Zinnemann felt that "being in the authentic barracks and seeing the Army life around us gave the actors a kind of framework that was very useful to them and helped them create characters who were reasonably authentic." According to the director, if extras had been used to play the soldiers, the film would "never have had the feeling of tautness, discipline or any of the other things that were part of the professional American Army. The picture would have been a caricature." Without cooperation, "the film would have been unthinkable."[39]

Zinnemann did not think the compromises, which he saw as imperative in obtaining military assistance, had significantly affected his artistic creativity or the dramatic power of the film. In the context of the 1950s and even without the barracks language of Jones' novel, he thought the film created "quite an impact on the audience." Zinnemann believed the film remained true to the spirit of the book, "which was not anti-Army. Prewitt is proud to be a good professional soldier, a thirty-year man, 'I love the Army' he says."[40]

Almost without exception, reviewers of the movie agreed with Zinnemann's judgments. According to the *New York Times*, the film "stands as a shining example of truly professional moviemaking." The critic saw the film as a "portrait etched in truth and without the stigma of calculated viciousness." Despite the deletion of the stockade chapters, he thought the film "fundamentally cleaves to the author's thesis."[41]

James Jones did not initially agree that *From Here to Eternity* captured the flavor of his book: "I hated it when it first came out and I thought I would never go to see it again." When he did look at it five years later, however, he was impressed. He explained his change in attitude by saying that when he saw the film the first time he was still too close to the book and was unhappy about the deletions. But after five years, those compromises had had time to fade from his memory. He recalled, "I liked it and I was pleased at how well they *had* done it."[42]

More than most movies, *From Here to Eternity* demonstrates that to do a film "well" requires a collective effort, not just the genius of the director. Harry Cohn contributed more to the creation of the project than studio heads usually do. Buddy Adler nursed the script through the complex negotiations with the Pentagon and helped to mute Harry Cohn's efforts to impose his ideas on the film. Daniel Taradash's script, which won him an Academy Award, is almost as much a masterpiece, as fine a piece of work, as Jones' novel. And unlike most scriptwriters, Taradash contributed to the production apart from the screenplay, becoming involved in the Pentagon negotiations, selection of the director, and the casting. Nevertheless, Fred Zinnemann's direction provided the catalyst for bringing all the elements together to give the film its scope, power, and impact.

In contrast to most movies about the Armed Forces, Zinnemann's direction of his superb cast made the characters, rather than the military organization, the center of attention. Clift, Lancaster, Sinatra, Deborah Kerr as Karen Holmes, and Donna Reed as Lorene—both women cast against type (their normal roles)—all created characters the audience could empathize with, could care about. Their interactions, their individual struggles to bring meaning to their lives, brought a richness to the film not found in most military movies, which rely on hardware, combat, or the color and romance of the services for their dramatic impact. Zinnemann remained in control of all elements of the film, conveying all the violence of the novel without ever showing it, creating the atmosphere of Army life in pre-Pearl Harbor Hawaii, and giving meaning to a climax that would have had the bathos of a soap opera in lesser hands. *From Here to Eternity* is one of the few Hollywood stories about the armed forces that ranks both as a great military film and a great American movie.

Reaction to the film was not all positive, however. It was criticized, as the novel had been, by those who resented what they saw as its anti-military perspective. A critic in the *Los Angeles Times* wrote that the film "goes all out in making the military situation look its worst, and could probably be used by alien interests for subversive purposes if they happen to want to make capital of this production."[43] Even the president of the United States and the Defense Department received complaints to which the Public Affairs Office could only answer that the film was made by a private company.[44] The Navy, however, took stronger action. A Board of Admirals banned the film from Navy ships and shore installations because it was "derogatory to a sister service." Of course this criticism ignored the fact of the Army's cooperation in making the film as well as the fact that both the Army and the Air Force had purchased prints for their motion picture service.[45]

As Baruch observed, *From Here to Eternity* did not portray the Army in a very good light even though neither Jones nor the filmmakers considered their work "derogatory." Like the novelist, Zinnemann saw the work as a study of an "individual striving to maintain his identity in the face of pressure from a huge organization." To him, the "organization is shown from the worm's eye-view as it were. The soldier in his articulate way says a man has to do what he has to do. . . . And he does it. He absolutely refuses to be a boxer. *Eventually he gets killed for wanting to be himself.* That is really what it is about.''[46]

The military clearly had not seen *From Here to Eternity* as a comment on the human condition. Throughout their negotiations with the studio, the Defense Department and the Army were concerned only with the image of the service that the film would create for its audiences. For this reason, the negative aspects of the portrayal always outweighed any dramatic or entertainment considerations. Admiral Lewis Parks, the Navy's chief of information, probably spoke for the majority of Pentagon officials when he said, "I enjoyed the movie as a dramatic motion picture. The acting was magnificent. Certainly, *From Here to Eternity* reflects credit on the actors, the writers, the director, and the producer as a dramatic achievement. And it definitely is not as objectionable as the book upon which it was based." Nevertheless, Parks maintained that the film "does not reflect any credit whatever on the Armed Forces of the United States.''[47]

The Caine Mutiny

Admiral Parks had been facing a similar confrontation in handling Stanley Kramer's request for assistance in transferring another novel, *The Caine Mutiny*, to the screen. From the book's publication in early 1951, the Navy had adamantly opposed cooperation on any film based on it. The service felt that Wouk's novel reflected poorly on Navy officers and men even though Wouk considered himself a total Navy man and had even sought technical advice from the service while working on his book. In contrast to Jones' novel, *The Caine Mutiny* contained no scenes of physical brutality, no whorehouses, no adultery, and no profanity. In a note at the beginning of the book, Wouk wrote, "One comment on style: The general obscenity and blasphemy of shipboard talk have gone almost wholly unrecorded. This good-humored billingsgate is largely monotonous and not significant, mere verbal punctuation of a sort, and its appearance in print annoys some readers.''[48] In fact, Wouk did not paint an unflattering portrait of the Navy as a whole and, until the military suggested otherwise, he believed he had written a complimentary story.

Despite its title, *The Caine Mutiny* actually focuses, not on a "mutiny" but on Willie Keith, one of the war's typical ninety-day wonders. He has joined the mine sweeper *Caine* as a newly commissioned ensign after finishing at Princeton and Officers Candidate School. In the course of his duty aboard the *Caine*, during the war in the South Pacific, Willie matures from a pompous and affected boy to a man who ultimately becomes the ship's captain. The reader observes Captain Queeg and the "mutiny" from Willie's progressively maturing viewpoint. While the young officer becomes an unwilling participant in the takeover of the *Caine,* he finally reaches manhood not through the mutiny or the subsequent court martial, but as a result of his actions when the ship is hit during a kamikaze attack in the closing days of the war.

While the mutiny and the court martial are the dramatic focus of the novel, the significance of *The Caine Mutiny* as a war story lies in Wouk's portrayal of life on a mine sweeper during wartime. He successfully re-created the experiences of men living in close proximity aboard ship, facing danger together for extended periods. Except for Captain Queeg's ultimate extreme behavior, many Navy men have testified to having served under officers of his type. Likewise, many high-ranking officers have indicated that Lieutenant Maryk's takeover of the *Caine* during the typhoon was a valid action under the circumstances Wouk created in his book.[49]

These opinions notwithstanding, the title of the novel itself prompted most of the Navy's opposition. The officer who served as technical advisor later observed, "I hazard a guess that if the book had been named *The Caine Incident* minus that inflammatory word 'Mutiny,' Navy cooperation would have been obtained speedily."[50] In fact, from the time of Wouk's first discussion of his proposed book with the Navy's Public Information Office in 1948, the service stated that it had never had a mutiny aboard any of its ships.[51] Whether Naval history could support the accuracy of that contention is debatable, since not all military occurrences on the high seas or elsewhere have become part of the public record. Nevertheless, the military has seldom demanded historical accuracy in the fictional films on which it has assisted. The criterion has usually been plausibility, with dramatic license providing flexibility. In military comedies, even probability often goes by the board. In *Jumping Jacks* (1952), for example, the Army permitted Jerry Lewis to be shown parachuting into Dean Martin's canopy even though in a real jump it would have most likely collapsed the chute.[52]

Realistic or not, to many Naval officers, *The Caine Mutiny* brought to mind *Mutiny on the Bounty* and the image of Fletcher Christian setting Captain Bligh adrift in a rowboat. In truth, nothing so dramatic happened to the U.S.S. *Caine.*

In his preface Wouk wrote, "It was not a mutiny in the old-time sense, of course, with flashing of cutlasses, a captain in chains, and desperate soldiers turning outlaws. After all, it happened in 1944 in the United States Navy." As Wouk explained, when he first came to the Navy for assistance in writing his book, the mutiny was a "mutiny of the mind," not of arms. While most Navy

In front of the film's story board, Commander James Shaw discusses shooting of The Caine Mutiny (1954) with producer Stanley Kramer and his staff.

men seemed to understand this distinction, they did not trust the American viewing public to do the same.[53] Wouk himself did not help the efforts of the film's potential producers. After the novel appeared, the author explored the mutiny issue in greater detail in a stage play, *The Caine Mutiny Court Martial*. Like the book, the play was a major success and reinforced the Navy's worries about the adverse effect of a movie.

Despite this obstacle, filmmakers were still lured by Wouk's story and the potential audience his works had created. However, when two studios made unofficial inquiries during the summer of 1951 to the Navy Department about possible assistance, they ran into a stone wall. The service denied it had ever had a mutiny and said it would refuse to cooperate on any film portraying such an event. Faced with this seemingly unbending position, Hollywood's major studios decided to forget about the project.

At that point, Stanley Kramer took an option on the screen rights to *The Caine Mutiny*. In the summer of 1951, Kramer was a young, independent producer who had a financial and distribution arrangement with Columbia Pictures. He also had a reputation for refusing to compromise his artistic and creative principles. Kramer himself concedes, "I was known as somewhat of a 'rebel' to the military establishment and to the government sources with whom

I dealt. If I weren't a 'rebel' then I was considered a radical, a man who was dealing in extremes and in bothersome material."[54]

To be sure, one of his earlier military films, *The Men* (1950), focused in a serious and controversial manner on hospitalized World War II paraplegic veterans and benefited the armed forces by showing the public how the government rehabilitated seriously wounded servicemen. But Kramer's *Home of the Brave* (1949) focused on the abuse of a Negro soldier by his fellow GIs during wartime and helped establish his controversial reputation. A Daniel Tara-dash–Buddy Adler team might have been able to assuage Navy worries about handling the "mutiny" on the screen because of their willingness to work with the military in developing a suitable script. But Kramer, because of his reputation, was destined to collide with the Navy as soon as he began work on *The Caine Mutiny.*

Nevertheless, he denied any "soapbox" intentions in producing *The Caine Mutiny.* He saw Wouk's book simply as "a very broad-based novel of the Navy. It's really a cross section of Navy life on a mine sweeper in the Pacific—officers and men and the crazy Queeg."[55] The Navy naturally saw little benefit in having one of its officers characterized as crazy, irrespective of the mutiny problem. As a result, Slade Cutter, director of the Navy's Public Information Division, said he was ordered "to drag the Navy's feet, so to speak, as long as possible to delay the inevitable and to get the script cleaned up as much as I could."[56]

Although Kramer wanted cooperation in making *The Caine Mutiny,* he started off on the wrong foot by selecting Stanley Roberts to write the screenplay. According to Cutter, when Roberts came to Washington to discuss the project, it was "like talking to Baby Snooks. My pride in the Navy was something absolutely impossible for him to comprehend or accept. He thought I was silly, unrealistic, irrational, and the possessor of that worst of all impediments to progress—the military mind, whatever that is." Roberts had an even more serious deficiency as far as the Navy was concerned. He had been caught up in the Red Scare that swept Hollywood in the late 1940s and early 1950s and had been accused of having ties to the Communist party. Whatever the truth of these charges, Cutter said the Navy Office of Information gave them credence and this "had no small part in the dragging feet operation."[57]

Kramer's most serious mistake in his efforts to win Navy assistance, however, was his decision to approach the Navy directly, which amounted to entering a lion's den unarmed. Both Baruch and Ray Bell, Columbia's lobbyist, attribute most of Kramer's problems to his refusal to follow regular military channels to obtain cooperation. According to Bell, Kramer believed that on the strength of his reputation as a filmmaker he could "probably obtain better and quicker cooperation from the Pentagon than working through me."[58] The producer saw the situation differently. He said he wanted no assistance from a lobbyist whose first responsibility was to his company and who believed in compromising to obtain military help. This "more adamant viewpoint" with which Kramer admitted he approached the military, perhaps as much as the book itself, forced the producer to spend eighteen months of on-again, off-again negotiations, sometimes in the Pentagon, sometimes publicly in the media, before he obtained assistance in making *The Caine Mutiny.*[59]

Kramer tried, of course, to keep as much control over the script as he could, but at the same time he prepared to ultimately make some concessions to the Navy to obtain assistance. In one early effort to capture the flavor of the novel and perhaps curry favor with the service, Kramer hired Wouk to work with Roberts on the initial treatment. As soon as Wouk realized the depth of the Navy's feelings about not wanting his book transferred to the screen, he urged Kramer not to make the movie and offered to return the money he had received for the film rights.[60] The producer responded with what he described as a "scathing letter calling him some sort of jellyfish."[61]

When Roberts completed his initial script and Kramer sent it to the Navy for consideration, the service found its worst fears fulfilled. Slade Cutter recalled that the "enlisted men were worse than bums, and the admiral was a stupid stuffed shirt." He conceded that it would have ruined "the picture to attempt to portray the *Caine* as anything but a 'honey barge.' And we didn't object to that. The problem was that there was no indication that the rest of the Navy wasn't as bad as the *Caine.*"[62] The Navy therefore took the tack of trying to encourage Kramer to develop a script that would indicate that both Queeg and the *Caine* were atypical.

Recognizing the problems he faced, Kramer hired a highly respected retired admiral to advise Roberts on the script and help bridge the gap to the Navy. And he finally turned to Ray Bell for assistance at Harry Cohn's insistence; as part of Columbia Pictures' financial arrangement with Kramer, the studio could exercise some control over production through the size of its budget. Ultimately, Kramer also "jumped the chain of command" to meet with the secretary of the Navy to make a passionate in-person plea for assistance.[63]

Kramer could have circumvented these problems by focusing on the court martial and making a small, "interior" film as Wouk had done in the stage play. He could also have resorted to miniatures, special effects, and combat footage for the exterior sequences, as other filmmakers had done when they couldn't obtain real ships. However, as Bell noted, by 1954 when *The Caine Mutiny* was released, filmmaking "had matured to the point where you could no longer phony something and feel that it was creditable to sophisticated audiences."[64] Kramer explained that *The Caine Mutiny* was set in the "massive environment of the U.S. Navy at war," and "to bring to the picture everything that is inherent in the book" required large-scale military assistance. To paint "this picture on a smaller scale would be to rob it of its value," he believed.[65] Therefore, he pursued Navy cooperation more resolutely than the Navy dragged its feet, until the service finally approved assistance in December 1952.

In reality, Kramer's meeting with the Navy secretary was unnecessary, since the service had already decided to cooperate on the film. While Admiral Parks, as chief of information, had bitterly opposed the film, most officers had

Producer Stanley Kramer (center right) discusses filming of The Caine Mutiny *with Fred MacMurray (Tom Keefer), Commander James Shaw (technical advisor), and Robert Francis (Willie Keith).*

enjoyed the book and only wanted any movie based on the novel to be as accurate and authentic as possible. Admiral Fechteler, the chief of naval operations, conceded after reading the book, "It's a hell of a yarn." He only wondered how Wouk in only two years of sea duty as a reserve officer had observed "all the screwballs I have known in my thirty years in the Navy." Moreover, Slade Cutter characterized his superior officer as not giving "a damn for public opinion or any of the media. He felt that doing a good job would be recognized eventually, and if it wasn't, so what?" Consequently, when Admiral Parks went to see Fechteler about Kramer's impending meeting with the Navy secretary, the chief of naval operations told him, "You had no business refusing cooperation in the first place."[66]

Parks recalled that Fechteler's comment "pulled the rug right out from under me after all this time," noting that the CNO had never mentioned the matter to him before. But recognizing that he had lost the fight, the chief of information set about to salvage what he could. After Kramer's meeting with the Navy secretary, who formalized Fechteler's pronouncement, Parks told the producer that the approval did not "mean that you are going to get any extra help from me, because I don't agree with [it]." Rather than allowing Kramer to use the retired admiral on his payroll as the Navy's technical advisor, he assigned James Shaw, an active-duty officer with experience on ships similar to the *Caine*, to serve as the official Navy representative on the film. And during the six months Shaw worked on the film, he strictly supervised the production, working with writer Michael Blankfort on revising Roberts' script, arranging for Navy assistance at Pearl Harbor and San Francisco, and insuring accuracy in the portrayals of actions and procedures.[67]

Despite the travails that accompanied Kramer's efforts to obtain assistance, he and his director, Edward Dmytryk, received "total" cooperation during the making of the film. In Hawaii, for example, the Navy put all its dockside derricks into operation simultaneously for one of Dmytryk's shots. As the script required, the Navy also provided use of attack boats, Marines, a carrier, and two destroyer mine sweepers (one in Pearl Harbor and one in San Francisco) to play the *Caine*. It would not, however, permit Kramer to acknowledge in the screen credits the cooperation he had received. Nevertheless, the last title stated, "The dedication of this film is simple: To the United States Navy."[68]

By working with Kramer and assigning one of its best officers as technical advisor, the Navy expected that it could achieve a more positive image of itself in the completed film. In writing to Ray Bell in September 1953, Admiral Parks said, "I am still hopeful that *The Caine Mutiny*, although it will show the seamy side of the Navy, also will include some decency and good and thereby be a good movie reflecting credit upon the armed services and the people in uniform."[69] And perhaps because their initial expectations had been so low, Naval officers were enthusiastic about the way Kramer had handled the story when they saw the finished film at a Pentagon screening in January 1954.

In its formal letter of approval, the Department of Defense Public Affairs Office stated: "We consider that Columbia Pictures fulfilled its obligations to the Department of Defense in bringing *The Caine Mutiny* to the screen in such a commendable manner." In a letter to Kramer, Don Baruch, writing on behalf of the Pictorial Branch, said, "We do want you to know, officially, that we believe you faithfully carried out your assurance to produce *The Caine Mutiny* in a manner which would be in the best interest of the Department of Defense. We consider the job well done, and will look forward to working with you in the future."[70]

Ironically, given all the smoke and fire that had accompanied the eighteen months of negotiations, the film they were praising did not stray very far from Wouk's book. To be sure, the author himself "thought it was a poor adaptation of my work."[71] But Wouk's reaction to the film echoed James Jones' when he initially saw *From Here to Eternity*. It is always difficult for an artist to see his work altered, and filmmaking necessarily demands that liberties be taken in translating a lengthy book to two and a half hours of screen time. In this case, except for the differences in the presentation of Queeg's actions as a Naval officer and the rationalization of the mutiny, the film probably adheres to the novel as closely as possible. The handling of Captain Queeg, however, like the handling of Captain Holmes in *From Here to Eternity*, simply illustrates how the military manages to improve its image in any film on which it assists. While Wouk's book and Kramer's film were ambiguous in their final treatment of Queeg, both the character and the Navy fare significantly better in the film than in the novel. In his version, Wouk reduces Queeg to virtual insanity and then half-heartedly tries to save him. After the court martial Barney Greenwald, the lawyer for Maryk (who has been tried for mutiny), seems to rationalize Queeg's breakdown by suggesting that he helped guard the country during the 1930s when most Americans ignored the Navy and its dedicated officers and men. But Wouk fails to connect Queeg's prewar service with his unstable behavior aboard the *Caine*. One literary critic pointed out that "Queeg is a goddamn maniac" and further observed that Wouk's justification would have validity only if it could be demonstrated that "Queeg worked himself down to the elbows for six years on this tin can in the North Atlantic and therefore he was crazy."[72] As the story is played out in the novel, therefore, the reader is ultimately left with the feeling that Queeg was sick and the Navy carelessly allowed a potentially dangerous man to command one of its ships.

Likewise in the film, Queeg is clearly a disturbed man who performs in an increasingly irrational manner. Most Navy men have acknowledged that Maryk was justified in taking over the *Caine*, given the structure of events leading up to the crisis during the typhoon. In the film, however, Greenwald's post-trial defense of Queeg is concerned with a conflict between the regular Navy on one hand and civilians-turned-sailors on the other. In confronting the *Caine*'s officers after Maryk's acquittal, the lawyer argues that they were responsible for Queeg's mental illness. When Willie Keith points out that Queeg did actually endanger the *Caine*, Greenwald retorts, "He didn't endanger anybody's life, you did, all of you. You're a fine bunch of officers!" When another officer reminds the lawyer that in the trial he had said Queeg "cracked" on the *Caine*, Greenwald responds that the captain had come to his officers for help and they had turned him down: "You didn't approve of his conduct as an officer. He wasn't worthy of your loyalty, so you turned on him. You ragged him. You made up songs about him. If you had given him the loyalty he needed, do you think the whole issue would have come up in the typhoon?"

When Maryk confesses the truth of this, Willie realizes that he and his fellow officers really were guilty of mutiny. Greenwald jumps on that: "Ah. You're learning, Willie. You're learning you don't work with a captain because of the way he parts his hair. You work with him because he has the job." Thus in the film, Queeg is as sick as he is shown to be in the book, but clearly, as Greenwald points out, "He couldn't help himself."[73] The civilians-turned-sailors have contributed to the disintegration of the regular Navy man, one who defended the nation when most Americans were comfortably at home making good careers and lots of money. In this context, Queeg emerges as a far better officer than Wouk's petty tyrant. Moreover, his breakdown is explained rationally, while the book's officer seems only slightly different from his fellow commanders. The Navy obviously preferred Kramer's version of the regular Navy officers to Wouk's more critical portrayal.

Kramer himself knew perfectly well that he had improved Queeg's character only to win Navy cooperation. In his pitch to the secretary of the Navy, he had said, "Fellows, you just aren't acquainted with dramatics. You cannot make white unless you make black. . . . Look, Captain Queeg was an officer who had battle fatigue and was going off his rocker. He did these things. Why did he do them? He did them perhaps because some of his officers were not patient enough with him and did not realize he was a sick man." In order to win cooperation, therefore, Kramer promised to show "simply that [Queeg] was an officer in the Navy who had gone off his rocker."[74] Years later, though, Kramer conceded that the ending he devised "was immoral." He said that a year after

Dick Powell, director of The Enemy Below *(1957), discusses film with Captain Herbert Hetu, the technical advisor, Frank McCarthy, Twentieth Century Fox executive, and the commanding officer of the destroyer on which shipboard shots for the film were made. In contrast to* The Caine Mutiny, The Enemy Below *was a "good" film for the Navy, showing a destroyer locked in mortal combat with a German submarine.*

he completed the film, he convinced himself that Maryk "*should* have taken over command."[75]

The success of the Navy and the Defense Department in modifying Captain Queeg's behavior probably had little effect on the public's perceptions of the Navy. They knew perfectly well that the Navy was not staffed by unstable officers. The United States could never have won the war if the armed forces had been led by Queegs or Holmeses. At the same time, audiences also knew that the military is not led only by the John Waynes or Gregory Pecks of *Sands of Iwo Jima* and *Twelve O'Clock High*. James Jones believes that the military benefits more from realistic portrayals like *From Here to Eternity* than the more typical, sanitized war films. He suggests that audiences recognize a falsely positive image as pure propaganda and so reject it out of hand.[76]

Whether *From Here to Eternity* and *The Caine Mutiny* benefited the armed forces, the military's struggles with the filmmakers seem to have drained the fight from the services. Some war films were made without cooperation, among them Robert Aldrich's *Attack!* (1956), which portrayed an enlisted man shooting an officer, and Kramer's *On the Beach* (1959), which showed the end of the world after an atomic war. But aside from these, the Department of Defense cooperated on virtually every major film made during the 1950s and into the

1960s. Only with the appearance during the mid-1960s of independent, anti-establishment producers and directors in the mold of the young Stanley Kramer, did the military refuse to assist on major productions that depicted the services unfavorably.

And if the image of the military suffered in the 1960s, these films were much less to blame than the nightly televised appearances of the armed forces fighting a real war 10,000 miles from home.

The Caine Mutiny

Van Johnson, flanked by Stanley Kramer and James Shaw, waves at camera during production of The Caine Mutiny.

CHAPTER EIGHT

THE MOST AMBITIOUS UNDERTAKING

★

With good reason, few people in Hollywood could understand why Darryl Zanuck wanted to make *The Longest Day*. Culminating the cycle of films about World War II and Korea that had begun in 1949, Zanuck was to make the largest, most expensive war movie up to that time.

Even Zanuck's son begged his father not to undertake the project, recalling, "What scared me was that we were getting into an eight or an eight and a half million dollar picture, which at that time was really fantastic." In addition, Zanuck seemed to be washed up as a producer, and his son thought *The Longest Day* was "liable to be really the end of the line." He asked his father, "Who cares about World War II?" noting that a good percentage of the movie-going public hadn't been born at that time. According to the younger Zanuck, trying to duplicate the battle scenes would be an "awesome" project.[1] Nevertheless, *The Longest Day* re-created the Allied landings on Normandy so faithfully that stills taken during the shooting are almost indistinguishable from photos taken on June 6, 1944. Many knowledgeable people, including military men who have seen *The Longest Day*, believe its visual authenticity results from use of actual combat footage. In reality, the entire picture was shot in 1961, with the assistance of the United States, British, French, and German military commands.

Of all the war films that preceded it, only *Wings* had received assistance of this magnitude, and as *Wings* set the standard for combat movies up to *The Longest Day*, Zanuck's film became the model for the war spectaculars of the

---

Darryl Zanuck with director Andrew Marton (foreground) prepares a shot on "Omaha Beach" during the making of The Longest Day *(1962).*

1960s and 1970s. But while Wellman's 1927 picture opened virgin territory for filmmakers and moviegoers, *The Longest Day* appeared to be the culmination of the genre that had begun in 1949. By 1960, World War II had been over for fifteen years, and Hollywood had nearly exhausted possibilities for films about that conflict. Moreover, World War II-vintage equipment was rapidly vanishing; not even the United States military had much materiel from the pre-1945 period.

★

Re-Creating The Longest Day

Darryl Zanuck described the film as the "most ambitious undertaking since *Gone With the Wind* and *Birth of a Nation*" when he announced in December 1960 that he had acquired the film rights to Cornelius Ryan's *The Longest Day*. He had paid $175,000 to French producer Raoul Levy, who had purchased the rights to the 1959 bestseller shortly after the book had appeared. Zanuck said he planned to use no stock footage in the film; he would re-create the entire invasion of Normandy. Although he had not yet calculated the cost of making a film of this scope, he estimated spending $1,500,000 just to restage the Allied landings on Omaha Beach. He expected that the greatest expenditure would be in the time needed to arrange logistics and locate equipment. With the exception of gliders that would be made especially for the film, he believed he could round up enough landing craft, amphibious tanks, planes, and other equipment for an accurate re-creation of D-Day.[2]

Zanuck claimed that he was being forced to restage the invasion in its entirety because no films of the Normandy landings existed in military archives. Actually, a limited amount of footage of the initial assaults did exist. According to Andrew Marton, one of the movie's three directors, the twenty-seven feet of film taken on Omaha Beach was "of a shockingly dramatic quality." However, it was of poor visual quality, and reprocessing it into Cinemascope dimensions and editing it into the newly-shot footage would have produced visually distracting results. Moreover, there was not enough quality footage of all the D-Day landings to reconstruct even a convincing small-scale landing. For *D-Day, the Sixth of June* (1956), actually a three-sided love story with only a small-unit assault as part of the film's climax, director Henry Koster staged a landing on a beach north of Los Angeles. Likewise, Arthur Hiller filmed James Garner's one-man landing on Omaha Beach for *The Americanization of Emily* (1964) in the same locale, because there was not enough footage for even that brief sequence.[3]

Colonel Dan Gilmer, the technical advisor, helps prepare for a shot in D-Day, the Sixth of June (1956), Twentieth Century Fox's initial effort to re-create the Normandy invasion. Essentially a romance, the film used the Southern California coast to represent Normandy for the brief battle sequence.

Zanuck was therefore correct in saying he could not use combat footage to re-create D-Day. And restaging a historical event of that dimension was truly a "most ambitious undertaking." But filming such a large-scale military battle was not the unique cinematic endeavor Zanuck seemed to suggest. Filmmakers had been shooting most of their ground combat sequences since the advent of wide-screen projection processes in the early 1950s. For combat spectaculars, like *Battle Cry*, directors photographed scheduled military training maneuvers. For smaller productions, like *Pork Chop Hill* (1959), they usually staged their own battles, relying on the armed forces' technical advice, some equipment, and occasionally a few men for a limited time. The resulting footage may have lacked some of the authenticity of actual combat film, but it presented none of the problems of visual quality that would have resulted from reprocessing the standard-dimension military film and then trying to intercut it with the non-combat portions of the movie.

Filmmakers did, however, continue to use old gun-camera footage, which was blown up to wide-screen size, when they needed to portray large-scale aerial combat because of the difficulty of acquiring large numbers of World War II planes. Even so, in *The Battle of Britain* (1969) Guy Hamilton staged all the combat sequences, since the production was a widescreen, color spectacular while the available footage was standard-dimension, black and white film. Fortunately, he was able to borrow fifty German Heinkel bombers from the Spanish Air Ministry to photograph on the ground and in formation. He also found sufficient numbers of British and German fighter planes in England, on the Continent, and even in Canada, to fill out the ranks of the opposing air forces.[4]

Even four years after the war it had been difficult to obtain B-17 bombers, as Darryl Zanuck had discovered when he made *Twelve O'Clock High*. Since the B-29 Super Fortress had made older planes obsolete even during the war, the Air Force had quickly scrapped their fleets of B-17s and B-24s as soon as fighting ended. (The B-24 Liberator bombers never acquired the romantic image of the B-17s, and no major film ever featured them.) Because of the cost of maintaining them in flyable condition, there were few plane collectors or dealers who could supply significant numbers of bombers to filmmakers. As a result, World War II airplane movies such as *The War Lover* (1964) and *The Thousand Plane Raid* (1968) used a few rebuilt B-17s for shots of individual planes on the ground and for specific maneuvers in the air, but the films obtained their waves of bombers and sweeping combat sequences from the same Air Force archives that had provided footage for *Twelve O'Clock High*. Of necessity, these films were all in black and white, since the Air Force had not used color film in their gun cameras until after D-Day and then not on a wide scale. *Fighter Squadron* (1948), one of the few color movies about the Air Force, is set in the post-invasion period, which enabled the producer to use color footage.

The Navy and Marines, in contrast, did use color film in the Pacific from the beginning of the war. As a result, most movies about the war in the Pacific could be made in color if the producer chose. In making *Task Force*, for example, Delmer Daves used rare black and white newsreel film to portray the early history of naval aviation. However, when the story reaches World War II, the film makes a dramatic transition to color in a scene that shows dawn breaking aboard ship.

World War II color footage gave producers of films about the Pacific War flexibility in deciding whether to make their movies in black and white or color. In addition, film companies could also generally shoot aboard Navy ships to obtain authentic locales to intercut with the combat footage and studio dramatizations. But they could not borrow whole fleets to restage their sea battles. For one thing, the composition of task forces and the types of ships in them changed during the 1950s. Battleships were mothballed, and straight-decked carriers became obsolete with the development of jet planes. These changes precluded the photographing of contemporary armadas to represent World War II flotillas. Therefore, in making movies about the World War II Navy filmmakers had the options either of reprocessing old combat footage with its attendant sacrifice in the quality of the visual image or of using miniatures and sacrificing authenticity. Walter Mirisch chose the first option in *Flat Top* (1952) and *Midway* (1976), while Otto Preminger in *In Harm's Way* (1965) and Elmo Williams in *Tora! Tora! Tora!* (1970) chose the second, all with limited success.

In contrast, Darryl Zanuck faced the challenge in *The Longest Day* to recreate authenticity on the land. The lack of suitable combat footage did give him the option of using color film for the production. He and Elmo Williams, however, his associate producer and the coordinator of the battle episodes, found from test shots that color would distract from the gritty, documentary style in which they intended to shoot the film.

If Zanuck couldn't plan to save money by using combat footage, he was well-versed in the Hollywood practice of cutting expenses by obtaining military assistance. As production chief at Twentieth Century Fox, he had supervised many war films in addition to *Twelve O'Clock High*. For *The Longest Day*, however, Zanuck realized he would need more help than he could obtain from only one nation. In his December press conference, he announced that cooperation had been promised from the NATO Command and the four governments that had been involved in the fighting at Normandy. To coordinate the actions of these armies, Zanuck said he would use directors from each of the four nations, supervising their work himself. According to Ken Annakin, the British director, Zanuck was like many American film people who "did not really like or trust Limeys and had only hired me because he'd made the promise that each section would be directed by the national of those armies." Nevertheless, Annakin quickly became part of the production team, which essentially functioned as a collaborative director. Annakin recalled that Zanuck "was a beaver for work" and tried to watch every scene being shot, ready to give suggestions, occasionally interfering with the directors' decisions and orders to the actors. As the British director stressed, however, Zanuck's concern was always "realism and accuracy, at almost any cost. . . . In my opinion, [he] was determined to make the greatest and truest film about the second World War which had ever been made."[5]

Zanuck ultimately claimed he had actually directed sixty-five percent of his film, but he admitted that "If anybody acts in *The Longest Day*, it is unintentional and not a result of my 'direction.' My job was to *prevent* actors from acting—to encourage them to play their individual roles realistically and without 'camera awareness.' "[6] Zanuck may have given himself too much credit for even this nondirecting. James Jones, one of the screenwriters for the film, thought that the size of the production was probably responsible for making *The Longest Day* the most true-to-life war film produced in Hollywood. "Simply because of its magnitude, the filming of it was like conducting a major military campaign. By its very scope it is precluded from concerning itself with basic human character, even as modern war itself is." To Jones, the film was basically a historical documentary. Like history, it recorded the personalities of the generals rather than the privates.[7]

Zanuck did not consider his film a documentary. At his press conference, he admitted that *The Longest Day* would have "no regular plot" as in a dramatic film. However, he asked: "What is a documentary? This is not a picture

Combined French and American military units help Darryl Zanuck reproduce the original Franco-American assault on the Casino of Ouistreham in The Longest Day.

about World War II, but about actual persons who participated in the Normandy landings." During a subsequent interview, he said that after reading Ryan's book, he had been "convinced that it would make one of the really great war pictures of our time." At his first news conference, though, Zanuck emphasized that "the production would not be a war picture as such." It would be "the story of little people, of the underground and of general confusion." "The stupidity of war" would be the theme of the film and, while it would condemn war, it would "be fair about it."[8]

Throughout the course of production, Zanuck repeated his belief that the film did more than simply portray history. He maintained that any picture "made on such a scale and with so much effort must say something." He felt it was important to convey through the film a message about the current world situation and the threat to "our way of life." His film was to be "a reminder to millions and millions of people that the Allies, who once stood together and defeated an evil because they stood together, can do so again in a different situation today which in some ways is similar to what they faced in 1940."[9] Most filmmakers like to think that their pictures make a significant comment on the human condition. In a film of the dimensions of *The Longest Day*, however, themes and messages often become lost in the rush of production demands.

In simulating the invasion of Normandy, the key ingredient was to re-create the kind of organization of men and materials that the Allies needed for the original invasion. The cost of making the film would have been prohibitive without cooperation from the four armed forces, who provided sufficient troops to re-create the magnitude of D-Day. Of all the planning, therefore, none was so crucial to the success of the film as the arrangements with each government for the use of its men and equipment.

Although Zanuck announced in December that cooperation was assured, he had only begun negotiations at that time. As his first step he wrote to Air

Force General Lauris Norstad, then Commander of NATO. In the controversy that later arose over the use of American troops in the film, the press described General Norstad as Zanuck's "friend," but both men denied the characterization. The producer pointed out that he had met Norstad only twice —the last time in 1952—and that he had never called him about cooperation. He had simply described his plans to make the film and asked Norstad whether he should apply to NATO for assistance or go directly to each of the four governments. Norstad advised him to deal directly with each government because going through NATO would "complicate things."[10]

Acting on the general's suggestion, Zanuck quickly reached agreements with the British, German, and French military authorities. From the British, he received promises of a fleet of World War II-vintage ships and 150 men from the East Anglia and Greenjackets Brigades. The Germans promised materiel and technical advice, but no troops. The French agreed to loan Zanuck 2,000 troops despite their war in Algeria. Later, when some of the promised American soldiers were not available for the final location shooting, the French Defense Ministry provided an additional 1,000 commandoes for almost five weeks and even permitted them to wear American uniforms.[11]

Despite the loss of American soldiers, Zanuck later denied having had any real difficulty obtaining help from the United States: "The fact is that the Pentagon was very cooperative and we were able, in one way or the other, to use a great many American troops."[12] General Norstad did send a telegram on February 1, 1961 to Assistant Secretary of Defense for Public Affairs Arthur Sylvester advocating support for Zanuck's film. Nevertheless, the producer claimed he "religiously followed" established Hollywood-Defense Department procedures in applying for assistance.[13]

According to Defense Department regulations, Zanuck's initial approach to General Norstad was "not an exception" to standard operating procedures. Nor was the general's telegram to the Pentagon in which Norstad recommended that Sylvester approve any request for assistance on *The Longest Day* saying, "I feel that this excellent book, brought to the screen with Zanuck's skill, could be very useful to the military services and to the United States. I think the German aspect could be handled in reasonable perspective and, on balance, the film would benefit the alliance." He recognized that the production would require a considerable amount of assistance from the American military at "substantial cost." But if the secretary approved cooperation, Norstad proposed to have the European Command work directly with the producer to clearly define requirements and ascertain problem areas for the military.[14]

Sylvester had been in office only a few weeks, and he acted primarily on assurances from his predecessor and the Public Affairs staff that Zanuck's request for assistance was routine. He later admitted that he responded "before

I knew what the hell I was doing." Sylvester cabled Norstad on February 8 that he agreed with the general's recommendations, and he asked Norstad to advise that Zanuck channel his request for assistance directly to the Pentagon. In response to the general's remark about "substantial costs" involved in Zanuck's request, Sylvester quoted the regulations governing military assistance to the film industry: "Cooperation will be at no expense to the Government." He further noted that his telegram did not imply approval of the project or that cooperation would automatically be forthcoming, but that it was merely "a courtesy preliminary survey without commitment."[15]

Following Sylvester's instructions, Zanuck began the process of obtaining assistance through negotiations in Washington and with the American Command in Europe. He was not above dropping names in his communications, once quoting a note in which President Kennedy had said, "I am delighted to learn that *The Longest Day* will now be a screenplay. I think that this is one of the finest books dealing with events of the Second World War, and I very much look forward to seeing your dramatization of this book." Despite such high level support for the project, Norstad's office extended no special treatment to Zanuck, refusing, for example, to switch regularly scheduled amphibious exercises from the Mediterranean to Normandy. But after extensive discussions in the Pentagon and with the military in Europe, Sylvester's office approved full cooperation on May 5 with the understanding that Zanuck would make certain minor changes in the screenplay that had been submitted in April.[16]

Coming up with a workable screenplay often resembled a battle on the magnitude of D-Day. Zanuck recalled that when he first read Ryan's book, "I went absolutely nuts about it." Even before he acquired the film rights, he and Elmo Williams had done a treatment that included the episodes they wanted to portray in the movie. Zanuck was "not interested in making a film that is only

Ken Annakin, director of the British sequences in The Longest Day, supervises the British landing on Sword Beach.

historically accurate. It just so happens that this one happens to be accurate. I am interested in following the brave, funny, bewildering, human and tragic events of the day." He not only attributed the book's success as a bestseller to its accuracy, but he also said "it gave the public a chance to see our own errors and our own successes, our own confusion and our own clear thinking." In addition, though, he wanted to show the events on the enemy side during D-Day and to avoid "a rosy, star-spangled banner drawing of D-Day," because that would lead to failure. According to Zanuck, the only way to make the film a box-office success would be to "tell audiences *what they do not know about what happened that day.*"[17]

To do this, Zanuck hired Cornelius Ryan in January to write the screenplay, a decision that proved to be a double-edged move. Ryan was an expert on the historic details of D-Day, but far from an expert on transposing them effectively onto film. The author had covered the Normandy invasion for the *London Daily Telegram,* and a return visit to the French Coast in 1949 had rekindled his interest in Operation Overlord, the invasion's code name. For ten years he researched the invasion, conducting more than 1,000 interviews with the participants. To him, the resulting book was "not about war but the courage of man."[18] Moreover, having spent much of his life becoming part of D-Day, he knew what had happened that day and wanted *The Longest Day* to portray events precisely—as he had written them. Ryan was not a filmmaker, though. Even the military, with its concern for authenticity, appreciated the tyranny of the movie camera, the need to move ships and men closer together than they operate in actual battle. The writer, however, did not recognize this need for compromise to ensure dramatic visual impact. Moreover, occasionally Ryan's knowledge was inaccurate. In his book, for example, he described a crucial skirmish at the Ouistreham Casino, although the building had been demolished two years before D-Day in an RAF bombing raid.[19]

In contrast, Zanuck was experienced in attempting to combine historical reality with Hollywood dramatics. By the time he found out about the nonexistent casino, his set designers had already begun constructing it, and the producer recalled that "because it turned out to be a great sequence," he left it in the film. Zanuck's biographer pinpointed the problem that led to continuing disputes between the producer and his writer, observing "One crucial difference between Zanuck and Ryan, it seems, is that Zanuck was usually aware when he was altering a truth for dramatic purposes, whereas Ryan could never admit to an error." Zanuck thought any inaccuracies in the film were minor, "They are close to the event that occurred. We did land. We did take the beach. We took dramatic license to make it effective. Anything changed was an asset to the film. There is nothing duller on screen than being accurate but not dramatic. There's no violation if you use basic fact, if you dramatize basic fact."[20]

The two men waged their own running battle during the months Ryan worked on the script, and Zanuck was often as inconsistent as the writer was stubborn. At one point, for example, Ryan suggested including in the film one or two romantic interludes that had actually occurred on D-Day. Zanuck responded in a blistering memo: "I do not want to badger you or cramp your style, but when you bring up, as you did at luncheon yesterday, an extraneous idea like love scenes between Gille [a French resistance fighter] and his fiancée, I have to speak up. These are just the things that we do not want and are the same things that have killed off so many other war pictures where they have tried to introduce a touch of sex."[21] By the time *The Longest Day* appeared, however, the fiancée's minor role in D-Day had been expanded, and Zanuck's current mistress, Irina Demick, had been cast in the part.

Despite these changes of direction and continuous disagreements, Ryan turned in a thick script on April 5. To Zanuck many things in it were out of proportion for a film. Consequently, he set to work redoing the screenplay to suit his purposes, and Ryan's *The Longest Day* became Zanuck's *The Longest Day*. While the filmmaker and Elmo Williams made most of the contributions to the revision, Zanuck sought additional advice from writers in the four countries involved in D-Day. Romain Gary and James Jones also made significant contributions to the final script.

Zanuck specifically wanted the author of *From Here to Eternity* to make Ryan's GI dialogue sound more authentic. But most of Jones' effort was wasted in the face of the industry censors.[22] When Zanuck submitted the script for approval, the Production Code Office refused to approve the "casual profanity" and the obvious substitutions for four-letter words that it contained. The censor objected to the use of dialogue like crap, muck it, motherlover, bastards, damn, hell, and even lines like "they couldn't sink this clucking can if they tried to." To make matters worse, the Code Office observed, "We are concerned with what seems to us to be an excessive amount of slaughter in this story. We realize that it is impossible to tell the story of the invasion of Normandy without indicating the staggering loss of human life. We do urge you, in those scenes you stage, to minimize the dramatization of personal killings. We think that such an effort on your part would avoid the 'bloodbath' effect." For the most part, Zanuck ignored these requests. Jones, however, was outraged at such strictures. Writing to the producer, he said, "I was *morally shocked* at . . . their 'concern' over the 'excessive slaughter' in the story. What the fuck do they think war is? What did they think Omaha was, if not a 'bloodbath'? . . . I find it incredible that these ostriches can go on like they do, building fallout bomb-

(Above) Ken Annakin discusses a scene in The Longest Day *with Darryl Zanuck.*

(Right) Filming the assault by United States Rangers on Point du Hoc for The Longest Day.

shelters with one hand, and not allowing honesty in combat films with the other. And if they tell me this is what American people *want*, I can only answer that they're full of *bullshit*."[23]

Faced with these reactions, a continuing dialogue with his writers, and the Pentagon's requests for changes, Zanuck admitted in mid-May that he was "going very slowly" on the final script. At the same time, work on other aspects of the production was proceeding toward an early summer shooting date. Zanuck brought together a general staff of seventy technical advisors headed by Ryan for the American sequences, General Koenig for the French, and Admiral Ruge for the German. Most of the experts had participated in D-Day; some had even been face-to-face combatants. (In one instance, only his death shortly before filming began prevented a former German pilot from working as an advisor with the French Marine he had strafed on the beach seventeen years before.) Zanuck even verbalized the hope that the original Commander-in-Chief General Eisenhower would consent to speak a few lines for a "faceless" actor in two brief but crucial scenes.[24]

Zanuck's "biggest problem" was to locate actual war equipment, and his staff conducted a vast scavenger hunt across Europe to find obsolete materiel.

Spain proved to be a repository of old German weapons, especially tanks. The sands of Normandy yielded a British tank that had been buried for seventeen years. Guns came from all over Europe. Zanuck located the British piano company that had built the original gliders for the invasion and had two exact replicas manufactured for the film. He also found three British Spitfires in Belgium and two German Messerschmitts in Spain. Fortunately for the producer, the skies over Normandy were thickly overcast on D-Day, and he was able to maintain accuracy without re-creating an entire Air Force. Uniforms for the Allies proved no major problem since battle dress had changed little since 1944. However, German uniforms had to be specially made because the West German Army had destroyed all vestiges of its Nazi past. In his efforts to re-create the past, Zanuck kept in mind that many potential viewers had been there and would recognize any sharp differences between history and its dramatic portrayal.[25]

During all these preparations, Zanuck adhered to his original concept of the film. "Remember our story is not a military picture," he repeated in mid-May. "It's not a war picture. It's the heartbeats on both sides." Ironically though, the producer had virtually assumed the role of a supreme commander in assembling his staff, in supervising all aspects of the production, and in all decision making. The filming was organized and planned as carefully as D-Day itself had been prepared. Even a similar tense excitement prevailed. As Zanuck noted, "All you can do is to get the buildup ready for the day we say 'Shoot'."[26] Unlike General Eisenhower, of course, Zanuck did not have to keep his preparations a secret.

But he did have limited resources. Zanuck had hoped to begin filming at Omaha Beach, using the promised British fleet to re-create the original invasion task force. When the Admiralty informed him that a $300,000 fuel bill accompanied the fleet, he turned to the United States Sixth Fleet, which had amphibious maneuvers scheduled at Corsica at the end of June.[27]

To prepare for this shooting, the producer sent Elmo Williams, Andrew Marton, and six camera crews to the Mediterranean, with a French LST providing the transport for the men and equipment. When Williams first approached the commander of the Marine assault force for permission to film its landing, the officer expressed serious reservations because of his men's inexperience. However, the producer convinced him to change his mind by pointing out that the landings would be more realistic for the men and so better for training purposes if the film company re-created the Normandy beaches and set off explosive charges. As part of this preparation, the film crews built fortifications on Saleccia Beach where the landings were scheduled to take place. By the time the fleet arrived, the company had built obstacles along a two-mile stretch of beach, buried explosive charges, and simulated machine-gun emplacements so that the shoreline looked like Omaha Beach as it had appeared on D-Day. The twenty-two ships of the Task Force, which represented the Sixth Fleet's largest concentration since it had been stationed in the Mediterranean, provided the background for the landing of 1,600 men of the Third Battalion, Sixth Marine Division. [28]

With his ships and a large-scale landing on film, Zanuck turned his attention to location work in Normandy. Shooting there began in mid-August when Zanuck took over the French town of Sainte-Mère-Eglise to re-create the disastrous American parachute drop of D-Day. For two weeks, seventeen French stuntmen wearing American uniforms made repeated jumps, dropping everywhere but in the town square. Finally, after several injuries but only a couple of successful landings in front of the cameras, Zanuck resorted to the traditional Hollywood method of dropping the parachutists into the square from cranes.[29]

At the same time, filming began on the Normandy beaches. They, like Saleccia Beach, required a makeup job to return them to 1944 conditions. Omaha Beach itself was useless: its D-Day monument was too large to be camouflaged, and it was still full of buried live ammunition. The battle on Omaha Beach was therefore shot at Ile de Ré in late October and early November. On the other hand, the American struggle to take Pointe du Hoc a short distance down the shore from Omaha Beach was filmed at the original site. Armed with French permission and original D-Day photographs, Zanuck's crew "burned the whole bloody place," fabricated shell holes, built fortifications, removed old mines, and sandbagged the monuments to look like bunkers. The invading force for the assaults on the German cliff positions was provided by the American Command in Germany, this time a unit of the 505 Infantry Battle Group and a battalion of Army Rangers.[30]

Numbering about 150, the GIs served for almost three weeks as supporting players to four of Zanuck's actor-soldiers in late August and early September. The Rangers were trained for both amphibious landings and mountain climbing, and it was their job to prepare the actors for the cliff assault. Zanuck had made their job harder by hiring three rock and roll singers, Paul Anka, Tommy Sands, and Fabian, along with Robert Wagner, a Hollywood veteran, to play soldiers in the four-minute sequence. According to Cornelius Ryan, Zanuck's casting was intended to attract young people to the film, but Elmo Williams admitted he was shocked to learn of his boss's choices for the physically difficult roles.[31]

The associate producer's reaction seemed justified during the early filming when Anka was immobilized, first by a speck of sand in his eye and then by a torn fingernail. One of the Rangers was moved to suggest that the actors didn't "have what it takes." After continued work with the Rangers, however, the four stars went up the cliffs side by side with the soldiers during the filming. By the end of the sequence, Williams had come to view the casting in a different light, observing that the "kids have done everything we've asked them. Anka had to fall off a ladder seventeen times before we got one scene right." If the director of the action, Andrew Marton, had any complaint about authenticity, it was that the soldiers were sometimes too proficient. Occasionally he had to remind them that things had not gone perfectly on D-Day and he didn't "want it to be perfect now."[32]

Marton's major problem, apart from minor injuries, flubbed lines at $35,000 a day, and unrealistic perfection, was the presence of Darryl Zanuck himself. Whenever the producer was on location he would stand behind Marton and breathe down his neck. During one scene, the producer rasped, "There's too much smoke, Cut!" Boss or no boss, the director turned on Zanuck bellowing, "Nobody says cut! Nobody says action but me when I'm directing. Nobody!" Despite such interruptions, spectators watching the filming at Pointe du Hoc could not help but admire Zanuck's invasion. One observer noted that the explosive charges shook the ground, water spouts soared 100 feet into the air as landing craft came in off the Channel, and the newly burned-out craters from the original shellings had "a sickening realness to them."[33]

One of the best judges of the authenticity of Zanuck's D-Day was a participant in the filming at Pointe du Hoc who had taken part in the original assault on Omaha Beach. Sergeant Joseph Lowe thought the re-creation was "very realistic." Was it like D-Day? "Oh. No sir, it wasn't nothing like this. Nothing will ever be like that believe me, sir." Trying to describe the difference, the sergeant said, "There was a good deal of confusion on D-Day and men were falling down into the water or down onto the beach everywhere you looked. There is confusion now. Lots of it. When we fall, it is because we are told to. The danger is not above us this time, it's below."[34]

Having re-created the "general confusion" of Normandy as planned, Zanuck felt he had left behind all the difficulties that had earlier plagued his production. By the second week in September, filming of the parachute drops at Sainte-Mère Eglise was nearing completion. British and French sequences were being shot or were in the final planning stages. And the producer had already scheduled final location shooting in Normandy for October and November, again using American troops promised by General Norstad. Even at this stage of production Zanuck had doubts about the possible success of the film: "I don't think anyone's ever had to spend so much time putting so little on film. Right here we're spending two and a half weeks and half a million dollars for

German soldiers attempt to repulse United States Rangers as they scale the cliffs of Point du Hoc during shooting for The Longest Day.

four minutes of film. . . . Moviemaking costs so much you lie awake all night worrying about it. I'd like this to be the best picture I've ever made. But I don't know."[35]

★
Sylvester's Re-Evaluation of Military Assistance

Without the military assistance, of course, Zanuck would not have been able to film *The Longest Day*. Nevertheless, at the same time he was using American GIs from Germany as advisors and extras in Normandy, the Defense Department had been mobilizing Army Reservists and National Guard units and was planning to immediately send 40,000 men to Europe to meet the Communist challenge posed by the building of the Berlin Wall. A direct phone line linking American headquarters in Germany with Zanuck served as a constant reminder that units assigned to his film could be recalled at the first sign of trouble.[36]

Although the 1961 Berlin Crisis constituted a threat to Zanuck's use of troops, the producer saw the Wall as a justification for his film's theme. To his mind the Communist threat in Berlin emphasized the parallel between the current situation and the one in 1944. His picture was fundamentally "the story of David and Goliath, the triumph of the seemingly weak over the seemingly invincible. There were the Allies, weary of long years of war, of humiliating defeats, divided, uncertain, the knife at their throats, uniting in a combined attack that first broke the hold of Nazism and then broke its neck." The defeatists of 1944

The Most Ambitious Undertaking

who spoke of "the wave of the future" were compared to those currently spouting the better-Red-than-dead line. "But," he said, "I believe that freedom will never be crushed as long as there are men as brave as the men of D-Day. That's what's implied—though not directly stated—in *The Longest Day* and that's why I'm making it and making it now."[37]

Zanuck was not the only person using American troops to convey this message. In early September, Jack Paar, then host of NBC's "Tonight" show, decided to provide his viewers with on-the-spot coverage of the Berlin Crisis. On September 7, with a television crew and four cameras, Paar travelled to Friedrichstrasse, a border crossing that had been the scene of several confrontations during the previous three weeks. Seven officers and about fifty men in seven Army jeeps arrived at the same time. The men took positions on the sidewalk and in a war-damaged building, and Paar filmed his program. When newsmen later questioned the Army about the unusual concentration of troops at the Wall, a spokesperson explained, "There was an operational changeover of units in progress this afternoon. In an effort to be accomodating, we permit-

The first wave of Marines, representing G.I.s, land on "Omaha" beach during first filming for The Longest Day *on Corsica in June, 1961.*

ted Mr. Paar to film these activities. Mr. Paar took advantage of this situation."[38]

By the next day, Paar's visit to the Wall had made the headlines in Washington where it caused an immediate outcry in the Senate. Describing Paar as a "TV comic," Majority Leader Mike Mansfield reminded people that the Berlin Crisis was not a TV spectacular. Majority Whip Hubert Humphrey added that the government had other things to do "besides provide a backdrop for television shows." These reactions were a forewarning of Hollywood's difficulty in obtaining further assistance from the military. Most ominously, Clifford Case suggested that "the practice of making facilities of the defense establishment available for any private ownership, for commercialization and commercial profit, is one to be examined, and should be permitted only in a situation in which their use would not in any way endanger the security of the United States."[39] Ironically, The Longest Day did not enter the discussion, although the September 8 issue of Time magazine contained an article describing the assistance Zanuck had been receiving from the military since June. After the Army announced on the 9th that it had taken disciplinary action against two Army officers in Berlin, the Senate lost interest in the Paar incident. But the controversy over Hollywood's use of military personnel had just begun.

The connection between Zanuck's use of the military and Paar's activities was made by David Brinkley in defending his network colleague from congressional and press criticism. By the 11th, Secretary Sylvester had begun to publicly express his reservations about Pentagon cooperation with the film industry: "I have grave doubts whether this sort of thing is a proper use for military equipment and manpower. It looks to me like a skunk in the military garden party." He said that the issue of military assistance had been on his mind for a long time, and he questioned Zanuck's making arrangements with the services at the same time the Army was complaining about a manpower shortage. He further noted, "Zanuck's isn't paying for any of the time our troops put in or for the equipment."[40]

The media's continued attention to the Paar incident and in Zanuck's use of troops in Normandy served to rekindle political interest in the matter. Congressman Bob Wilson, head of the Republican Congressional Committee and a member of the House Armed Services Committee, wrote to Secretary Sylvester on the 13th, asking a series of questions about the Paar incident and its relationship to The Longest Day. His letter was clearly politically motivated, and he lost interest in the subject as soon as Sylvester answered him on the 25th with the standard public relations justification of military cooperation to Hollywood.[41] When later asked about the controversy, Zanuck commented, "I think that story got out of hand and was exaggerated by people who thought they could get headlines out of it."[42]

From his perspective in France in September 1961, however, Zanuck did not realize that the uproar had arroused Sylvester's concerns about cooperation. The press soon discovered that General Norstad still intended to loan Zanuck 700 soldiers for his final shooting at Ile de Ré, a small island 200 miles south of Normandy. In confirming the assistance, a spokesman for the United States Command in Europe said on October 16 that the Defense Department had approved the request. He explained that the troops were considered to be on a training exercise involving a movement by vehicles and an amphibious assault. He added that Zanuck would be paying at least part of the cost of transporting the troops from their base hear Frankfurt.[43]

Responding to inquiries, the Pentagon issued a statement that both the White House and the Pentagon were "reviewing any further cooperation with Darryl Zanuck." The White House, however, refused to take part in reviewing Norstad's agreement. When questioned about continued cooperation, an aide to Congressman Wilson replied, "What's okay with General Norstad is okay with us." The general believed his decision to assist Zanuck was his own business and declined to act on the Pentagon's "suggestion" that he send fewer soldiers to Zanuck. Ultimately, Secretary of Defense Robert McNamara ordered a cut in the size of the force from 700 to 250 men. According to the Pentagon, "This decision was based on the fact that the number originally planned was much larger than is normal in military cooperation. The curtailed participation is being authorized on the basis that it is in the national interest to do so and that the U.S. and its allies are cooperating in helping to film a great story of American, British, and French heroism."[44] According to Zanuck, the loss of the 450 men would have meant he could not have re-created Omaha Beach, except that the French government, loaned him 1,000 French commandoes for five weeks and allowed them to wear American uniforms. The 250 GIs who were provided cost the producer $300,000 because he "had to pay every penny of their expenses" as a result of Sylvester's closer scrutiny of cooperation.[45]

The reduced number of soldiers and Zanuck's payment for their transportation and expenses were the first tangible signs of the secretary's re-evaluation of the Pentagon's policy toward cooperation. To actually effect significant changes in the regulations, however, Sylvester needed to overcome opposition from both the military and the film industry. His commitment to make these changes was further strengthened by another controversy stemming from the military's help to The Longest Day. In November, while filming was in progress at Ile de Ré, United Press reported that Robert Mitchum, portraying General Norman Cota in the movie, had complained that during a major action scene some of the American soldiers used by Zanuck were afraid to board a landing craft in high seas. Mitchum was quoted as saying, "I had to

Robert Mitchum, portraying General Cota, lands on "Omaha" beach, at Ile de Re, off the French coast, in November, 1961. Mitchum's comments about the Army assistance during this scene added to the controversy surrounding the making of The Longest Day.

hop aboard first myself with some other actors and stuntmen before they gave in." To make matters worse, Mitchum also said he had seen two top officers watching the landing operation from the beach, "Unfortunately they got cold as we were wading in the icy water and asked for a good fire to get warm." While both Mitchum and Zanuck subsequently denied the inferences drawn from the actor's remarks, the newspaper accounts kept the cooperation issue alive.[46]

To exacerbate the situation further, Senator Sam Ervin, chairman of the Senate Subcommittee on Constitutional Rights, announced about a month later that some soldiers were claiming they had been forced to take part in the filming at Ile de Ré. At first the Army insisted that all men used by Zanuck had come from Germany as reported in the press and so were there on regular assignment. In the follow-up report, however, the Army acknowledged that some soldiers attached to a transport unit near Ile de Ré had been used in the film, and some of these men had refused to participate in the shooting.[47]

If Sylvester needed any more evidence to harden his conviction that policies should be changed, Zanuck himself provided it. When the producer sent The Longest Day to Washington for final approval on September 21, 1962, the Defense Department found that the print contained a brief sequence it had specifically requested that Zanuck delete. The sequence portrayed an American soldier machine-gunning a group of German soldiers who were apparently trying to surrender. The Germans advanced toward the soldier calling "Bitte!

American forces break through the sea wall on "Omaha" beach, filmed at Ile de Re, and move inland, assuring Allied success on The Longest Day.

Bitte!'' (''Please!''), but the American did not understand German and fired. After the screening, the Defense Department Public Affairs Office and the Army reiterated that the scene should be deleted, and Don Baruch informed Zanuck's Washington representative to that effect. The Pentagon's chief of the Production Branch explained, first by phone and then by letter on September 24 that the original script had been approved only with the understanding that the scene be changed or deleted. Zanuck had advised the Pentagon that he would do the sequence in a way he felt would satisfy all parties, but Baruch stated that ''the scene still is objectionable. Unless this objection is overcome, the film is not approved for public release.''[48]

The subsequent correspondence took on an air of surrealism and finally became a moot debate. By the time one of Zanuck's aides answered Baruch on October 1, 1962 *The Longest Day* had had its world premiere in Paris with the controversial scene intact; more than 100 prints had been made and circulated. Through his aide, Zanuck defended the release of the film. According to him, the portrayed killings had actually occurred, and he had done the sequence in such a way as to show the GI had not deliberately killed soldiers attempting to surrender. He said he had screened a rough cut of the film for many high-ranking officers in Europe and none had objected to the scene; General James Gavin, then ambassador to France, had not objected to the sequence; and no one at the Paris opening had objected to it. The aide further suggested that the problem was a sincere ''difference of opinion,'' not an attempt by Zanuck to skirt regulations. He did mention the issue of the number of troops, which had been ''arbitrarily'' reduced, and the problems this caused Zanuck. The aide also asked that the Pentagon again screen the film and judge it not on the basis of one scene, ''but on its overall impression and on its authenticity as a sincere and realistic portrait of D-Day and of the triumph of the combined efforts of the Allied forces.''[49]

In responding for the Defense Department, Baruch repeated the Pentagon's objections and cited regulations that required ''a film to be approved prior to multiple printing and public release unless otherwise determined.'' Noting that no such discussions had occurred, Baruch said that Zanuch had taken a calculated gamble in making the 100 prints before receiving Pentagon approval. He repeated, ''The scene still is not considered in our best interest and, therefore, in accordance with the policy under which assistance was extended on this production, we assume it will be deleted.''[50]

Of course, Darryl Zanuck had no intention of recalling all the prints to delete the offending scene, and the Pentagon had no way of stopping the film's distribution. The sequence itself, running less than seventy seconds, was done realistically and had a strong dramatic impact. It could have had little adverse effect on "the best interest" of the Army or the military establishment. Nevertheless, Zanuck clearly violated his agreement with the Defense Department. The time for him to object to the requested deletion was before, not after, he had completed the film. Through proper negotiations, Zanuck could have had both this scene and military approval. Instead, Zanuck's methods only reinforced Sylvester's determination to increase Defense Department supervision of policies governing cooperation.

Clearly, *The Longest Day* had become Zanuck's sacred cow. Neither Cornelius Ryan, nor the military, nor his directors, nor Twentieth Century Fox executives were going to tell Zanuck how to make his film. In the end, the movie returned more than $17,500,000 in domestic rentals on an investment of close to $10,000,000, the most expensive black and white film ever made. Usually, foreign sales equal or slightly outdo the American-Canadian market. Given the subject matter, *The Longest Day* undoubtedly did better, making it one of the most successful black and white films produced and, up to that time, the best war film in box-office terms. Its success meant the rebirth of Zanuck's career and the financial salvation of Twentieth Century Fox.

The film that did all these things presents many faces to its viewers. Perhaps because it attempts to be both a pseudodocumentary history and a commercial drama, *The Longest Day* exhibits a split personality. As James Jones observed, it ultimately worked because its production so closely resembled the combat it was trying to portray. And like the Allies' success on D-Day, the film succeeded in spite of great obstacles, even errors. If, for example, a film should limit its focus to two or three individuals to achieve a significant dramatic impact, then *The Longest Day* should have failed. It has no star but rather a galaxy of stars appearing in cameo roles. If a successful dramatic film should relate a story with a beginning, a middle, and an end, building tension as the plot unfolds, then the movie should have failed. It had no plot and portrayed what might be termed only a slice of life, one day lifted out of history. Moreover, every audience knows the story's ending, knows further that it was only a beginning of eleven more months of struggle in Europe. Finally, like *Tora! Tora! Tora!* and *Midway*, which imitated *The Longest Day* and were dramatic disasters, Zanuck's film spends too much time getting to the action, too much time talking, planning, preparing for battle.

Despite all these burdens, however, *The Longest Day* works not only as reasonably accurate history, but also as powerful drama. The film owes much of its success to the great skill with which Zanuck, Williams, and his codirectors re-created the battles on the Normandy beaches. As Bosley Crowther noted in his *New York Times* review, there has been no other dramatic film in which "the labor and agony of warfare, the sheer, awful business of getting there and going into battle and being blasted with shot and shell while you struggle to kill other people has been shown more lengthily or graphically described."[51] *The Longest Day* became the quintessential war film because of the authenticity of the battle scenes, but even more so because Zanuck followed the lead of Cornelius Ryan and focused on men before, during, and after battle. Although no character's role is developed fully, most of the characters are human in their fears, pride, courage, and misery. In the end the film, like the book, leaves a lasting impression of the human element of war, where men on both sides do their best to carry out orders and try to survive their longest day.

Sylvester's Re-Evaluation of Military Assistance

CHAPTER NINE

A MARRIAGE ENDS

★

The *Longest Day* served as the model for all subsequent combat spectaculars. Like Zanuck's film, *Battle of the Bulge* (1965), *Bridge at Remagen* (1969), *Tora! Tora! Tora!* (1970), *Midway* (1976), and *A Bridge Too Far* (1977), among others, told the story of great battles of World War II from the viewpoints of its combatants. These films traced the events leading up to a particular battle, with the participants speaking in their own tongues as was done in *The Longest Day*.

However well each film re-created history, the narrative served only as a framework for the film's objective: the spectacular combat scenes. Individuals seldom counted for much in the stories; the major historical characters were usually played by top stars in cameo appearances. Visual drama, violence, and noise replaced personal drama, the stories of men and their struggles, and the kinds of portrayals that had made *Twelve O'Clock High*, *Sands of Iwo Jima*, and *From Here to Eternity* significant movies irrespective of their genre. That few imitators of *The Longest Day* found the same box-office rewards suggests that a film must focus on believeable human beings with whom the audience can empathize if it is to succeed critically and commercially.

To succeed, of course, a film must not only tell a dramatic story and tell it well, but also it must tell one that interests people. As a biography first and a war movie second, *Patton* did all these things. But in general, the combat spectaculars that followed *The Longest Day* did not tell their stories as well

A B-52 bomber roars skyward during filming of A Gathering of Eagles *(1963), a film about the Strategic Air Command which received full Air Force cooperation despite stricter supervision of the Hollywood/Pentagon relationship by Assistant Secretary of Defense for Public Affairs Arthur Sylvester.*

either narratively or visually. Worse, with the exception of *Midway*, which became a major box-office hit despite both a dull script and poor visual effects, the large-scale war movies that imitated Zanuck's production related stories that failed to interest enough people to make the films financially successful.

Even before Zanuck undertook his project, most Hollywood filmmakers believed the market for movies about World War II had become saturated. (The Korean War market had died with *Pork Chop Hill* in 1959, if not earlier.) *The Longest Day* succeeded at the box office because it was based on a popular book and attained a unique visual and dramatic authenticity. By 1962, however, there was an apparent thaw in the Cold War, a realization after the Cuban Missile Crisis that the Super Powers could not resort to nuclear war to solve their disagreements. In this atmosphere, people were less interested in reliving past battles. At the same time, the new generation of Hollywood filmmakers had little commitment to the traditional relationship with the military that had produced an almost unbroken string of movies glorifying the armed forces.

In practical terms, the problems involved in attempting to make films about World War II by the early 1960s also played a major role in ending the cycle of movies about the conflict. As Zanuck's searches and expenditures for materiel demonstrated, it had become increasingly difficult to find the equipment needed to authentically restage the war. *In Harm's Way, Tora! Tora! Tora!*, and *Midway* depicted their battles primarily with miniatures, mockups, and combat footage. However, most of the spectaculars that followed *The Longest Day* were shot in Europe, where film companies could still find usable World War II equipment and even armies available for rent. Even so, the cost and the logistics involved in these overseas productions limited the number of major projects that were undertaken.

Paradoxically, then, *The Longest Day* marked the end of the cycle of traditional World War II films that had begun in 1949, while at the same time it spawned the era of the combat spectacular. The movie also brought about the end of the free and easy marriage between Hollywood and the military that had existed since the early days of the film industry. The controversies the film created because of the amount of assistance Zanuck received from the Army and the producer's own disregard for Pentagon regulations left the relationship in temporary disarray. As a result, a period of retrenchment took place between 1962 and 1965 during which time the Pentagon reexamined the process of cooperation. While the regulations were being rewritten, filmmakers became wary of approaching the Pentagon for assistance, and this also contributed to the decline in the number of films made not only about World War II, but about all aspects of the military establishment.

★

A New Look at Cooperation

Over the years, an occasional member of Congress or of the media had questioned the armed forces' policy of loaning of men and equipment to film-makers. But nothing much had ever come of these queries. Now, because *The Longest Day* had brought the issue of cooperation before the public and because Arthur Sylvester had been drawn into the controversy on so many occasions, he initiated a reevaluation of Pentagon regulations governing military assistance to commercial filmmakers. As the study progressed, Sylvester became convinced that the Public Affairs Office had to assume tighter control over assistance to the film industry. His determination to change the regulations was reinforced in February 1962, when a sailor was killed while preparing explosives for use in *No Man is an Island,* a movie being made with limited military cooperation. Although the sailor was on leave, Representative Walter Norblad reacted to the incident with a declaration that filmmakers should hire their own extras and employ civilian experts for dangerous special effects.[1]

Arthur Sylvester.

The film industry did have its defenders. Late in February, Senators Vance Hartke and Thomas Kuchel praised the documentary *A Force in Readiness,* which Warner Brothers made at cost for the Marines. On the Senate floor, Hartke gave particular credit to Jack Warner, who "put all the facilities of his company" into the making of the film.[2] Nevertheless, during the first half of 1962, cooperation between the film industry and the military slowed measurably as Sylvester's office continued its policy review.

The Motion Picture Association, unsure of the secretary's intentions, solicited the help of Hubert Humphrey, who wrote Sylvester in mid-June to inquire about the current status of the relationship between Hollywood and the Pentagon. The secretary responded that he was "cognizant of the benefits of cooperating with the film industry to more fully inform the American public of the activities of the Department of Defense." He also cited criteria that filmmakers would have to meet before the Pentagon would agree to assist them in the future. These included an evaluation of the dramatic quality of the potential movie, the need to assure safety for servicemen working on the films, and the requirement that assistance not interfere with the operational readiness of the armed forces. Sylvester told Humphrey that his office had already developed new guidelines to insure that these criteria would be met and would "serve the best interests of the taxpayers and the nation." Sylvester also assured Humphrey that the new guidelines would not stand in the way of continued assistance to filmmakers, citing his office's recent approval of cooperation on *A Gathering of Eagles* and *PT-109.*[3] In fact neither of these examples was valid

Norman Stuart, the dialogue coach, Delbert Mann, the director, Rock Hudson, and an Air Force officer discuss filming in Missile Silo for A Gathering of Eagles.

evidence that the film industry could still expect to receive assistance without red tape and inhibiting restrictions.

A Gathering of Eagles, a direct descendant of Air Force, Thirty Seconds Over Tokyo, and Twelve O'Clock High, had the backing of General Curtis LeMay, the father of the Strategic Air Command (SAC) and one of the most powerful men in the Pentagon. Sy Bartlett, the producer, had been an Air Force officer in World War II and had established his filmmaking credentials with the Pentagon as a result of Twelve O'Clock High, Pork Chop Hill (1959), and The Outsider (1961). Also, A Gathering of Eagles was being made by Universal Studios, whose Washington representative, John Horton, had helped Donald Baruch set up the Motion Picture Production Office in 1949 and was one of the most effective studio representatives in Washington. In line with Sylvester's new requirements, Bartlett had submitted a detailed list of the men and equipment he would need to make the film and a precise schedule of when he would need them. This was the first time such a strict accounting had been requested, and Don Baruch later said he had labeled the list "the Bible." Even so, Sylvester initially had refused to approve cooperation on the film because he considered it simply another Air Force public relations movie.[4]

At this point, General LeMay took a personal hand in the matter. He had become concerned with criticisms of SAC's safety procedures then being

John Wayne on bridge of U.S.S. St. Paul during location filming of Otto Preminger's In Harm's Way *(1965), which received Navy and Marine assistance immediately after the issuance of new Department of Defense regulations governing cooperation.*

raised by both Peter George's 1958 novel *Red Alert* and Stanley Kubrick's *Dr. Strangelove*, then in the planning stage. In conversations with Bartlett, a long-time friend, the general talked about the possible detrimental effect of the movie on SAC. Bartlett recalled that he "instantly" saw the possibility of doing a film that would explain SAC's function. He wrote the story himself, without any direct request from LeMay, combining the informative aspect of the film with dramatic flying sequences and a plot centering on the tensions under which the wives and families of the fliers lived.[5]

LeMay's feelings about Hollywood films were ambivalent. He liked Hollywood because people played up to him but admitted that he "never did like any movie that came out of Hollywood about our activities. They always had to throw this Hollywood stuff into it, a little sex, the hero had to have a problem he had to surmount and conquer and so forth." He conceded that Air Force people did have problems but noted they weren't the type that were "of particular interest to a moviemaker," no people "with mental problems and things of that sort." Since Hollywood emphasized those elements to make good stories, LeMay felt their films, "really didn't tell the story of what we were trying to do." At the same time, he appreciated the public relations and recruiting advantages of the films. When he discovered that Sylvester had rejected Universal's request for assistance with *A Gathering of Eagles*, LeMay wrote a memo to the secretary saying the Air Force wanted the film made. His aide hand-delivered it to Sylvester, who approved cooperation almost immediately.[6]

Sylvester's new regulations gave him no more control over the actual assistance extended than he had had before. According to Bartlett, the film company was able to do things the secretary "sure as hell" didn't know about when it went on location at Beale Air Force Base in California. The producer said he dug up a runway, had a special training take-off exercise repeated when a camera malfunctioned, and, in general, made the film as assisted military movies had always been made. The film company even had access to SAC's underground command center in Omaha, and during their visit, Rock Hudson, the movie's star, was permitted to speak his lines over the SAC worldwide radio alert network. Given such cooperation as well as a script written by Bob Pirosh and directed by Delbert Mann (both previous Oscar winners), *A Gathering of Eagles* realistically captured the conflicts and tensions in the peacetime Air Force. More important for the service, it accurately portrayed its fail safe procedures. Despite Bartlett's need to include the "Hollywood atmosphere" of women and family problems, General LeMay thought it was "the closest any of [the Air Force films] ever came to showing a true picture of what the military was all about."[7]

In contrast, *PT-109* offered little "truth" in portraying military life aboard PT boats in the South Pacific in World War II. In the pre-Sylvester era, the Navy would have routinely agreed to assist on a similar, but fictionalized story because of the innocuous nature of the script and the limited help needed. But if the film had been a test case of Sylvester's new policy as the secretary had suggested to Senator Humphrey, the request for cooperation would likely have been turned down. Because it dealt with the wartime experiences of the incumbent president, however, the new regulations had no apparent influence in the ultimate decision to assist Warner Brothers.

The film necessarily portrayed a two-dimensional character. It could not contain the typical war movie romantic interlude, and it could not very well show a man with warts, since the president would be running for re-election soon after the film's projected release date. Consequently, it offered little in the way of potential dramatic quality—one of Sylvester's criteria for approving a script. Moreover, if the story had not been about President Kennedy, the script probably would not have interested filmmakers. According to Lewis Milestone, the movie's original director and one of Hollywood's best (*All Quiet on the Western Front, A Walk in the Sun, Pork Chop Hill*), the script contained a lot of "cornball jokes" and was "just another adventure story." He believed that if it had been a fictional film, the studio would have abandoned it: ". . . why bother? We've got better stories than this." But Jack Warner, president of Warner Brothers and a long-time friend of the Democratic party, had liked Robert Donovan's book *PT-109*. And Brian Foy, Jr., the producer, believed the film would make money.[8]

Ordinarily these political and commercial factors would have reinforced Sylvester's opposition to assisting on any film. But when President Kennedy indicated that he did not object to the Navy's participation, the secretary had no choice but to approve assistance. Even with stricter guidelines on coopera-tion, Sylvester would have had a difficult time turning down Warner Brothers' request for assistance. Over the years, the studio had made more commercial military films with armed forces assistance than any other company. In addi-tion, Warner Brothers had regularly produced military documentaries such as *A Force in Readiness* at little or no cost to the various services.[9]

PT-109 needed relatively little in the way of men or equipment, and so satis-fied Sylvester's criterion that assistance be on a non-interference basis. Since the Navy no longer had any World War II PT-boats, the film company planned to construct reasonable facsimiles. For actual shooting, the studio needed only about 100 sailors and a few ships and planes for a short time on location near the Key West Naval Base. But even this limited request proved to be too much. While the controversies surrounding *The Longest Day* undoubtedly influenced the Defense Department's action, White House fears of Republican criticism clearly dictated the Pentagon's decision to cut the amount of assistance.[10]

President Kennedy, while agreeing to allow Navy participation on the film, stated through his press secretary that the service "should not extend a single bit more cooperation to do this movie than it would to do any movie in which it determined that the interests of the Navy as a fighting service were involved." With this advice in hand, the service provided less than a dozen sailors and re-jected the studio's request for planes. Warner Brothers was forced to hire off-duty sailors and to rent the needed aircraft. The Navy did provide a destroyer, six other ships, and some equipment for the filming.[11] It is doubtful that any amount of assistance would have improved the quality of *PT-109*. In the end it resembled a dull campaign propaganda film more than a Hollywood commer-cial release.

Certainly neither *PT-109* nor *A Gathering of Eagles* was greatly affected by Sylvester's new regulations. Nevertheless, Sylvester cited them as positive examples in his letter to Senator Humphrey. He concluded with the hope that his proposed controls would be "a means of assuring the film industry that equitable arrangements can, in fact, be developed between the industry and the Department of Defense."[12]

Neither the letter nor any of Sylvester's actions in formulating a new Defense Department Instruction on military assistance during the next eighteen months did in fact assure the film industry. Shortly after the secretary's reply to Senator Humphrey, Kenneth Clark, executive vice president of the Motion Picture Association, observed that the industry would manage to work things out, "but cooperation will be more difficult in the future than in the past. The old easy, informal ways are over."[13] Sylvester's proposals for a new set of regulations offered virtually no changes from the 1954 Instruction which he intended to replace. It was not surprising, therefore, that in October, Sylvester repeated that the "United States military can't be rented by anyone. They are not going to be turned over to motion pictures indiscriminately." While his office would continue to provide assistance, he stressed that in the future, he wanted "all Hollywood requirements spelled out in advance. And whether the training is necessary or merely make-believe, we don't want to be put in the position of writing to any parent that 'your son was killed in making a picture.' "[14]

The film industry leaders doubted that Sylvester would have a lasting effect on the Hollywood-military relationship. Eric Johnston, president of the Motion Picture Association, wrote to Darryl Zanuck in October 1962 that Sylvester was "not the last word. In this case I would say that he was merely the first word. If we find that the revisions are objectionable and Sylvester is unyielding, we shall carry our case to the highest authorities in the Department of Defense and in the White House."[15] In Robert McNamara's Pentagon, however, the assistant secretaries did have almost complete authority over their own departments; as a result, Sylvester was the last word as well as the first word in determining new policies on military assistance to Hollywood.

The new regulations issued in January 1964 reflected Sylvester's intention to impose tighter control over the cooperation process. First verbalized in September 1961 at the height of the *Longest Day* uproar, the new Instruction did not stop military assistance to filmmakers in any sense. According to Sylvester though, "they got it on our terms." Under his new regulations there was "less ordering stuff all around and more precise definition beforehand of what cooperation was to involve. It was not a case in which we just went whish, come take anything you want."[16]

Initially, the film industry responded to this tighter control with cries of anguish. Stan Hough, a production supervisor at Twentieth Century Fox, wrote to Richard Zanuck in 1964 saying that the new regulations gave the Defense Department "a very strong voice in the creative controls of any film requiring their cooperation." And from a production standpoint, the policies were "quite rigid." A studio was required to "not only designate equipment and material, but also the date, location and the *time of day*." He conceded that there "would be some 'give' but it is frightening that we must name months in advance the time of day we expect to make a shot of some military equipment or personnel."

Darryl Zanuck's The Longest Day *in large measure captured the emotions of what it was like to be under fire in scenes such as the landing on Omaha beach.*

Hough later admitted that the new regulations "did not prove to be as awkward as they seemed. More practical minds prevailed."[17]

If the new policy ultimately proved workable, its immediate effect was to reduce the number of films made with military assistance. Otto Preminger was able to obtain a reasonable but reduced amount of help with *In Harm's Way*

(1965), but only after some effort. Sylvester himself approved limited assistance to nonmilitary films such as *Thunderball* and *Goldfinger*. Even so, Hough advised Zanuck that the studio "should weigh very carefully whether it would be feasible to undertake any project which requires intensive military cooperation."[18] John Horton, who had arranged cooperation between Hollywood and the Pentagon for almost twenty years, specifically attributed the decline in films about military subjects to Sylvester's 1964 regulations.[19] And Ken Clark of the Motion Picture Association noted that "the new regulations produced decisive changes in the manner and history of cooperation between Hollywood and the American military establishment."[20]

If Sylvester's actions gave impetus to Hollywood's move away from combat movies, America's changing attitudes toward the military greatly influenced the content of those films that were made. By 1962, audiences were less interested in reliving past military glories via the movie screen. John Kennedy had proclaimed a new era of peace, the Cold War was apparently thawing, and a nuclear test-ban treaty was being negotiated. Despite the Bay of Pigs, the Berlin Crisis, the Missile Crisis, and a minor war in Southeast Asia, military preparedness seemed less important than it had during the 1950s when nuclear war posed a continuing threat. In the midst of this semipeaceful interlude, World War II and Korea seemed inappropriate topics for Hollywood films.

In actual fact, the fear of nuclear holocaust was ever-present in the early 1960s. The military continued to talk of new weapons, of intercontinental ballistic missiles to replace long-range bombers, of nuclear submarines and aircraft carriers. Despite the talk of a thaw in the Cold War, the Pentagon was conducting business as usual. The contradictions between the talk of peace and the reality of continued preparedness, as well as the growing distance from the wars of the forties and early fifties created a new atmosphere, one in which it was possible to voice at least subtle criticism of the military in films.

Meanwhile, in Hollywood the defenders of the traditional relationship between the film industry and the military—Louis B. Mayer, Harry Cohn, Harry and Jack Warner—were disappearing from positions of authority. Only Darryl Zanuck retained his power throughout the 1960s. Television was bringing to an end the old studio system. Hollywood was being taken over by bankers and conglomerates who were more interested in financial returns than in fostering images. The new industry leaders were willing to invest in a project with any kind of story line as long as the proposed film had potential appeal. Often this new generation of independent producers had no contact with or commitment to the traditional relationship with the military. More important, to the younger generation of filmmakers nothing was sacred. Film was the medium in which to create drama, and neither the Production Code's view of sex and the family nor the military's view of its own infallibility were respected or perpetuated.

★

Antiwar Themes in Hollywood Films

Until the early 1960s, with only a few exceptions, Hollywood had consistently portrayed our armed forces positively. Admittedly, history, the model filmmakers had to work from, offered little of a negative nature. In both World Wars I and II, American forces had fought bravely and emerged from the conflicts with glorious victories. If American history books and movies slighted the Allies' contribution (especially the Russians') to victory in World War II, there is no question that the United States was largely responsible for the defeat of Germany and Japan. If the armed forces had not exactly won in Korea, most people blamed the stalemate on political decisions, not military shortcomings. But in the new climate of the 1960s, Hollywood began to present another view of the services, one that often differed greatly from the image suggested by its earlier collaborations with the military.

Antiwar, antimilitary themes have always had an honored place within the war film genre. Lewis Milestone's 1930 classic *All Quiet on the Western Front* and Stanley Kubrick's 1957 *Paths of Glory* both expressed strong antiwar themes, and both were critically acclaimed. However, neither movie portrayed the American military and both dealt with World War I. Stanley Kramer's *On the Beach* (1959) did strive for a pacifist message by dramatizing the consequences of nuclear holocaust. But the film showed no destruction, contained little explicit criticism of the American military, and was set for the most part in the remoteness of Australia.

Only an occasional film like Kramer's *Home of the Brave* (1949) or Robert Aldrich's *Attack!* (1956) dared show American officers and men performing in less than an exemplary fashion. Neither film received Pentagon assistance, and *Attack!* was one of the few war movies on which military officials refused even to discuss possible script revisions that might have made it acceptable for cooperation. After reading the screenplay, which included an enlisted man killing an incompetent officer, Don Baruch told Aldrich that there was no way of keeping that situation in the movie if he wanted assistance. Since the whole story built up to this dramatic high point, there would have been no movie without the scene. As a result, Aldrich made the film without military support. He ended up with a highly dramatic story that presented another side of military life, albeit a rare one. Nevertheless, he made it clear that the military as a whole was not at fault. The soldier who killed the officer explains at one point: "The Army is not a mockery! The war is not a mockery! It's just this small part!" He also ended up with a movie obviously shot mostly on a soundstage. Visually, the film lacked the authentic feel of men in combat, and without that realism the film failed to attract large audiences, however meritorious its story.[21]

A Marriage Ends

The portrayal of negative human qualities such as cowardice, pettiness, and self-aggrandizement does not necessarily make a movie antiwar or anti-military. In fact, Hollywood filmmakers seem to lack a precise understanding of what constitutes an antiwar theme. Virtually everyone in the industry purports to be against war. But in seeking to make their antiwar statements, filmmakers have usually depicted the brutality and violence they oppose without considering either their general impact or specific use in the context of the movie's overall structure.

Darryl Zanuck, for example, clearly stated that *The Longest Day* conveyed antiwar sentiments because of the manner in which it portrayed combat. Better than most Hollywood productions, the film does create a very real sense of the horrors of war, the waste of lives and resources, the senselessness of attempting to use violence to solve ideological problems. In Zanuck's production, these images are reinforced because the film is not simply another fictionalized portrayal of combat. The men who die in the film are real people, not the product of some screenwriter's imagination. The audience knows that the paratroopers who are shot as they drop into the town square at Sainte-Mère-Eglise are French stuntmen, and perhaps they even know they are descending from Zanuck's hired crane. But unlike the stuntmen in a typical war film, they represent real human beings who died on June 6, 1944, precisely as portrayed in the film. The men who "die" in 1961 on the beaches of Corsica, Pointe du Hoc, or Ile de Ré, the Germans who "die" because an American soldier does not understand "Bitte! Bitte!" represent soldiers who actually died on D-Day.

The impact of this reality on audiences undoubtedly had a sobering influence. If the film's original ending had not been deleted, its antiwar thrust might have been shattering. A soldier sits on an ammunition box at water's edge, staring at the incoming waves. In the background are two rows of bodies and other flotsam of the battle. However, Zanuck thought the scene was "too downbeat" and wrote a new closing montage. In the first scene, Richard Burton as a downed RAF pilot and Richard Beymer as an American soldier sit crumpled on the ground beside a dead solider. Beymer begins: "You know something? I haven't fired my gun all day." Burton responds: "It's funny. He's dead. I'm crippled. And you're lost." Beymer asks: "I wonder who won?" A quick cut to Omaha Beach. Robert Mitchum, having blown the seawall obstacle to the interior, climbs in a jeep and says: "O.K., run me up the hill, son."[22]

Whatever feeling of revulsion has been engendered by the combat sequences is dissipated with this upbeat ending. Instead of the vision of mentally and physically exhausted soldiers and dead bodies (unbloodied ones to be sure, since not one drop of believeable blood is seen on the screen), the audience leaves the theater with the image of men going "up the hill." The soldiers are off the beaches, and a giant step has been taken toward defeating Hitler.

Original ending for The Longest Day *that Darryl Zanuck decided not to use because he thought it was "too downbeat."*

In trying to make their antiwar statements, filmmakers have too often juxtaposed images of war's brutality with war's successes. Violence and excitment, the horrors of war, and its adventure and romance, too often cancel each other out. The costs of war are too often justified in the filmmakers' efforts to use their medium to create patriotism and build morale. The escapist entertainment that war films offer their audiences often outweighs the negative images of combat that the movies visualize.

Filmmakers have, of course, always been aware of the difficulty of presenting an "anti" message on the screen, whether about war in general or violence in particular. Norman Jewison, for example, intended *Rollerball* (1975) to be a critique of violence: "The statement of the film is surely against the exploitation of violence. If the film itself is accused of exploiting violence, then I would ask how you make a statement about violence without showing any violence." In translating word pictures to the screen, however, he acknowledged that "the images are so much more vivid that the film may be open to misinterpretation. That's why I just don't know how effective films are. I know certain people will be excited by the violence in *Rollerball*. I just hope they understand why they're being excited, and by the end of the picture perhaps realize that the violence is appealing to their more base instincts."[23] Audiences usually don't have time to think during a movie, especially one as filled with action as *Rollerball*. For the most part, they came away from the film with an appreciation for the visual beauty of the action. That the action was extremely violent did not seem significant to many viewers, who found the film simply exciting and escapist entertainment rather than a message against violence.

Similarly, films that claim to condemn war produce in the audience a sense of patriotism, of adventure, of camaraderie, but seldom a sense of repulsion. *Paths of Glory* plainly presents a negative picture of the French officer corps and seeks to provoke horror at the random execution of French soldiers for mutiny in the front lines. Nevertheless, no one in the film (or probably in the audience) questions the validity of the executions as a means of suppressing the revolt. This punishment has always been considered a legitimate means of maintaining discipline. Moreover, the closing image is not of the senselessness of war or even the tragedy of innocent men's execution. Instead, the surviving soldiers are seen drinking and singing, preparing to fight another day for the glories of France, not philosophizing about their dead comrades. They may be drinking to put the executions out of their minds, and Kubrick may have intended to condemn war by juxtaposing the executions with the relaxing soldiers. But there is sufficient ambiguity at the end of the movie to mute the film's antiwar sentiment.

Likewise, Sy Bartlett's *Pork Chop Hill* (1959) suffers from the ambiguity of its conflicting images, the bravery of men who find themselves in an untenable situation because of the irrationality of war. Set in Korea during the final hours of peace negotiations, the film documents the true story of the American

John Garfield, as the blinded Al Schmid, receives a medal for his actions in Pride of the Marines *(1945).*

capture of Pork Chop Hill, an action ordered only to demonstrate to the Communist negotiators that the United States still had the will to fight on if an agreement was not reached. The GIs vaguely understand the ultimate meaninglessness of their action, but as well-trained soldiers they go out to fight and die, obeying military orders. To Bartlett, this portrayal clearly represented an antiwar statement, that no man should have "to face a situation like that during his lifetime." Nevertheless, Bartlett said that the Pentagon strongly approved of the film for two reasons: it showed the Army carrying out its mission, but more than that, it answered the post-Korean "world-wide gossip that the American soldier broke and ran." Consequently, the film was seen from rather different perspectives. While Bartlett claimed to be "very, very antiwar," others saw his film glorifying the determination of the military in battle.[24]

Some filmmakers have tried to overcome this paradox by showing the impotence of death in battle. *All Quiet on the Western Front* (1930) offers the classic example of this kind of antiwar statement. At the film's close, the hero reaches for a butterfly, a symbol of hope and beauty, and is shot by a sniper as the armistice is about to begin. In a more contemporary setting, *Beach Red* (1967) also attempts to create this sense of the futility of war. The director-producer-star, Cornel Wilde, explained that he tried to "show people what war was really like whichever side you are on. The enemy is not a faceless extra who gets mowed down while the heroes charge up the beach gung ho, and we feel sorry for those who are hurt." According to Wilde, he was not trying to make a "war as hell" film in which men are "torn apart by shrapnel, or maimed by 50mm machine guns or cut in half, [or] have an arm blown off." Instead, he "tried to show that war, even without the killing and maiming, just the physical and mental stress is horrifying."

Wilde recognized that "Deadly combat is always exciting to people," and his ending implied "that war was terrible and a waste of human life, of youth, and of human relationships and that it accomplishes nothing." *Beach Red* closes with a confrontation between a Marine and a Japanese soldier who have wounded each other severely. They lie twenty feet apart, both in agony and incapable of moving. Staring at each other, they realize they are alike, young and in pain. The Marine senses the agonizing thirst of the Japanese who is dying from a stomach wound, and he throws the soldier his canteen. To reciprocate, the Japanese tries to throw the Marine his one remaining cigarette. As he does, an American patrol arrives, sees only that the Japanese is about to throw something, and kills him. According to Wilde, his meaningless death illuminated the horrors of war without showing any positive value.[25]

These scenarios still portray aspects of war as an exciting romantic escape. Yet they do come close to conveying the absurdity and uselessness of war. Recognizing the thrust of Wilde's script, the Marines extended only limited assistance to the film, in the form of combat footage from the Marine film archives. (The Marines probably benefited more from this assistance than Wilde, since the footage had deteriorated and he had it restored in the process of blowing it up to wide-screen dimensions.) To obtain the men and equipment needed for his battle scenes, Wilde went to the Philippines and arranged to use its armed services for the large-scale action sequences.[26]

While these re-creations are as realistic as any done for an American war movie, Wilde managed to avoid picturing combat as adventurous. Instead, his war is a grim, desperate business; his Marines have no time for typical Hollywood antics. They are in a struggle for survival with an enemy little different from themselves, and they are willing to die for their cause, but, as shown in the final confrontation, they also possess humanity and compassion. Unlike so many antiwar movies, this interpretation of combat conveyed the message the director intended. According to Wilde, at the first sneak preview the audience watched the film in virtual silence. Afterward, a weeping woman came up to him and said, "I want to thank you, Mr. Wilde, for showing people what it's really like. I lost one of my two sons in Vietnam." At another screening, Wilde reported that a serviceman left the movie "sobbing uncontrollably."[27]

Reviewers were equally moved. One critic described *Beach Red* as "a grim, wryly humorous, gripping, and emotion-packed drama of war." In taking a "fresh approach to both the purpose and purposelessness of war," Wilde made a picture in which "Neither preachment, chauvinism, nor cynicism gets the upper hand . . . as it explores the human sacrifice that war imposes on both sides." To the reviewer, the film came "close to being the definitive drama on human expendability in war." Similarly, another critic said that *Beach Red* showed "War without glamour; death without glory; hatred without reason. [It] is so frighteningly real in its portrayal of war in the Pacific that it could be a shouting sermon against militancy." As a third reviewer noted, while "there are practically no mock heroics as the men writhe and bleed and yell or moan," this "is not what makes it such a powerful antiwar document." Rather, its statement came from showing "that the men don't want to kill, want to live themselves, and that they are frightened most of the time."[28]

Fright is, of course, the other aspect of the excitment war offers men who challenge death in combat. By focusing on the negative side of the war experience, Wilde's antiwar theme did not get lost in a wave of gratuitous violence, adventure, or romance. Nevertheless, the frightened men were only actors in a fictionalized story. Their emotions were merely a performance. For a movie to convey the full impact of fright, the camera must capture the faces of men who are caught up in actual combat, men who may actually die the next moment.

Marines land on Pacific Island in Beach Red *(1967), Cornel Wilde's effort to make an antiwar statement by showing combat as it really is, without the typical war film excitement and escapist entertainment.*

Such visualizations are of necessity found only in documentaries, and even then, only in an honored few. Of these, John Huston's *The Battle of San Pietro* remains probably the best film—whether documentary, pseudodocumentary, or pure fiction—about the experience of men in combat. While the Army saw the film as the record of a single battle in Southern Italy, most viewers have seen it as an antiwar statement, because it so well captured the fear on men's faces as they went into battle, so well showed the meaningless of death, so well conveyed the reality that there is no glamour in actual combat. Yet *The Battle of San Pietro* succeeded not only because it showed war from the perspective of the men who did the fighting, but also because it showed the victims of war, the men who died and the civilians whose lives were shattered by the battle that swept over them, their homes, and their land. Perhaps in conscious or

Cornel Wilde examines a natural obstacle during the filming of Beach Red *in the Philippines.*

A Marriage Ends

unconscious recognition of the message these images portrayed, the War Department deleted some of the shots of soldiers dying or being killed. And the film spends a few moments showing civilians returning to their homes and later it shows their land again in bloom.

If *The Battle of San Pietro* ends on this upbeat note, the overall effect remains one of revulsion at war and the horrors it brings to all people, soldiers and civilians alike. In focusing on the victims of the battle, Huston provides perhaps the best answer to Norman Jewison's question of how to make a statement about violence without showing any violence: focus not on the violence but as much on the victims as possible.

Huston's *Let There Be Light* (1945), one of the strongest antiwar statements ever put on film, succeeds because it focuses exclusively on victims, not on soldiers in combat, but on soldiers who have returned from war suffering the psychological effects of their combat experiences, soldiers with mental damage as severe as any physical wounds. Huston's narration in the film describes them thus: "Born and bred in peace, educated to hate war, they were overnight plunged into sudden and terrible situations." The film document illustrates the horrors of combat much more graphically than any film claiming to condemn the brutality of war by showing scenes of battle, either real or recreated. Yet *Let There Be Light* has never been released to the general public. Huston claims the Army is repressing it more than thirty years after the end of the war because of its antiwar content. The Pentagon denies the accusation, pointing

out that the rights of privacy of soldiers appearing in the film prevent its showing. In any case, the film remains the prototype of the antiwar movie that con-
veys its message through the victims of war rather than through combat.[29]

Several Hollywood dramas have tried to convey the negative side of war in
similar but less drastic ways. Delmer Daves' *Pride of the Marines* (1945) portrays a blind Marine's adjustment to civilian life, while William Wyler's *Best
Years of Our Lives* (1946) portrays three veterans, one of whom has lost both
hands in battle, trying to bring order to their lives after the war. In *The Search*
(1948) Fred Zinnemann shows German children as the victims in postwar Germany, but his direction of Stanley Kramer's production of *The Men* (1950) returned to the soldier-as-victim theme. Portraying a group of paralyzed veterans
who attempt to adjust to a life of permanent helplessness, the film depicts a
story of war victims seldom talked about let alone shown on the screen. *The
Men* received the full cooperation of the Army and the Veteran's Administration, who saw it as a means of informing the American people of the government's efforts to rehabilitate wounded soldiers. The images Zinnemann
created suggested another message, that war was destructive to human beings
and was not the glamorous adventure implied by most other films with a military background.[30]

Although the Army did not realize the significance of the victim approach
in 1950, the Air Force was quick to recognize it when they saw the script of
Limbo (1973). The film told the story of POW wives waiting for their husbands
to return from North Vietnam or for word that they had been killed. According
to director Mark Robson, *Limbo* was a true antiwar film because it shows the
suffering of the women, but none of the excitement or adventure usually found
in a war movie. The producer, Ellen Gottlieb, stated that the Air Force refused
to provide even limited assistance because the plot included unfaithful wives.
The Air Force felt the movie would be bad for the morale of fliers in Vietnam
and for the American POWs, who might somehow be treated to a screening of
the film within a few days of its release in the United States. The Air Force
further contended that less than two percent of POW wives had cheated on
their husbands. Without making a judgment on the women, Gottlieb said that
her research showed the figure to be much higher.[31]

Of course the point of the film had to do not with precise numbers but with
the tragedy of the women's situation. However, to the Air Force, the point that
emerged was the unflattering image of the service and its wives. As a result,
the Air Force not only refused to provide assistance, but also went out of its
way to make sure the film company was denied help even of an informational
nature. Ironically, the service's concern about the effect of *Limbo* was rendered moot when the POWs began to return at almost the same time the film

Robert Redford during a respite from combat in War Hunt (1962), a film that attempted to make its antiwar statement by showing the corrosive effect war has on its participants.

A Marriage Ends

was released. With the story irrelevant, few people bothered to see the film and whatever antiwar message it may have had was lost. Still, the movie illustrated an important means of presenting the negative side of war without portraying any of the glamor or excitement.

Only rarely in the 1960s in films such as *War Hunt* (1962), *The Victors* (1963), and *The War Lover* (1964) did filmmakers attempt to suggest an antiwar message by portraying the futility of combat. *War Hunt*, for example, illustrated the destructive nature of combat through a character who loved war because he lived to kill. In the film John Saxon is considered a good soldier because he is adept at killing North Koreans. Even after the truce he continues his forays because he likes to kill. His actions, now deviant, are no longer in the best interest of his country; they now jeopardize the truce. Saxon's commander must ultimately dispose of the killer who cannot adjust to peacetime conditions.

Terry Sanders, the producer of *War Hunt*, sent the script to the Pentagon "on the remote chance that they might not read the script and might give him a few tanks or something." Being realistic, however, Sanders recognized that the Army would probably find the script incompatible with any image it hoped to portray. His belief was confirmed when the Army objected to many elements of the script, including the portrayal of an enlisted man as a professional killer who, as a result of his killing ability, is catered to by an officer. They also objected to an enlisted man's portrayal as a coward, to a scene in which a captain calls a sergeant an idiot, and to scenes it considered too gruesome to be in

Robert Redford in War Hunt *looks on after his commander has been forced to kill John Saxon, playing a compulsive killer who cannot adjust to peace and has continued his forays despite the cease fire.*

good taste. The Army's recommendation was for the producer to "explore other avenues of approach to a new story line which would be acceptable."

War Hunt is notable, however, because it illustrates the problems of making even a small-scale war movie without military cooperation. The movie has a significant statement to make about war and killing, but it lacks the dramatic impact of *The Longest Day*, which has no plot and a known ending. Unlike Zanuck's film, *War Hunt* did not have authentic military equipment and used extras instead of trained soldiers. To help disguise these physical deficiencies, much of the film was shot at night. Despite noisy explosions the film lacked a realistic atmosphere and authentic-looking battle sequences. The resulting "back lot" feel of the movie at a time when *The Longest Day* offered "reality" continually intruded on the story. The audience cannot suspend disbelief, cannot pretend it is watching war, and so the message is weakened.

Although *War Hunt*, *The Victors*, and *The War Lover* show a negative side of war, they tried too hard to make audiences aware of their message. In *The Victors*, for example, the execution of an Army deserter, shown in graphic detail, is accompanied by Frank Sinatra's crooning of a Christmas carol on the sound track. And the final confrontation, in which an American GI and a Russian soldier kill each other over an insignificant right of way, is too heavy-handed in its symbolism. Moreover, each film depicted the excitement and the fellowship of men in combat, which further muted their antiwar statements. What these films confirmed compared to *Beach Red*, *Battle of San Pietro*, or *Let There Be Light*, was the need to focus on the victims of war, not the war itself, in attempting to create antiwar feelings in the audience.

CHAPTER TEN

THE MILITARY AS ENEMY

★

A major problem in using World War II and even Korea as vehicles for attacking war was that the armed forces had been successful, the American fighting man had performed bravely, and the nation as a whole thought the conflicts were necessary. Even America's great defeat at Pearl Harbor was excused in Zanuck's *Tora! Tora! Tora!* (1970). Instead of focusing on the errors of judgment that resulted in the devastation there, the film dealt sympathetically with the men responsible for our ill-prepared armed forces and portrayed December 7 as a brave response to a sneak attack. If filmmakers were going to make an antiwar statement, therefore, they not only had to avoid combat situations and separate the fighting men from military leadership, but they also had to find suitable scapegoats to justify their attacks on militarism.

Filmmakers found their targets in two previously sacred subjects, the Bomb and military leadership. During the 1950s Hollywood portrayed the Bomb as an instrument of peace. *Above and Beyond* (1952) told the story of Paul Tibbets and the dropping of the first atomic bomb on Hiroshima, which had ended World War II. *Strategic Air Command* (1955) portrayed Curtis LeMay's bomber force as the major deterrent to Communist domination of the world. *Bombers B-52* (1957) was an informative film about SAC and its newest weapon for maintaining peace. Only at the end of the decade did Stanley Kramer's *On the Beach* (1959) suggest that the Bomb was a force that could

---

The Enola Gay ushered in the atomic age over Hiroshima in 1945. Above and Beyond *(1953), depicting the story of Colonel Paul Tibbets and his mission, became the forerunner of a series of Air Force movies about the Bomb as a deterrent to war. Today, Tibbets' plane sits in a Smithsonian shed awaiting restoration.*

destroy the world. Protesting that Kramer's vision of doomsday could not happen, the Pentagon refused to provide him with a nuclear submarine during shooting of the picture.

Films about the Bomb provided a perfect means of attacking war and the military without having to portray combat or raise the issue of so-called necessary wars. The Bomb's potential to destroy all of modern civilization suggested to many that its threats outweighed its military benefits. The armed forces had nevertheless committed themselves to its development and use, so any criticism of the Bomb would imply a criticism of the military. Moreover, since the Bomb had enjoyed "good" public relations through most of the 1950s, it was virgin territory for filmmakers who wanted to develop stories about its negative features. Having lived for more than a decade under the tensions of a peace maintained through the threat of nuclear destruction, Americans were ready to look at another aspect of the Bomb and its relationship to the future of civilization.

Likewise, military leaders could be used as convenient scapegoats in attacking war. With the exception of Captain Holmes or Lieutenant Commander Queeg, filmmakers had rarely portrayed military officers with significant frailties. To be sure, some characters made mistakes, showed pigheadedness, or dealt with peers or subordinates in less than ideal ways. But by the end of the film the character had changed and matured to become a typically dedicated and successful officer. By ignoring the deficient officer, Hollywood war movies until the early 1960s helped create the impression of the infallible American military man.

As their reactions to Hollywood scripts showed, the armed services were immutable in their insistence that films portray officers performing their duties properly. The Navy had even objected to films that had been made without its assistance. On at least one occasion, its Public Information Office had gone so far as to complain to the Motion Picture Association about a Boston Blackie film in which Navy men were shown in a bad light. An Air Force officer in the Pentagon voiced his objections to Sy Bartlett about the script of *Twelve O'Clock High* because it portrayed pilots who were unwilling to fly for their new and demanding commander. Bartlett recalled, "He turned to me and said, 'Colonel Bartlett, you mean to tell me that an Air Force officer like you is actually going to make a film which says and shows that a group refused and would not answer a field order and refused to fly?' I said, 'Colonel, if that's all you read into the book and that's all you read into the script, I guess that's what I'm going to do.' And, he said, 'Well, it'll be over my dead body.' And I said, 'Perhaps it will be over your dead body.' And he was obstructionist."[1]

By the early 1960s, changing American attitudes gave Hollywood for the first time the courage to ignore the possible wrath of the Pentagon. Filmmakers

General Curtis LeMay (with author in 1975), the father of the Strategic Air Command, encouraged Hollywood productions about the Air Force.

began to produce a series of pictures that focused on the negative side of military leadership, but without the usual combat scenes that detracted from their messages. The producers expected military assistance despite these antiwar themes and continued to approach the Pentagon for the necessary cooperation.

To the military, the threat of a radically different handling of its image presented a public relations challenge unfaced since *From Here to Eternity* and *The Caine Mutiny*. Generally the Pentagon's response to the current requests for assistance was simply to cite the long-standing Department of Defense regulations which stipulated that the armed forces could help on a movie only when it benefited the services being portrayed or when cooperation was in the best interest of the military. Also explicit in the regulations was the requirement that military procedures and personnel be pictured authentically and that events portrayed be historically and technically accurate. The disagreements between the Pentagon and filmmakers over the assistance issue centered more on the authenticity requirement than on the other questions. (Whether a particular film benefited the armed forces was a subjective judgment of the individual services and the Department of Defense.) The criterion of historical and technical accuracy, or at least plausibility, was the one most often used by the Pentagon in refusing to help with films about nuclear war.

The armed forces had always allowed some dramatic licence on films receiving assistance. In most combat sequences, as in *Sands of Iwo Jima*, directors were permitted to move landing craft and GIs closer together than they would have been in battle in order to aid camera work and heighten the visual effect of the action. In military comedies and science fiction movies, directors had generally been given more leeway in portraying procedures and events than in serious combat films. In assisting on films like *The Day the Earth Stood Still* (1951), the military maintained that although the stories were improbable fantasies, the services would be expected to defend the earth from alien attack. In that context the movies portrayed the hypothetical actions correctly. On the other hand, the Air Force refused to assist Steven Spielberg on *Close Encounters of the Third Kind* (1977) because the director was attempting to create reality, not fantasy. The service had repeatedly denied the existence of flying saucers and so felt it would be counterproductive to cooperate on a film that treated UFOs as "science fact" rather than science fiction.[2]

★

Dr. Strangelove

In films dealing with the Bomb, the Air Force always insisted on a serious and factual presentation of its procedures and preparedness, and the competence of those operating the switches of the nuclear arsenal. The service used films such as *Strategic Air Command, Bombers B-52,* and *A Gathering of Eagles* to inform the American people not only of SAC's military potential, but also of its precautions against accidental launchings of a nuclear attack. Consequently, Curtis LeMay had every reason to be concerned over the possible injurious effect of *Dr. Strangelove, Or: How I Learned to Stop Worrying and Love the Bomb.* Based on Peter George's 1958 novel *Red Alert,* Stanley Kubrick's 1964 film portrayed an Air Force general who orders a squadron of planes to bomb Russia in hopes of triggering a war that will obliterate the Communist menace.

As if one such story was not enough, the Air Force soon had to face a second picture with essentially the same plot. In *Fail Safe,* based on the Eugene Burdick and Harvey Wheeler novel of the same name, a faulty computer rather than a deranged general launches the strike force. As in *Dr. Strangelove,* neither the United States nor Soviet armed forces is able to stop all the bombers. One reaches Moscow and delivers its hydrogen bombs. Both films imply the military does not truly control the Bomb, and thus they suggest that a nuclear accident is inevitable. However, the two movies approached their common thesis in diametrically opposite manners. *Dr. Strangelove* took on not only the Bomb, but military and government leaders, American and Russian alike, using satire and black humor to attack virtually everyone and everything.

Kubrick peopled the film with incompetents, bigots, and warmongers, with the military characters bearing the brunt of the criticism. In contrast, *Fail Safe* developed its message through a serious, taut melodrama. The filmmakers characterized both government and military personnel as dedicated people who were genuinely stunned by the catastrophy facing the world.

Kubrick did not set out to convey his message comically. Having made one major antiwar statement in *Paths of Glory*, he had for some time "been keen on the theme of a nuclear war being started by accident or madness." He came across *Red Alert* (written by a retired R.A.F. pilot) in 1961, and decided almost immediately that it would serve as the basis for his statement about the Bomb. Although Kubrick tried to follow the serious tone of the novel in beginning work on the screenplay, he soon found that each time he created a scene, it turned out to be comic. He later recalled, "How the hell could the president ever tell the Russian premier to shoot down American planes? Good Lord, it sounds ridiculous."[3] Consequently, the film turned into a satirical nightmare, a surrealistic portrait of humans blundering through war rooms, carrying on absurd dialogues on a hot line, and committing sheer lunacy while the world moved inexorably toward destruction.

Opening with a poetic, rhythmic, sexual scene of a B-52 bomber being refueled in midair, the film unfolds in a rapid-fire sequence of events that leaves the audience breathless. A SAC general orders a squadron of bombers to attack Russia; the president informs the Soviet premier of what has happened; the crew of the lead bomber prepares for its mission; the governments of both nations attempt to stop the attack both in the air and by trying to capture the insane general; efforts meet with failure, and one plane reaches its target. At the fadeout, bombs explode like fireworks, filling the screen with mushroom clouds.

In creating his biting denouncement of man's inability to control the ultimate weapon of war, Kubrick uses potent visual and verbal imagery. The sexual coupling of the two planes at the opening of the movie is followed regularly by shots of a bomber flying gracefully, sensually over a snowcovered landscape toward its target. The beauty of the plane in motion contrasts starkly with the absolute destructiveness of its mission. When the bombs go off, the explosions assume their own sensuality, which Kubrick reinforces ironically with the soothing sounds of a popular World War II ballad, "We'll meet again, don't know where, don't know when, but I know we'll meet again some sunny day."

The symbolic visual effects of the movie are reinforced by language, from the singing and music to the names of the characters which establish their personalities. The demented SAC commander is Jack D. Ripper; the president is Merkin Muffley; the Russian premier is Dimitri Kissof; the Russian ambassador is de Sadesky; the chairman of the Joint Chiefs of Staff is Buck Turgidson; the colonel ordered to storm General Ripper's headquarters at Burpelson Air Force Base is Bat Guano; the British officer assigned as Ripper's executive officer is Group Captain Mandrake. And then there is Dr. Strangelove himself, a "rehabilitated" Nazi scientist whose character is developed both visually and verbally. Strangelove makes his entrance into the Pentagon's underground war room in a wheelchair, struggling with an artificial right arm that has a mind of its own. Periodically, Strangelove reverts to his German background, addressing President Muffley as "Mein Fuhrer," while desperately trying to restrain his arm from either giving a Nazi salute or strangling himself.

The scene that best captures the tone of *Dr. Strangelove*, however, comes when President Muffley calls Premier Kissof on the hotline to tell him of the impending disaster. After tracking him down at his mistress' residence with the help of Ambassador de Sadesky ("Our premier is a man of the people"), the president tries to explain what has happened: "How are you? . . . Oh fine. Just fine. Look, Dimitri, you know how we've always talked about the possibility of something going wrong with the Bomb? . . . The Bomb? The HYDROGEN BOMB! . . . That's right. Well, I'll tell you what happened. One of our base commanders did a silly thing. He, uh, went a little funny in the head. You know, funny. He ordered our planes to attack your country . . . let me *finish*, Dimitri." But there is nothing else to say. The deed has been done. The perpetrator of the crisis, General Ripper, is a caricatured right wing fanatic who is tormented by the "Commie plot" to fluoridate American drinking water and debilitate the people by destroying "the purity and essence of our natural fluids." He has severed all communications with the outside world and only he knows the code for recalling the bombers.

What follows resembles a tour through every insane asylum that has ever appeared on the screen. When General Turgidson starts wrestling with Ambassador de Sadesky, who has been taking pictures of the underground command center, President Muffley reproves both men: "You can't fight in here, this is the War Room." In arguing that the president should seize the opportunity and launch an all-out attack, Turgidson admits, "I'm not saying we won't get our hair mussed." Going over their survival kits containing rubles, dollars, gold, Benzedrine, cigarettes, nylons, chocolate, chewing gum, prophylactics, and tranquilizers, one of the crewmen remarks, "I could have a pretty fine weekend with this in Vegas."

Under other circumstances, the Russians might have been willing to accept the accidental loss of one missile site. But Kubrick's plot has another twist. The

A Gathering of Eagles (1963) shown being filmed at Beale Air Force Base in California, was made with the service's full cooperation despite Arthur Sylvester's initial refusal to approve assistance. In contrast, Dr. Strangelove and Fail Safe had to be made in studios using miniatures, mock-ups, and newsreel footage because the Air Force would have nothing to do with either production.

Soviets have a Doomsday Machine, set to go off if any nuclear bomb explodes on Russian territory. The radioactivity the machine will generate will make the earth uninhabitable for ninety-nine years. Yet to have worked as a deterrent from enemy attack, the enemy has to know of its existence. This the Russians had not yet done, as Strangelove ironically observes in suitably gutteral tones.

The only hope that remains is to either destroy the attacking planes or force them to turn back. Burpelson Air Force Base is besieged by Army units, and the battle rages under a SAC billboard proclaiming that "Peace is Our Profession." Inside, Mandrake alternately pleads with General Ripper to recall the planes and tries to figure out the proper recall code based on the general's rantings and doodlings. When he does discover the code after Ripper has killed himself, Mandrake tries to call the president. But he has no money and the White House will not accept collect calls from an unknown group captain. In desperation, Mandrake pleads with Colonel Bat Guano to shoot the lock from a Coke machine to get the needed change. But the officer recoils in horror: "That's private property."

In the end, just one plane eludes all the Russian missiles and heads toward its target. In a seeming last-minute reprieve, the bomb will not drop from the plane. In *Red Alert*, the bomb was damaged and didn't go off, but Kubrick's film does not cop out. The pilot, a Texas cowboy, climbs onto the bomb, shakes it free, and rides it downward as if it were a bucking bronco, yelling exuberantly and waving his Stetson. This paradox of pure joy juxtaposed with the scene of absolute destruction that immediately follows symbolizes the two sides of *Dr. Strangelove*. On the one hand, it produces side-splitting laughs; on the other, it creates a horror of the ramifications lurking just around the corner.

As ridiculous and comic as the story appears on the screen, the threat of nuclear accident still comes across as a plausible reality. Kubrick observed, "The greatest message of the film is in the laughs. You know, it's true. The most realistic things are the funniest." To Kubrick, *Dr. Strangelove* was realistic. He estimated he had read seventy books on the subject of the Bomb, and he maintained an extensive file of relevant articles. He had also talked to nuclear war strategists such as Thomas Schelling and to Herman Kahn, the author of *On Thermonuclear War* and *Thinking About the Unthinkable*. Consequently, he believed that a psychotic general could unleash a squadron of bombers against Russia and maintained that "for various and entirely credible reasons, [if] the planes cannot be recalled, the President [will be] forced to cooperate with the Soviet Premier in a bizarre attempt to save the world."[4] To the military, however, the film was no laughing matter. Nor did they think it bore any resemblance to reality.

During preproduction, Kubrick had made unofficial contact with the Air Force to discuss possible cooperation. The service told the filmmaker that, apart from the portrayal of its officers as insane, bloodthirsty, and ludicrous, the misrepresentation in the script of the Positive Control safeguards precluded official Pentagon assistance.[5] The Air Force maintained that a SAC base commander cannot order a single plane to undertake a nuclear bomb attack. Furthermore, only the president or his surrogate knows the attack code, and he must relay it to SAC Headquarters, which in turn issues the appropriate orders. According to officials, the Positive Control System could not be subverted; it was fail safe.

Kubrick naturally disagreed—he was making *Dr. Strangelove* to warn of the possible dangers in the safeguard system. Consequently, literal accuracy of Air Force procedures had little relevance. His intention was to convey a message, not make a pseudo-documentary. With the military's refusal to provide assistance, Kubrick became the film's sole technical advisor, using knowledge gained from a youth spent watching war movies in New York City. His re-created B-52 cockpit was based on a magazine picture and probably on impressions gained from the earlier Air Force films. The war room was built out of his and the art director's imagination, since no one had ever acknowledged the existence of an underground crisis center in the Pentagon, much less released a picture of it. The sequences of the bomber in flight were produced by placing a ten-foot model of a B-52 in front of a moving matte made up of shots taken over the Arctic. If the end result bore little resemblance to actual Air Force procedures or equipment, most people accepted it as reality in spite of the film's comic motif.

Dr. Strangelove does not portray reality, Kubrick's intentions notwithstanding. Instead, he produced satire, a genre which depends on exaggerated visions of reality to expose humanity's and society's foibles. To succeed, satire (or any social commentary) must reach its intended audience, and *Dr. Strangelove* proved to be highly successful at the box office. Whether its popularity had more to do with its message or its cinematic qualities remains unanswered. In any case, the picture is one of the highest achievements of Hollywood filmmaking.

Although clearly an American movie, *Dr. Strangelove* was shot in England to accommodate Peter Sellers, who was indispensable to the film. Sellers assumed the roles of President Muffley, Group Captain Mandrake, and Dr. Strangelove and managed to instill in each a unique personality in a tour de force of character acting. George C. Scott as General Turgidson and Sterling Hayden as General Ripper were equally superb. The actors, however, performed within the structure that Kubrick created, manipulated, and directed. His interweaving of the visual and verbal images, the use of sound and music, the imaginative production all combined to produce a rare film experience, one that retains its impact even though missiles have for the most part replaced bombers as the United States' first line of defense and people have all but stopped thinking about accidental nuclear warfare.

If *Dr. Strangelove* has a fault, it is that Kubrick creates his impact with a story based on inaccurate premises and factual errors, requiring an audience to suspend disbelief if it is aware of the Positive Control System. Unfortunately for the United States Air Force, few viewers either knew or had the time and interest to ascertain how the system worked, and most were willing to accept Kubrick's version of the system as well as its implied deficiencies. Some people might well have emerged from the theatre not only entertained, but also concerned over the future of the world. In fact, because *Dr. Strangelove* was, for most people, a comedy rather than a message film, relatively few took the movie as seriously as Kubrick had hoped. *Fail Safe*, which appeared later in 1964, was a different case altogether.

Fail Safe

Max Youngstein, the film's producer, had also long been concerned with the issue of nuclear safeguards. He was a member of SANE and other groups concerned about the possibility of accidental nuclear war. He believed that the government was withholding critical information about the potential for failure of the United States' safeguard system. Consequently, when he read *Fail Safe* in manuscript form in 1962, Youngstein said that "it hit a very important nerve with me." Having just become an independent producer after years as an industry executive, he set about to acquire the property for his first picture, even meeting with the authors to convince them that he had the same worry about the problem they had described in their novel.[6]

To Youngstein, the book, "whether or not it was a fictionalized description of reality . . . was close enough to the information I had come across in my own research so that I could give the film validity."[7] To Wheeler and Burdick, their book was more than a fictionalized novel: "Thus the element in our story which seems most fictional—the story's central problem and its solution—is in fact the most real part. Men, machines, and mathematics being what they are, this is, unfortunately, a "true" story. The accident may not occur in the way we describe but the laws of probability assure us that ultimately it will occur. The logic of politics tells us that when it does, the only way out will be a choice of disasters."[8] This statement helped make the novel controversial from the moment the *Saturday Evening Post* began serializing it in October 1962, shortly before it was published. This, along with a good publicity campaign, made the book an immediate bestseller and so offered Youngstein good commercial prospects as well as a forum for his antibomb message.

All claims to the contrary, however, *Fail Safe* did not tell a "true" story of the United States Positive Control System. In fact, the term "fail safe" had actually become obsolete long previously. Despite Wheeler and Burdick's claim that their "research was endless," the authors had not bothered to take a trip to SAC Headquarters in Omaha to understand how the Positive Control System really worked. If they had, or if they had used the basic unclassified material readily available from the Air Force, they probably would not have written a novel about the failure of the system. Technicalities aside, the Air Force maintains that the safeguards designed to prevent a nuclear accident are virtually foolproof. The president or his stand-in must give SAC the correct code, which is then transmitted to the bombers and missile silos. Whether the orders are given verbally, as the military explains, or mechanically, as described in the book, they must be given positively, not by default. Any failure in the system, such as a malfunctioning computer, would automatically result in the recall of the bombers and not in a signal to attack as presented in the novel. While the military would undoubtedly concede, if pressed, that nothing is absolutely certain, officials have always maintained that the odds of an accident occurring are infinitesimal. If Wheeler and Burdick had understood and accepted the validity of the Positive Control System, they would have had no story. Nevertheless, they operated on the assumption that if something is not absolutely impossible, it becomes probable, and on this tenuous foundation they built their story.

While the authors claimed their book was close to the truth, it was truth only in the minds of those to whom truth is an intellectual creation rather than an approximation of reality. According to Max Youngstein, Wheeler and Burdick were the first to acknowledge that their description of SAC procedures was not totally accurate. But they also insisted that in principle an accident could happen, and there was a damn good chance of it.[9] Nevertheless, the foundation of their story was a false premise. Apart from the crucial misrepresentation of the Positive Control System, their description of SAC's underground headquarters is erroneous. A single unidentified object could not trigger the entire SAC force into action as portrayed. Since attack signals are relayed to the bombers by verbal command, not by electronic computer, there is no "black box" receiver in each plane as described in the book. Clearly, the facts had little relevance to Wheeler and Burdick. Their purpose was not to write an informative book about SAC operations but to warn the American people about what they saw as the potential threat of nuclear accident.

Max Youngstein had the same concerns, and for him, as for Wheeler and Burdick, the story—rather than objective truth—became the primary consideration in transferring *Fail Safe* to the screen. Walter Bernstein's script followed the novel much more closely than most movies based on books. As a result, when Youngstein attempted to get Pentagon assistance, the military turned his request down cold. In addition to pointing out the script's incorrect portrayal of the Positive Control System, officials said that the accident situation was not possible. In response to these criticisms, Youngstein went to see Wheeler and Burdick, who insisted that they had done extensive research. Since they had no pretense of writing anything but a novel, albeit a novel they hoped would have an impact, they felt they were not tied to accurate technical descriptions of the system's operation. Their concern was that people accept their story because it sounded right, because of their reputations as academics, and because of their research on the subject. As a result of Youngstein's conversation with the authors, the issue became not the accurate portrayal of the Positive Control System, but the question of whether any system could be foolproof. From his own research and contact with people in organizations like SANE, the producer said, "I would simply not accept the fact that it could not happen." To him, the point of the film was whether the system was 100 percent safe for the American people."[10]

After seeing the script, the Pentagon refused to provide Youngstein with a

description of the way Positive Control procedures actually functioned. From
the military's point of view, it would not help to have the system portrayed correctly if the producer's intention was to show the system's failure. Also, Youngstein would not agree to alter the script even if the Pentagon provided him with
the necessary information—he could not delete the accidental launching of
the attack and still make his film, at least a film based on *Fail Safe*. Even with a
prior awareness of the controversial nature of the novel and the Pentagon's
rejection of its premise, Youngstein recalled that the military's turndown of his
request for assistance was "kind of staggering, since it meant revising those
scenes which required Air Force cooperation to insure visual authenticity." In
particular, the producer needed shots of bombers on the ground and in the air.

Youngstein approached several of the large film libraries that maintained
collections of stock shots of most subjects. At first, he found them cooperative.
But when it came time to furnish the footage, the libraries didn't return his
calls: "It was like trying to punch our way out of a paper bag when we would
inquire if they had found anything. It became a nightmarish thing that you
could never pinpoint."[11] In trying to make *Attack!* without military assistance,
Robert Aldrich had experienced a similar reluctance of private sources to provide him with needed equipment.[12] Finally Youngstein asked one of the film
libraries to explain its reluctance to give him the requested footage. He was
told, "I'm probably not supposed to tell you, but orders have come down that
we're not to cooperate on the making of this film." When the producer asked if
the orders had originated with the government, the librarian responded, "I'm
not at liberty to tell you. But they are orders from people that I cannot afford to
disregard." Ultimately, a source apparently missed by the orders provided
Youngstein with about 100 feet of film showing bombers in formation, and
through optical work in a film laboratory he obtained enough footage to meet
the needs of the film. Nevertheless, he had to discard his original plan to show
formations of planes flying toward their readiness positions in all parts of the
world.[13]

Without military assistance, Youngstein had problems reproducing
authentic sets. To create the cockpits of the planes in the picture, the film company rented an old commercial plane at LaGuardia Airport and made it over.
The limited space inside the plane made it necessary to shoot the cockpit
sequences through open windows from the outside. In contrast, films approved
by the Air Force usually use cockpit mock-ups (provided by the plane's manu-
facturer), which come apart, facilitating interior shooting. The military's
refusal to help Youngstein also created problems for him in reproducing the
SAC war room, one of the movie's main sets. Although his request had already
been turned down, Youngstein asked the Air Force to allow him to send his art

director on a research trip to SAC Headquarters so that he could re-create the facility as exactly and authentically as possible. The Air Force had recently allowed Sy Bartlett to shoot a sequence for *A Gathering of Eagles* in the war room itself, and the Pentagon had routinely given filmmakers permission to make research trips to military facilities and to ride on planes, ships, and even nuclear submarines. Nevertheless, Youngstein received "as cold a turn-down as you ever saw in your life. Under no circumstances would they allow anybody connected with the project to go out there and look at the war room." Consequently, as had been the case with Kubrick, Youngstein's war room was created by the art director, using suggestions from several people including a man who had once been in the SAC facility.[14]

In the end, *Fail Safe* provided enough semblance of authenticity so that the visual image did not intrude on the story. Yet Youngstein felt that the lack of cooperation "hurt the whole look of the picture. It affected the atmosphere, the size, the validity that you get if you have cooperation." It also affected the budget, especially with the cost of building the war room rather than shooting on location. While the producer would not attempt to estimate the effect of the lack of authenticity on the film's success, he was "firmly convinced of the fact that if we had gotten the material from the government, it would have enhanced the picture and I am a believer that the better the picture . . . the better the box office, the better the acceptance the picture has from the public."[15]

Most viewers did accept *Fail Safe* as an exciting account of a potential nuclear accident. To be sure, not even the producer considered it a work of art

Models of "Little Boy" and "Fat Man," the bombs dropped on Hiroshima and Nagasaki, became scapegoats for film-makers in their portrayals of the military as enemy during the mid-1960s.

in a class with *Dr. Strangelove*. While he thought his company had turned out "a good picture," Youngstein conceded that Kubrick had "turned out a brilliant picture. It's as simple as that. . . . It was a brilliant type of black humor, so far ahead of its time."[16] Nevertheless, *Fail Safe* had a greater chance of conveying its message because of its serious tone and seemingly factual depiction of military procedures. Bosley Crowther observed in his *New York Times* review that unlike *Dr. Strangelove, Fail Safe* does not make its characters out to be maniacs and monsters and morons. It makes them out to be intelligent men trying to use their wits and their techniques to correct an error that has occurred through over-reliance on the efficiency of machines."[17]

Except for the military and the few people who had knowledge of the Positive Control System's actual operation, most viewers weren't concerned with the issue of the film's accuracy, with the fact that the system was not entrusted to machines. Even Hubert Humphrey, the Democratic vice-presidential candidate in the 1964 election, was more concerned with the film's message than with its "controversial phase as to the possibility of malfunction of 'fail-safe' mechanisms." Ignoring the fact that the government had refused to have anything to do with making the film, Humphrey wrote to Press Secretary Bill Moyers that he was glad it had been brought to President Johnson's attenion: "Many people feel that the more millions of people who might see it in these next few weeks, the better will be their understanding of the crucial role of the Chief Executive in preserving the peace."[18] Echoing Humphrey's letter, Moyers sent a memo to President Johnson the next day saying that the film "should have pretty good impact on the campaign in our favor, since it deals with irresponsibility in the handling of nuclear weapons."[19] The film's theme did tie in perfectly with several of President Johnson's television commercials linking Barry Goldwater to the irresponsible use of the Bomb. His one-minute campaign film that showed children playing, followed by the appearance of a mushroom-shaped cloud, made nuclear safeguards one of the central issues of the 1964 presidential campaign. In the sense that *Fail Safe* contributed to that dialogue, it performed a useful function. Nevertheless, it did so through a distorted and inaccurate portrayal of Air Force procedures and equipment.

Ironically, though people were willing to ignore the implausibility of the story, few viewers found the ending believable. Once the president realizes that neither the United States nor Russia may be able to stop the destruction of Moscow, he orders an American bomber loaded with two hydrogen bombs to circle over New York City. When the Russian capital is demolished, he has New York bombed to prove to the Russians that the destruction of Moscow was truly an accident. Crowther did not think the film's resolution was "a sensible or likely one, but it is, at least, a valid shocker that induces the viewer to think."[20]

Youngstein said there was "legitimacy to it. But even if I did not believe it was a legitimate situation, I don't think it should be dismissed just because it doesn't coincide with popular thinking."[21]

Such thinking naturally found it difficult to accept a president's ordering the destruction of the nation's largest city under any circumstances. But, in the context of the film, or even in the real world, a president would have few alternatives with which to demonstrate good faith. A Russian leader could not confront his people solely with an American apology or even an offer of reparations and expect to prevent demands for retaliation, let alone stay in power. In contrast, with the awesomeness of the calamity facing both powers, the film's conclusion, a commitment to meet as quickly as possible to reach a disarmament agreement, has a feel of believability. In fact, the message of the movie may not be that an accident is possible, but that until a nuclear accident provides the impetus, the world will not bring itself to disarm.

★

Seven Days In May

Even when motivated by the fear of world destruction, many people did not accept disarmament as a viable alternative. Fletcher Knebel and Charles Bailey used the military's dissatisfaction with a crisis-initiated disarmament treaty as the starting point for their novel of an attempted coup against the president of the United States. *Seven Days in May* (published in 1962) details the discovery and successful stifling of a plot by a popular chairman of the Joint Chiefs of Staff and his cronies to seize the government. A disarmament treaty has been hammered out and barely ratified, following a Soviet incursion into Iran which has led to that country's partition and has almost caused a third World War. Air Force General James Scott and other top military commanders have opposed the treaty, believing it indicates a policy of appeasement at a time when President Lyman's 29 percent rating in public opinion polls shows him to be an ineffectual leader. They see his lack of leadership as an invitation for Russia to cheat on the new treaty (an eventuality that comes to pass as the story unfolds) and further weaken the United States. To prevent this, Scott, several high-ranking officers, a conservative senator, and a right-wing television commentator plan to seize control of key communications, isolate the president, and take control of the government.

Without question, the novel requires the reader to accept as probable a series of events which taken together strain credibility. The conspirators' base of operations is big enough to handle the largest Air Force transports, but it remains a secret from the president, Congress, noninvolved military men, and local residents. A Marine colonel stumbles across bits of suggestive information and immediately suspects the coup. Although only a colonel, he secures a meeting with the president within a few hours of discovering the plot. Subsequently, an obscure diplomat recovers a crucial piece of evidence against the conspirators from a plane wreck (one of the events used to heighten the melodrama), recognizes its significance, and brings it directly to the president without telling a single person. Despite these implausibilities, the authors' book worked because they were able to create the atmosphere of the Washington political scene, write a suspenseful story, and dramatize the then-current national concern about the military's role in politics. As a result, *Seven Days in May* remained on the *New York Times* Best-Seller List for forty-nine consecutive weeks.

Typically, Hollywood wanted to turn the book into a movie. The military, though, saw *Seven Days in May* as a virtual travesty because it portrayed the highest ranking command officers plotting the overthrow of the United States government. Arthur Sylvester, then developing the Pentagon's policies on cooperation with the film industry, told Ray Bell, still Columbia's Washington representative, that any film based on the book would never receive Defense Department assistance. Bell, whose studio had obtained an option on the novel, felt that Sylvester's decision was based on his interpretation of the novel as the depiction of an ineffective government.[22]

While the book portrays some military men as traitors, it does show the constitutional government surviving. Most people, both inside and outside the Pentagon, continue to respect the tradition of civilian control of the military. To be sure, a film showing military leaders plotting a coup would offer little benefit to the armed forces. And since the plot of the novel would of necessity form the basis of the movie, the military had little leverage in requesting script changes as it had been able to do with *From Here to Eternity* and *The Caine Mutiny*. Unlike *Dr. Strangelove* and *Fail Safe*, however, *Seven Days in May* did not give the military a strong case on grounds of implausibility.

The setting of the story is twelve years in the future (1974), in a political climate where well-meaning military men could conceivably believe an immediate change in leadership is necessary to save the country. Historically, the nation had witnessed two military men defying civilian authority not long before the novel appeared. President Truman had removed General Douglas MacArthur from his command because of the general's public opposition to presidential decisions. More recently, General Edwin Walker had formed an alliance with the far right and had attempted to indoctrinate his men with his political beliefs. While General Walker was atypical, the armed services would have been hard-pressed to categorically deny that under the right circumstances a group of military men might plot to seize power. In fact, Ray Bell said high ranking officers told him that if the country ever fell asleep, a coup similar to the one described in *Seven Days in May* could very well be a possibility.[23]

With this in mind, Bell asked Pierre Salinger, President Kennedy's press secretary, to read the novel as a personal favor. When Salinger had finished it, Bell related Columbia's problems with the Pentagon and asked if he thought the book was detrimental to the country's best interests. "Hell, no!" said Salinger. Moreover, he could see "absolutely" nothing that would hurt the military. On the contrary, he thought that a few revisions in the script would create a strong document, showing that a plot to overthrow the president would undoubtedly be nipped in the bud, as Knebel and Bailey demonstrated in the book.[24]

Given Salinger's reaction, Bell asked the press secretary to meet with himself and Sylvester at the White House to explore further the possibility of military assistance to the film. Bell "[wanted] Sylvester, from an objective third party, to get these views which I hoped would be persuasive." As a result of the meeting, Bell felt certain that Sylvester's perspective had been "somewhat modified," but before he could formally request assistance, the studio decided the cost of the project was prohibitive. It relinquished its rights to the story.[25]

At that point, Edward Lewis and Kirk Douglas acquired the rights and set out to produce the film. They hired Rod Serling as the screenwriter and John Frankenheimer as director. Lewis said in October 1962 that he "anticipated noncooperation and stumbling blocks from the Pentagon," but he expected the executive branch would be in favor of the film. He planned to make the film despite any objections believing "it is important that we have the strength to see that such a problem exists and meet it; this is a patriotic film."[26]

President Kennedy apparently agreed. According to his aide, Ted Sorenson, Kennedy enjoyed the book and joked that he knew a couple of generals who "might wish" to take over the country.[27] With Kennedy's approval, Frankenheimer and his assistants were allowed to tour the White House so they could accurately reproduce the living quarters and the Oval Office. The director later received permission to film entrance and exit scenes at the White House and stage a riot between opposing treaty factions in front of the mansion. Ironically, the demonstration was filmed two days after the initialing of the 1963 Nuclear Test Ban Treaty in Moscow, and real pickets had to be moved aside for the fictional riot.[28]

Frankenheimer did not, however, follow up Ray Bell's efforts to obtain military assistance for the movie—"because we knew we wouldn't get it." The filmmakers did ask to visit the office of General Maxwell Taylor, then chairman of the Joint Chiefs of Staff, but permission was made contingent on their submitting a script. Frankenheimer refused this covert form of censorship. His reluctance to even show a script to military officials may have provided him with a sense of creative freedom. But it also generated problems in producing visual authenticity in scenes involving military locales and equipment. Without asking permission, Frankenheimer planted cameras in the back of a parked station wagon to shoot a sequence of Kirk Douglas walking into and out of the Pentagon in his role as the Marine colonel who discovers the planned coup. In editing the film, however, Frankenheimer cut the segments, finding them extraneous.[30]

Another time, Frankenheimer needed to shoot aboard an aircraft carrier for the sequence in which the president's key advisor meets with a nonparticipating admiral to ascertain details of the conspiracy. Edward Lewis and Frankenheimer talked their way aboard the USS *Kitty Hawk* in San Diego Harbor by asking the duty officer to allow them to shoot a small boat from a high vantage point. Once the sequence was completed, they asked to film an actor disembarking from the small boat and walking along to the bow of the *Kitty Hawk*. Then Lewis asked to shoot a scene of the actor crossing the flight deck and entering the island of the carrier. In this sequence, he even used one of the ship's officers as a messenger. Before leaving the carrier, Frankenheimer was able to shoot still another scene utilizing two sailors as extras and filmed the small boat approaching the ship from a lower angle.[31]

When the Defense Department discovered what had happened, it protested to the Motion Picture Association that Lewis had "acted unethically" in obtaining his footage: "We believe that he was fully aware of our policy covering assistance on such productions but took the calculated risk that someone in the field might be unaware of the policy and from a seemingly innocent request involved the Navy in a situation that is embarrassing."[32]

Lewis disagreed. He explained that the request to shoot aboard the ship was "a simple, unplotted, natural location request" that he made to see if "the wishes of the director could be fulfilled" to obtain a better vantage point. Lewis said he had given the ship's officer all the information about his project: the name of the book, the studio involved, the stars, and the director. He assumed that because *Seven Days in May* had been a best seller for over a year, the officer would have full knowledge of the subject matter. Moreover, because he had never discussed possible cooperation with the Pentagon, Lewis questioned the Defense Department's contention that he was "fully aware" of its policy governing assistance. Nevertheless, he conceded that the Pentagon had no obligation to assist on projects with which they do not agree.[33]

The military's involuntary assistance and the White House's willing help gave *Seven Days in May* an authentic visual atmosphere in which to tell the story of General Scott's attempted coup and President Lyman's successful efforts to preserve democracy. To Edmund O'Brien, who played a Georgia senator and close friend of the president, the story needed "to have one tremendous emotion—the survival of the United States. If that can be attained, it will have the same emotional pull as a war picture. In this one, the American ideal must become a living person."[34] How much, if any, damage the film actually did to the military image cannot be measured. Given the climate of the times and the unfavorable portrayals of the military in contemporary films, *Seven Days in May* undoubtedly engendered a greater awareness of the relationship between the military and the civilian government. For most viewers, however, the film functioned primarily as a gripping suspense thriller pitting the good guys against the bad guys, with the latter just happening to be military leaders.

For those willing to look deeper, the film offered a perceptive comment about the mood of the country in the mid-1960s. President Lyman sadly notes that the motivation behind the coup was not the military's lust for power but the consequence of the growing fears and anxieties of the nuclear age. That, not General Scott, was the true enemy. In an observation equally appropriate to *Dr. Strangelove* and *Fail Safe*, Lyman suggests that the Bomb "happens to have killed man's faith in his ability to influence what happens to him."

★

The Bedford Incident

Within this framework, *The Bedford Incident* returns to the classic theme of an obsessed ship captain. Like Ahab and Queeg before him, the *Bedford's* captain, played by Richard Widmark, loses touch with reality as he pursues an elusive enemy, a Russian submarine. Although the cause is unstated, Widmark's unrelenting chase grows out of his antipathy to Communism as well as the continued pressures of commanding nuclear weapons directed against the enemy's similar weapons. Like his seagoing predecessors, who couldn't drop their pursuit of white whales and strawberry eaters, Captain Finlander cannot let go of his prey once he has begun the chase. Having detected the Russian submarine in Greenland territorial waters, Finlander continues his tracking even after the undersea craft has returned to international waters and apparent safety.

Richard Widmark modeled his portrayal of Captain Finlander in The Bedford Incident *(1965) on the mannerisms and speeches of Senator Goldwater during the 1964 Presidential campaign.*

As the pursuit changes from a game of cat and mouse into a virtual war, the captain of the *Bedford* loses touch with reality. No longer involved in just another Cold War confrontation, he sees the Russian submarine as a dangerous enemy that must be forced to the surface. Orders to break off the hunt are ignored in Finlander's war, a war which no one can persuade him to end.

Like *Dr. Strangelove* and *Fail Safe, The Bedford Incident* suggests that man can no longer control the forces he has created. The film ends with the accidential triggering of nuclear weapons, reinforcing the warning of the two earlier movies. Finlander's explanation that he does not intend to attack first is misinterpreted as a command to fire: "The *Bedford* will never fire first. But if he fires one, I'll fire one!" The weapons officer, hearing only "Fire one," thereupon presses the button. Picking up the sound of the missile entering the sea, the Russian submarine then fires its torpedoes. Suddenly realizing where his obsession has taken him, Finlander refuses to take evasive measures. Like his prey, the hunter is destroyed in the explosion of the Russians' nuclear torpedoes.

Script preparations for the film were extensive. James Harris, the producer-director, and James Poe, the screenwriter, were allowed to take a five-day cruise on a destroyer. They also met in November 1963 with military officials at the Pentagon and incorporated their suggestions into the script. The screenplay then went to an admiral who made corrections of a technical nature in Navy operations and dialogue. Poe took the script back to the Pentagon in June 1964, at which point the Defense Department and the Navy objected to the script's cataclysmic ending for the first time.[35]

Officials said they did not want an atomic explosion implied in the accidental firing of the ASROC, even though it was public knowledge that the missile had nuclear capability. They also objected to Finlander's passivity after the torpedoes were fired; they felt his "calm stoic acceptance of termination is apt to be misinterpreted by the public." To provide motivation for the captain's zealous pursuit of the Russian submarine, officials suggested having the craft "exhibit an unusual and strange device." While the Pentagon did not want the American ASROCs in the film to be armed with nuclear warheads, the military did suggest that the filmmakers "introduce the strong possibility that the Russian submarine's torpedoes are armed with nuclear warheads," then not part of the script. Finally, the Pentagon wanted the commanding officer of the *Bedford* to clearly state: "Only if the enemy fires first will we fire."[36]

Poe incorporated the suggestions into his revised script of June 14, which he then sent to Harris, to Richard Widmark, and to Ray Bell, who had been working on the project for Columbia Pictures. Harris and Widmark, however, refused to accept the Pentagon's version of the ending. Harris thought that the message of accidental nuclear warfare was "worth saying again and again." Since the Pentagon and the State Department did not want an American movie to show the United States Navy provoking a nuclear incident, the Department of Defense rejected the filmmaker's request for use of a destroyer and other assistance.[37]

Harris had recognized the ramifications of the Pentagon's refusal, saying in August that if necessary, "we'll either use models, miniatures, and process, or fake it with some other kind of destroyer."[38] The deadlock with the Pentagon forced him to resort to all these expedients. Since he had intended to make the film in England in any case, Harris was able to obtain use of a British destroyer and helicopter for his opening sequence in which Sidney Poitier, playing an American journalist, arrives aboard the *Bedford* to do a story on Captain Finlander and the new Navy. The British also allowed the company to shoot establishing shots with a miniature American-type destroyer in the model test basin on Malta. The shipboard sequences were then done on a mock-up of a destroyer built in a studio in England.[39]

At the same time, Harris and Widmark hired Captain James D. Ferguson, a recently retired Navy officer, as technical advisor to insure as much accuracy in the film as possible. Ferguson himself was not bothered by the Pentagon's refusal to assist or by the film's ending, although he did feel the climax "was stretching things pretty far. . . . It possibly could happen, but it would be really far-fetched." As the story was structured, the fail-safe mechanisms built into the destroyer's system were accidentally overridden by the dialogue between Finlander and the *Bedford*'s weapons officer. Ferguson claimed that in a normal situation a captain would not be in a position to have his words misinterpreted, but he acknowledged that the film didn't portray a normal situation. The *Bedford* initially had come upon the Russian submarine in territorial waters. While a more stable captain would not be likely to force the final confrontation, Ferguson believed that the whole point of the story was that Finlander "was driving himself nuts."[40] Harris thought the story could be more accurately described as Finlander "driving eveyone else nuts," which caused the weapons officer to misinterpret the captain's comment about not firing first.

The characterization itself, however, had a firm basis in reality. According to Richard Widmark, he used Barry Goldwater as his model, because the 1964 Republican presidential candidate was "one of my pet peeves," even though he liked him personally. Widmark said he compiled a rather extensive folder on Goldwater and his statements during the campaign, which was in progress while the film was in preproduction. Admitting that he "enjoyed playing Barry Goldwater," the actor said, "it gave me an added dimension to play with. Actually, his statements were not unlike the captain's actions."[41]

In any case, as with Captain Queeg, the motivation for Captain Finlander's actions is not really given. One possible explanation for his developing madness is found in President Lyman's observation that in the nuclear age man has lost faith in his ability to influence what happens to him. The *Bedford*'s captain endured long and seemingly fruitless patrols in the North Atlantic, and his frustration, when combined with a hatred of the Russians, turns him into an obsessed man.

To Captain Ferguson, Finlander's enforced removal would not have offered a viable resolution to the confrontation. While he believed that Maryk acted correctly in removing Captain Queeg, he explained that the situation on the *Bedford* was "completely different." Finlander's irrational behavior developed only during the pursuit of the submarine, while he was on the bridge, where a captain is in complete control. In contrast, Queeg's behavior on his bridge during the typhoon crowned a long series of deviant actions. In any event, Ferguson's primary concern was to ensure an authentic military atmosphere, and while he continued to believe the story was essentially implausible, he believed his role as technical advisor was to try to make the film "look like it could happen as much as I could." As a result, his script modifications, both at the beginning of his film work and during the shooting, focused on matters of

Filming the Bedford *at night in the test basin on Malta.*

procedure and dialogue which the filmmakers readily incorporated into the script.[42]

What neither Ferguson nor Harris could change, however, was the need to use a British destroyer and helicopter to represent American counterparts. The technical advisor pointed out that when the helicopter delivers Poitier to the deck of the ship, "you can see it is a British ship. All Navy men will notice it. . . . [but the] only people who would know are those familiar with ships and helicopters."[43] In any event, opening the film with a live shot enabled Harris to establish a sense of reality, which then allowed him to use models and mock-ups without much loss of authenticity.

To prevent possible recognition of the British destroyer in the repeated full-ship shots, the film company photographed a miniature U.S. Navy frigate for the open sea sequences. By using the British test basin in Malta for these sequences, Harris was able to create waves of the right frequency and size to fit the model. To provide the illusion of being in the North Atlantic, the special effects men also floated "icebergs" in the water and had the *Bedford* sail between them. Ferguson, who did not go to Malta, felt that a destroyer would have been incapable of these feats. He would have preferred to eliminate the shots.[44] Even so, the basin allowed Harris to shoot the real sea as background and gave more realism to the film than any other available method. Shooting the deck shots and interiors in a studio had little adverse effect on authenticity. (Even when filmmakers use Navy ships for exterior sequences, they make most dialogue shots on mock-ups built on sound stages to enable them to control lighting and sounds. They also avoid prolonged interference with Navy opera-

The Bedford sails past an iceberg during filming of the story of Captain Finlander's compulsive pursuit of a Russian submarine. (Note the perimeter of test basin and Mediterranean Sea in the background.)

tions.) For *The Bedford Incident*, the mock-ups were built on a huge British sound stage and Harris could move from one set to another with a minimum of delay.

Ray Bell thought the filmmakers "did turn out a very credible picture. They maintained the authenticity." He said the Pentagon failed to realize that most people believe what they see on the screen and therefore would conclude that the military had given assistance whether it had or not. To Bell, both *Fail Safe* and *The Bedford Incident* showed "that things could be done authentically by imaginative people who have limited budgets." Captain Ferguson believed that an audience becomes "so engrossed in the action that they don't care whether it is real or not." He thought the movie "had a feel of authenticity even if it wasn't 'real!' " For his part, Harris believed that striving for authenticity is worthwhile only as a supportive base to the drama and the issues dealt with in the film. In other words, if there are glaring errors in authenticity, it could jeopardize the audience's willingness in accepting the more important parts of the overall film. Authenticity for the sake of authenticity alone is merely an exercise and has very little to do with film as an art form.[45]

Unlike a typical combat film *The Bedford Incident* relied less on visual authenticity than on its story for dramatic impact. Ironically, the build-up of tensions during Captain Finlander's obsessive pursuit of the Russian submarine obscured the filmmaker's intended message. Despite Harris's hope that his movie would repeat the warning of a possible nuclear accident, the story focuses more on man's irrationality than on the instrument of his destruction. The strong impression created by the destruction of the two ships would undoubtedly have remained even if the mutual extinction had resulted from conventional weapons rather than nuclear warheads.

★

The Americanization of Emily

Survival, not destruction, becomes the theme in *The Americanization of Emily* (1964) as it comments on the absurdity of war and the irrationality of military men. Using World War II for its setting, the film became the first major Hollywood production to portray an American serviceman proudly professing the virtues of cowardice. When confronted with such a radically different military image, many reviewers reacted with stunned outrage. According to one critic, *The Americanization of Emily* was "so hypocritical—because it dares to call itself funny—so callous, so cruel, and so crass, that it provokes only anger and a feeling of resentment that we, as Americans, have allowed ourselves the 'luxury' of permitting such encroachment against our very heritage as it were."[46]

The script was in fact, uneven; its thesis undoubtedly was presented too verbosely, and its message contained inconsistencies and fallacies. Nevertheless, through alternating satire, slapstick, and serious drama, the film attempted to question the glorification of war and to ridicule the idea that to die for one's country was a positive good. Beginning with William Bradford Huie's novel *The Americanization of Emily*, Paddy Chayefsky used a rather conventional love story as the framework in which to reexamine the premises of war. Rather than state his antiwar observations in a traditional dramatic script, Chayefsky used "savage comedy with brash and irreverant situations."[47]

The biggest change Chayefsky made in transferring the book to the screen was to make the hero (played by James Garner) into a professed coward, a "charming churl whose principle it is to be without principle."[48] Garner, a junior Navy officer in pre-D-Day London, serves as a "dog-robber" for his admiral, one of the planners of the invasion. In return for the security of a safe position, Garner procures luxuries for his boss—from liquor to food to women. In the course of his assignment, Garner meets an English war widow who hates Americans (played by Julie Andrews in her first non-singing and probably best screen role).

Garner woos her with a mixture of charm and his philosophy of cowardice, which takes advantage of her bitterness over her husband's combat death. He tells her, "I preach cowardice. Through cowardice we shall all be saved. . . . If everybody obeyed their natural impulse and ran like rabbits at the first shot, I don't see how we could possibly get to the second shot." He talks about the unreasonableness of waiting to be killed "all because there's a madman in Berlin, a homicidal paranoid in Moscow, a manic buffoon in Rome, and a group of obsessed generals in Tokyo." Garner ignores the possibility that if he and those like him were to run away, the "paranoids" and "buffoons" might take over. Nonetheless, his espousal of cowardice suggested on the screen for the first time that one thing people could do toward eliminating war was "to get rid of the goodness and virtue" they usually attribute to combat.

Ultimately, Andrews responds to the American's philosophy: "I am glad you are yellow. It is your most important asset, being a coward. Every man I ever loved was a hero and all he got was death." But as Garner wins the battle of love, his efforts to stay alive are thwarted by his admiral's brainstorm: the first dead man on Omaha Beach should be a sailor so that the Navy can show it has no peer for bravery among the services. Despite his efforts, Garner in a comic scene is forced onto the beach at gunpoint at the head of the assault force. At this juncture, he is saved by the filmmakers. At first reported dead, he reappears in England as a wounded hero and, after initially refusing, he agrees to return to the United States to take part in a victory bond drive.

Despite this traditional heroic ending, *The Americanization of Emily* stirred up wrathful criticism not only in the media, but among moviegoers. According to Arthur Hiller, the film's director, he even lost a few friends "because their heroic vision of the goodness, virtue, and nobility of war has been tarnished" by the movie's disrespect for the traditional American view of combat. As a result of the controversies stirred up during the film's sneak previews, Hiller attended the first public screening in New York to hear reactions from an actual audience. He found many people "hopping mad." One viewer thought it was "a pretty deadly joke making a comedy episode out of the D-Day landing and having laughs at the expense of an admiral who had a breakdown." Others objected to the message that there is no virtue in war, no goodness, that death in war isn't noble, that women who wear their widows' weeds like nuns help to perpetuate the very wars that gave birth to their sorrows, that men who die in war are not necessarily brave or noble but probably victims of societies that glamorize war. The consensus of these people was that the film perverted some American institutions and misrepresented some human foibles. They felt it should never have been made.[49]

In response, Hiller suggested that dead heroes are simply dead men and that more could be achieved by living cowards. He emphatically believed that "a wild, satiric, cynical comedy" was the way to comment "on the lunacy of the attributes we attach to war. . . . Goodness and virtue and nobility are so out of place in the context of war that satiric laughter is the only logical response." At the same time, Hiller argued that *The Americanization of Emily* did not ridicule those who had to go to war, did not argue that all wars were bad, did not say that there aren't times when lives must be sacrificed for good cause. In fact, he said the film shows "war for what it is, a barbaric, inhuman act of man—a miserable hell. It says one thing we can do toward eliminating war from our world is to get rid of the goodness and virtue we attribute to war. Be grieved by death, but not proud of it. Stop naming streets after generals, stop erecting statues. It says stop applauding death—stop celebrating war. [These celebrations are] helping to perpetuate circumstances in our world that will bring our heroes, again and again, into situations where they must give their lives." He argued that war was not a fraud but that the fraud "is in the virtue and goodness we attribute to war. If you glorify war you create a climate for more wars."[50]

Not everyone agreed with Hiller about the essence of his film. One retired Army officer answered the director's published remarks with his own essay. He said he was not against the portrayal of military men as cowards, but disagreed with Hiller's "didactic preachment about the meaning of the film and his specious or naive reasoning that the deglorification of nobility and virtue in war and the glorification of cowardice will contribute to lessening the climate for future wars."[51] Melvyn Douglas, the eccentric admiral in the film, disagreed, suggesting that there was value in looking at the military with some irreverence: "I often wish that we were like the British, who have a capacity to laugh at themselves and their own institutions which far exceeds our own." He felt that all organizations "should be able to look at themselves with humor as well as with seriousness."[52]

Douglas, who was in both World Wars, said he had "seen first-hand some of the excesses that were exploited in the film," including the part Garner played.[53] Nevertheless, in 1964, the Navy was not ready to laugh at itself or openly acknowledge the existence of officers even approximating Garner's role. Knowing this, the producer did not even bother to seek the limited military assistance he needed for the brief Omaha Beach sequence. And when the film was released, the Navy discouraged distribution to its bases because the "story and characterizations do not present the Navy accurately."[54]

Ironically, in the end, Garner accepts his hero's mantle in the best tradition of the American fighting man. Bowing to his love for Emily, Charlie Madison/Garner seemingly embraces her argument that "war isn't a fraud. . . . It's very real. . . . We shall never get rid of war by pretending it's unreal. It's the virtue of war that's a fraud. Not war itself. It's the valor and the self-sacrifice and the goodness of war that need the exposing. And here you are being brave and self-sacrificing and positively clanking with moral fervor, perpetuating the very things you detest, merely to do the right thing." But what is doing the "right thing" in this instance—telling the truth about what happened on Omaha Beach, or letting "God worry about the truth" and knowing the "momentary fact" of his love for Emily?

Madison may sell out to the establishment, but Emily also accepts the traditional values of society. When she first meets Madison, she says, "I don't want oranges, or eggs, or soap-flakes, either. Don't show me how profitable it would be to fall in love with you, Charlie. Don't Americanize me!" But she changes. Where she previously found Madison's cowardice a virtue, she now finds it a failing if it means he will go to prison for telling the truth about Omaha Beach. Having become Americanized, Emily wants her man home even if he must play the hero, however falsely.

In changing its characters' values so quickly, the movie may have copped out. As Douglas says, the filmmakers "lost their courage at the end. They didn't go as far with it as they could. The tried to sweeten up the end."[55] But if the film weakened its message, it did so with such rapidity, so close to the end, that most viewers missed the transformations completely, or found them so ambiguous that they ignored the switches. As a result, the general feeling remained that *The Americanization of Emily* contained a pacifist statement.

According to Bosley Crowther of the *New York Times*, the film was "a spinning comedy that says more for basic pacifism than a fistful of intellectual tracts. . . . [It] gets off some of the wildest, brashest, and funniest situations and cracks at the lunacy of warfare that have popped from the screen in quite some time."[56] Other critics noted, however, that the film's "preachiness" sometimes slowed its pace. More important, the film's then-unique message and the ambiguity of its apparent change in direction created confusion about the film and caused some people to find it distasteful.

As a result, the film initially had an indifferent success at the box office. It was subsequently re-released with its title shortened to *Emily* in an attempt to capitalize on Julie Andrews' success in *Mary Poppins* and *The Sound of Music*. Not until the rise of the antiwar movement of the late 1960s, however, did the film find its place as a cult film that voiced the ideals of the Vietnam War protesters. More than any of the contemporary antimilitary films, *The Americanization of Emily* addressed the generation's disillusionment with the armed forces and the growing realization that the armed forces could no longer sweep all enemies before it.

The films discussed in this chapter portrayed a side of the military not previously known in Hollywood films. The four Cold War, anti-Bomb movies dealt in one way or another with a cosmic issue, the possible end of the world, an abstraction difficult for most people to grasp. Moreover, the black satire and slapstick humor of *Dr. Strangelove* and the melodramatic build-up of tensions in *Fail Safe, Seven Days In May,* and *The Bedford Incident* tended to obscure the intended message of the films. Unlike them, *The Americanization of Emily* had one fundamental idea with which people could readily identify: It was better to be a live coward than a dead hero. Much of the social ferment in the late sixties focused on this issue, and during the period a significant segment of the American population came to reject the long-standing notion that the highest calling a man could have was to die for his country.

The Americanization of Emily

CHAPTER ELEVEN

WAYNE, WOMEN, AND VIETNAM

★

Essentially a masculine genre, the American combat movie aimed its adventure, romance, and camaraderie toward the male audience, providing an arena for John Wayne and his fellow actors to establish norms of bravery and heroism for young men. This emphasis on the male as hero also contributed to the overall Hollywood image of women as inferior, as the satisfier of man's sexual needs and, especially in combat films, as useless baggage who interfered with the men's true companions, their fellow men. Seldom has the presence of a woman in a war movie contributed significantly to the development of the plot or to the success of the military operation.

Women's Roles

In *The Americanization of Emily*, James Garner represents the antithesis of the classic John Wayne fighting man—the strong, determined cowboy, soldier, sailor, flier, or Marine who does his best to defend the United States and liberty. Likewise, Julie Andrews' portrayal of Emily is atypical for an American war movie. Emily does ultimately "cop out," does become Americanized, does want her man even at the cost of his having to renounce the very characteristics she had originally found so appealing. Nevertheless, Emily is a strong wo-

---

John Gilbert leaves Renee Adoree behind as he and the American army depart for the front in The Big Parade.

man, even dominating her man, convincing him to change his most dearly held tenets for her sake. Emily, a major figure, does more than fill the spaces between the battle scenes. In contrast, the typical heroine in a Hollywood military movie is submissive, long-suffering, and long-waiting, a woman who satisfies her man's sexual desires and provides loving care and relaxation away from the true excitement of combat. These women's lives are subordinated to their men's military careers or wartime missions—the job has to be done, the nation's needs come before love.

So Proudly We Hail (1943) is one of the few exceptions to the standard presentation of women in combat situations. While the film tells the story of a typical group of Army nurses in the Philippines in 1941, it does show one nurse actually waging war against the Japanese. Veronica Lake, in her role as an embittered war widow who has been a divisive force in the company, places a grenade in her blouse, lets her famous shock of blond hair fall over her eye, and walks down to meet the advancing enemy. The resulting explosion allows Claudette Colbert and the other nurses to escape to fight another day. Since the American people "knew" what Japanese soldiers did to American women, the scene and the film produced the appropriate patriotic reaction. However, like many other combat films of the early war years, *So Proudly We Hail* was fantasy.

If women only rarely fought and died in war films, they were only a little more often portrayed as complaining about the long separations from their men or as interfering with their military careers or combat missions. In these few instances, the movies were either based on fictional works that delineated the characters' actions or on biographies that even more defined the parameters of the story. For example, in *From Here to Eternity*, Lorene (Donna Reed) does help Prewitt (Montgomery Clift) remain AWOL and does try to keep him from joining his unit after the attack on Pearl Harbor, arguing that the Army has tried to destroy him. To have changed James Jones' plot and have Lorene encourage him to return to the base would have destroyed the power of the novel.

In *Above and Beyond* (1952), the documentary-style account of the dropping of the atomic bomb on Hiroshima, the wife of Colonel Tibbets is shown as so bitterly unhappy that he cannot confide in her about what he is doing. She sees his secret mission as the problem destroying their relationship. After repeated clashes, she is exiled from the training base and Tibbets' life, at least until the bomb is dropped and the nature of his mission can be revealed. Since Tibbets and his wife were the primary sources for the screenplay, the story had to follow actual events.[1]

For the most part, however, women are characterized as the understanding wives or girlfriends who bravely stay in the background—while the hus-

Having protected her from the German menace, Raymond McKee sends Marguerite Coutot to his parents in America as he returns to his fellow Marines and combat in The Unbeliever *(1918).*

band goes off to war—and wait to receive him home even if he is maimed in combat. Whether in the fictional *The Big Parade* or *Battle Cry* or in the biographical *Thirty Seconds Over Tokyo* or *Pride of the Marines*, the women gladly accept their men home however crippled they may be. Virtually no American war film has raised the question of whether these women have wanted to spend the rest of their lives with a disabled veteran, though the conflict is suggested when the men offer to renounce their ties because of their changed condition.

Despite this noble image, John Wayne recognized that if women's place was not in war, they should not be in war films, and complained about the requirement to usually include a romantic interest in films merely to attract audiences. He recalled that the original script for *The Fighting Seabees* was "a good story," even though it had no female character in it. The studio, however, insisted that the producer put some romance in the film. As a result, the script was rewritten to include a woman journalist who arrives on the island where Wayne is working and fighting. For Wayne, the addition to the script "took all the reality out of the picture. They really had a fine picture, kind of a lost patrol story to begin with. But it just ended up the usual type of film."[2]

Even John Ford, whose reputation was based on his action, male-oriented movies, included a love interest between Wayne and Donna Reed in *They Were Expendable* (1945). Wayne and Reed, a nurse on Corregidor, begin their romance while he is recuperating from a wound received in an early Japanese attack on the Philippines. However, when the time comes to evacuate General MacArthur from Corregidor, Wayne boards his PT-boat and rides off to do his duty. While he shows a deep feeling for Reed, the romance does little for the film except provide a minor dramatic complication. There is never a moment's doubt that Wayne will be able to save Reed; she always knows she is only filling a momentary gap in Wayne's life, that he must soon go off to war.

While this interlude falls into the typical male-female pattern in war movies, it is not Wayne's usual military film relationship. Ironically, despite his image as the symbolic fighting man, Wayne's women are generally not the sub-

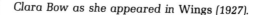

Clara Bow as she appeared in Wings *(1927).*

missive, understanding females of most American war films. In *Sands of Iwo Jima*, his character is significantly influenced by his relationships with two women, neither of them typical. His brief affair with a prostitute while on leave after the Battle of Tarawa is used as a device to explain Stryker's apparent callousness. He tells the woman about his ex-wife, how she left him because of his commitment to the Marines, and how she refuses to allow him to communicate with their son. Stryker's outer shell seems to soften during the affair, the woman's child reminds Wayne of his son, and he becomes more human, perhaps even vulnerable. Before the battle on Iwo Jima, Wayne finally writes a letter to his son trying to explain his feelings. But, in what was probably an unwitting comment about the dangers of such a transformation for a "true" fighting man, Stryker is killed by a sniper after helping to lead the advance up Mount Suribachi.

In the next fifteen years, Wayne continued to have romantic relationships in his military films even though they seldom interfered with his primary concern, his career. In *Operation Pacific*, Wayne's wife has left him because of his commitment to the Navy. In *Wings of Eagles*, Wayne plays Spig Wead, an early Navy flying hero and later a Hollywood screenwriter, whose wife actually left him for the very reasons Wayne's fictional wives had left—Wead's commitment to his career, in this case, the development of Naval aviation in the 1920s. Although they are shown as beginning a reconciliation, the attempt is cut short when Wead is paralyzed in a fall and insists his wife leave him because he can no longer be a husband to her. By the time Wayne appeared in *In Harm's Way* in 1965, he has been promoted to admiral, but he continues to fail as a husband and father. Early in the film, his embittered son shows up to remind him of still another lost family. The meeting seems to affect Wayne and during a relationship with Patricia Neal, who plays the understanding nurse, he begins to mellow. In this film, he loses only a leg in the great climactic sea battle and at the end he seems ready to settle down in retirement.

★

The Green Berets

If World War II had been won by 1965, the Vietnam War was escalating. Off the screen, Wayne had always supported the government's actions in Southeast Asia and, having recovered from the removal of a cancerous lung, he was ready to support the war on the screen. In December, he wrote directly to President Johnson about his interest in making a movie based on Robin Moore's best-selling novel *The Green Berets*. In advising the president on how to respond to Wayne's request for assistance, presidential aide Jack Valenti wrote that "Wayne's politics [were] wrong, but insofar as Vietnam is concerned, his views are right. If he made the picture he would be saying the things we want said."[3]

John Wayne was not the first filmmaker to seek military assistance to produce a movie about the Green Berets. As early as January 1963, Columbia Pictures had written to the Army indicating a desire to make a film about a Special Forces Team. The studio intended "to show the formation, military training, and indoctrination of the men who make up this particular team, stressing, among other things, the importance of the work that the Special Forces are doing."[4] The Army found the proposed film to be "very desirable" and recommended that the Defense Department Public Affairs Office encourage the filmmaker to visit Special Forces training installations. By the end of 1965, however, the studio had failed to come up with an acceptable script, and in June 1966, the Defense Department cancelled the studio's priority.[5]

Robin Moore's novel *The Green Berets* had appeared in the spring of 1965. Focusing on the exploits of the Special Forces in Vietnam, the best-selling book angered Pentagon officials because of Moore's descriptions of Green Beret forays into North Vietnam. Although the Defense Department denied these excursions had taken place, Moore claimed his narrative was based on first-hand knowledge gained while accompanying Green Beret units in Vietnam. Moore later said the Pentagon refused to cooperate with filmmakers who wanted to purchase the rights to his book because the military was unhappy with the novel. David Wolper, among others, denied these accusations. He said that though he had been very interested in acquiring *The Green Berets*, his failure to make the movie had nothing to do with Pentagon intransigence. Wolper explained that Columbia's priority had still been in effect when he approached the Defense Department about cooperation. In addition, he said he had not been able to acquire the necessary financial backing for the project.[6]

In any event, by the end of 1965, John Wayne had learned that the film rights to Moore's book were still available, and he wrote to President Johnson setting forth his interest in making a film about the Green Berets. He explained that while he supported the administration's Vietnam policy, he knew the war was not popular. Consequently, he thought it was "extremely important that not only the people of the United States but those all over the world should know why it is necessary for us to be there. . . . The most effective way to accomplish this is through the motion picture medium." He told Johnson he could make the "kind of picture that will help our cause throughout the world." While still making money for his company, he could "tell the story of our fighting men in Vietnam with reason, emotion, characterization, and action. We want to do it in a manner that will inspire a patriotic attitude on the part of fellow-Americans—a feeling which we have always had in this country in the past during times of stress and trouble." To make the film, Wayne explained he would need the cooperation of the Defense Department, and in support of this request, he cited his long film career and specifically his portrayal of the military with "integrity and dignity" in such films as *They Were Expendable*, *Sands of Iwo Jima*, and *The Longest Day*. He concluded that his film could be "extremely helpful to the Administration" and asked Johnson to help "expedite" the project.[7]

Wayne's extended plea to the White House was actually unnecessary. Ultimately the Pentagon decided to cooperate because they viewed the final screenplay as another Wayne action-adventure film and thought the movie would benefit the services and the war effort.[8] Nevertheless, Michael Wayne, John Wayne's son and the film's producer, required eighteen months to secure approval of a script and begin shooting the film.

Developing a script acceptable to the military proved to be a major obstacle to getting production started. In February 1966, as a first step in this direction, he hired James Lee Barrett, an ex-Marine and successful scriptwriter, to start work on the screenplay. Barrett's selection relieved Pentagon fears that Robin Moore would be asked to adapt his own novel to the screen. In fact, Michael Wayne assured Don Baruch that Barrett would do "what amounts to an original screenplay using only a few incidents from Moore's book."[9]

From the beginning, however, John Wayne's own views on the conflict gave the script and ultimately the movie its focus. Responding to encouragement from the White House, he repeated his hope that *The Green Berets* would tell Americans what was happening in Vietnam. He wanted "to show such scenes as the little village that has erected its own statue of liberty to the American people. We want to bring out that if we abandon these people, there will be a blood bath of over two million souls." According to Wayne, the film would portray the professional soldier "carrying out his duty of death but, also, his extracurricular duties—diplomats in dungarees—helping small communities, giving them medical attention, toys for their children, and little things like soap, which can become so all-important." He thought these things could be inserted into the picture "without it becoming a message vehicle or interfering with the entertainment."[10]

In early April, both Waynes and Barrett visited the Defense Department to discuss details of the film and then traveled to the John F. Kennedy Special Warfare Center at Fort Bragg, North Carolina on a research expedition. Afterward, John Wayne wrote to Baruch thanking him for leading his party through the Pentagon and its bureaucracy. He admitted they had "arrived with trepidation [but] left with a feeling of confidence that the Department was sincerely sympathetic and would cooperate within any reasonable limits."[11]

The senior Wayne also wrote to Bill Moyers about his visits and commented on the strong impression the men at Fort Bragg had made on him. He attached a copy of a letter he had written to several senators including Richard Russell and J. W. Fulbright, in which he advocated continued support of the government's policies in Vietnam. He asked Moyers if these views were "reasonably close to the thinking of our Administration." The letter itself amplified Wayne's position on the type of guerrilla activity he intended to portray the Green Berets fighting against in his film. He asked the senators to remember that if such guerrilla-type warfare was successful in Vietnam, it could also take place in South America.[12]

Wayne still had a long way to go before actually getting these ideas on film. As one step in his preparations he made a three-week USO tour of Vietnam, where he was able to see firsthand some of the action he intended to show. In fact, the action came almost too close when Vietcong snipers fired into an encampment where he was talking to Marines. Wayne made light of the incident, saying "They were so far away, I didn't stop signing autographs." Landing within seventeen yards of where he was standing, however, the bullets did bring the war close enough to give him a true feeling of the conflict.[13]

In the meantime, Barrett continued working on the first draft of the screenplay. By the end of May 1966, Michael Wayne informed Pentagon officials that he hoped to have it finished by mid-July. The producer was also working on the

financial and distribution arrangements of the film and by the end of June had
reached an agreement with Universal Pictures.[14]

When Barrett finally completed the first rough draft of the screenplay in
early August, Michael Wayne told Baruch that before revising the script he
wanted to send the writer to Vietnam for some firsthand information. Like all
producers of war movies, Wayne was concerned with the need of military help
to ensure the right ambience. Moreover, television and news coverage had
brought the war into American homes, and Wayne explained that he couldn't
"afford to come up with anything less than the real thing." Consequently, he
felt the trip was necessary for Barrett "to familiarize himself with all the jar-
gon, attitudes, equipment, and procedures indigenous to the war."[15]

The request was granted. But Michael Wayne quickly discovered that,
while visual and verbal authenticity might be important to him as a filmmaker,
the Defense Department was more concerned with the movie's plot. Baruch
asked Wayne to submit the rough draft of the screenplay so that his office
would have some indication of the direction the writer was taking. When it
arrived, Baruch found the story disappointing. The script portrayed a covert
mission into North Vietnam to blow up a bridge and power plant and to seize a
highranking Communist official. According to Baruch, this plot conflicted with
normal Green Beret actions of "reconnaissance, surveillance, and training"
which the Army had described to both Waynes during their trip to Fort Bragg.
Consequently, Baruch advised Wayne that the fictionalized mission was "not
one that the Green Berets would participate in."[16]

The Army's reaction was even more negative: the "development of plot is
not acceptable in that the type mission evolved is not one which Special Forces
would be involved in under present policy." The Army recommended that "the
producer be informed that substantial plot changes would have to be made to
conform with the mission of Special Forces in Vietnam before cooperation by
the Department of the Army could be made."[17]

Barrett began revisions as soon as he returned from Vietnam in September, and he wrote Baruch that the suggested changes would cause no problem.
In light of his experiences in Vietnam, he stressed that he wanted to "write a
meaningful, exciting, and enlightening motion picture, portraying our Special
Forces as accurately and honestly as possible." Because the film would be the
first movie about the Green Berets, Barrett said he wanted it to be "the best,"
and so was sure his second draft would be done "to the satisfaction of all concerned."[18]

To ensure this, Michael Wayne and Barrett went to Washington on September 29 to discuss the script's problems with Pentagon officials. Amplifying
what Baruch had told him, the Army denied that the Green Berets went into

Mitzi Gaynor as Nellie For-
bush and Captain Herb
Hetu, the technical advisor,
talk during the shooting of
South Pacific (1958), a
musical set in a military
environment. Unlike the
feminine leads in typical
Hollywood military musi-
cals, Nellie falls in love
with a French planter
rather than an American
fighting man.

France Nuyen as Liat, the native girl in South
Pacific, on the film's set in Hawaii with Captain
Hetu. Because of the social conventions of the 1940s
and 1950s, Liat's love affair with an American officer had to end with his death rather than marriage.

North Vietnam as described in the script. The service admitted, however, that Special Forces units would conduct raids across the border if asked to by South Vietnam. The officials stressed that Green Berets would take no part in a specific mission into the North, only in conjunction with other actions.[19]

Wayne had felt the script contained a "legitimate" account of events that either had happened or could have happened. In fact, he thought it "was a better script than the film we made in terms of dramatic value for the screen." Nevertheless, at the meeting, he agreed to delete the across-the-border kidnapping, explaining later that he had no choice: he needed the Army's cooperation to supply required equipment. Perhaps more to the point, he did not want to face his father with news that the Defense Department had refused to cooperate on a John Wayne war movie. According to the younger Wayne, he never told his father the Army had rejected the initial script: "I was actually afraid to because he would have said, 'You dumb son of a bitch!' " Also, he said that it had already been announced that Batjac, the Wayne Production Company, was making *The Green Berets*, and he didn't want any negative publicity.[20]

Although Wayne told Pentagon officials at the meeting he would have the revised script done by the end of October, Barrett began to fall behind schedule. Finally he finished his draft at the end of December. He wrote to the Army Office of Information that he realized the script still had "technical inaccuracies" that were "unavoidable" because of his "ignorance of military matters and procedures." But he assured the Army that all these errors could be corrected with the help of a Special Forces technical advisor and expressed confidence that the Army would be pleased with the final script.[21]

Despite his hope, the Army found many things in the revised screenplay not to its liking when it finally received the script in February 1967. Some of the problems pertained to technical matters like the wrong height for a free fall tower and the wrong type of aircraft. Other matters, however, related to question of image and propriety. The Army suggested, for example, that one character's line be changed from "Well, sir, I'm a soldier and it's the only game in town" to something like ". . . when I came in the Army a wise infantry sergeant always told us to 'move toward the sound of the guns because that's where we'll be needed most.' " The Army felt that the reference to war as a game would "degrade the image we are attempting to project with the movie."[22]

Michael Wayne again readily agreed to the changes requested, and on March 1, he sent copies of a third draft to Baruch with a note saying he was working on a list of requirements the film would need from the Army "if and when the script is approved." Although the Army and the State Department all requested changes in the revised script, the Defense Department formally agreed on March 30 to assist Wayne's Batjac Company, provided the modifications were made.[23]

The Defense Department changes were, as before, both substantive and technical. Instead of referring to the war as "North against the South," the Pentagon recommended: "We do not see this as a civil war, and it is not. South Vietnam is an independent country, seeking to maintain its independence in the face of aggression by a neighboring country. Our goal is to help the South Vietnamese retain their freedom, and to develop in the way they want to, without interference from outside the country." The Public Affairs Office also pointed out that the brutal treatment of a prisoner by a Vietnamese officer, and its approval by the Americans "is grist for the opponents of U.S. policy in Vietnam. It supports some of the accusations of these opponents against the U.S., and is of course a clear violation of the Articles of War." On a technical level, the Pentagon noted that the incident which causes the journalist to change his views on the war and begin to support it is "objectionable." The Defense Department said that the writer's seizing a gun and becoming a combatant "violates the rules under which he operates as a news correspondent, and to the extent that the incident is considered realistic by those who might see a film

"Woman as decoration," one of Hollywood's typical roles for women in military films, is illustrated during the filming of The Outsider *(1961). Delbert Mann directs Tony Curtis, playing Ira Hayes, a hero of the Iwo Jima flag-raising.*

John Wayne as Colonel Kirby in The Green Berets *(1968).*

based on this script, might indicate that it would not be unusual for a newsman to perform such violations.'' Despite its objections, the Defense Department said it looked forward to working with Batjac ''on what promises to be a most worthwhile and, we trust, successful production.''[24]

Although the Pentagon was satisfied with the state of the production, Universal Studios had become disenchanted with their involvement in a film about an increasingly unpopular war. According to Michael Wayne, the studio claimed to be unhappy with the proposed budget. But when he and his father sat down with officials to resolve the difficulty, studio executives raised questions about the script. As soon as the senior Wayne realized the studio was looking for a way out of its contract, he said goodbye and walked out of the meeting. Apart from the issue of the Vietnam War a Universal executive subsequently called the screenplay the worst he had ever read.[25]

Even without considering the dialogue and character development, the final screenplay Barrett submitted to the Pentagon was not a dramatic triumph. *The Green Berets* portrayed the activities of Lieutenant Colonel

Michael Kirby (John Wayne) during a tour of duty in Vietnam. His actions as commander of a Special Forces unit are covered by a liberal journalist (David Janssen) who is at first skeptical of American involvement in South Vietnam but is later won over to the military's point of view. Kirby is shown working closely with his Vietnamese counterparts. In the course of the story, the Viet Cong overrun Kirby's Special Forces camp before they are driven back in a furious attack by American helicopters and planes. In the movie's climax, a small Green Beret force kidnaps a leading Viet Cong officer—basically an anticlimactic episode because the battle for the Special Forces camp is actually the dramatic and visual highlight of the story. If it had come before the battle sequence or been left out altogether, the movie would have had a much stronger dramatic impact regardless of the artistic aspects of Barrett's script.

While the Pentagon generally limits its advice to technical matters of one kind or another, Don Baruch did talk to Michael Wayne about restructuring the script to improve its impact. The producer agreed with Baruch's observations but felt it expedient to leave the screenplay as it was—John Wayne's name alone would make *The Green Berets* project attractive to most studios. His son was right. Batjac found a new financial backer and distributor almost immediately with Warner Brothers in June 1967. Shooting was then scheduled to begin in early August.[26]

Batjac had been searching for a suitable site for the exterior filming ever since the Army had agreed to cooperate on the movie. John Wayne would have preferred to shoot the film in Vietnam but admitted that "if you start shooting blanks over there, they might start shooting back." Okinawa offered tropical terrain and an Army helicopter facility, but on an inspection trip, Wayne and his codirector, Ray Kellogg, found that the aircraft would not be available on a regular basis.[27]

The Army strongly suggested that Batjac consider shooting the film at Fort Benning, Georgia. At first, the company showed little interest in the location, believing that Georgia would not look like Vietnam. But after a scouting trip to the base, Kellogg called John Wayne to say that the Georgia terrain would serve their visual needs. More important, the codirector found that the Army regularly had twenty to thirty Huey helicopters in the training program at Benning, and these would be available during filming. Since the Hueys were an essential part of the story, this was a crucial factor in their decision. Wayne made his own inspection tour of Benning, then told his son to go ahead with a formal request to use the facility.[28]

In approving the request, the Army indicated that "there will be a minimum of difficulty in acceding to Mr. Wayne's request." As was always the case on military cooperation, however, final approval of assistance rested with the local commander. In light of the Army's interest in making a film about Vietnam and in light of John Wayne's involvement in the project, the Fort Benning command provided the filmmaker with most of the assistance he needed. The only major problem Wayne had as director was coordinating his shooting schedule with the base's training schedules and the availability of the helicopters.[29]

Following Arthur Sylvester's new regulations, the Pentagon watched the production closely. Unlike earlier films which had had one technical advisor who supervised all aspects of military assistance, *The Green Berets* had three contacts with the Army, a technical advisor to supervise actual military procedures, a liaison man with the Fort Benning command who arranged for equipment and men when needed, and an overall liaison man who informed Baruch's office of progress on the production.[30]

While the Army could no longer provide on-duty soldiers to work as extras or set up special exercises (Wayne could still film regularly scheduled training maneuvers), the service did do as much as possible to ensure the visual authenticity of *The Green Berets*. Among other things, the Army brought a platoon of Hawaiians down from Fort Devens, Massachusetts, and placed them on administrative leave so that Wayne would have enough Orientals to fill the screen. To help create the proper atmosphere in which both the Green Berets and the "Vietnamese" could perform, Batjac built a Vietnamese-type village at a cost of more than $150,000 which the company later left standing for the Army's use as a training facility. In addition, following the new regulations, Batjac paid the government $18,000 for fuel and other items used exclusively in the shooting of the film.[31]

Hawks and Doves

Despite the producer's careful efforts and the Army's attempts to implement Defense Department instructions, *The Green Berets* did not avoid controversy. In June of 1969, a year after the film opened, Congressman Benjamin Rosenthal of New York launched an attack on Wayne for having made only a "token" payment to the Pentagon; he demanded a General Accounting Office investigation. Although the GAO said Wayne had followed regulations as they were written, Rosenthal charged that the Army had subsidized Wayne in making his hawkish film. In response, Wayne called Rosenthal "an irresponsible, publicity seeking idiot." Denying that he had received more than $1,000,000 worth of weapons and man hours in return for his token payment, Wayne said, "I wish this were the 1800s. I'd horsewhip him."[32]

Wayne's major problem in making *The Green Berets* had nothing to do with government regulations or congressional criticism, however. He faced the task of portraying the Vietnam War in the manner he had promised to the president and senators—as the good guys against the bad guys. The conflict in Southeast Asia differed from earlier American conflicts in which the nation had for the most part enjoyed the support of its people. As David Halberstam, author of *The Best and the Brightest*, put it, "Vietnam simply wasn't a very patriotic war. It was a lie." As a result, it was "a terribly difficult thing for John Waynism." To Halberstam; the key ingredients in Waynism are that "all the other guys are richer, more powerful and dominate the town, and you are part of the smaller group. You are leading the way for the numerically smaller group, weaker, don't have much ammunition, guns, whatever. Now, you suddenly have to take Waynism and transfer it to a place where you are bringing on the heaviest carnage in the history of mankind, to a peasant nation." According to Halberstam, Wayne was able to transfer Waynism to the Vietnam War by singling out a single microcosm within the conflict. By sending a small Special Forces unit to fight with the Montagnards, Wayne created a classic Wayne situation: a few good guys surrounded by a sea of enemy bad guys.[33]

In a sense, Wayne himself was practicing Waynism simply by making *The Green Berets*. Because opposition to the war was becoming increasingly bitter, because its body counts and battles were brought into American homes every night through television, and because of the continuing negotiations that might end the war at any moment, no one in Hollywood wanted to make a film about the conflict. Even doves who might donate large amounts of money to the anti-war movement wouldn't finance an anti-Vietnam film that might lose money. Likewise, except for Wayne, the supporters of the war wouldn't make a pro-Vietnam film because they also recognized it would probably be bad box office.

Michael Wayne explained, however, that he and his father saw the controversy surrounding the war as "a natural subject for a film." Beyond that, he didn't see the story itself as controversial: "It was the story of a group of guys who could have been in any war. It's a very familiar story. War stories are all the same. They are personal stories about soldiers and the background is the war. This just happened to be the Vietnam War." For Michael Wayne, the film may only have told "a fresh story because there were different uniforms, a different unit, and a different war."[34] The Department of Defense may have seen the film as simply another John Wayne adventure film that would benefit the military and the war effort. The White House may have believed the film was saying the things it wanted said. And John Wayne may have played his standard soldier role, carrying out his mission while trying to survive in a hostile atmosphere. But he also saw the movie as "an American film about American boys who were heroes over there. In that sense, it *was* propaganda."[35]

*John Wayne with
author (1974).*

For his efforts and for his patriotic intentions, Wayne received nothing but
criticism from film reviewers. The most extreme attack came from Renata Adler
in the *New York Times.* She wrote that *The Green Berets* was a film "so un-
speakable, so stupid, so rotten and false in every detail that it passes through
being fun, through being funny, through being camp, through everything and
becomes an invitation to grieve, not for our soldiers or for Vietnam (the film
could not be more false or do a greater disservice to either of them) but for
what has happened to the fantasy-making apparatus in this country. Simplicities of the right, simplicities of the left, but this one is beyond the possible. It is
vile and insane. On top of that, it is dull."[36]

Even the trade journals, which are usually gentle with the films they review, found *The Green Berets* wanting. The *Hollywood Reporter* called the film
"a cliche-ridden throwback to the battlefield potboilers of World War II, its
artifice readily exposed by the nightly actuality of TV news coverage, its facile
simplification unlikely to attract the potentially large and youthful audience
whose concern and sophistication cannot be satisfied by the insertion of a few

snatches of polemic." The reviewer thought the film was "clumsily scripted, blandly directed, and performed with disinterest" and predicted it would have a "chill run" domestically and "an even colder reception abroad."[37]

Wayne and his film also had their defenders. Responding to Adler's *New York Times* review, Senator Strom Thurmond told the Senate that the first paragraph of her remarks "was enough to convince anyone that this was a good movie," suggesting that Adler's calling the film "dull" was the tip-off. Declaring that he found it "hard to believe that John Wayne could ever be dull," the senator called Wayne "one of the great actors of our time. He is a true and loyal patriot and a great American. It is men of his caliber and stripe who have built America and made it what it is today—the greatest country in the world."[38]

Moreover, Green Berets who saw the film seemed to find it authentic. One lieutenant colonel commented that "when Hollywood's doing it, you have to expect some dramatization—some exaggeration. But I thought it was a real fine film." Another officer enthusiastically said, "I think it caught the essence." According to a Green Beret sergeant major, the film "was just God, Mother, and the Flag. Now who the hell could have any opposition to that? It was a good, low-key, accurate picture. . . . The accuracy was there, and the photography was real great."[39] Anyone seeing himself or a reasonable facsimile of himself portrayed on the screen admittedly lacks some objectivity. A Marine general who fought in Vietnam and commanded a Special Forces unit in his area undoubtedly put *The Green Berets* in better perspective. He found the film so bad that it almost made him sick. Among other things, he noted that Georgia simply did not look like Vietnam.[40]

If both Waynes had stuck to their stated goal of making an authentic and entertaining film rather than compromising with the military to obtain needed equipment, *The Green Berets* might have had some artistic merit. As it was, the film was no more or less than another John Wayne adventure film, in fact one of his lesser efforts. In many respects, it resembles one of his typical westerns but set in a different locale. Michael Wayne went so far as to say it was a "cowboys and Indians" film. "In a motion picture you cannot confuse the audience. The Americans are the good guys and the Viet Cong are the bad guys. It's as simple as that. . . . when you are making a picture, the Indians are the bad guys."[41]

In *The Green Berets*, John Wayne relied on Army helicopters rather than a stagecoach or horses to transport the good guys through Indian territory. Nevertheless, the seige of the Special Forces camp literally resembled thousands of Indian seiges that had long been a staple of Hollywood westerns. And, as in those films, the struggle in Vietnam pitted white men against colored men, in this instance, yellow men rather than red men. But, as David Halberstam noted, the conflict in Vietnam had produced a switch in roles. Americans were no longer universally perceiving themselves as the good guys in the struggle. It just might be that we were the many bad guys surrounding a few good guys. Moreover, the war offered no easy way out for Americans; it was too complex and impersonal for pat solutions. Consequently, Wayne could not solve the problems of Vietnam with a sudden burst of violence in the last reel of *The Green Berets* as he could in most of his previous roles.

The film's epic size also worked against Wayne's being able to play his typical character. Most of his movies had relied on the Wayne image and his physical presence to carry the story. Trying to direct the film and at the same time act in it, Wayne now had to compete for star billing with helicopters, planes, and all the other instruments of modern war. In the end, he succeeded only in becoming lost in the cast of thousands and military gadgetry. Audiences came away from the film remembering the spectacular firefight and the Viet Cong general being snatched by plane out of the air far more than any of Wayne's actions. To be sure, like so many of his western characters, Wayne is heading off into the sunset at the end of the film. Symbolizing the difficulty he had in finding the proper direction for the film, however, Wayne's sun is setting in the east, into the South China Sea, rather than in the west.

Despite such geographic errors, dramatic problems inherent in the script, the controversial nature of the subject, and virtually unanimously poor reviews, *The Green Berets* proved to be a box office hit. Confounding critics and Hollywood insiders who had predicted the film would flop, it brought in $8,700,000 in film rentals during the first six months of its run. Against a production cost of $6.1 million, *The Green Berets* generated a total domestic theatrical film rental of $9,750,000, which constituted Warner Brothers' share of the theater box office for the United States and Canada.[42] Foreign distribution and sale to television brought in additional revenues.

The film's success confirmed Wayne's statement that although he had made it "from a hawk's point of view," he had also made it "strictly for entertainment." At the same time he credited the criticism of the movie with helping to make it successful: "Luckily for me, they overkilled it. *The Green Berets* would have been successful regardless of what the critics did, but it might have taken the public longer to find out about the picture if they hadn't made so much noise about it."[43] Irrespective of the artistic merit of the movie, most reviewers directed their criticism more at Wayne's hawkish views than at the film as entertainment. And John Wayne's long-established reputation gave him an advantage over the critics' opinions.

Ironically, the Vietnam War itself marked the beginning of the end of America's glorification of war and the virtue of dying for one's country, ideals at the core of the Wayne image. For the first time since the War of 1812, large numbers of Americans refused to support the government in waging a foreign war. And also for the first time since that conflict, the United States pulled out of a war. The ramifications of this withdrawal for the nation are still unclear. What is apparent is that the shock of our failure in Vietnam has caused many Americans to re-examine the so-called virtues of war as well as roles in life that are based on conflict, brutal action, and martial success. Despite the questions raised by the the American role in the war, John Wayne and his image emerged from the controversies not only unscathed but seemingly more popular than ever.

Hawks and Doves

CHAPTER TWELVE

FILM BIOGRAPHY
AS REALITY

★

John Wayne's box-office success with *The Green Berets* did not encourage other filmmakers to use Vietnam as a subject for military movies. Despite the growing antiwar sentiment in the country during the second half of the 1960s, however, the film industry continued to produce movies about World War II. Though their numbers declined, the size and cost of the films generally increased as studios attempted to lure people away from their television sets with "spectaculars." With the exception of an occasional *Beach Red*, most American-produced combat movies were of the dimension of *Battle of the Bulge* (1965), *The Dirty Dozen* (1967), *The Devil's Brigade* (1968), and *The Bridge at Remagen* (1969). At the same time, European filmmakers also turned out spectaculars such as *Operation Crossbow* (1965), *Where Eagles Dare* (1968), and *The Battle of Britain* (1969), which focused on the Allies' fight against Hitler.

With the exception of *The Devil's Brigade*, partially shot in the United States, the Pentagon provided little or no assistance to the American productions. By the mid-1960s, the armed forces had virtually no World War II-vintage equipment in service. In most cases, retired officers who had fought in the war could arrange directly with a studio to work as technical advisors on a production. Moreover, following the release of Arthur Sylvester's new regulations in 1964, Hollywood had become reluctant to approach the Defense Department for assistance. Otto Preminger could ignore normal channels, scream a little, and obtain cooperation on *In Harm's Way* (1965). But most filmmakers did not want to go through red tape and delays, preferring to negotiate for as-

---

George C. Scott, film crew, and military men discuss the re-creation of Patton's landing on Sicily, staged with Pentagon assistance on Crete.

sistance with countries such as Spain, Italy, and Austria, which had World War II equipment and men available for rent. Spain had even compiled a thick price list covering every type of military hardware; their price for a soldier depended on his rank.

Despite the lack of Pentagon assistance and supervision, the image of the American military in these productions did not radically differ from the earlier portraits. To be sure, *The Dirty Dozen* did not portray a group about whom the Army would want to boast. Nevertheless, historical basis existed for a story about a unit made up of soldiers convicted of serious crimes; the men were to perform a highly dangerous mission in return for their freedom. The military itself had cooperated on films that had portrayed units of misfits who become rehabilitated through their combat experiences. In *Twelve O'Clock High*, for example, General Savage orders one of his planes—named "The Leper Colony"—to be manned by incompetents. While the men are not the rapists and murderers of *The Dirty Dozen*, the crew is comprised of the squadron's losers and oddballs. In the end, there is little dramatic difference between their becoming one of the best crews in Savage's group and Lee Marvin's suicide squad successfully destroying a German High Command pleasure retreat.

In contrast to these fictionalized stories, *The Devil's Brigade*, made with Pentagon assistance, portrayed the actual story of a unit of American rejects who join with a highly disciplined group of Canadian soldiers to assault a virtually impregnable German position high on a mountain. Shot near the actual battle site in Italy and in the mountains of Utah, the film received armed forces cooperation in Europe and National Guard assistance in the United States. In Utah, a National Guard engineering unit bulldozed a road to the mountain used in re-creating the actual assault, helped build the fortress, and then participated in the filming. The resulting combat sequence captured the intensity of the struggle to the satisfaction of the commander of the actual unit, who also served as the movie's technical advisor.[1]

David Wolper relaxing with William Holden during the shooting of The Devil's Brigade *(1968).*

★

Bridge at Remagen

Bridge at Remagen

Bridge at Remagen, another film based on an actual event, was less successful in duplicating history. The book's author, Congressman Ken Hechler, thought the movie could have been more accurate. The problem had little to do with the lack of Pentagon assistance. Hechler said that some of the scenes were hoked up with excessive military action that had not actually occurred during the capture of the Ludendorff Bridge. He particularly objected to a fictional fire-fight at the end of the picture that he thought was unnecessary. If the film had not been "so Mickey Moused" up, Hechler believed it would have made a more exciting drama.[2]

While also disagreeing with many of the details in the script, Cecil Roberts, the technical advisor and a retired colonel, thought that "the major events were there. The personalities as portrayed in the script were simply fiction for the most part." Roberts did try to hold down the excessiveness of the film-makers but recalled that the director, John Guillermin, regularly disagreed with him over the size of the explosions: "He always wanted one tank round to destroy a complete building." In the face of Guillermin's claim of "dramatic

Austrian tanks were rented and brought to Davle, Czechoslovakia, during the filming of David Wolper's The Bridge at Remagen *(1969).*

David Wolper hastily constructed a bridge set at Castel Gondolfo, Italy, for **Bridge at Remagen** after the film company was forced to flee from Czechoslovakia because of the 1968 Russian invasion.

Director John Guillermin (foreground with cap, next to camera) prepares one of the closing shots in **Bridge at Remagen** as Bradford Dillman and Ben Gazzara study script.

licence," Roberts admitted that he usually lost the arguments. If an active-duty officer had served as technical advisor on a Pentagon-assisted film, he would have had reasonable leverage in supervising the accuracy of the film's military aspects. David Wolper, however, had not requested Defense Department assistance and so was not bound by Pentagon regulations of historical and technical veracity. As a result, Roberts saw his role as concerned primarily "with the uniforms and vehicles and the authenticity of the scenes from a military point of view" rather than matters of story, personality, and literal accuracy.[3]

Frills and fictionalized drama notwithstanding, *Bridge at Remagen* recreated with reasonable accuracy the American dash to the Rhine in March 1945 and the capture of the last surviving bridge across the river. The bridge, which remained standing for ten crucial days after its seizure, enabled the Allies to establish a beachhead in Germany and so bring the war to a quicker ending. Although Hechler's book was historical, Wolper's film fictionalized the characters on both sides to facilitate the drama and avoid problems obtaining releases from the battle's actual participants. Nevertheless, Hechler said that most of the film characters were patterned after real people and that perhaps seventy-five percent of them were readily identifiable to those who had fought for the bridge or read his book.[4]

Some of the battle's survivors did ultimately object to what they felt were inaccurate portrayals. Even so, Hechler saw nothing in the script that he felt would make Pentagon cooperation impossible in terms of historical veracity. But when Wolper submitted the script for comment to the Army's Public Relations Office in Los Angeles, officers gave him an unofficial opinion that assistance would not be forthcoming as long as the script included a scene in which an American sergeant takes binoculars and a wrist watch from a dead German soldier. Wolper "was not shocked" by the opinion, believing that the military should not assist on a film it finds "violently anti-Army."[5]

While the objection might have been resolved if Wolper had formally requested assistance from Washington, he had no reason to do so given the film's requirements and his means of satisfying them. Wolper said the movie needed "one thing more important than any men or equipment: a bridge. We found the bridge in Czechoslovakia." Wolper did admit that if he had found a suitable bridge in the United States, he would then have had to deal with the Pentagon to obtain military equipment: "I don't know what would have happened. It would have been difficult." Finding the bridge had not been an easy task. After a year and a half of searching, Wolper located the Davle Bridge, which looked like the Ludendorff and was on a site that resembled Remagen, Germany in 1945. Fortunately also, Czechoslovakia was in the midst of Dubcek's efforts to liberalize his country, and government officials wanted Western contacts and money. Wolper was therefore able to reach agreements with the government to use soldiers to play both Americans and Germans and to have river traffic suspended during the filming.[6]

The selection of Czechoslovakia, more than problems with the script or lack of appropriate equipment, made United States military assistance impossible as well as unnecessary. American uniforms and weapons were easily obtained from costume rental agencies in Europe and the United States. German uniforms and weapons were available in Czechoslovakia, since its film and television industries often produced films about World War II and Hitler's occupation of the country. For tanks and other heavy equipment, Wolper turned to the Austrian Ministry of Defense, which rented him World War II materiel, purchased as war surplus from the United States after the war. The collected arsenal of equipment and supplies was shipped without difficulty into Czechoslovakia in May 1968, shortly before filming began.[7]

The dated armaments, trained soldiers, and a reasonable facsimile of the Remagen area enabled the director to depict the essence, if not the total accuracy, of the capture of the Ludendorff Bridge. In re-creating the atmosphere of combat, Guillermin had unexpected assistance from the Soviet Union. With the filming only two-thirds completed, Russian armies moved into Czechoslovakia to crush the liberal Dubcek government. Congressman Heckler, then on location as a part-time technical advisor, managed to get out of the country on one of the last planes from Prague. The film company itself left in a fleet of taxis the afternoon of August 22 and walked across the border into Austria that evening in a rain storm. Ultimately, Wolper completed the movie at sites in Austria, Germany, and Italy, and a second unit returned to the bridge at Davle where they filmed some long shots with the tanks, armor, and Czech soldiers as extras, all performing under the watchful eyes of the Russian Army.

Despite the unintentional warlike atmosphere, the equipment, and the men, all of which produced an authentic atmosphere, *Bridge at Remagen* ultimately failed as drama. As Congressman Hechler noted, the filmmakers' efforts to expand a singular event into a large-scale spectacular caused the second half of the movie to drag. Instead of building tensions by focusing on the American forces racing against time to capture the bridge before the Germans could blow it up, the film jumps back and forth between the two sides. The technique of detailing the decisions and actions of the opposing forces so carefully dissipates the drama inherent in the story, and the capture of the bridge becomes anticlimactic. At the same time, individuals become lost in the sweep of events, and the result is an impersonal, two-dimensional visual image that leaves the audience uninvolved in the story.

★

Battle of the Bulge

Battle of the Bulge failed for much the same reason as *Bridge at Remagen*. In trying to relate the entire story of the German surprise attack in December 1944, the film ended up telling little of the human experiences of the pivotal battle. It failed to capture the desperate struggle for survival between the Germans, who were making their last major effort to stop the Allied advance through Europe, and the Americans, who were suddenly confronted by an overwhelming force. In contrast, by focusing on a single unit surrounded at Bastogne, *Battleground* captured the urgency and the desperation that was the Battle of the Bulge. But Dore Schary's film was a standard screen, black and white movie, and filmmakers in the mid-sixties believed that only wide-screen, color spectaculars would draw people into theatres.

Battle of the Bulge failed at the box office for more reasons than simply its bloated size and hollowness. Its characters were fictional, and in contrast to those in *Bridge at Remagen* or *Battleground*, they seemed artificial and one-dimensional. More important, the story itself lacked credibility. While professing to re-create history, the film seemed phoney, a feeling that was reinforced by the choice of location. The dusty plains of Spain simply did not look like the snowy December of Belgium in 1944. The palm trees in the background were no substitute for the evergreens of Northern Europe.

The film was shot in Spain for two very practical reasons. The financial backers had money in the country that could only be spent there, and the Spanish Army had a fleet of World War II tanks of both American and German manufacture. Moreover, the Spanish government readily rented its Army to filmmakers, since it had little else to do except enforce domestic tranquility. Given the availability of this equipment and men, the producers did not need the Pentagon's help. Still, the film's image of the American military was essentially positive. Although caught off guard and initially driven back, the Army ultimately wins the battle. Yet the film's army was made up of faceless men. Audiences could not care about them, could not believe they were suffering the bitter cold of winter, could not forget they were simply actors. Ultimately, *Battle of the Bulge* failed not because of the phoney location, not because of doubts about the validity of its history, but because audiences did not empathize with the characters, did not believe they represented American fighting men.

★

Patton: The Nineteen-Year Struggle

Film Biography as Reality

Patton did not suffer from this deficiency, at least in regard to its title character. Even though the film was also a large-scale combat spectacular, was also made for the most part in Spain, used the same tanks and equipment, and portrayed history (partly the same history), its theme was sharper and narrower than that of *Battle of the Bulge*. In focusing only on the wartime exploits of General George S. Patton, Jr., the film avoided the pitfalls of most movie biography, which tends to clutter the story with unnecessary personal entanglements. An authoritative study of the military career of one of America's great generals, the film never lost sight of its subject. Consequently, George C. Scott became Patton to those people who had never met the general, and to many of the men who knew the general, Scott became more like Patton than Patton himself. General James Gavin, who knew Patton "awfully well," explained that this happened "because the movie seemed to accentuate his idiosyncrasies, and in that way somehow the real Patton was left behind."[8]

Patton succeeded as a biography and as a war movie because of Scott's study of the general and his virtuosity as an actor, because of a superb script, because of excellent direction that combined Scott's acting with effective use of the Spanish military and locales, and perhaps most important, because the film was a labor of love for the producer, Frank McCarthy. McCarthy, who had served as secretary to General George C. Marshall during the war and eventually rose to the rank of brigadier general, became a film industry executive after the war and later a staff producer at Twentieth Century Fox. McCarthy had come to know Patton during the war when he accompanied General Marshall on his trips abroad. Of all the generals McCarthy had known, he thought that Patton was "the guy you ought to do a movie about." It was possible, he thought, to prove mathematically that Patton was the most successful Army field commander in the war. More important, as far as a movie was concerned, he said that Patton "was very theatrical and very flamboyant and had several Achilles heels. All these things put together made for fine drama." Having produced one critically acclaimed, if not financially successful war film, *Decision Before Dawn* (1950), McCarthy sent a memo in October 1951 to Darryl Zanuck, then head of production at Twentieth Century Fox, proposing a film about Patton. Even though Zanuck gave his immediate approval, McCarthy needed nineteen years to bring the biography to the screen.[9]

He met with immediate problems. The Army was afraid that any story about Patton would necessarily be derogatory in light of the general's reputation as a rebellious man who had slapped soldiers, had been a difficult sub-ordinate throughout the war, had wanted to fight the Soviet Union once Germany had capitulated, had refused to de-Nazify Bavaria. But the Pentagon was not McCarthy's only obstacle. Patton's family objected to any film about the general, claiming invasion of privacy and arguing that any biography would portray him inaccurately.

Given this opposition, Twentieth Century Fox did not pursue the project, and Warner Brothers obtained a Defense Department priority in 1953 for a Patton film, but ultimately allowed it to lapse because of the same obstacles. After the death of Patton's widow in 1960, however, McCarthy's interest in doing a film about the general's career was renewed. He wrote to Baruch's Office in November, inquiring about the old Warner Brothers' priority, and Baruch advised him that Warner Brothers was no longer interested in the project. He also informed the Army of McCarthy's renewed interest in a Patton biography, suggesting that it should consider cooperating on a film even if the family was still opposed. McCarthy, though, was not yet willing to proceed without the family's approval.[10]

By this time, McCarthy had become a brigadier general in the Army Reserves, with his active duty assignment as Deputy Chief of Information in Washington. During his two weeks of duty in 1961, McCarthy spent considerable time convincing his boss that the Army should allow Twentieth Century Fox to make a Patton film. Apart from the obvious fact of his fortuitous Army connections and sympathies, he argued that the Army had no right to oppose the movie, since Patton's military career was in the public domain. He also suggested that the Army was on shaky ground if its opposition continued only as a favor to Patton's family.[11]

His arguments and the Defense Department's now-favorable position began to "warily" change the Army's stance. In July 1961, it informed the Patton family that it would probably cooperate with Fox if the studio submitted a suitable script. At a meeting the same month, the Army told McCarthy it could assist on the film and that no legal liability would result if he proceeded without the family's permission. The Army nevertheless encouraged him to seek their "blessing."[12] The family, however, remained adamantly opposed, advising Twentieth Century Fox in September that its position had not changed from that of the early 1950s. Their lawyer wrote that they objected "not only on the ground of possible invasion of privacy but, equally important, on the ground that it is their considered opinion that such motion picture could not portray the character of General Patton as it actually was." As a result, they regarded "the making of such picture with great distress and assure your company that such motion picture will be most repugnant to them, and further assure your company that they have opposed strenuously and continue to oppose strenuously the production of such a picture so distasteful to each of them.[13]

When the controversy over the Pentagon's assistance to *The Longest Day* erupted in Washington the same week, Arthur Sylvester informed the Army that if cooperation on a Patton film was "going to involve any large use of troops, I would back away from it at this time." And despite the Army's conclusion that the Patton family had no grounds for a court case, he expressed concern over the family's threat of legal action.[14]

With Sylvester's reluctance to commit the Pentagon to another major production and continued opposition from Patton's family, McCarthy made little headway in the next months. In February 1962, he advised Don Baruch that he was experiencing an unexpected delay in developing a script but that the research was progressing on both Patton's military career and the accumulation of appropriate anecdotal material. Because of the studio's own financial problems and its failure to win approval from Patton's family, Fox shelved the project by the summer. When the studio did not answer Don Baruch's June 1963 inquiry about the status of the film, the Pentagon cancelled Fox's priority in July. Shortly afterward, McCarthy moved to Universal Studios as a staff producer.[15]

The appearance of Ladislas Farago's *Patton: Ordeal and Triumph* (1964) rekindled Fox's interest in a filmed biography. Darryl Zanuck, now in control of the studio, had been looking for a military subject with which to duplicate the box-office success of *The Longest Day*. Having had a year to digest the Pentagon's new regulations governing cooperation, Zanuck and his son Richard, now in charge of production, bought the rights to Farago's book, and in March 1965, they announced that Frank McCarthy was returning to Fox to produce the "major budget" biography.[16]

While *Patton: Ordeal and Triumph* served as basic source in developing the screenplay, McCarthy also drew on his original research for the project and, even more important, on his personal contacts, including correspondence and visits with former president Dwight D. Eisenhower. During one meeting in Palm Springs, Eisenhower asked McCarthy why he had chosen to portray Patton rather than Omar Bradley. McCarthy later pointed out that Eisenhower had answered his own question in his book *At Ease*. Eisenhower wrote that of all the ground commanders he had known or read about, he "would put Omar Bradley in the highest classification. In every aspect of military command . . . Brad was outstanding . . . Patton was a master of fast and overwhelming pursuit. Headstrong by nature and fearlessly aggressive, Patton was the more colorful of the two, compelling attention by his mannerisms as much as his deeds. Bradley, however, was master of every military maneuver, lack-

Frank McCarthy, the producer of Patton, *checks a shot during filming.*

ing only in the capacity—possibly the willingness—to dramatize himself."[17] According to McCarthy, Patton's dramatic qualities, his spectacular military success, his flamboyance, and his maverick nature all made him "ideal theatrical material."[18]

In early 1966 General Eisenhower sent McCarthy a "Personal and confidential" letter that provided a "personal evaluation of my old friend." He described a friendship that had "remained strong and close" despite the "many differences of opinion" engendered by Patton's "volatile character, accompanied by a strong trait of exhibitionism." Eisenhower stated that only his intervention on several occasions had kept Patton in positions of command during the war: "Indeed the most serious of these occasions never had any publicity whatsoever." Eisenhower felt that Patton's "temperament made him a headliner in the press but he was not the kind of all-around, balanced, competent, and effective commander that Bradley was. . . . But he was a genius in pursuit. Recognizing this, I was determined to keep him in my war organization no matter how often the public might scream for his scalp because of some publicized and foolish episode." Eisenhower submitted that Patton "disliked, intensely, the heavy fighting necessary to break through, and because of this I did not even use him during the slugging match that finally brought about the breakout from the beachhead in late July 1944. . . . [But Patton] was a natural

to put in for exploiting the weaknesses of the Nazi forces on our right flank"
once the Allies had broken through, as he had done in Sicily and as he did after
the crossing of the Rhine in 1945. Eisenhower noted that when the Allies "got
into dirty ding dong fighting in Moselle and later, when [Patton] was trying to
fight his way to the relief of Bastogne, he was apt to become pessimistic and
discouraged. In such instances he liked a great deal of moral 'patting on the
back.' "[19] Officers who served with Patton may have disagreed with Eisenhower's judgments, and the film may not have incorporated all of his observations. Nevertheless, his information greatly aided McCarthy's script preparations.

Based on his own research, McCarthy wrote that he agreed "without
qualification" with Eisenhower's comments and stated that the script would
"reflect General Patton accurately rather than glamorize him unduly or gloss
over troublesome incidents which are matters of public record." Acknowledging that Patton's "controversial nature" made him a worthwhile dramatic
subject, McCarthy anticipated what was to become the completed film's hall-
mark: "The best parallel I can think of at the moment—and it is by no means an
exact one—is *Lawrence of Arabia.* One left that film intrigued by the character, perhaps understanding him a little better, but certainly not condoning his
excesses, which had been amply presented."[20]

Early 1966 was still, however, a long way from McCarthy's shooting schedule. After his return to Twentieth Century Fox in 1965, he had begun the
process of reestablishing the studio's Defense Department priority for the project. In formally confirming its renewal that July, Don Baruch made it clear that
the Defense Department's agreement to grant protection for the project did not
constitute a commitment for eventual assistance. He also restated the Army's
position that it would "not assist in the making of a film which depicts General
Patton in any manner that would detract from the roles and accomplishments
of his senior commanders."[21]

Despite the Army's approval of the project, the Patton family's opposition
continued, and in August its lawyer wrote directly to Secretary of Defense
Robert McNamara requesting that the Pentagon "withhold any cooperation or
assistance to Twentieth Century Fox or any other motion picture company
which may request a priority for the commercial exploitation of the General's
life and military career in a motion picture."[22] The Defense Department's
general counsel once again pointed out that Fox did not need consent or cooperation to make the film, but that the Pentagon "considers that its cooperation will undoubtedly result in a better picture, since only then will the
Department be given the opportunity to review the script for accuracy.... [The Department] will make every effort to assure that the picture

accurately presents the life and military career of General Patton and that it is otherwise in the best interest of the Department."[23]

★

Delays and Disagreements

McCarthy found that producing a script that would satisfy Defense Department requirements was a major problem. Although he had initially signed Calder Willingham to write the screenplay in April 1965, nothing came of the effort. By June 1966, he had turned to Francis Ford Coppola, then newly out of film school, to write a second version. McCarthy explained that Coppola's youth would be an advantage—he would not be influenced by recollections of Patton. While he did not expect to have the new screenplay done until early fall, McCarthy also hired William Wyler (*Best Years of Our Lives, Ben Hur*) to direct the film. At the same time, the studio informed Don Baruch that it had budgeted *Patton* at more than $10,000,000 and intended to make it a road show picture in 1967. By November though, problems with the script and Wyler's availability had combined to push production back at least until the summer of 1967.[24]

The delay resulted in large measure from disagreements over the script between Wyler and George C. Scott, whom McCarthy had selected to play Patton. Originally, in 1951, McCarthy had envisioned Spencer Tracy in the title role. Later, he considered Burt Lancaster. In 1966, Darryl Zanuck screened *The Bible* for McCarthy and told him, "There's your Patton," pointing to Scott, then hidden under the beard of Abraham. While Scott liked Coppola's script, Wyler didn't. In an attempt to resolve the impasse (conducted through McCarthy, since Scott and Wyler never met or even talked on the phone), McCarthy hired Jim Webb to write a new screenplay by the fall of 1967.[25]

When it was completed, McCarthy found that he still had the same problem, but in reverse. Wyler liked Webb's screenplay, but Scott didn't and said he wouldn't play the part. He wanted to portray Patton "as multifaceted as he really was. Recalling the disagreements over the scripts, Scott said: "I simply refused to play George Patton as the standard cliché you could get from newspaper clips of the time. I didn't want to play him as a hero just to please the Pentagon, and I didn't want to play him as an obvious, gungho bully either. I wanted to play every conceivable facet of the man." Scott believed the conflicts on the film "grew out of trying to serve too many masters. We had to serve the Pentagon, we had to serve General Bradley and his book, we had to

Filming one of the panoramic shots of Patton's advance in Sicily, on location in southern Spain.

serve the Zanucks. If you ride that many horses at the same time, you're going to have problems.''[26]

Frank McCarthy's problem with Scott was soon exacerbated by the problem of finding a new director. Wyler decided to resign from the project when he realized that the film, which was to be shot primarily in Spain, would be too physically strenuous at his age. McCarthy offered the job to Richard Brooks, John Sturges, Henry Hathaway, and Fred Zinnemann, among others.[27] Zinnemann said he turned down the picture because he had already made his military movie, was interested in another project, and didn't ''have tremendous sympathy and admiration for Patton as a man, aside from his obvious military genius.''[28] McCarthy offered Scott's role to Burt Lancaster, Robert Mitchum, Lee Marvin, Rod Steiger, and John Wayne, all of whom turned it down. Wayne later told the producer that he had made a big mistake in doing so, while McCarthy observed that *Patton* would have been a difference picture if Wayne had played Patton.[29]

At that point, Scott again expressed interest in the role—provided McCarthy would go back to Coppola's script. With this impetus, the producer hired Franklin Schaffner to direct the film and Edmund North to rewrite Coppola's script. Starting to work in mid-June 1968, North retained elements that he, Schaffner, and McCarthy agreed on and added new elements as ''necessary or desirable.'' North, who never met Coppola, felt his original ''contribution was as large as it was obvious, and we made every effort to retain the many brilliant things in his script. In addition, his basic approach to the material was the correct one—and that is no mean contribution.''[30]

As with any complete rewrite, North said ''this one involved a good deal of new creative material. The development of a strong central story line between

Patton and Bradley—who served with him first as subordinate, then as his superior—is one major example." North drew on Farago's book as well as General Bradley's autobiography *A Soldier's Story*. He also worked daily with Bradley for about a month, going through the script to ensure perfect technical detail. In October, Bradley, Schaffner, and McCarthy visited the principal battlefields scheduled to be re-created in the movie, and to further ensure accuracy, McCarthy hired retired general Paul Harkins to serve as technical advisor. Harkins, who read five scripts before he agreed to work on the film, had served as Patton's deputy chief of staff from the time of Casablanca until his death. With all this attention to accuracy, McCarthy felt he submitted "an almost perfect" script to the Pentagon in December 1968.[31]

With McCarthy readily agreeing to make two minor corrections, the Defense Department approved the script in less than five weeks. McCarthy pointed out "there wasn't very much they could say," given General Bradley's involvement in and approval of the screenplay.

★
Developing the Character: Devil or Saint?

If the Pentagon had little to question about the film, other people did ask about the movie's purpose. Why was *Patton*, clearly a war movie, being made while the country was involved in an increasingly unpopular war in Vietnam? When he accepted his Academy Award, Edmund North said, "I hope those who see the picture will agree with me that it is not only a war picture, but a peace picture as well." Franklin Schaffner saw it as an antiwar film.[32]

Even Frank McCarthy, whom North described as being "thoroughly integrated into the military" and as having a different viewpoint, insisted that the film's contents imply an antiwar attitude: "The horrors of war are nothing new. But you can't look at what we shot at Almeria and think of it any other way." McCarthy saw Patton himself as very violent, talking of shooting up the enemy and greasing the treads of his tanks with them. Nevertheless, the producer also pointed out that he was "a very genuinely religious man. With women he was very courteous. With people in his immediate staff, he was quite affectionate. With people with whom he had no personal relationship, he was a martinet, a very tough taskmaster. All of these things put together made a fascinating character for me." While *Patton* was clearly a war film that included battles, to McCarthy they served primarily as the "tapestry in the background" against which Patton's character could be developed.[33]

The long process of creating an accurate and dramatic script had not
brought about an agreement among McCarthy, Scott, and Schaffner on just
how to develop that portrait. With the film his labor of love, McCarthy served
as the fulcrum: "I knew Patton and admired him—dramatically, theatrically.
I'm not talking about him as a man. Mrs. Roosevelt thought he was a devil with
horns. Hedda Hopper thought he was a saint. I wanted to get all the facts into
the script." With these facts, McCarthy thought audiences could judge for
themselves the "enigma" that was Patton.[34]

Scott created that character through his acting, but he was also concerned
with guarding what he considered the authenticity of his portrayal. From books
and 3,000 feet of film, Scott studied the man he was to interpret: "I watched
the way he moved and talked. Some of it I absorbed, some I threw out. For instance, he had a high, squeaky voice, like a football coach. The more excited he
got, the higher it got. I didn't use that. People are probably used to my gravel
voice and if I tried to use a high little voice it would be silly." His main consideration "was to not distract the audience with eccentric (albeit factual)
mannerisms. I didn't want the medium to be more arresting than the message."
Scott tried to avoid interjecting his judgments of Patton into his portrayal:
"Hell, you get paid for acting, for giving the *illusion* of believing, not for
actually believing. For chrissakes, no, I didn't believe in what he did any more
than I'd believe in the Marquis de Sade or Frank Merriwell! This is a schizoid
business to start with. The biggest mistake an actor can make is to try to resolve all the differences between himself and the characters he plays."[35]

Scott did develop an "enormous affection" for Patton, "a feeling of amaze-
ment and respect for him," and his only goal was to produce "a fair and
respectful portrait." Given the nature of the man, however, Scott's task sometimes seemed impossible. The ambiguity of Patton's character and actions produced in him mixed feels about the man, the role, and his own performance: "I
studied General Patton as comprehensively as humanly possible. He was a
very complicated human being, and I never came to any conclusion about what
I wanted the character to say, though everybody thought I did." According to
Scott, "Patton actually believed what he was doing was right. . . . But he
wasn't a hypocrite. Even though war was all he cared about, it was what he did
for a living. It was a profession." Scott noted, moreover, that Patton's war
"was unavoidable," not like Vietnam, which the actor called "an obscenity."
In trying to develop the controversial as well as the positive aspects of Patton's
character, Scott told McCarthy he didn't want to play another Buck Turgidson:
"I already played that goddamn part." He also rejected "the glory-hunter
cliché. Patton was a mean sonofabitch, but he was also generous to his men."
In the end, Scott concluded that his portrait was fair: "There are still things

A man of many facets, Patton often took time to pray before and after combat.

about him I hate and things I admire—which makes him a human being, I guess."[36]

To make Patton into a human being—"the point of the whole goddamn thing" according to Scott—he had to make himself over externally and keep "screaming" about dramatic aspects of the characterization until he had a script that finally enabled him to capture the "essence" of the man. While not resembling Patton physically, Scott used his body and the art of film make up to create a realistic impression of the general. He shaved his head daily and used a half-bald hair piece; he straightened his nose with plastic and net; he had his dentist make false teeth to fit over his own, which lengthened his jaw and simulated Patton's longer, patrician jawline; and he added two moles, even though the one on his left ear was hidden.[37]

The physical transformation was simple compared to developing the character. At one point during the shooting, he complained, "It's an unactable part, and I'm not doing too well. It's an inadequate script, and it's very difficult for me." Scott felt Patton "was misunderstood contemporaneously, and he's misunderstood here—and I'm ashamed of being part of it." As an actor, he said he was doing the best he could "to load the part with pyrotechnics, with smoke screens, with every dirty sneak actor's trick to bring out what I want to bring out, but I'm thoroughly disgusted with the entire project."[38]

Of necessity, Franklin Schaffner had most directly to bear the brunt of Scott's animus against the script and the project. As director, he not only had the responsibility for helping Scott create his role, but also he had to work with the rest of the huge cast while also orchestrating the battle scenes. He was more willing to take dramatic license with certain episodes than Scott, whose only concern was with Patton's character and its visual portrayal. On occasion, Schaffner shot around a controversial scene until Scott had calmed down, or he tried to compromise with him. Scott, who felt Schaffner "did a superb job in an extremely difficult assignment,'' recalled that he ''was personally kind to me and tolerant of even my worst peccadillos,'' Scott said his only real unhappiness with the director resulted from Schaffner's ''apparent lack of clout with Fox.''[39]

In fact, *Patton* was not a director's film of the 1960s, one in which the director had total control through the final cut, such as Stanley Kubrick's *2001: A Space Odyssey* or Mike Nichols' *Catch-22*. It much more resembled a movie made in the heyday of the Hollywood studio system, when the director's contribution was only one of several inputs. In *Patton* influence came from Scott, McCarthy, the Zanucks, Generals Bradley and Harkins, and the Pentagon. As a result, Schaffner found it difficult to impose his will on the film, a reality that Scott himself documented.

In one key scene, for example, Patton tells General Lucien K. Truscott, Jr., ''If your conscience won't let you conduct this operation I will relieve you and let someone else do it.'' Scott believed that the way the scene was structured was too harsh, that it created an image of Patton as a megalomaniac, that it suggested he had a callous disregard for the lives of his men, that he was vain and self-serving, that it juxtaposed Bradley's humanitarian devotion to his men against Patton's intransigent lack of flexibility and his indifference to the loss of human life. Feeling ''it was slanderous and false and one-dimensional,'' he refused to do the scene. ''My repugnance drove me to the laborious rewriting of the scene, using the guidelines of Farago's excellent reconstruction of what actually happened and why.''[40]

According to Scott, Schaffner ''was accommodating, if not enthusiastic. He said he did not have the power to alter the text.'' Scott said that McCarthy also ''pleaded a similar unfortunate impotence'' when he received the proposed changes and ''bucked it upstairs to the Zanucks. Word came back to shoot it like it is. I asked to confer with someone—anyone!'' However, he said he met with a curious phenomenon that years of experience had caused him to label ''executivitis transmigrati. . . . The disease sets up a resistance to cablegrams and letters. In fact, [the victim] actually *dematerializes* for relatively short albeit harrowing periods of time.'' Scott explained that the ''malodorous symptoms are shortlived. Most cases clear up completely . . . after the crisis of decision has passed, the scene shot, the frustrated and distraught actor (a carcinomic lump in the studio's corporate breast) removed from the premises.'' As a result, Scott had no choice but to speak the lines as originally written.[41]

Nevertheless, Scott found a way to express his displeasure with the scene. With the agreement of Schaffner, he ''did it supine. Not only as a private (however impotent) little protest of my own, but in the hope that anyone who ever knew General Patton would recognize the falsity of the technique. To my knowledge, *no one* ever witnessed Patton lying down either psychologically or physically in a command situation." General Harkins' reaction confirmed Scott's hopes: "Imagine General Patton lying down on a couch. Oh, me!"[42]

Whatever their differences, Schaffner felt that Scott was "the only American who could play the part. He has no strong screen image as a personality and he has the required vigor, anger and insanity" to become Patton. Schaffner did not begin by admiring the general, but as he read through the research, he found that "one develops an enormous empathy for this man." He saw Patton as "a warrior, a throwback to the 16th century. He was misguided and a man after a headline. He hated peace and wanted to start trouble with the Russians. . . . After the war, he began to fall apart, but we were lucky to have him during the two years that we needed him."[43]

★

Production of Patton

While the script and character development were fomenting, McCarthy also had to work out the practical aspects of his production. Though the film focused on Patton, the producer realized that it would require visual authenticity. Ironically, despite McCarthy's long involvement with the Pentagon in getting the project underway, the Defense Department actually provided very little assistance during production. Throughout the 1950s, the military's refusal to become involved with a Patton film had effectively prevented any studio from undertaking the project, because only the armed forces could then provide the needed tanks and other equipment. By the mid-1960s, the situation had reversed. The services no longer had surplus World War II equipment in any quantity. The Army had changed its position on a Patton film because it knew that a company could now make the movie abroad, and yet the Pentagon could have input into the script only by offering to assist.

McCarthy had decided by June 1966 that the only suitable terrain for shooting the bulk of his film was in Spain and, more important, given Arthur Sylvester's continued presence as assistant secretary of defense for public affairs, Spain had for rent the only available army, World War II tanks, and other equipment he would need. Its government had received the tanks in exchange for American air and naval bases there and, unlike other recipients of obsolete equipment, the Spanish military had maintained it in excellent condition. The Spanish Army also had some old German equipment dating from Franco's friendship with Hitler.

Seeking the use of these men and weapons, McCarthy took Coppola's script to Spanish officials, only to be turned down. According to Spanish military authorities, the screenplay defamed Patton and so discredited soldiers everywhere. McCarthy soon discovered that the translation of the script, done at UCLA, was "perfectly terrible." Once it had been redone with the help of a retired bilingual Spanish general, military authorities readily agreed to assist on the film. When he asked about the cost of such help, the military replied, "That's easy," and produced a mimeographed memorandum stating rates per day for each soldier by rank. McCarthy also paid for transportation, gasoline for the tanks and other vehicles, and subsistence for the soldiers while working on the film. Ultimately, about $6,000,000 of the film's $12,500,000 cost went to the Spanish Army. But in return, McCarthy got his combatting armies.[44]

While *Patton* is first of all a character study, the combat sequences provide the framework within which the actors function; they are in the finest tradition of the Hollywood war movie. As often is the case, the movie was not shot in chronological order, the last battle being done first. In early February 1969, Schaffner and his crew went to Segovia in Central Spain to film Patton's daring dash across France to relieve the siege at Bastogne. After waiting a week, enough snow fell for them to duplicate the wintery conditions of December 1944. Unlike the soldiers in *Battle of the Bulge*, Schaffner's army looks cold because it is cold. From there, the crew went to the Pamplona area to film Patton's campaign across France into Germany, and to Almeria in southernmost Spain to shoot the battles of Kasserine Pass, El Guettar, and the Sicily invasion, with the principal photography being completed by the end of May. According to General Harkins, the goal in all this location work was to create as realistic battle scenes as possible.[45]

To accomplish this, Schaffner had practically a whole army at his disposal—in military terms, *Patton* was filmed at infantry battalion strength. The Air Force consisted of four Heinkels, four Messerschmidts, six T-6s, three Nords, and one observation plane; the armor of thirty-four German Tiger Tanks (converted M-48s) and twenty American M-41s and M-42s. The special effects crew made its usual contribution, blowing up jeeps, burning tanks, and simulating airplane strafing. Schaffner received additional help from the Sultan of Morocco, who loaned him his 10,000-man honor guard, colorfully uniformed, with horses and camels richly decorated, to re-create the review staged for Patton by the Sultan in return for liberating his country. Schaffner also went to Crete to film with Navy assistance an amphibious landing for the black and white "newreel" shots of Patton and Bradley coming ashore in Sicily. Finally, the film company went to Knutsford, England to film Patton's controversial speech there in 1944, in which he warned of the threat he perceived Russia posed to the West.[46]

With the exception of the few simulated newsreel segments, *Patton* was filmed in 70-millimetre, Dimension 150, with color by Delux. The process produced an awesome sense of depth and grandeur, especially in the long, open battlefield shots. Despite the antiwar material McCarthy found in these scenes, the very beauty of the pictures tends to dissipate the feeling of horror created by the images of death and destruction that are portrayed. Moreover, because the battle sequences were reproduced as giant, impersonal panoramas rather than hand-to-hand, small unit struggles, the viewer ultimately becomes detached from any sense of war's brutality. If any feeling emerges from the sweeping vistas of combat, it is the impression that war is beautiful, whether fought in the boiling desert or the freezing snow. The vastness of the landscapes reduces to virtually nothing the conflicting armies, the tanks, the civilians caught up in war. The audience's attention is focused on one man, George C. Scott, who becomes Patton and totally dominates the film in a great screen performance.

Interpretations

To Franklin Schaffner, contributing to the success of this performance, not staging the huge battle scenes was the most impressive task he had to face. He saw *Patton* as "the personal story . . . the intimate story of a man involved in great events." And he considered that man "our necessary evil." To Frank McCarthy, Patton was an "enigma." Karl Malden, who portrayed General Bradley, would not have wanted to serve under Patton, but he felt "it was lucky he was on our side." And within George C. Scott's characterization rest all these interpretations, all these reactions to Patton, the general and the man.[47]

When he began the project, McCarthy had hoped he could present a many-faceted Patton, a man in whom people could see what they wanted, and he believed he had succeeded. While he considered *Patton* a war film "because it had battles in it," he also left it up to the viewer to decide whether it was a war film or an antiwar film. He thought people came out having "fulfilled their own wishes as to what they wanted to see. Some people came out saying, 'What an antiwar picture,' meaning wasn't it grueling, wasn't he rough. Other people came out saying, 'If we just had somebody like that in Vietnam.'" McCarthy, himself, disagreed with both North and Schaffner, who thought they had made an antiwar movie.[48]

Ironically, McCarthy himself was ambivalent about what kind of film he had in fact made. He contended that his first purpose had been to make enter-

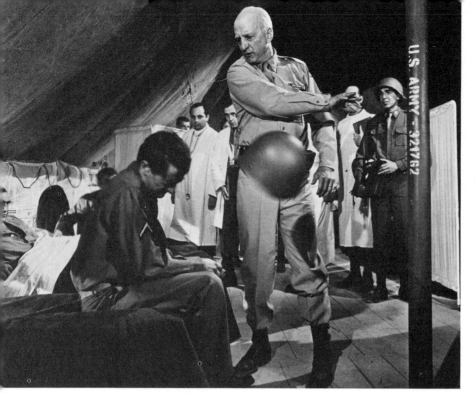

George C. Scott re-creates the slapping incident, Patton's most controversial action.

tainment, not a war film. He wanted to depict "a close-up portrayal of this man. Patton was the most explosive commander in the war, or perhaps in military history. He was pious and profane, brutal and kind—and we show him with all his faults as well as virtues." But he conceded that once "you say this is a military man and a war, you instantly evoke a feeling of urgency." Though he disagreed with Schaffner as well as North, the screenwriter, about the film's thrust, he did insist that the graphic filming would be antiwar material: "The horrors of war are nothing new. But you can't look at what we shot at Almeria and think of it any other way."[49]

Even though Edmund North has always seen the film as making an antiwar statement, he admits, "I see other interpretations possible." Patton's own personality, his ambiguities and beliefs, all captured by Scott, contributed to these divergent reactions. North said that he had attempted "to be as objective as I could in whatever contribution I made to the film. The easy thing to do would have been to make a monster. All the material in the world was available." He recalled that he constantly had to catch himself and say, "But, wait a minute. He also did this which was positive and good and necessary." In summing up his feelings, North said he felt that the "strongest comment the picture makes is that war is the kind of business that requires *this* kind of man. I think this is a commentary on the institutions of war itself, condemnatory of its brutality, mindless glory-seeking, and insensitivity to the value of human life."[50]

Whether people actually came away from *Patton* perceiving this commentary and so seeing the film as an antiwar statement is another matter. The blood and gore were too beautiful and too remote to create a sense of revulsion. More important, the combat sequences conveyed a sense of the excitement rather than the horror of war. At times, Patton muses on the negative aspects of combat, the death of good men, the waste of energy. But from his opening monologue onward, Patton sees war as an adventure for himself and his men, a game to be played and won. Despite the losses, he can't help but admit, "I love it. God help me, I do love it so." If the film had ended with Patton's fatal accident shortly after the war's end, his death would have reinforced the images of death and destruction throughout the film. But at the close, audiences are left with a triumphant, if restless, general and a glorious victory in a necessary war.

The film would undoubtedly have made its comments on war and brutality much more powerfully if Schaffner had been permitted to shoot two scenes that North had included in his script. In one that George C. Scott described as "beautifully written," Patton becomes so "revolted" by his examination of a death camp that he forces the local citizens to inspect it one by one and clean it up. The hamlet's mayor returns to his office and commits suicide. Scott said, "I had seen Patton's face countless times in the newreel footage as he emerged from the ovens—his eyes wet, struggling to control his gorge, a handkerchief held to his mouth, and the most chilling expression of revulsion coupled with vengeance I have ever beheld in a human being's eyes. It could easily have been the paramount sequence in the film—perhaps of any film." In reply to Scott's inquiry about why the scenes were eliminated he was told that Darryl Zanuck felt they were inappropriate because "we've seen that sort of thing before."[51]

North's ending, another scene that was eliminated, would have created a strong final impact in an antiwar statement that created its image by focusing on the victims of the conflict. According to North, his script called for a closing shot of Patton's grave in the huge American Military Cemetery in Luxembourg: "From his grave the camera was to pull slowly back and upward, finally including the graves of all the 6,000 dead of the Third Army. I thought then—and I think now—that this would have been the right ending—one that would have made a powerful statement. But I couldn't get anyone to agree with me. They said it was too downbeat."[52]

The ending aside, if *Patton* had appeared any time before the mid-1960s, people would have seen it as simply another glorification of a great military leader and a confirmation of America's military superiority in the world. Because it was released while the Vietnam War still raged, *Patton* offered the viewer other options. Having been exposed to antiwar rhetoric and an increasingly unpopular war, people had new perspectives on war and the military. Perhaps for the first time, they could see the negative aspects in a Patton-type character and his philosophy of combat. On the other hand, at a time when people were beginning to realize that the United States had been defeated in Vietnam, *Patton* offered a ready explanation for the quagmire in which the military was caught. If only we had a Patton, we could go through the North Vietnamese and Vietcong as Patton had gone through the Germans. Edmund North provides his own answer to why people saw both explanations in a film he considered antiwar: "I believe it was because each person brought to it his own underlying feelings about the Vietnam war. Those who were appalled by Vietnam found Patton a fascinating antihero. Those—like Richard Nixon—who regarded Vietnam as a noble enterprise could find comfort and support in Patton's self-righteous and dedicated savagery."[53]

In the final analysis, people were left with the power of Scott's performance, which overshadowed all the scenes of combat, all the ambiguities of the film, all the other actors. His portrayal was enough to dissolve the twenty-year opposition of Patton's family to a movie. His daughter, Ruth Totten, went to see McCarthy's rendering of her father's career "screaming and kicking inside, but, I hope, in a calm and ladylike fashion outside." She expected the worst because the publicity that the press had given Patton for years "was so disgusting and so unfair that we could not imagine a medium as vulgar as the movies giving him any kind of break at all. We had a mental block that they would picture him as a coarse, cursing, nosepicking, belching gorilla of a man, none of which things he was."

After seeing the film, Mrs. Totten had to admit that the family had been wrong to assume that any film would necessarily present a brutal picture. But she found some virtue in the family's prolonged opposition, believing that if the movie had been made sooner, Scott might not have played her father. She was impressed that the actor "had obviously made a deep study of General Patton both on film and in his writings and books written about him. So many of his gestures, particularly his 'mirthless smile,' were so true to life that it gave me quite a start." According to Mrs. Totten, Scott's deep study also enabled the actor to get under Patton's skin and indicated to the family that Scott "not only liked General Patton, he understood him—which few people did, do, or ever will." She thought his performance was a "tour de force and he has made a great contribution, not to the so-called Patton legend but to film history." More than that, she thought Scott conveyed her father's dedication to his country better than she had ever seen it done before—a dedication that put country before wife and children.[54]

Patton advances.

Not everyone would of course agree with Patton's priorities. Nevertheless, *Patton* illuminated all aspects of the general's personality and stimulated a wide diversity of reactions to the man and the movie. Nowhere was the multiplicity of responses more evident than among reviewers. While they universally praised Scott's performance, the critical response to the film ranged from accolades to outrage, sometimes within the same review and even in the same sentence.

In the *New York Times* Vincent Canby wrote, "The real surprise is that the film, though long (and from my point of view, appalling) is so consistently fascinating." He thought the film "looks and sounds like the epic American war movie that the Hollywood establishment has always wanted to make but never had the guts to do before." The film was "an incredible gas, especially in this time and place." In one long sentence, he then managed to capture the entire flavor of the movie: "*Patton* is a loving, often sentimental, semi-official portrait of a man it characterizes as a near schizo, a man who admitted that he damn well loved war, was surprised and somewhat taken aback when men near to him were killed, who quoted the Bible, believed in reincarnation, had the political acumen of Marie Antoinette, and according to the movie, somehow so touched General Omar Bradley with his folksy honesty ('I'm a prima donna—I know it!') that Bradley went through the war looking always as if he were about to weep." Canby found that for a "supposedly sympathetic character in a superspectacle" to admit his love of war was "in a negative way, a refreshing change from the sort of conventional big-budget movie claptrap that keeps saying that war is hell, while simultaneously showing how much fun it really is." Canby didn't think that *Patton* marked an advance "in the civilizing processes of our culture," but he thought it was "a good deal less hypocritical than most patriotic American war movies." Recognizing his contradictory responses to the film, he conceded, "If I sound ambivalent about *Patton*, it's because the movie itself is almost as ambivalent about its hero."[55]

The *New Yorker* reviewer, Pauline Kael, also pointed out the ambiguities of the title character and of the movie. But she had much less trouble deciding what she thought of *Patton*, writing that in its almost three hours, "there is not a single lyrical moment. The figure of General George Patton, played by George C. Scott, is a Pop hero, but visually the movie is in a style that might be described as imperial. It does not really look quite like any other movie, and that in itself is an achievement (though not necessarily an aesthetic one)." She seemed to be unhappiest with the film's refusal to take a position on Patton, which she concluded was probably as "deliberately planned as a Rorschach test. He is what people who believe in military values can see as the true military hero—the red-blooded American who loves to fight and whose crude talk is straight talk. He is also what people who despise militarism can see as the worst kind of red-blooded American mystical maniac who *believes* in fighting; for them, Patton can be the symbolic proof of the madness of the whole military complex."

Because the film plays Patton "both ways—crazy and great—and more ways than that, because he's a comic-strip general and even those who are antiwar may love comic strips," Kael suspected that people would most likely see in the film what they wanted, with the result that "a lot of them are going to think *Patton* is a great movie." However, she thought the film "strings us along and holds out on us. If we don't just want to have our prejudices greased, we'll find it confusing and unsatisfying, because we aren't given enough information to evaluate Patton's actions." She pointed out that Patton is treated "as if he were the spirit of war, yet the movie begs the fundamental question about its hero: Is this the kind of man a country needs when it's at war?" She further suggested that "every issue raised is left unresolved."[56]

Despite their equivocations about the film and its hero, in the end, both reviewers revealed their antipathy toward the man in objecting to the movie's subtitle: *A Salute to a Rebel.* Kael asked, "Whom does Twentieth Century Fox think it's kidding? What was Patton a rebel against except humanitarianism?" Canby thought Scott dominated the film, "even its ambiguities," and was "con-

In the snows of northern Spain, Scott portrays Patton's brilliant rescue of the Americans surrounded at Bastogne during the Battle of the Bulge.

tinuously entertaining and, occasionally, even appealing," but he concluded that the actor "never quite convinced me that Patton, by any stretch of the imagination, could be called a rebel against anything except the good, gray, dull forces of bleeding heart liberalism."[57]

Perhaps it was this arch-authoritarianism that appealed to Richard Nixon. Perhaps it was Patton's rabid anti-Communism, his desire to turn against Russia after the defeat of Germany, his lust for combat and compulsion to emerge victorious from every struggle. Perhaps the president simply appreciated the film's excellent character study of Patton. In any case, Nixon saw the film on April 1, 1970 and again on April 25, just five days before he ordered American forces into Cambodia. In his 1977 interview with David Frost, the ex-president denied that the film had had any effect on his decision to order the incursion. Nevertheless, while the troops were still in Cambodia, Nixon commented on the film to a group of businessmen and financial leaders he had called to the White House. He talked about Patton's accomplishment of the impossible in rescuing the men trapped during the Battle of the Bulge, an action that other generals said was impossible. He also cited Patton's asking the chaplain to pray for good weather and then decorating him when the sun came out. He said that now every chaplain in Vietnam was praying for early rain so that the Communists could not easily re-occupy the sanctuaries then being destroyed. He observed, "You have to have the will and determination to go out and to do what is right for America."[58]

Why did Nixon find Patton and the movie so intriguing? Hugh Sidey, then *Life* magazine's presidential correspondent, suggested that Nixon may have empathized with a man who had lived through criticism, endured rejection, and was in the end still willing to try what seemed impossible, to take the bold stroke. Sidey also pointed out that like Patton, Nixon had faith in God and was a complex man, one who had as many ambiguities and facets as the general. According to Sidey, Nixon was "an insecure man. He had an inferiority complex. . . . He cast around for stronger people. He was fascinated with Kennedy. Part of this was the sureness with which Kennedy moved through this world. He liked Kissinger and Connolly for this reason. And I am sure that he thought that the Wayne model, the old-fashion courage [offered the same strength]. Then the *Patton* film comes along. Here's a man in battle. Here is an argument for boldness, innovation, ready-made . . . It was just a marvelously articulated argument for precisely what Nixon fancied he was doing in Cambodia."[59]

The film's influence on Nixon went farther than his decision to invade Cambodia. Ladislas Farago, author of the book on which *Patton* was based, asked Margaret Mead why she thought Nixon was so fascinated with Patton. According to the anthropologist, Nixon "thrives on opposition. It is a form of stimulation for him. His enemies should take heed. Any figure who had had to make decisions in the face of opposition as he has done will seem appealing to him." Dr. Mead also observed that the mementos of the president's career were relics of his fights, his victories. Similarly, his book was concerned with challenges and crises, perhaps matching those Patton went through in his career and in the film.[60]

Like Nixon, some people undoubtedly went to see *Patton* to empathize with the man and to find strength to act. Some went to see a major antiwar film, others to learn how war should really be fought. Most, however, went simply to be entertained by a superb actor and an excellent film. Whatever their reasons, thousands saw *Patton* and it became a smash hit, giving Twentieth Century Fox two concurrent box-office successes about war. Ultimately, McCarthy's film became the most profitable or second most profitable military film of all time, depending on how one classifies *M*A*S*H,* the other Fox hit of 1970.

CHAPTER THIRTEEN

ILLUSION AND REALITY OF WAR

★

Whatever its message, *Patton* was perceived by audiences as a film about war and, more specifically, as a biography of one man in war. Most people also perceived *M*A*S*H* and *Catch-22* as portraying men in battle, or at least men's relationship to battle. While both films comment on relationships in society, neither in fact looks at men in combat, external appearances notwithstanding. In contrast, *Tora! Tora! Tora!* looks at the failure to prepare adequately for battle, but its dramatic and visual shortcomings negate its conscious effort to portray war. Ultimately, each movie says far less about men in combat than its military framework suggests or than most audiences probably concluded.

★

M*A*S*H

For most people *M*A*S*H* is a war film or at least a spoof of war films; some have seen it as a war comedy, others as an antiwar statement. One critic called it "an animated cartoon with the cartoon figures played by real people." Although the story's setting is the Korean War, many thought its director, Robert Altman, was making a comment about the Vietnam War. One reviewer suggested, "A strong case could be made for *M*A*S*H* as a clinically ambigu-

Commander Ed Stafford, the technical advisor, discusses the filming of the miniature sequences for Tora! Tora! Tora! *with producer Elmo Williams and Fox's miniature expert. Note edge of painted backdrop.*

ous study of the way Joe College and Fred Pre-med adjust—sell out—to a pervasive, corrupting system like War."[1] In fact, M*A*S*H is simply a portrayal of people interacting within a structured bureaucracy that just happens to be a military hospital. Altman himself observed, "It's told with war as a background—we hear the firing, but the only gun we actually see in the entire picture is that used by the timekeeper at the football game to mark the end of each half."[2]

The only real connections the film has to combat or the military are the uniforms the characters wear and references to the battles that provide the MASH (Mobile Army Surgical Hospital) doctors with their patients. The setting could just as easily be any war or even any disaster area or crowded freeway for all the relationship the mutilated bodies have to war. The characters make infrequent comments about combat, but they show no concern for the progress of the war they are supposedly involved in. As much as anything else, M*A*S*H can be described as a satire on doctors and the medical profession, closely related to Paddy Chayefsky's Hospital or Otto Preminger's Such Good Friends. George C. Scott, who starred in Hospital, observed, "Half the budget was raw meat. Every time he [Robert Altman] got in trouble he flashed back to the operating room with the blood. Cheap tricks. To me, the worst sin of all is cheapness and shoddiness."[3]

The producer, Ingo Preminger (Otto's brother), saw no need to create an authentic military atmosphere. After an initial inquiry to the Pentagon about acquiring MASH tents from the Army, he never returned with a script or made further requests for assistance. Instead, he shot the film on the Twentieth Century Fox Ranch outside Los Angeles, renting helicopters and other equipment from commercial sources. Ironically, despite the movie's irreverent portrayal of the relationships between officers, the rowdy military discipline, some of its language, and its explicit sexuality, Don Baruch indicated that the Defense Department might have provided some limited assistance if Preminger had followed up his initial inquiry.[4] His reaction suggests that the Public Affairs Office saw the film primarily as a comedy that implied little, if any, judgment about war and the military, pro or con.

M*A*S*H had its origins in a comic novel of the same name by an Army surgeon writing of his experiences in an Army field hospital during the Korean War. Altman ultimately fashioned a screenplay written by Ring Lardner, Jr. into a film that portrayed the adventures of three surgeons in a MASH hospital. Lardner felt the film would have been better if some things had not changed. He was critical of the movie's opening, saying that "the Keystone Kops spill and slapstick" indicate a "too self-conscious effort to establish the film as a comedy." He faulted the football sequence for being "too long and ending too abruptly," and he thought the barrage of abuse heaped on Major Burns after his "broadcast" lovemaking with "Hot Lips" was too extended. He also regretted the implication that Lieutenant Dish was having an affair with Hawkeye, feeling that it vitiated her supreme sacrifice of giving herself to the impotent dentist to restore his virility.[5]

Lardner's criticism of Altman's portrayal of women in M*A*S*H mirrored feminist attacks that condemned his films for "an adolescent view of women as sex objects." Altman, however, defended his treatment of "Hot Lips": " the precise point of that character was that women *were* and *are* treated as sex objects. They can't blame me for the condition because I report it. We're dealing with a society in which most of the significant activity until now has been initiated by males. If you make a western or a sports story or a story about big business or gangsters, it's automatically going to reflect the secondary positions women hold."[6]

Altman has seen himself reporting on society in his films. But he perceives that society and the people who interact within it in a largely unfocused, unstructured manner, and he sees it as a cruel society. To him, M*A*S*H was "supposed to be a cruel film. That's what it was. That's what I see constantly. Certainly that time and certainly that situation breeds that." For Altman, the settings he uses to show this cruelty are irrelevant. M*A*S*H has no more to do with war than *Nashville* has to do with country and western music. When asked if it were true that M*A*S*H was bitterly antiwar, he replied: "Do you know anybody who is prowar?" To the charge that some viewers had perceived the film as a prowar statement because of its lack of structure and the emphasis on emotional rather than literal accuracy, Altman assumed that "they are people who need to see children burning to think something is antiwar." He dismissed them as "people who want a political statement rather than an artistic one."[7]

With few exceptions, reviewers and moviegoers accepted M*A*S*H as a superior artistic statement and as a movie about men in war. But as with *Patton*, people saw in the film what they wanted to see. To most viewers, the uniforms, military forms of address, and military-type equipment constituted a war film. These visual and verbal devices are necessary ingredients in films about war, but a movie about combat or even about the military in general requires more. It must have some visual and dramatic connection to combat or to a military bureaucracy, and it must clearly establish the direct influence of these on the characters' actions. M*A*S*H focuses on doctors who happen to be wearing Army uniforms but who show no interest or concern about the Korean War or any war or about the military establishment. While M*A*S*H may say something about man in an artificially structured society, it makes a comment about men in combat or in the military only insofar as the military reflects society as a whole.

★

Catch-22

Catch-22, also released in 1970, has little more to do with war than *M*A*S*H*. Based on Joseph Heller's 1961 novel, it focuses on man versus the system, human relationships, survival, dying. War serves only as the framework for the characters' actions, although the story originated in Heller's own World War II experiences as a B-25 bombardier. Unlike Yossarian, the hero of his novel, however, Heller didn't try to avoid combat: "I actually *hoped* I would get into combat. I was just nineteen and there were a great many movies being made about the war; it all seemed so dramatic and heroic. . . . I felt like I was going to Hollywood."[8] Perhaps the gap between the image and the reality inspired him. In any case, Heller wrote one of the most original comic novels of its time. But its images do not deal with men in combat. Nor do the movie's, despite the filmmakers' efforts to ensure visual authenticity of the locales and the aerial sequences.

John Calley and Martin Ransohoff, the producers, acquired a squadron of B-25 bombers, which Frank Tallman restored to their World War II configuration and flying condition. Calley and production designer Richard Sylbert found a site near Guaymas, Mexico, that resembled Heller's fictional airbase in Corsica. They built a runway, base, and roads to represent the book's island of Pianosa. With the planes and pilots that Tallman brought together, director Mike Nichols staged and filmed the air action in a style befitting *Twelve O'Clock High*, or even *Wings*.[9]

Nichols did see a couple of movies about the air war because his film would have flying sequences. But he found nothing useful because the book "isn't a literal rendering of what happened. It's a dream." According to Andrew Marton, who helped stage the flying sequences, Nichols had no intention of making a flying epic. He saw airplanes in flight as a cliche representative of most combat extravaganzas, and to have included them might have made *Catch-22* just another aerial war picture. Even so, the opening montage is one of the great flying sequences in all of film history. From total darkness, the screen gradually becomes lighter as the sun comes up through time-lapse photography. The barking of a dog gives way to the sound of plane engines coughing to life. Finding the bombers as they warm up, the camera follows them, seemingly without a cut, as they rumble down the runway, take off into the lightening sky, and pass one after another in perfect order behind a shattered control tower. In a later aerial sequence, filmed with a telephoto lens, the bombers are shown taking off fully loaded. The camera makes the air shimmer as the planes rise, seemingly one on top of the next, shaking as they climb into the sky. One wonders if the war could have been fought with such machines.

It was, but not in Heller's novel or Nichols' movie. The author himself confessed, "I wrote it during the Korean War and aimed it for the one after that." He had warned that *Catch-22* was no more about the Army Air Corps than Kafka's *The Trial* was about Prague, that "the cold war is what I was truly talking about, not the World War."[10] Nicholas saw the movie as a story about dying: "And the theme is about when you get off. At what point do you draw the line beyond which you won't go? . . . that you can't live unless you know what you'll stop at."[11]

Catch-22's characters wear uniforms, fly planes that drop bombs, die in combat unseen, receive medals for bravery, and chase women during their free time as in most traditional war movies. But combat only symbolizes the threat to Yossarian that all of civilization poses to his survival. The continuing visual image of that threat, the dying Snowden, an image that is repeated in ever greater detail as the movie progresses, had its basis in actual combat. On Heller's thirty-seventh mission, his gunner was wounded and bled copiously into his flight suit. As a consequence, Heller grew petrified of flight: "War was like a movie to me [until then]. I suddenly realized, 'Good God! They're trying to kill me too.' War wasn't much fun after that." He took a ship home when his tour was over and didn't fly again for another fifteen years.[12] Snowden's wound initiates a similar realization for Yossarian. It tells him it's time to get off, to get himself grounded. As presented in the movie, however, Snowden's wound is inflicted by some distant impersonal war, and the recurring scene is surrealistic, the images part of a dream.

In trying to draw the line, trying to stop the insanity that confronts him, Yossarian meets his Catch-22: "In order to be grounded, I've got to be crazy. And I must be crazy to keep flying. But if I ask to be grounded, that means that I'm not crazy anymore and I've got to keep flying." In the end, Yossarian does the only thing possible, he deserts: "It's the only sensible thing for me to do." After fighting for his country for three years: "Now I'm gonna start fighting for myself." When he is warned that he will "be on the run with no friends! You'll live in constant danger of betrayal!" Yossarian yells: "I live that way now!" And he is off, carrying a yellow rubber life raft past the row of bombers, into the sea, inflating it as he goes, to paddle to Sweden.

Yossarian is Everyman, confronting a world that seems to control his destiny and seems to render him powerless, but it is a universal world, not the distinct world of war or combat. Perhaps Heller's words capture Yossarian's moment of truth better than the movie's dialogue with its visual images of the bombers and the base: " 'But you can't just turn your back on all your responsibilities and run away from them,' Major Danby insisted. 'It's such a negative move. It's escapist.' Yossarian laughed with buoyant scorn and shook his head. 'I'm not running *away* from my responsibilities. I'm running *to* them. There's nothing negative about running away to save my life. You know who the escapists are, don't you Danby? Not me and Orr.' ''[13]

The nature of this message combined with the book's structural complexities made for a seemingly impossible task in transferring Heller's novel to the screen. Heller himself thought the film sacrificed most of his humor "in a vain attempt to establish a 'story line'—something the novel didn't have to begin with." He had had "virtually no hope" that *Catch-22* would become a good film: "And if I had participated in making it, I would have been compelled to care how it turned out." He did get to know Alan Arkin (Yossarian) and Nichols before shooting began and found them "so concerned about doing 'justice' to the book—which is, of course, impossible in *any* film—that I found myself rooting for them."[14]

His rooting and the $15,000,000 cost of the movie were not able to produce a film that attracted large crowds, and it became one of the financial disasters of 1970. Heller thought that *Catch-22* turned out "OK" despite his initial lack of expectations. He also believed that if the film "had been foreign, in black and white, without stars and based on an unknown novel, it would have been a major critical success. This is not a comment on the quality of the film but on the consistency of film reviews.[15] As it was, reviews ranged from Vicent Canby's "quite simply the best American film I have seen this year" to Stanley Kauffmann's opinion that the film broke most of the promises the opening sequence made and ended up "a disappointment." Canby put his finger on one of the problems when he said, "Great films are complete in themselves. *Catch-22* isn't, but enough remains so that the film becomes a series of brilliant mirror images of a Strobe-lit reality."[16]

Like Canby, the readers of Heller's novel could bring his words to the theater and merge the two cultural forms. Because they did not expect a war movie, they were not disappointed by the lack of combat. Many other people probably came expecting to see aerial warfare, given the film's advertisements and publicity campaign, which had focused on Nichols' fleet of bombers. However beautifully they appeared taking off and in flight, audiences quickly discovered the planes had little to do with the story, which turned out to be a serious and reverent attempt to pictorialize the abstract, satiric, and sometimes philosophic ideas that were densely packed in Heller's novel. The screen, in general, resists such efforts, and ironically, Nichols only complicated his task by visually stressing the war film genre as the vehicle for visualizing Heller's themes. Nothing is more central to a consideration of war than life and death.

But with few exceptions, combat films have dealt with the subject in raw, basic terms— people fight and die.

While *Catch-22* offered little to people who were looking for escapist entertainment, it impressed those opposed to the war in Vietnam. To them, Yossarian's paddling away to Sweden, to life, made sense. To them, combat or no combat, *Catch-22's* message was clearly antiwar. Nichols did ''suppose'' this was true, but he noted, ''Nobody wants to make a pro-war film. And I don't know what an anti-war film is. It's like 'Fuck Hate.' Nobody likes war. It'd be like making an anti-evil film. Or a pro-good film.''[17]

Hardly anyone likes war. But for a majority of the American people in 1970, heroes didn't run away either, even to live. Patton might harrangue his men with the idea that ''no bastard ever won a war by dying for his country.'' But death had always been an unavoidable and noble part of Patton's life. For most Americans, the message proclaimed hundreds of time on the motion picture screen had always been: a man can have no higher calling than to fight and die for his country. Yossarian's actions, his desire to stop flying, his escape to save his life would alienate the average moviegoer, just as James Garner's philosophy of cowardice in *The Americanization of Emily* had done six years before. While five million people may have read *Catch-22* by 1970[18], a combination of readers and Americans opposed to the war in Vietnam did not comprise a large enough audience to make Nichols' film successful at the box office.

In addition, *Catch-22* had many flaws. Nichols attempted a serious inquiry into human survival and death. Yet his concept was a hazardous undertaking, because Heller's novel encompassed too many ideas and levels of meaning to deal with visually in a brief time. Consequently, for most viewers, *Catch-22* failed intellectually—if not artistically and dramatically. Because it could not offer people Heller's ideas effectively, and because it did not attempt to depict the typical war film's action, it failed commercially. Still, *Catch-22* contains much beauty and even more meaning and remains a noble failure.

The same cannot be said of *Tora! Tora! Tora!*

Tora! Tora! Tora!

In the hyperbole of the ad writers, *Tora! Tora! Tora!* was ''The Most Spectacular Film Ever Made.'' The headlines over Vincent Canby's review in the *New York Times* described the movie less exuberantly: ''Tora-ble, Tora-ble, Tora-ble.''[19] Seldom has a studio spent so much money on a film—at least

Illusion and Reality of War

$25,000,000—and received so little visual and dramatic effect in return. Darryl Zanuck and Twentieth Century Fox adopted the style and scale of *The Longest Day*, attempting to duplicate its box-office success. Using the same technique as *The Longest Day* (and its imitators, *Battle of the Bulge* and *Bridge at Remagen*), *Tora! Tora! Tora!* re-created a historical event, the sneak attack on Pearl Harbor, by crosscutting between the opposing forces as their actions led to confrontation. *Tora*, Japanese for tiger, was the code word used to notify the carriers that surprise had been achieved and the raid could go forward as planned.

U.S.S. Arizona explodes during re-creation of Pearl Harbor in Tora! Tora! Tora!

Done in a pseudodocumentary style with close attention to historical accuracy, the film fails to create any dramatic tension as events lead up to Sunday morning, December 7. Its characters seem to be marking time, waiting for the film's highlight of sweeping destruction that is portrayed in vivid color and designed to attract audiences. *The Longest Day* ultimately overcame this dramatic problem because it portrayed D-Day authentically, because it dramatized a glorious victory, and because its characters were believeable. But despite four years of effort and at least $25,000,000, no one could instill the same illusions of reality into *Tora! Tora! Tora!* Even more important, no one could disguise the fact that the film depicted the Japanese killing American men, sinking American ships, and destroying American planes, materiel, and facilities with virtually no American response. Pearl Harbor remained a "Day of Infamy."

Why would Americans want to be reminded of such a day? Before the film went before the cameras, Darryl Zanuck explained, "Audiences may not think they are waiting for *Tora! Tora! Tora!* but audiences never know what they want until it's put in front of them. *Tora! Tora!* will say something about today."[20] When the film became embroiled in controversy while still in production, Zanuck took out full page advertisements in the *New York Times* and the *Washington Post* to further justify portraying the defeat. He wrote that in his film he hoped "to arouse the American public to the necessity for preparedness in this acute missile age where a sneak attack could occur at any moment. You cannot arouse the public by showing films where Americans always win and where we are invincible. You can only remind the public by revealing to them how we once thought we were invincible but suffered a sneak attack in which practically half our fleet was lost." He claimed that *Tora! Tora! Tora!* was not "merely a movie but an accurate and dramatic slice of history that should never have occurred but did occur, and the purpose of producing this film is to remind the public of the tragedy that happened to us and to ensure that it will never happen again."[21]

While Zanuck was attempting to give significance to *Tora! Tora! Tora!*, his son Richard, vice president in charge of production at Twentieth Century Fox, was expounding on the studio's philosophy in other terms: "We go for idea pictures which contain a lot of entertainment. We don't get involved with the message pictures or anything very preachy. We don't try to do anything terribly intellectual—that can be dangerous." For the most part, he said, Fox made "sheer entertainment pictures" compared to other studios.[22] Elmo Williams, the producer of *Tora! Tora! Tora!*, rebutted Darryl Zanuck's claims of social significance for his movie in blunter terms: "There is only one reason why studios make films and that is to make money. Nothing else." He did admit, though, that filmmakers have "consciences: [We] are concerned with telling stories fairly and presenting the truth as much as we can, especially in the case of films that require cooperation of a government agency."[23]

The failure of *Tora! Tora! Tora!* had nothing to do with its accuracy or truthfulness. It reflected the contemporary historical interpretation of events that led up to December 7 and the reasons for the military's lack of preparedness for the surprise attack. Even though the film showed a military defeat, Williams said that no one in Washington asked him to distort the facts or "play anything down." The screenplay was based on two contemporary books about Pearl Harbor, Ladislas Farago's *The Broken Seal* and Gordon Prange's *Tora, Tora, Tora.* When Fox first circulated *The Broken Seal* (the story of the breaking of the Japanese code) throughout the studio, readers found the Pearl Harbor section of the book most exciting. However, the production received its primary impetus when Fox acquired Prange's best-selling book shortly after it was published in Japan in 1966.[24]

Developing a screenplay that portrayed both sides of the story fairly and yet did not "take years" to tell required great effort, but turning the script into a movie seemed an insurmountable task. One producer to whom the studio initially offered the project turned it down, asking, "Do you want to bury me?" Elmo Williams finally received the job, largely because of his success in handling the production logistics on films such as *The Longest Day*, *The Blue Max*, and *Those Magnificent Men in Their Flying Machines.* Also, his early career as a film editor and his Academy Award for *High Noon* gave him the expertise necessary to supervise the editing of a long and complex movie. Actually, he had to edit two films, one made in Japan portraying the Japanese story of the attack, and one shot mostly in Hawaii, re-creating the attack on December 7. The separately made stories were then edited into one integrated film.

To bring order to a project of this scope, Williams explained that he took "a very simple approach. . . . I used the Japanese point of view, the airman's point of view because it allowed me to use miniatures and to get around the problem of ships and planes that no longer existed, things we couldn't build." However important the "things" might be, actual filming had to take place at Pearl Harbor if the re-creation of December 7 was to have any sense of authenticity. Consequently, in July 1967, Williams and Richard Fleischer, the film's director, went to Hawaii with Defense Department approval to scout the necessary locations. They found that Hickman Field, now Honolulu's international airport was unavailable but that Ford Island and other airfields and military areas that had been involved in the Japanese attack could be utilized during filming.[25]

At the same time, Williams faced the problem of accumulating "things" with which to dress up his locations in Hawaii and Japan. While he was forced to resort to miniatures for establishing shots of the Japanese fleet and the American ships at Pearl Harbor, Williams managed to create reasonable facsimiles of a few key ships for onboard sequences. In Japan, the studio built full-size replicas of parts of the Japanese battleship *Nagato* and aircraft carrier *Akagi*. Constructed on dry land out of pine and bamboo, and seemingly held together with miles of wire, the ships were situated on the shore so that in filming, the sea formed the background. A replica of the aft half of the U.S.S. *Arizona* was built on two barges close to where the original *Arizona* had been moored on December 7. The mock-up also represented other battleships at Pearl Harbor that day and was constructed so that it could be "destroyed" during shooting. The cost of these and other replicas and miniatures came to $3,500,000.[26]

Williams had no choice but to use these re-creations for his two fleets. To restage the attack itself, however, he needed operable planes. Only a handful of airworthy Japanese planes, vintage 1941, still existed, and Williams needed an entire airforce. Moreover, the aircraft lacked spare parts and were not reliable enough to withstand the many hours of strenuous flying that the script demanded. Consequently, Williams ruled out the original Japanese planes and decided to remodel American planes to resemble the Japanese aircraft that had flown over Pearl Harbor.[27]

Although Hollywood had used the expediency of disguised American planes ever since *Air Force* and *Sahara*, Williams' goal of authenticity demanded that he do more than simply paint Japanese ensignia on his aircraft. For example, filmmakers had always used AT–6s as Zeroes, to which they bore only a slight resemblance. However, the AT–6s (and the SNJs and Harvards, the Navy and Canadian counterparts) could, with varying degrees of difficulty, also be rebuilt to approximate Japanese Kate torpedo bombers and Val dive/bombers. So AT-6s substituted for all three types of aircraft that had participated in the Pearl Harbor strike. In addition, Williams had to come up with two flyable and two "taxiable" P-40s, five flyable B-17s, and one flyable PBY as well as nonflyable derelicts and mock-ups of all three American planes (designated for destruction during the attack). The cost of the air operations came to $2,500,000.[28]

The American ships, planes, and equipment had to be constructed, located, and reconditioned because the United States military had none dating from Pearl Harbor. Nevertheless, Twentieth Century Fox could not have made *Tora! Tora! Tora!* without Pentagon assistance. Williams secured approval to utilize facilities in Hawaii subject to usual requirements of safety and noninterference with regular activities. He also needed a few active and inactive ships in Pearl Harbor, use of men, and most important, access to an aircraft carrier to film the scenes of Japanese takeoffs and landings on December 7. To ensure this assistance, Fox had kept the Defense Department informed of the progress of the project from its inception in September 1966. The Pentagon had provided research assistance in the form of information, stock footage, and comments on the several versions of the script as it developed. In July 1967 Williams submitted a revised screenplay for approval. With only minor requests for changes relating to technical and historical accuracy, the Defense Department approved the script in mid-September and asked the studio to submit an up-to-date list of required assistance.[29]

Williams thought it was to the military's credit that it went along with the making of a film about its most humiliating defeat: "After all, what is a defeat? Sometimes you've got to lose a little battle to win a big one."[30] According to Richard Fleischer, the military's decision to assist showed its willingness to accept a necessary evil: "I think it was just one of these things where they had no choice because they're damned if they do and damned if they don't. I think they would have been more damned if they hadn't cooperated because then there would have been the accusation that they had something to hide and something to cover up."[31]

The military saw its decision to cooperate in more positive terms. J. M. Hession, the director of the Navy's Los Angeles Public Affairs Office, advised the chief of naval information that the service should cooperate because "the [July 1967] script is apparently an accurate document of the events leading up to the Japanese attack on Pearl Harbor. It is in the best interests of the Navy that this film be completed in order that it may impress the public with the importance of seapower and the necessity of maintaining a strong Navy."[32] In October 1968, during the debate over whether to allow the filmmakers to stage takeoffs and landings on a carrier, R. M. Koontz, the Navy's director of the Media Relations Division, wrote to the chief of information: "This film can and should be an accurate portrayal of a vital moment in our history. . . . Additionally, despite the fact that it was a Japanese Carrier Task Force, it will be a most effective and dramatic portrayal of a resoundingly successful carrier task force operation."[33] Elmo Williams agreed that the positive image of a successful carrier raid figured in the Navy's decision to cooperate. Moreover, as Fleischer pointed out, the film showed the bravery of the men at Pearl Harbor once the attack began. Yet he also conceded: "I don't know if there is any great positive value in the whole film for the Navy."[34] In any case, Tora! Tora! Tora! presented a historically accurate account of events leading up to December 7 and of the attack itself and, as Fleischer suggested, the Navy probably had no real choice but to cooperate.

While the Pentagon had approved the revised script in September 1967, it did not formally agree to cooperate on the film until it approved the final cor-

Pearl Harbor burns following Japanese attack in Tora! Tora! Tora!

rected screenplay in February 1968. Mindful of the legacy of Arthur Sylvester, who had left office in early 1967, the military was careful to analyze all of Fox's requirements lists as they were submitted. In his 1967 memo to the chief of information, Captain Hession had suggested stipulating to the studio that they assist "only on those sequences portraying American Navy forces, and then only within reasonable limits for sequences requiring the utilization of ships and aircraft, so that operational efficiency will not be impaired."[35] Throughout the production, both the studio and the Pentagon tried to avoid any hint of inpropriety that might trigger controversy like the one that occurred during filming of *The Longest Day*. Ultimately, the General Accounting Office ruled that all military cooperation on the film had followed the guidelines set forth in Sylvester's 1964 regulations and that the studio had paid all the costs it had incurred.[36]

The only significant problem that arose between the studio and the Pentagon during the entire production had to do with using an aircraft carrier to stage the takeoffs and landings of the Japanese attack force with the made-up American planes. In formally approving cooperation on February 2, 1968, Daniel Henkin, deputy assistant secretary of defense for public affairs advised the studio that the issue of landing studio aircraft was still under advisement and suggested that "it would be best to consider an alternate plan."[37]

With the production finally scheduled to begin in late 1968, Fox requested in August that it be allowed to use the carrier U.S.S. *Valley Forge*. In response, the Defense Department advised Ellen McDonnell, the studio's Washington representative, that although the request had received "every consideration," it had "determined that such use of an operational carrier cannot be authorized under the provisions of current Department of Defense Instructions." Since the carrier would represent a Japanese ship, assistance would have to be on a courtesy basis rather than part of the normal cooperation. According to the Pentagon, this assistance would involve "improper utilization of manpower and equipment" even if the studio could afford the cost of a carrier and crew for the period needed. At the heart of the matter, however, was the issue of safety: "Flight deck crews perform demanding and hazardous duties under the best conditions, and to require them to work with old equipment with which they are unfamiliar would add unacceptable risks for them and the pilots." Nevertheless, the rejection did not preclude filming nonflying sequences aboard an available carrier on a noninterference, no-special-arrangement basis.[38]

Though Elmo Williams had an inoperative carrier in Japan, to re-create the attack authentically, he needed a carrier from which he could launch and receive his reconstructed planes before the cameras. Consequently, he went to Washington on September 5 to present his case to Daniel Henkin and to formally request reconsideration of the decision. What followed was almost two months of spirited debate within the Pentagon. The Navy wanted to allow Fox to stage its landings and takeoffs, while the Defense Department Public Affairs Office was concerned about the dangers of the action and the uproar that would result if a Navy man were killed or injured during the filming.[39]

Acting on Williams' request for reconsideration of its decision, the Public Affairs Office again asked the Navy to comment on its ability to supply a carrier on which to film takeoffs and landings. Navy commands at all levels stated that the request was "feasible," and on October 11 the chief of information advised Phil Goulding, the assistant secretary of defense, that the Navy "strongly recommended" it be permitted to provide a carrier for the studio's needs.[40]

Goulding's main concern was the possible danger of the operations to the carrier's crew. Having spent some time on carriers as a journalist and as a government official, Goulding had found them "really terrifyingly dangerous places. The idea of crews, who were accustomed to dealing with jets taking off and landing, being put in a situation where they would be dealing with propeller-driven planes I thought was scary." Not only did he feel this was an unnecessary risk, but also he believed "very very strongly" that men were not in the Navy to take part in Hollywood films. He did not see how the government could "explain to the family of the kid who backed into a propeller and lost his head what he was doing in the service of his country."[41] Goulding's staff reinforced his concern when they advised him that "cooperation would be difficult to defend from a noninterference standpoint or if there should be an accident involving injury or death."[42]

Captain Koontz, director of the Navy's Media Relations Division, had anticipated this continued resistance and provided the Navy with answers to potential Defense Department objections. Koontz said that since the carrier was involved in a "precedent-setting way," he expected Goulding's office "to say no and base it on safety considerations determined by non-professional, non-aviation, and non-Navy personnel." He rejected the argument about the propriety of a United States carrier representing a former enemy carrier, citing the many instances in which American men and equipment had depicted enemy forces, including John Wayne's *The Green Berets*. Koontz also expressed concern that a refusal to provide a carrier for *Tora! Tora! Tora!* would establish a precedent for disapproving cooperation on a film about Midway, then in the early stages of development, that would portray a glorious Navy victory.[43]

The intra-Pentagon debate became more complicated when Jack Valenti, formerly an aide to Lyndon Johnson and now president of the Motion Picture Association, brought to bear the weight of the film industry. Acting on a request for help from Darryl Zanuck, Valenti wrote letters on October 3 to both Goulding and Clark Clifford, secretary of defense, in support of Fox's request. Citing a possible "slight hang-up—resistance of some kind" to the use of a carrier, he asked Goulding to assist in "making sure that this request is granted." In his letter to Clifford, Valenti said he was writing for "his personal knowledge and because it may be that I may need your help." Mentioning "some minor resistance" to the Fox request, Valenti explained that he "just wanted you to know this in case this request gets to your level."[44]

On October 23, Valenti followed up a phone conversation with Clifford by responding to the Public Affairs Office's objections against a United States carrier portraying an enemy ship and to the safety issue. Valenti's strongest argument was the long-established precedent that under certain circumstances, American military personnel and equipment had been permitted to represent enemy men and armaments. He cited John Wayne's *The Green Berets* as the most recent example of this practice. He then recounted the measures Fox was taking to ensure the safety of the flying sequences. As an "incidental issue," he mentioned that the studio had already spent $5,000,000 on the project and anticipated a total expenditure of more than $20,000,000 on the film. He added, "I need not point out the catastrophic consequence to a major motion picture from the denial by the Defense Department in this instance."[45]

The Public Affairs Office was not swayed by Valenti's arguments. In a long memo to Clifford on October 24, Phil Goulding reiterated his arguments against approving the Fox request. Despite the Navy's stated reasons for cooperating on the film—that it would help recruiting, serve as a historical document, evoke a patriotic response, and be a reminder of the need for strong armed forces to deter or defend against unexpected military attack—Goulding said, "I have yet to see a reason why a U.S. carrier steaming at taxpayers' expense should represent a Japanese ship." He advised Clifford that Elmo Williams had informally sacrificed the need for carrier landings, "which represent the greatest danger," and was willing to settle for filming only takeoffs. Goulding rejected the compromise, arguing that no possible benefit to the military was worth the risk involved. He continued to recommend disapproval of Fox's request for the carrier, while he supported cooperation on other aspects of the film.[46]

Clifford, of course, had more important things on his mind, and he turned over the matter to his deputy, Paul Nitze. Nitze, a former secretary of the Navy, quickly decided in favor of the Navy. He noted that the present secretary of the Navy approved of the film because he thought the service should continue to cooperate with Hollywood. Nitze himself believed the film would be helpful to the Navy: "I thought we would be better off with the film being made than not being made even though there were risks involved." He acknowledged Goulding's concern for the risks, saying the issue "was whether or not to accept these risks, whether the benefits would be greater than the risks. I felt the benefits would be greater." To him, Pearl Harbor was part of United States history: "You have victory and you have defeat."[47]

Fox and the Navy did not, however, win a complete victory in their confrontation with the Defense Department. Clifford accepted Nitze's decision, but specifically ruled out any landings aboard the carrier. Even with this limitation, Elmo Williams and Richard Fleischer obtained the footage they needed. At the end of November, thirty carrier-qualified naval aviators on authorized leave or inactive duty convened at El Toro Marine Air Base south of Los Angeles to familiarize themselves with the reconstructed aircraft and to prac-

Tora! Tora! Tora!

Japanese planes take off at dawn for attack on Pearl Harbor. Originally filmed for Tora! Tora! Tora!, the sequence appeared several times in Midway (1976).

tice Japanese-type formation flying. On December 1, thirty planes were loaded aboard the U.S.S. *Yorktown* docked at the Naval Air Station in San Diego, and the carrier departed on a regularly scheduled training exercise.[48]

During the first two days aboard, the filmmakers and the pilots rehearsed the takeoffs, and Captain George Watkins, the Navy's technical advisor for the carrier operation, re-created the landing of Air Group Commander Fuishida's Zero aboard a Japanese carrier. Since the studio planes could not actually land, the Zero was first photographed rolling down the deck and then as Watkins made a touch-and-go landing. Elmo Williams later created the illusion of the actual landing in the editing room. On the 4th, under the supervision of Commander Ed Stafford, the overall technical advisor, and Watkins, the other twenty-nine planes took off in the dawn light, went into their formations, and flew by the carrier to provide Fleischer and Williams with all the carrier shots. Everything went smoothly during this phase of the filming.[49]

Thanks to the Navy's assistance, the carrier sequences conveyed an authentic feeling for the excitement of the moment when the Japanese launched their attack, and for the beauty and grace of planes taking off from a carrier into the morning light. Likewise, the flying scenes done in Hawaii and over Pearl Harbor re-created the shock of the sudden appearance of the Japanese planes as they began their bomb and torpedo runs. In particular, the film came alive during the sequence in which the aircraft momentarily surround a civilian biplane out for an early morning flight. The scene combines humor with the forboding of events to come. As long as the movie follows the planes over Hawaii and into Pearl Harbor, *Tora! Tora! Tora!* maintains a strong sense of reality.

Likewise, the full-size mock-ups of the Japanese ships as well as of the *Arizona* were carefully constructed and visually realistic in every sense. In fact, some of the leased Navy ships were less believable than the mock-up of the *Arizona*, because the ships were post-1941. (In at least one shot, the angle-deck of the *Yorktown* is visible during the carrier sequence.) The staged explosions at Pearl Harbor were realistic because actual locales and buildings were used—the filmmakers even blew up an old hanger that had been scheduled for demolition. The destruction of the *Arizona*, which took only thirty seconds, was the visual climax of the movie. It was more realistic than most cinematic explosions. But when the filmmakers cut from live action to the special-effects shots and miniatures photographed in the lake on the Fox Ranch, the illusion of reality collapses. The miniatures and the painted backdrops look like miniatures and painted backdrops, and the viewer cannot possibly pretend otherwise.

Elmo Williams and Twentieth Century Fox cannot be faulted for their effort. The studio spent millions of dollars building the miniatures, which were as accurate as the art and special effects departments could make them. The filmmakers simply faced an impossible task in matching the stunning live aerial shots over Pearl Harbor with the miniatures. The explosions of the miniatures and the destruction in Hawaii of the P-40 mock-ups look like what they were—special effects explosions and disintegrating fiberglass models.

Since the scenes of havoc were the core of the film's visual impact, their shortcomings vitiated the success of the flying sequences and the explosion of the *Arizona*. But the real problem was not the film's visual failures but its impotent drama. In *The Longest Day*, history and drama had ultimately merged. The actors became historical figures, real people with whom the audience could identify. Through them the film portrayed a story of human struggle, of life and death. But in *Tora! Tora! Tora!* people and their actions are secondary to the event, to the exploding bombs, to the ships, planes, and other instruments of war, "toys" which the director moved around for his camera. As a result, the actors remain actors, wooden caricatures of people, simply reading their lines. Admiral Kimmel, the Navy's commander at Pearl Harbor who was narrowly missed by a bullet, remarks in the film: "It would have been merciful if it had killed me," but the tragic implication of his comment fails to move audiences. If the explosions, mock-ups, miniatures, and actual ships and planes had become integrated on the screen, the lack of realistic characters might have passed with less notice. But all the construction, special effects, and military assistance never meshed. Consequently, *Tora! Tora! Tora!* failed as drama and as entertainment even as it re-created the history of Pearl Harbor with reasonable accuracy.

In doing so, the film could not, of course, exonerate the American military for its lack of preparedness or the government for its failure to alert Hawaii in time to meet the attack. As a pseudohistorical documentary, *Tora! Tora! Tora!* showed the ironies and errors that produced Pearl Harbor, the bureacracy and blind tradition that amplified each mistake beyond calculation. It also explained the Japanese intentions and showed the attack for what it was, a skillful military mission, planned by skillful tacticians—a far cry from the image of the Japanese in the Hollywood films of the war years.

No single person emerges as the American scapegoat, and no heroes appear. Once the attack begins, however, the film portrays American bravery under fire and the can-do attitude that has typified the majority of American war movies. Moreover, though the film portrayed an American defeat, the audience knew that the military would ultimately win a great victory. As Admiral Yamamoto, the Japanese commander of the attack, observed after the completion of the mission, Pearl Harbor served only to "waken a sleeping giant." The closing image is therefore one of American resolve, of determination to fight back and overcome adversity. In this way the film may have indirectly conveyed a positive image of the military.

★ Renewed Controversy

Tora! Tora! Tora! directly rekindled the controversy over military cooperation to the film industry, despite the fact that both Twentieth Century Fox and the Defense Department had taken extensive precautions to avoid trouble. Apart from the problem of obtaining the aircraft carrier, the shooting of the film itself had gone so smoothly that Fleischer finished his location work in Hawaii eleven days ahead of schedule. Working with Commander Edward Stafford, the technical advisor and Defense Department liaison man, Fleischer had obtained just about everything he needed, sometimes on short notice. Stafford also had made sure Fleischer's requests were met at no cost to the taxpayer by billing the studio for all expenses.[50]

As with *The Longest Day*, however, the controversy surrounding *Tora! Tora! Tora!* grew out of media coverage of the production, which focused on the Pentagon's commitment of men, equipment, and facilities to Fox. Television's "Sixty Minutes," acting on a tip from a serviceman, went to Hawaii ostensibly to do a feature on the film's re-creation of the attack on Pearl

Harbor. In its May 1969 broadcast, Mike Wallace raised questions about the decision to provide the carrier, about using it to transport the studio's planes to Hawaii after the launching sequence off San Diego, and about the Navy's assistance to the company at Pearl Harbor. He concluded by asking: "Should the taxpayer, and the serviceman, help to subsidize the undertaking?"[51]

Bill Brown, the producer of the *Tora! Tora! Tora!* segment of "Sixty Minutes," later admitted that there was "subterfuge" in his research in Hawaii, because both the military and Fox thought he was doing a feature on how the filmmakers were re-creating history. More serious, he embarked on the project already convinced that the studio was taking advantage of the Navy and the American taxpayers. He refused to accept the Navy's explanations that the carrier which transported the studio planes to Hawaii had already been scheduled to go there on its way to recover an Apollo spacecraft or that the studio had agreed beforehand to pay all costs: "But I didn't know that. They claimed they were doing that. I am still not convinced that was so."[52] In fact, even a minimum of research would have revealed that the *Yorktown* had been assigned to the Apollo mission before the Navy agreed to carry the planes and that the studio had ascertained that suitable commercial transportation could not be arranged. Moreover, stories published the week the planes arrived in Hawaii reported that Fox was paying regular commercial freight rates for the carrier transportation.[53]

At the time of the broadcast, "Sixty Minutes" was not yet an established program, and the *Tora* segment, because of the controversy it stirred up, helped make it a continuing success. But the feature did so by playing loose with the facts, by refusing to give credence to the Navy's statements, by editing to "prove" the broadcaster's case. Documentary evidence verifies that the

Men at the beginning of the attack on Pearl Harbor, in Tora! Tora! Tora!

Navy went out of its way to provide a full accounting of services rendered and that Twentieth Century Fox paid for all bills presented.[54] This is not to say that the Navy charged for every gallon of fuel used or every piece of material expended, something that has never happened during the history of the military-film industry relationship. Such an accounting would be virtually impossible. Without question, Fox wasn't anxious to reimburse the military if it could avoid a charge. But the studio could not have made the film without assistance and so generally accepted the military's figures as appropriate. Furthermore, both congressional and General Accounting Office investigations concluded that the Navy's aid to Fox had followed Pentagon guidelines and that the studio had paid for all assistance received outside normal military expenditures.[55]

Congress has never been slow to recognize the political value in a controversy, the facts notwithstanding. Coming at a time when the military was being attacked in Congress and in the press because of Vietnam, the "Sixty Minutes" program triggered a wave of congressional criticism that was reminiscent of the uproar surrounding the making of The Longest Day. The renewed controversy raised filmmakers' fears of additional red tape and more congressional criticism of large-scale Pentagon assistance to other war movies. At the same time, the Defense Department became even more cautious in considering requests for assistance on productions that required a major expenditure of time and men. As a result of these issues, the financial failure of Tora! Tora! Tora!, and the growing antimilitary sentiment in the country, Hollywood ended the cycle of war films that had begun more than twenty years before.

CHAPTER FOURTEEN

FICTION AND HISTORY IN THE 1970s

★

Despite Hollywood's pause in the production of war films after 1970, the American people did not lack for a visualization of combat. In addition to the regular appearance of old war movies on the late show and of documentary series such as "Victory at Sea," television continued to saturate the nation with combat footage from Vietnam until the final American withdrawal in 1973. Unlike Hollywood's re-creations, the evening news had no difficulty providing all the authentic details of war—firefights, body counts, zippo lighters torching bamboo huts, medical helicopters evacuating wounded GIs, napalmed children, and even a serviceman, on cue, cutting the ears off a dead Vietnamese for the camera. Hollywood had never matched the realism of these images, all presented in living color. Not only did the recurring pictures contribute significantly to the nation's revulsion against the Vietnam War, but they also helped erode the respected image the military built up for almost fifty years in Hollywood war movies.

Those few films with a military setting that were produced in the early 1970s owed their irreverent portrayals of the armed forces to the country's growing antipathy to the military and to the new realism that had developed in Hollywood with the breakdown of the Production Code during the 1960s. Swearing, drinking, and explicit sex scenes had become normal elements in

Facsimiles of Japanese Zeroes practicing in formation for Tora! Tora! Tora! *and, later,* Midway *(1976).*

American films; characters could even live happily ever after without benefit of marriage or fear of retribution. Fictional servicemen taking part in these activities on the screen undoubtedly better represented reality than the sanitized behavior of Hollywood's earlier fighting men. But the armed forces were bound to see that their already fragile image was only worsened by the screen portrayal of military men who were hard-drinking, swearing, and fornicating. Filmmakers who intended to include such characters in their movies found themselves considered sympathetic to the antiwar movement and their scripts unacceptable for assistance.

Because the ground war and close air support in Vietnam had been so well covered by the news services, and because the bombing had remained impersonal, unglamorous, and symbolic of evil, Hollywood turned to the Navy for its first postwar subjects. The Navy, however, adamantly refused to cooperate with the producers of *The Last Detail* and *Cinderella Liberty*, because the films conveyed the impression that military regulations counted for little, that sailors spent their time drinking and womanizing, and that their language consisted primarily of four-letter words. Together the films created an image of the modern Navy that was strikingly different from portraits created in earlier peacetime films of the 1930s or in the innumerable musicals and comedies of the 1940s and 1950s. Moreover, these new films suggested that the discipline and patriotism shown in combat films such as *They Were Expendable*, *Task Force*, and *Tora! Tora! Tora!* had become obsolete.

The Last Detail

The Last Detail tells the story of two Navy MPs detailed to escort a young prisoner from the Norfolk, Virginia naval base to the Navy prison in Portsmouth, New Hampshire. The youth, about to serve eight years for attempting to steal $40 from a charity box, is a big, pitiful slob. Along the way, the two Navy MPs initiate him into manhood through a series of drinking bouts and a sexual encounter. Much of the texture and tone of the movie's military realism is established in its first three minutes, when the audience hears a string of obscenities uttered with dazzling speed. Jack Nicholson is extremely proud of his nickname, "Badass," and Otis Young and Randy Quaid trade lines throughout the film such as: "Tell the M.A. to go fuck himself," "I ain't going on no shit detail," and "You're a lucky son of a bitch." Even its mild words (by recent standards), such as "crap," "bastard," and "badass," would have gotten the film banned by the Production Code fifteen years before.

The Navy's reaction to the script and to the efforts of the producer, Gerald Ayres, to obtain even limited military assistance illustrate the service's extreme sensitivity about its image during the early 1970s. After visiting the Norfolk Naval Base in August 1972, Ayres called Don Baruch to discuss the project and the process of obtaining cooperation. In his cover letter accompanying the script, he explained he had found that the way "the Navy has responded to a changing society is impressive and should be noted in the film." With revisions he intended to make in the screenplay as a result of his research trip, Ayres thought the film "will be a credit to the Navy." He requested minimal cooperation, since the movie would require only a few day of shooting on the naval base. Ayres said he could fake the Navy facilities if he didn't receive assistance, but he noted, "Given the extraordinary showcase appearance of the Norfolk base, that would be a shame."[1]

Baruch responded by recommending that Ayres not submit the original screenplay to the Navy, objecting to the image it suggested by showing the prisoner participating in various inappropriate escapades with his escorts; he also said the eight-year jail term was not factual. Nevertheless, in asking Baruch to forward the script to the Navy, Ayres expressed a willingness to delete some of the profanity and discuss correcting any inaccuracies. He wrote to Baruch, "I sincerely hope that the Navy understands that I am as anxious to cooperate with them as to receive their cooperation."[2]

Despite Ayres' willingness to cooperate, the Navy decided it could find "no benefit" from assisting on the film. Its Information Office felt that while Ayres had indicated he would "delete some of the profanity and correct some inaccuracies. . . no minor modification to the script can produce an acceptable film for the Navy."[3] After failing to change the Navy's mind by phone, Ayres wrote to the Navy pointing out that he did not consider himself "irresponsible in the representation of reality nor in any way hostile to our armed forces."[4]

Ayres stressed he was trying "to show a human drama with a Navy background," and wanted help "to make the script all the more accurate and, as a consequence, all the more effective." He expressed "shock" at the Navy's suggestion that he save his airplane fare and not come to Washington to discuss the portions of the screenplay that it found "unsympathetic or unreal." He asked for an explanation of what the Navy meant by telling him: "[You would] have no plot left by the time you altered the script sufficiently to get our cooperation." While Ayres agreed that his characters broke some Navy regulations, he pointed out that most films that received military assistance showed the same thing. In his case, these occurrences were "shown in a most humorous light." More important, he said the two escorts "show themselves first and foremost to be humane and compassionate." He closed by saying he refused to believe that the Navy "would not want men in positions of leadership who are humane and compassionate. Our times are too much in need of such men."[5]

The Navy rejected Ayres arguments, saying that "it is very unlikely we could arrive at a mutually agreeable script without emasculating the premise of your story." While conceding it would make an entertaining movie, the Navy repeated that it did not consider the plot "in the best interest of the Navy, or for that matter a reasonable occurrence within today's Navy." Furthermore, although the Navy found the escorts "sympathetic in their own fashion and somewhat enthusiastic about the Navy, they do not reflect the best of the service and in many cases perpetuate a false derogatory stereotype."[6]

Given the finality of the response, Ayres and his director, Hal Ashby, made the film without cooperation, managing to give it a sense of authenticity by taking some exterior shots of the entrance to the Portsmouth Navy base. They were so successful in creating the illusion of being on the base that Admiral John Will, the technical advisor for *Men Without Women*, became furious after seeing the film, believing it was disgusting and that the service had assisted in making it.[7]

Despite Will's reaction and the belief of one of the film's financial backers, a Navy veteran, that "it had the ring of truth,"[8] the movie did distort Navy procedures to such an extent that its story was implausible to anyone familiar with Navy regulations and activities. For the average viewer, however, *The Last Detail* seemed to show the Navy as it currently existed. And given the humor and good-natured friendship that developed among the three main characters, it is hard to see how the film could have hurt the Navy, especially since the service had over the years assisted on even more implausible comedies, ones that totally disregarded Navy procedures and regulations. During the 1970s however, at the highest levels, the Navy manifested a sensitivity to its image that precluded virtually any cooperation except to a traditional World War II-type combat film, which Hollywood was not yet ready to make.

★

Cinderella Liberty

Cinderella Liberty met a fate similar to *The Last Detail's*, even though the producer-director Mark Rydell went to greater lengths to secure assistance than had Gerald Ayres. *Cinderella Liberty* also used the Navy primarily as background, in this case for a love story between James Caan, as a sailor, and Marsha Mason, as a prostitute. Because the story's setting was a Navy base and a ship, Rydell sought Navy assistance, making his initial contact through its Information Office in Los Angeles.

The script Rydell brought with him depicted sailors whose thoughts and actions followed decidedly unmilitary directions. The love story left something to be desired from the Navy's viewpoint—a prostitute did not represent the ideal girlfriend for a sailor, particularly when she had a son from her black former lover. The screenplay also included inaccuracies in Navy procedures as well as a good deal of profanity. Finally, the ending, which showed James Caan deserting the Navy, should have been so repugnant to the service that it alone should have precluded cooperation. The plot has Caan switching places with an old sailor who had been mustered out of the Navy, a good sailor who knows his job and wants to get back into the service.

Ironically, however, the desertion did not become an issue during Rydell's initial discussions with the Navy in Los Angeles or with officials in Washington. Focusing on the script's other problems, Rydell and lower level Navy officers revised the story until it was approved for cooperation by Don Baruch's office and the Navy's Public Affairs Office. At that point, top Navy brass stepped into the picture and demanded further revisions that would have totally changed the character of the film.[9]

Baruch himself thought the Navy had not acted in good faith with Rydell. He said that the revised script had been a great improvement and that the film would not have been detrimental to the Navy, especially if a project officer had overseen the appearance and actions of the characters. Nevertheless, his only possible option would have been to ask the assistant secretary of defense for public affairs to order the Navy to cooperate—something that had never been done before. Besides, the Defense Department itself had no direct involvement in the project, since Rydell's needs were limited assistance from the Navy alone.[10]

Because Rydell had fulfilled his end of the negotiations, he was in a position to appeal the decision to higher Navy authority. With this in mind, he contacted Jack Valenti, president of the Motion Picture Association, who in turn called the Navy. Valenti, however, was not willing to dispute high level feeling that the incorrect portrayal of the service and its men demanded further script revisions. Unlike his extensive efforts on behalf of Darryl Zanuck only a few years before, Valenti suggested to Rydell that he forget about cooperation and find a nonmilitary ship. Despite his refusal to intervene further, Valenti did believe the government should not base its decision to cooperate simply "on whether or not they liked the director or the star or the story: "I think the government should cooperate on the making of a film if it is not a costly thing for the government [and is] not going to interrupt training. . . ." Rydell's limited requirements would have fallen into this framework, and Baruch felt Valenti could have reversed the decision if he had tried harder because Rydell "had shown good faith, was led down the primrose path, and had wasted time and money doing what the Navy asked, only to be told that it was useless!"[11]

In any case, Rydell returned to his original script, obtained additional financial backing from Twentieth Century Fox, and made the film without Navy cooperation.[12] Whether the earthy language, unconventional love story, and Caan's desertion projected a realistic or a negative image of the service, *Cinderella Liberty*, like *The Last Detail*, did not show the Navy as it would have liked. Moreover, since there were no positive-military-image films being released, the essentially irreverent image in these two films furnished the only fictional picture of the military during the 1970s.

The closest the Pentagon came to presenting itself positively in these years was in nonmilitary films like *Airport 1975* and *Towering Inferno*, both major disaster movies, the most popular genre of the '70s. The military agreed to cooperate on these films because they showed the services performing as they would in an actual disaster. As with combat films, the Defense Department demanded an accurate portrayal of the military. Before agreeing to assist on *Airport 1975*, for example, the Air Force conducted a test to determine whether one of its helicopters could actually fly as fast as a 747 jet under the conditions described in the film. Only when it had ascertained that a person actually could be lowered from the helicopter to the "stricken" airliner did the Air Force approve use of its aircraft and personnel to simulate the rescue.[13]

In *Towering Inferno*, Navy helicopters answer a request to assist in rescuing people from a burning skyscraper. The Navy felt its involvement in this plot would help inform the public that a military emergency assistance network existed to meet such situations, and for this reason the Pentagon requested that the filmmaker include lines in the script describing the network. The explanation did not get into the movie because the request was not made mandatory, but the screen credits nevertheless acknowledged the Navy's and Defense Department's help.[14]

Not all filmmakers felt the need to seek official assistance. While the 1936 disaster film *San Francisco* had used Marines to help re-create the scenes of chaos during the 1906 earthquake, Mark Robson, the director of *Earthquake* (1975) preferred to use actors and extras rather than request assistance from the National Guard, and undergo its red tape.[15] The Guard would undoubtedly have been reluctant to help anyway, given the film's portrayal of a deranged guardsman. In any event, during the early 1970s, the Defense Department continued to be accomodating when films—combat or otherwise—benefited the services.

★

World War II Nostalgia

Frank McCarthy had begun work on *MacArthur* in mid-1972, hoping to duplicate his success with *Patton*. He admitted that he had resisted the subject for a long time, fearing it might seem "self-imitative." A comment from General Robert Eichelberger, who had fought under MacArthur but had not liked him very much, provided McCarthy's inspiration. Eichelberger said that in view of MacArthur's love of publicity and his ego and his great success, if Patton, instead of serving under the more modest Eisenhower had served under MacArthur, then Patton would have emerged from World War II as the unknown soldier.[16]

McCarthy decided that if *Patton* had been a good film because its subject had had those qualities, then a film about MacArthur could be even better. He would make an appealing screen hero because he had been "enormously successful" and was the great hero of the conflict. Furthermore, "Every woman was in love with him and eventually, when he was relieved in Korea for insubordination, which you ordinarily would think is a disgraceful thing, he came home and got the biggest hero's welcome that anybody ever had. This is fascinating, I think."[17]

McCarthy's first step, to interest financial backers, was accomplished by September 1972. He reached an agreement with Richard Zanuck and David Brown and their newly-formed independent company to make the film in association with Universal Studios. In announcing the project, Zanuck (who had been in charge of production at Twentieth Century Fox when the studio made

Captain George Watkins re-created the landing of Air Group Commander Fuishida's Zero aboard a Japanese carrier in this reconstructed AT-6. The sequence later appeared several times in Midway.

Patton), said that the film was a "long-range project," which he hoped to have under way within a year. By March 1974, however, the script had not been completed, though a decision had been made to do the exterior shooting in South Korea and the Philippines, where armies had World War II equipment. Ultimately, the cost of sending a film company to the Far East ended those plans, and the movie, much scaled down in scope, did not go before the cameras until August 1976.[18]

In the meantime, Walter Mirisch had begun work on *Midway*. Portraying the first major American victory of World War II, the Battle of Midway was the turning point in the Pacific Theater. Mirisch conceived of his project as a tribute to the American Bicentennial, with the story symbolizing the nation's spirit and will to triumph in the face of great odds. At Midway, American forces had faced a vastly superior Japanese task force but had sunk four enemy aircraft carriers and emerged victorious. From that point onward, United States strength continued to grow while Japan was unable to mount another offensive equal to that of Midway.

From their respective standpoints, the Navy and the Defense Department anticipated no problems in working with Mirisch. Unlike *Tora! Tora! Tora!*, *Midway* would reveal no skeletons of unprepared military leaders, no unchallenged attacks, no victorious enemy. The film would show a successful carrier-based attack and a significant victory over the Japanese. In his initial reaction to the script in December 1974, the head of Navy Aviation Periodicals and History wrote to the Navy's chief of information that the film "could be useful in recruiting efforts as part of the Bicentennial and as an adjunct to the Sea-Air Operations Hall of the new Air and Space Museum which will focus on carriers."[19] Subsequently, the Navy informed the assistant secretary of defense for public affairs that it believed "cooperation is both feasible and in the best interests of the service."[20]

Although the Pentagon found that both *MacArthur* and *Midway* merited its cooperation, actual assistance was necessarily limited, given the paucity of World War II equipment. Because *MacArthur* dealt with one man's career, primarily in command positions, Frank McCarthy did not have the problem of re-creating large-scale battles that he had experienced with *Patton*. Ultimately he utilized some combat footage, a few small-scale re-created combat scenes, a couple of facsimile PT-boats, a few rented planes, and some Navy ships to produce the illusion of a military atmosphere.

In contrast, Walter Mirisch had to show two major naval task forces on the screen. Fortunately for Mirisch, in actual history the Japanese and American fleets had never come within sight of each other—the entire battle was waged by the planes of each side attacking the enemy ships. To re-create this air-to-sea battle, Mirisch resorted to several expediencies, primarily the use of Navy combat and gun-camera footage. Mirisch also acquired some sequences from *Thirty Seconds Over Tokyo* as well as *Tora! Tora! Tora!*, used miniatures and mock-ups, and rented two World War II F4F planes. The only significant Navy assistance he received was use of the U.S.S. *Lexington*, the one World War II aircraft carrier still on active duty. The film company spent several days shooting aboard the ship while it was dockside at Pensacola, Florida. Then fifty members of the cast and crew and the two planes spent a week aboard the carrier during one of its regular training cruises, filming exterior sequences and interior atmosphere shots. The Navy refused to allow Mirisch to fly his two planes off the *Lexington*, even though they had flown to Pensacola from Texas and Illinois.

Despite their airworthiness, Jack Smight, the film's director, used the aircraft solely as props for the actors. With only two planes, he was forced to shoot the sequences so as to create the illusion that the flight deck or hanger deck contained the full complement of planes. To do this, the camera was compelled to restrict its vision and could not capture the huge size of the *Lexington*. As a result, the film's visual authenticity was not as successful as the filmmakers had hoped, given Navy cooperation. Considering the rigidness of the scenes that featured the old planes, Smight might just as well have shot them on a sound stage as Mervyn LeRoy had done thirty years before while directing *Thirty Seconds Over Tokyo*.

The problem of duplicating life aboard the carrier during the Battle of Midway paled when compared with Mirisch's task of re-creating the actual battle. The scarcity of World War II planes gave him no choice but to use footage from earlier Hollywood productions and Navy archives. The film's opening montage, Doolittle's raiders skimming over the waves and flying inland over a Japanese city, came from *Thirty Seconds Over Tokyo*. While the footage was tinted to blend with the color of the rest of *Midway*, the sequence remains second-hand, easily recognized material. Likewise, the crash of a B-17 returning to Midway after a mission against the Japanese fleet came from the 1970 Fox production. (The crash itself is an example of creative innovation, since it resulted from a malfunction in the plane's landing gear during a training flight. The pilot informed Williams of his difficulty, and the producer had the cameras ready when the plane landed on one wheel.) The Japanese planes taking off from their carriers in search of the American fleet were outtakes from Twentieth Century Fox's *Tora! Tora! Tora!*

To get the American planes off the carriers and into the air to re-create the Battle of Midway itself, Mirisch relied on Navy combat and gun-camera footage. Fortunately, the Navy had used color stock almost exclusively during the war and had preserved and catalogued the processed film in its archives. Without this footage, Mirisch would have had to resort to models and process shots. More positively, he saw "two great advantages" in using the Navy footage: "It gives you a feeling of validity that I find tremendously dramatic" and it made possible "real, full-size planes, not models."[21]

Although the Navy footage was real, *Midway* itself provided only an illusion of war, and often not a very convincing one. The problems with the production began with the combat footage itself. In blowing up the 16mm standard dimension film to 35mm Cinemascope proportions, it was necessary to cut off the bottom and top of the frame. Mirisch thought this produced "a much more exciting effect" because it placed the viewer in the center of the picture and made the action "much more dramatic than it was originally."[22] Even so, the combat footage is immediately recognized by its deep blue cast and grainy quality that resulted from enlarging it. While the battle sequences are impressive, the film loses its sense of realism because the viewer is constantly aware of the old footage as the screen image switches from "live" action to studio re-creations.

At the same time, for anyone who had seen any of Hollywood's older films about the war in the Pacific or documentaries such as "Victory At Sea," the recognition of the borrowed sequences would necessarily lessen the impact of the visual image. Rather than becoming absorbed in the action, many viewers undoubtedly spent their time recalling where they had previously seen the sequences. Moreover, many of the Navy combat scenes postdated the Battle of Midway and so contributed to the film's lessened authenticity. (One spectacular and often-used crash sequence, in which a returning plane breaks in two on landing, actually occurred in October 1944, during the Battle of Leyte Gulf. The F6F Hellcat did not even make its maiden flight until three weeks after the Battle of Midway.)

For the most part, only airplane enthusiasts, military historians, and World War II veterans could pick up these flaws or notice the repeated shots, which the filmmakers attempted to disguise by reversing the film from left to right. Much of the movie's ultimate box-office success resulted from people who went to see the battle sequences irrespective of their chronological accuracy. Most of the viewers either had not seen the original dramatic films and combat documentaries from which the battle scenes had been borrowed or had found them unimpressive on their television's small screen. In addition, use of the Sensurround sound system gave a new dimension to the images even if the sound track did not always synchronize with the action. Unfortunately, *Midway* had aspired to be more than a series of World War II combat clips enhanced with technological gimmicks. Mirisch had claimed to relate a dramatic story within the framework of a major historical event. While the film succeeded as history as well as any Hollywood commercial product had, *Midway*, like *Tora! Tora! Tora!* before it, failed as drama.

The two films suffer the same basic problem. The historical figures fail for the most part to become living people with whom the audience can get involved. Only Henry Fonda, who plays Admiral Nimitz, successfully captures the essense of the man: a commander who has grown accustomed to the isolation that comes with the responsibility of four stars on his collar. The other Americans are all rumpled, informal, and skilled in the art of war. The Japanese, led by Toshiro Mifune as Admiral Yamamoto, are more formal and stoic. This proved to be a wise casting decision, since Mirisch elected to dub their lines into English rather than use subtitles as was done in *Tora! Tora! Tora!* and *The Longest Day*. The filmmakers treat both sides with an evenhandedness that refuses to explore the abilities and decisions of the combatants. Even though the Americans win and the Japanese lose, the difference is attributed to luck. No one makes a major mistake or even voices serious fears about the outcome of the battle. This lack of emotionalism dissipates the drama inherent in the developing confrontation.

Recognizing the problems of creating a dramatic film within the framework of historical events, Mirisch chose to graft a fictional character onto the factual story. Captain Matt Garth, played by Charlton Heston in his bigger-than-life style, finds himself at the center of events throughout the film. If Garth's character could "have been stolen from some terrible movie made shortly after World War II,"[23] his role was the means of introducing dramatic complications through a love interest into the film—in the tradition of the soap-opera. Garth's son, also a Navy flier, informs his father that he has fallen in love with a Japanese-American girl who is interned in Hawaii with her family. The Romeo and Juliet story is highlighted by some of the most ludicrous dialogue to appear in any Hollywood movie: Son: "Dad, I've fallen in love with a Japanese girl. I want to marry her. Dad, I need your help." Garth: "I damn well guess you do, Tiger." The romance draws on every cliché found in a Hollywood war movie: the girl is willing to give up her man for the good of his career and his country; nevertheless, she waits for him as any good serviceman's woman does; and in the end, she welcomes him home, eager to love him even despite his terrible burns suffered in the battle.

Garth the elder stands around looking grim about both the romance and the impending battle. He never becomes a believeable character or any less wooden than the historical figures with whom he mingles. His role, intended to provide human drama in *Midway*, simply accentuates the film's lifelessness in anything except the Navy's combat footage. In the end, Garth dies after leading the final attack on the Japanese fleet—perhaps only because Mirisch had one more fiery crash (albeit a Korean war-vintage jet plane crash) left in the editing room—and few people cared.

The film's scriptual ineptitude is not limited to the American historical and fictional characters. When an aide informs Admiral Yamamoto of Doolittle's raid on Japan, he adds: "This raid is a blessing in disguise. The Americans have done us an invaluable service. They have proven you correct. Our homeland is not invulnerable to attack. After today there will be no more foot dragging by the general staff." This dialogue, combined with the badly-matched battle sequences that cut from combat footage to miniatures to exploding mockups, made *Midway* little more than a competent, dull, and occasionally confusing history lesson. Nevertheless, the film became one of the major box-office successes of 1976, suggesting that the viewing public's nostalgia craze and desire to see a victorious military were able to surmount a characterless story and purloined visual images.

As historical biography, *MacArthur* did not lack a strong central character around whom to create a dramatic film. As Frank McCarthy had concluded when he decided to make the film, General Douglas MacArthur had at least as many facets to his personality and was probably more controversial than George Patton. Unfortunately, the completed movie only hinted at the ambiguities and controversies that surrounded MacArthur. As Richard Schickel observed in his *Time* review, the filmmakers "tiptoed up to the most fascinating enigma of his character, and then quietly backed away from it."[24] Consequently, the film remains at best a bland, official biography, at worst, a dull, unconvincing, often confusing story about one of America's greatest generals.

General MacArthur was a consummate egomaniac. He regularly had his staff send back to the United States films of his exploits for exhibition in the nation's theaters. Like James Garner's admiral in *The Americanization of Emily*, who wanted to make a movie about the first dead man on Omaha Beach, MacArthur always wanted to give the impression he was the first American on every beach. In one instance, the Army Signal Corps submitted to the Office of War Information for possible release to commercial theaters, a 30-minute film portraying the invasion of New Guinea. An OWI official recalled: "Though a full-length shot of MacArthur was not shown wading ashore, his figure in profile or his hat or pipe was shown in all three landings" which supposedly had been made simultaneously. The official speculated that perhaps the film was meant to suggest MacArthur had been "there in 'spirit' if not in person." In any case, the footage arrived six or eight months after the invasion and was much too long to be suitable for theatrical release.[25] When MacArthur landed in the Philippines, the cameramen and sound equipment were carefully placed

to record his "I have returned," not "We have returned"—even though an American fleet and landing force surrounded him. In the movie, however, Mac-Arthur's public relations efforts seem more the product of an eccentric than an egotist.

Midway burns, thanks to footage provided from Tora! Tora! Tora!

If this and other aspects of MacArthur's personality lack development or insight, the screenwriters' failure is perhaps understandable. MacArthur's Army career spanned fifty-two years, the longest in American military annals. According to Hal Barwood, he and his coscreenwriter, Matthew Robbins, "faced an enormous task in narrowing his life to the confines of a feature film." By deciding to open the movie with MacArthur's departure from Corregidor under Japanese fire in 1942 and end it with his dismissal by President Truman in 1951, the writers focused on his greatest years. This prevented them from probing into the origins of his personality or tracing its development, although they tried to "show the light and dark" in MacArthur's life. Robbins observed that the general's decisions "were frequently brilliant, but the way he carried them out was often ludicrous. He had a great capacity for self-delusion." The authors also attempted to illustrate that after the "grandeur" of ruling a conquered Japan and setting it on the road to spectacular recovery, MacArthur felt "he should be making the decisions instead of a former artillery captain who happened to be president."[26]

Portraying even the nine years from the ignominy of his retreat on a PT-boat to MacArthur's removal from the Supreme Pacific Command presented the writers with a huge task. *Patton* focused on less than three years of Patton's career and so the film could explore the ambiguities in the general's personality at some length. In contrast, Barwood and Robbins could only suggest the complexities in MacArthur's personality. Perhaps an actor with George C. Scott's ability could have added his reading of MacArthur's life to the script to provide a complex picture of the general, but Gregory Peck simply did not get inside MacArthur; he spoke his lines rather than lived them. Where Scott became Patton both mentally and physically, Peck could not merge himself with MacArthur. Part of the problem was that many people remembered MacArthur; he had been visible for a longer time than had Patton. MacArthur had generated more publicity, had had a longer career, had been on television, and had died only thirteen years before his biography was filmed. In addition, Peck could not completely submerge his own acting mannerisms or seem to age visually as MacArthur aged chronologically. Consequently, audiences found it difficult to forget that they were watching Gregory Peck play Douglas MacArthur.

The film would also have worked better if McCarthy and his director, Joseph Sargent had supported Peck with better visual surroundings. Because of budgetary problems, McCarthy shot *MacArthur* in the United States on a limited scale. For all practical purposes this meant that the film became an interior, dialogue movie rather than an exterior, action war film on the grand scale of *Patton*. The few staged combat sequences resemble the battles Hollywood waged on its backlots for early World War II period films like *Bataan*, *Wake Island*, and *Marine Raiders*. As a result of Sargent's failure to create any illusion of reality in these scenes, the actual combat footage used (supplied in large part by the Marine Corps) becomes even more obvious than in *Midway*.

Sargeant was relatively successful in re-creating events on location and in meetings between MacArthur and historical figures. MacArthur's farewell address at West Point in 1962, filmed at West Point, and the Japanese surrender aboard the U.S.S. *Missouri*, photographed aboard the ship where it is moth-balled at Bremerton, Washington, are visually authentic, almost documentary in style. In the general's meetings with Presidents Roosevelt and Truman dramatic license facilitates the sharp confrontations and clarifies personalities and issues, and the scenes come alive through the interactions of Peck, Dan O'Herlihy (Roosevelt) and Ed Flanders (Truman).

The dramatic highlight of the film is MacArthur's reunions with the survivors of the Bataan Death March, including General Jonathan Wainwright. The meetings are believable and even moving, but because the filmmakers failed to develop MacArthur's character, even these sequences produce confusion. Early in the movie, MacArthur refuses to recommend Wainwright for the Congressional Medal of Honor because he had surrendered Corregidor rather than hold out to the last man. Yet when he meets the now-frail general after his liberation, MacArthur treats Wainwright with apparent affection and later arranges for him to be part of the surrender ceremony. It never becomes clear whether MacArthur regretted his early denouncement of Wainwright or whether he was being hypocritical.

MacArthur also suffers from some structural and historical defects. MacArthur's years as ruler of occupied Japan represent perhaps his greatest and most enduring success. Yet both historically and in the movie, the Japanese surrender marked the high point of MacArthur's life. Everything that followed was necessarily anticlimactic. The general could never achieve a greater role than as orchestrator of the American victory in the Pacific, and the film had to treat his years in Japan and as United Nations commander in Korea as a series of vignettes. This episodic treatment precluded a build-up of dramatic tensions toward the film's conclusion. And the filmmakers intensified the problem by using the general's farewell speech at West Point as their starting point rather than climax and then flashing back to Corregidor to start the biography.

The filmmakers worked diligently to produce a historically accurate and even-handed biography. Even so, inaccuracies crept in. For example, MacArthur and his party left Corregidor aboard four PT-boats, not two as shown in the film. His return to the Philippines was made on Leyte Beach, not Luzon as portrayed on the screen. MacArthur probably did not answer President Osmena's comment, "Suppose the people learn I can't swim?" with "Suppose they learn I can't walk on water?" as the two men prepared to embark. MacArthur shunned visits to wounded servicemen in hospitals, but in the film he visits wounded in the tunnel hospital on Corregidor. He was not on Buna during the fight for the island, again contrary to the film.[27] And Truman lived at

Blair House when he decided to remove MacArthur from his Korean command not in the White House as shown—it was then in the process of being renovated.

In the end, however, the failure of *MacArthur* as a dramatic, insightful, and moving film was not the fault of historical errors or even poorly re-created battle sequences. As a movie biography, *MacArthur* could only be as success-ful as the actor in the title role. Whatever Peck's acting talents (and they were clearly demonstrated in films such as *Twelve O'Clock High* and *To Kill a Mock-ingbird*), he suffered in inevitable comparison with George C. Scott. Where Scott brought out all of Patton's ambiguities, his ability and his weakness, Peck simply could not capture the grand MacArthur style and so could not indicate why he became the center of so much controversy. According to Richard Schickel in *Time*, MacArthur deserved "a robust life made of him: something that really attacked its subject, taking a strong point of view about him—whether for or against would not have mattered. The Great Commander never operated in a climate of caution, and there is no good reason why this movie should. Something of the spirit of *Patton* is what is required."[28] More suc-cintly, Robert Sherrod, a MacArthur biographer, observed, "MacArthur was a better actor than Peck."[29]

★ A Bridge Too Far

Regardless of their dramatic qualities, both *Midway* and *MacArthur* presented the American military at its best, fighting and winning battles, and emerging with its reputation unblemished. As far as the United States Army was con-cerned, Operation Market Garden, described in Cornelius Ryan's *A Bridge Too Far*, was also a success. In the operation, which took place in September 1944, American forces captured all of their objectives and held them. Overall, how-ever, the enterprise proved to be a tragic fiasco. Of the 10,000 men of the Bri-tish First Airborne Division who landed at Arnhem in the Netherlands (the "Bridge Too Far"), fewer than 2,000 made their way back to Allied lines. More men died in the operation than on the Normandy beaches. Most important, the combined Allied effort failed to open the road to Germany in the fall of 1944, and the war dragged on until the following May.

Joseph E. Levine's $27,000,000 *A Bridge Too Far* (1977), which brought Ryan's best seller to the screen spectacularly, focuses more on the British ef-forts to capture the Arnhem Bridge than on the American role in the battle. In the tradition of *The Longest Day, Tora! Tora! Tora!*, and *Midway*, the film followed the battle from its inception through its implementation to its conclusion. Like its predecessors, the film used two dozen or so leading actors, for the most part in cameo roles, and several received huge salaries. Robert Redford, for one, reportedly received $2,000,000 for ten minutes of screen time. It is debatable whether the expenditure of such amounts of money for actors helps or hinders a film. Instead of getting caught up in the action, audiences tend to look for their favorite stars, who cannot develop their characterizations in any case because of the brief nature of their roles.

Most of the actors gave credible performances for their large salaries. According to most critics, however, Ryan O'Neal, as General James Gavin, was miscast. Richard Schickel suggested that O'Neal "looks as if he is about to inquire, 'Tennis, anyone?' like a summer-stock juvenile."[30] General Gavin himself acknowledged that O'Neal "tried very hard, could not have been more serious in trying to carry out the role in which he was cast, and I admired his effort. . . .[but he was] perceived as a matinee idol, and it may have been very difficult for him to carry out the role that I had." Part of the problem was that O'Neal had not been drilled in military procedure. Gavin noted that he "carried a rifle like a broomstick over his right shoulder, the butt well to the rear behind him and holding the rifle by the metal part, near the muzzle." He was totally unprepared for action, according to Gavin, who recalled that "being engaged by fire as soon as we landed, we all carried our rifles in a very ready position, knowing that we would need them."[31]

In the context of the film, this was a small matter that would bother only people who came to it with a knowledge of military procedure. A more serious problem was the film's inability to keep the audience adequately informed of what was happening, where, and when. Levine spent his money well in re-creating the battle sequences. Given his problems in accumulating the World War II planes and tanks, the combat sequences are remarkably realistic and, like *The Longest Day*, use no old World War II footage. The William Goldman script clearly explains the origins of Operation Market Garden, the planning, the military risks, the expectations of success. It also delineates the mistakes in planning and errors in judgment that doomed the attack before it began. However, it could have emphasized more General Montgomery's failure to heed intelligence reports that showed a German build-up at the precise point the British were to land—landing in fact in full view of German Field Marshal Model's window, where he happened to be standing at the exact moment. And the screenplay could have been more explicit in explaining that Montgomery disregarded the reports, hoping that Operation Market Garden would enable him to beat Patton to Berlin.

The film's problems begin once the battle is launched. Events happen too quickly over too broad an area for director Richard Attenborough to handle effectively. Confusion reigned in 1944 Holland, and it reigns again in the movie. Military men as well as readers of Ryan's book admitted to bewilderment during the film.[32] Moreover, while the script attempts to humanize the struggle by following individuals as they try to survive the bloodbath, the scope of the actions overwhelms the effect of individual characters. In trying to follow the course of events while watching the stars go through their paces, the viewer has little time to consider the possible meaning of the images on the screen. Attenborough had thought *A Bridge Too Far* would be a "very moving" film that would "prove to be one of the greatest antiwar pictures ever made" through the war-is-hell theme. Relaxing between takes of one of the more ambitious combat scenes, he observed, "The marvelous thing in this film is that the facts shout for themselves."[33]

What seemed an antiwar "shout" to the director during production seldom appears that way in the completed product. In part, it failed to make its statement because it was filmed in color; it often seems too pretty, too much like a typical Hollywood combat epic and not enough like a portrayal of a tragic debacle. As a result, the blood and gore fail to create a repulsion with the scenes of death and destruction.

The individual episodes too often ended up conveying a sense of excitement, adventure, and humor rather than the terror of being under constant attack. Paddling a boat across a river under heavy fire, for example, obviously shows the dangers of combat. Performed by Robert Redford, who mumbles "Hail Mary" all the way, the sequence becomes almost comic. Building a temporary bridge in a few hours so that the advance can continue is a tension-filled operation when hundreds of lives are in the balance. But the drama of the sequence is dissipated by Elliot Gould's performance, which has the aura of a Dean Martin comedy routine on a television special. There are elements of high tragedy in a Polish general's concern for the success of his assignment and the safety of his men and his later pain over the needless losses. Played by Gene Hackman, the general is reduced to a Polish joke. Apart from the issue of using violence to create antiwar sentiment, the portrayal of combat in a comedic, almost surrealistic manner effectively destroys the film's pacifistic message. What remains are visual images of random exciting action. Viewers can only respect Levine and Attenborough for attempting to re-create the battle on such a broad scale so many years after the event.

Ultimately, *A Bridge Too Far* failed as an antiwar statement because people recognized the necessity for World War II, and in their minds it re-

mained a successful and even good war. Operation Market Garden may have
been a disaster, but the battle is remembered mainly in terms of the bravery
and fortitude of the men who fought and died. V-E Day served as their tribute
and memorial.

The same cannot be said of the United States experience in Vietnam, the
subject of *Apocalypse Now* (1978).

CHAPTER FIFTEEN

HOLLYWOOD AND VIETNAM: A BEGINNING

★

America's wounds from the war in Southeast Asia have healed slowly. Particularly in the face of defeat, the war's 55,000 American combat deaths seem to have been futile sacrifices, and maimed veterans remain stark reminders of the war's continuing price. These lingering memories have made Hollywood reluctant to use the war either as the setting for an action-adventure movie or even as the motif for an antiwar statement. Until the mid-1970s, only an occasional television drama or film like *Limbo* touched on the subject.

Not until 1975 did a major filmmaker turn to the subject of Vietnam. Having completed his second *Godfather* film, Francis Ford Coppola told an interviewer that his next movie would deal with Vietnam, "although it won't necessarily be political—it will be about war and the human soul. . . . I'll be venturing into an area that is laden with so many implications that if I select some aspects and ignore others, I may be doing something irresponsible. So I'll be thinking hard about it."[1]

As the vehicle for his expedition, Coppola selected a six-year-old script by John Milius, which shifted Joseph Conrad's *Heart of Darkness* from the jungles of Africa to Southeast Asia. Milius' screenplay transferred Conrad's theme of civilization's submission to the brutality of human nature to the story of a Green Beret officer who defects and sets up his own army across the Cambo-

---

Captain Willard sets out in his search for Colonel Kurtz in Apocalypse Now (1978).

dian border, where he fights both American and Vietcong forces. Working with "Agency" representatives, the United States Army orders an officer to find and "terminate" the renegade and eliminate his band of deserters.

Throughout the production, Coppola characterized his film as pro-American, denying it was anti-Pentagon or even antiwar. One day, while filming in the Philippines, he said, "It is an anti-lie, not an antiwar film. I am interested in the contradictions of the human condition." In his intellectual attraction to the contradictions in man, to the good and evil that are inherent in all humans, Coppola said that he was trying to make a war movie that would somehow rise above conventional images of valor and cowardice. When asked why he was attempting to show this in a film set in Vietnam, he responded that it was "more unusual that I am the only one making a picture about Vietnam."[2]

In May of 1975, during the early development of the project, Coppola and producer Fred Roos visited the Pentagon to advise officials of their plans for the film. Coppola provided a copy of Milius' script and explained that it still needed considerable revision. He said he would personally work on the last portion of the screenplay in particular, which he described as "surrealistic." He also indicated that he wanted to work with the Pentagon as closely as possible to obtain background information, stock footage for study purposes, and possibly physical assistance during actual filming. But he also admitted he had yet to decide where he would shoot the film or whether he would formally request military assistance.[3]

For several years, Defense Department officials had believed the Vietnam War would make an attractive setting for a good action-adventure movie that focused on soldiers doing their assigned jobs professionally. They hoped that such a film would avoid the political issues of the Vietnam conflict, but they also recognized the inevitability that any film about the war would present negative as well as positive aspects.[4]

With this in mind, the Pentagon's Public Affairs Office sent the script for *Apocalypse Now* to the Army Office of Information, advising it that the military should have the opportunity "to present factual corrections and recommendations to put the story in proper perspective." Since Coppola had indicated he would make the film under any circumstances, Defense Department officials recommended that the Army work with him "towards preparing a final script that will be an honest presentation" whether the Pentagon ultimately agreed to provide assistance or not.[5]

The Army immediately objected to the script as "simply a series of some of the worst things, real and imagined, that happened or could have happened during the Vietnam War." It informed the Public Affairs Office that there was little basis for cooperating "in view of the sick humor or satirical philosophy of the film." Several "particularly objectionable episodes" presented its military actions "in an unrealistic and unacceptable bad light." These scenes included U.S. soldiers scalping the enemy, a surfing display in the midst of combat, and an officer obtaining sexual favors for his men and later smoking marijuana with them.[6]

The Army and the Defense Department probably would have been able to live with at least some of these negative incidents—in the proper context. But from the initial script onward, the military strongly objected to the main plot situation in which Colonel Kurtz (Marlon Brando) sets up his independent operation in Cambodia and Captain Willard (Martin Sheen) is sent to "terminate" him. In its initial response to Milius' script, the Army said Kurtz's actions "can only be viewed as a parody on the sickness and brutality of war."[7]

Both in the Army's original response and in subsequent comments, military men asserted that an officer would desert only if he had become mentally unbalanced. In an actual situation, officials insisted, the Army would attempt to bring him back for medical treatment rather than order another officer to "terminate" him. Moreover, they explained that any such problem would be handled within the military chain of command, not by a civilian "Agency" as called for in the script. Consequently, the Army Information Office said that "to assist in any way in the production would imply agreement with either the fact or the philosophy of the film."[8]

While the Army washed its hands of the project, Defense Department Public Affairs officials attempted to keep communications open with Coppola, as he had hoped they would. Officials explained to Gray Frederickson, Roos' co-producer, that the Army felt the basis for the film was not factual and invited Coppola to return for discussions that might make the script more acceptable.[9]

In July 1975, Frederickson called the Public Affairs Office to arrange a research trip to Fort Bragg to look at a simulated Vietnamese village used in training. Officials agreed and suggested that after his visit, Coppola should stop in Washington to discuss script changes. Although the Army subsequently scheduled the visit and agreed to talk to the filmmakers, Coppola never appeared at Fort Bragg or in Washington.[10]

Instead, he headed to the Far East in search of suitable locations and military assistance. Going first to Australia, Coppola showed a lack of knowledge of American arms sales in asking the Australian government for use of B-52 bombers—which have never been sold abroad. When he also requested use of 10,000 troops and 400 helicopters, the government turned him down cold, saying its Army was "not a film-extra agency." Coppola then turned to the Philippines, where he reached an agreement with the government in December 1975, for suitable filming locations and use of its Army and equipment.[11]

During his trip, Coppola also visited a U.S. naval base in the Philippines, where he inquired about the use of planes, helicopters, and men. There, he was advised to first obtain Defense Department approval of assistance. When it received the report of Coppola's visit, the Pentagon's Public Affairs Office wrote to remind him that he could expect little or no assistance based on his original script. The Pentagon also said it would be willing to review any future script and discuss a request for assistance based on an acceptable revision.[12]

At the end of December, Fred Roos submitted a revised script to the Pentagon, although he "honestly" doubted it would change the military's stance regarding formal assistance. Still, Roos told officials he wanted "to keep the communication between us open. Any constructive advice or suggestions you wish to give us unofficially will be welcome and considered." Essentially, the revision was little different from the original, and the Pentagon saw no reason to comment on it. However, Roos was advised to visit the Information Office of the commander-in-chief of the Pacific if he planned any military contact of a research nature.[13]

In mid-April 1976, with filming under way, Coppola discovered that the Philippine Army could not supply him with all the needed helicopters and jets. At that point he made his first official request for American military assistance, submitted still another script, and asked for the needed aircraft. He persisted in ignoring the regulation that any screenplay had to be approved before the military could formally discuss assistance.[14]

Defense Department officials repeated their willingness to consider his request if Coppola would agree to eliminate certain objectionable scenes, including the sending of one officer to "terminate with prejudice" another officer. They suggested changing the film's springboard to an officer who is "investigating and bringing those guilty of wrongful action back for a courtmartial or medical/psychiatric treatment." The Defense Department felt these changes "would be of mutual benefit by making the film more logical and factual." The officials also warned that even if the script were approved for assistance, the needed military hardware might not be available in the Philippines when Coppola needed it.[15]

Coppola responded almost immediately with an offer to make several changes in the script including making "it an unspecified civilian who sends Willard on his assignment, rather than an Army officer, and I will present the situation in such a way that it will be obvious that there is no alternative but to terminate Kurtz if he does not comply." He also said he would make it clear that the "desire to secure a surfing beach is secondary to some bona fide military mission." The Defense Department did not find the proffered changes satisfactory, particularly with regard to the issue of terminating Kurtz. Neverthe-

Francis Ford Coppola became the first American filmmaker to undertake a film about the Vietnam War since John Wayne made The Green Berets *in 1968. Like the war, the production of* Apocalypse Now *seemed to have no end.*

less, Pentagon officials remained willing to reach some accomodation, and a series of telegrams was exchanged. The Pentagon indicated that Willard must be sent to "investigate" with no reference to "termination." Furthermore, officials suggested that in the screen titles Coppola include a statement "honoring those who served in Vietnam." If he agreed in principle to the revisions, the Pentagon felt that detailed changes "could probably be negotiated." They also suggested that the best way to resolve differences would be for Coppola or his representative to come to Washington.[16]

Finally, in early June, Assistant Secretary of Defense for Public Affairs William Greener telegraphed Coppola that he would be willing to send one of his assistants to the Philippines to discuss "all aspects of possible Defense Department support. . . . if there was some affirmative indication that the suggested script modifications are being considered positively and constructively." Greener said that if Coppola agreed to the "general thrust of the suggested modifications," the agreement on detail would not distract "from the overall impact of your production."[17]

Coppola did not respond to Greener's telegram, perhaps because filming was too far along for him to modify the basic story line, or perhaps because of the chaos following a typhoon in May, which had destroyed many of the movie sets. Finally in February 1977, Coppola again turned to the American government for assistance on the final stages of *Apocalypse Now.*

Claiming that the film was "honest, mythical, prohuman, and therefore pro-American," Coppola telegraphed President Carter requesting "some modicum of cooperation or entire government will appear ridiculous to American and world public." He explained to the new president that "because of misunderstanding original script which was only starting point for me," the Pentagon "has done everything to stop" the production of the first major Hollywood film about Vietnam since the end of the war.

Coppola asked Carter for use of one Chinook helicopter for one day, citing the assistance John Wayne received on *The Green Berets* as justification for his request. He also said he needed "immediate approval" to purchase ten cases of smoke markers, which the Pentagon had denied along with all other requests for assistance. In closing, Coppola told President Carter that his movie "tries its best to put Vietnam behind us, which we must do so we can go to a positive future."[18]

Since neither Coppola nor his public relations staff would comment on any aspect of *Apocalypse Now* during the final year and a half of its production, it was impossible to ascertain what the director meant when he stated that the "entire government will appear ridiculous to American and world public" if he didn't receive Pentagon assistance. But from the records, it seems clear that the Pentagon did not do "everything to stop" *Apocalypse Now*. Except for the Army's initial intransigence regarding the original script, Pentagon officials continued to communicate openly with Coppola and his staff, hoping to agree on a script that would qualify for assistance. In contrast to the Navy's sensitivity about its image in *The Last Detail* and *Cinderella Liberty*, both the Army and the Defense Department recognized that any film about Vietnam would necessarily contain elements that would not reflect favorably on the military's experience in Southeast Asia. Nevertheless, the Pentagon remained willing to assist—within the limits of its regulations—on scripts that were accurate.

The interdepartment memos written from April to June 1976, during the exchanges between Coppola and the Defense Department, show that officials were willing to take an extra step to avoid a confrontation. In one memo on May 10, an official indicated that the Public Affairs Office believed that "if we could come to a mutual agreement to changes, even if only to the opening sequence (springboard of the story) and to the closing episode at the Green Beret camp, it would be a worthwhile bargain to grant assistance by making four aircraft available on the basis of non-interference and no-additional-cost-to-the-government." Because of the problems of negotiating by correspondence, the official urged that a meeting be set up in the Pentagon with Coppola or his representative. In a subsequent memo on the 20th, questions were raised about whether the military would be able to provide assistance even if an agreement were reached. But the official recommended that if negotiations were successful, the Pentagon should "provide such assistance, as we are able, in consideration of no cost to the government, no interference with missions, and all safety factors taken into account."[19]

Just as the Pentagon had not closed the avenue to assistance during the first half of 1976, it had not "denied" Coppola's request to purchase smoke markers or use a helicopter in February 1977—as he charged in his telegram to President Carter. At the time he made his accusation, the Pentagon was in the process of considering the request, and its subsequent decision to do nothing about it resulted from Coppola's own failure to negotiate in good faith and because no assistance could be given until the script had been officially approved.

Coppola did not follow up his telegram to President Carter. In June 1977, however, a San Francisco attorney wrote to the Pentagon seeking to obtain for an unnamed client "certain soundtracks or recordings" to use for a motion picture. Since Coppola's headquarters were in San Francisco and the request was for rifle fire, rocket launchers, jet fighters, and Chinese ordnance, it was not difficult to figure out who the client was. When the attorney called the Pentagon, Don Baruch advised him that the sound effects were available from any number of commercial sources—including Radio Shack. The lawyer later sent a thank-you note saying the technical people were "pleased with the cooperation they have received."[20]

Coppola's difficulties with *Apocalypse Now* multiplied. Like the American intervention in Vietnam, which had bogged down in a quagmire, Coppola's project seemed to slowly sink beneath the weight of its problems and a budget that escalated from an original estimate of about $10,000,000 to a figure approaching $30,000,000 by 1978. First scheduled for release in April of 1977, the premiere was postponed until November and then finally delayed a full year to November 1978.

With a virtual blackout on information about the film, and with Coppola continuing to reshoot exterior combat scenes even after his return from the Philippines in February 1977 (he filmed sequences in the Napa Valley in July 1977) expectations grew about the final form of the film. While in the Philippines, Coppola had said, "I can allow the film to be violent because I don't consider it an antiviolence movie. If you want to make an antiviolence film, it cannot be violent. Showing the horrors of war with people being cut up and saying it will prevent violence is a lie. Violence breeds violence. If you put a lot of it on the screen, it makes people lust for violence."[21]

Coppola's earlier films all showed his propensity for portraying people's lust for violence. *Patton*, for which he wrote the original screenplay, contained broad scenes of bloody slaughter. *The Rain People*, ostensibly a cross-country odyssey, contained in it the threat of impending violence, a threat Coppola ultimately delivered. *The Conversation* as well as the two *Godfather* films utilized violence as a major theme, and Coppola splattered the screen with blood in them. And all reports indicated that he intended to outdo himself in *Apocalypse Now*.

Vietnam provided Coppola with all the examples he might want. To duplicate its carnage, he went to great lengths to insure visual authenticity. To create a village devastation scene, Coppola hired dozens of South Vietnamese refugees and according to a crew member, "We literally stacked them up like logs, dangled a few arms and legs around, and poured gallons of blood over them." Another crew member said, "It will make *The Godfather* look like a kid's story."[22] One of Coppola's spokesmen claimed, however, that the director had "no intention or interest in making *Apocalypse Now* grisly or gory," and he attributed the stories to personnel who were "unqualified to assess the film's eventual tone and content."[23]

Precisely what that tone would be remained perhaps the longest running battle during the production of *Apocalypse Now*. Marlon Brando's stand-in (Brando showed up in the Philippines weighing 285 pounds, so Coppola decided to make Colonel Kurtz six feet, five inches and use a double for Brando's body shots) suggested, "What Francis is trying to say is that the military people were not second-class citizens and idiots. They were good hometown boys, but the war changed them. The whole military image is going to be changed after this." The special effects chief observed that the "whole movie is special effects. You got three stars but the action's gonna keep the audience on the edge of their seats. It's a war movie." The production designer said, "This movie's about how wrong it was for Americans to go against their nature."[24] Except to inform his staff that in his "personal opinion. . . *Apocalypse Now* is going to be a very fine film, possibly even a great film. I have never worked on a film before that truly had that possibility,"[25] and to describe the film to President Carter, Coppola refused to publicly discuss the film after the completion of principal shooting in the Philippines.

His apparent fascination with violence in his earlier movies, reports that filtered back from the Philippines, and his statements during production and to President Carter all indicated that Coppola was using images of violence in *Apocalypse Now* to create a catharsis in the viewer and so purge Vietnam from the American psyche. He himself answered the question as to why he wanted to "scratch old wounds," by saying, "I'm cauterizing old wounds, trying to let people put the war behind them. You can never do that by forgetting it."[26] Whether repeated scenes of blood and guts and massive destruction will "help America put Vietnam behind us, which we must do so we can go on to a positive future" as he told President Carter, is another matter. Yet as Coppola himself observed, rather than repulse them, the portrayal of violence usually makes people lust for violence. Moreover, it is doubtful that the re-creation in living color of Vietnam's horrors can be considered "pro-human and therefore pro-American." Even if Coppola had significantly reworked Milius' original script, it is unlikely that the depiction of the fighting in Vietnam, whether in *Apocalypse Now* or any other movie, could significantly change the image created by ten years' television coverage of the war. It definitely cannot help the image the armed forces have been attempting to develop since 1973 as an aid in recruiting for the all-volunteer military.

In any event, while *Apocalypse Now* was the first film about Vietnam to go into production since *The Green Berets*, the postponements in its release prevented it from being the first Hollywood film about the war since 1968 to reach American theaters. Coppola and his production spawned a number of movies that used the Vietnam War as their starting point, either to tell stories about returning veterans or simply to serve as a new site for combat stories.

The first of these to appear, *Rolling Thunder* (1977) and *Heroes* (1977), developed the theme of the returning fighting man as the victim of war and focused on the scarred veterans' efforts to adjust to their peacetime environment. *Rolling Thunder* is the story of a POW who returns home and seeks revenge on the killers of his family. The producer's request for assistance from the Air Force was flatly rejected, and the Defense Department advised him: "There are no known cases of Air Force officers becoming schizophrenic as happens . . . in the story. Yes, there are cases of returnees coming home to marital problems, but there is nothing beneficial for the Department of Defense in the dramatization of this situation." The Pentagon agreed, however, that there were positive elements in the officer's stoic behavior while he was a POW.[27] Essentially the film used the murder of the officer's family as a springboard to a stereotyped revenge plot, with his Vietnam experiences the justification for his crazed and vengeful rampage. Most reviewers found the violence excessive, and audiences had already seen the story in the recent movie, *Death Wish*.

In contrast, *Heroes* (which received some limited Pentagon assistance) was basically a typical "road" film in which the hero, played by Henry Winkler, is a demented veteran who roams the country trying to find himself. *Heroes* attempts to convey an antiwar message by characterizing its hero as a victim of Vietnam. The film opens promisingly enough with his insane efforts to drag potential enlistees from the grasp of a recruiting officer who is telling the youths that "war is better than sex." But for most of its length, the film is little more than another romantic comedy, filled with Winkler's antics and efforts to woo Sally Field whom he has picked up along the way. Only in the closing sequences, during which the cause of Winkler's insanity is finally visualized in a brief but

(Above and right) Ted Post talks to Burt Lancaster during filming of Go Tell the Spartans (1978), one of the first combat movies about Vietnam to reach American audiences.

well-done firefight, does the film make a meaningful statement about the terrible effect of the war on at least some of its participants.

Coming Home (1978), with Jane Fonda, was a more serious attempt to explore the problems of returning veterans. It combined elements of *The Men* with drug problems and a three-sided romance. Fonda, who plays a middle-class American wife, must choose between two Vietnam veterans, her hallucinating war-hero husband or a radicalized paraplegic. Like *The Men*, many scenes were shot in a hospital for severely injured veterans, which helped the film visualize its antiwar statement through the war's actual victims.

In contrast, movies such as *Deer Hunter*, *Boys in Company C*, and *Go Tell The Spartans*, all released in 1978, focused on actual combat in Vietnam. *Deer Hunter* tells the story of a restless veteran who leaves his job in a steel mill to return to Vietnam, where he hopes to find his missing buddy. He arrives just in time to be caught up in the fall of Saigon, staged in Thailand. Max Youngstein, the producer of *The Boys in Company C*, believed that by 1978 the American public had reached the point where they were willing to "take a look back at what happened in Vietnam, warts and all." His film showed the warts by concentrating on a unit of young American Marines.[28]

Ted Post, director of *Go Tell the Spartans*, felt that after Watergate the American people "are open to disillusion. It's now safe to cope with the issues the war raised."[25] In fact, it took seven years for Wendell Mayes to find a producer for his script about a group of American soldiers during the early days of the United States involvement in Vietnam. Burt Lancaster plays Major Asa Barker, a "crusty officer who has been through too many wars to be a hero, but not too many to remember his duty to his men." According to the producers, the concept of surrounding Lancaster with young, little-known actors "coincides with the American consciousness of those early years in Vietnam, when we knew little more than what the president or the generals told us and the battle lines were being manned by the anonymous volunteers of our special combat forces."[30]

The film was shot in the foothills outside Los Angeles and used dozens of Vietnamese refugees as South Vietnamese soldiers, peasants, and Vietcong. Many had been soldiers in the war and were able to contribute their advice on technical details as well as perform realistically in the battle scenes. Nevertheless, the film is not one of major battles but of the experiences of a small patrol of Americans, their working relationship with their Vietnamese counterparts, and what happens when they meet the enemy in combat.

Their "moment of truth" comes in a minor battle fought with grenades and small arms, and finally hand-to-hand. In fact, the story is not unique to the Vietnam war, and as such, audiences may view it as a traditional war film offering

**Hollywood and
Vietnam: A Beginning**

adventure and escapism. If so, then it would hardly be a test of whether Americans are ready to look back on Vietnam, "warts and all." In any case, the future production of films about the war in Southeast Asia will most likely be determined not by the success or failure of these first movies but by the reaction to *Apocalypse Now*.

If Coppola's epic proves successful, American filmgoers will undoubtedly be treated to a full cycle of movies about all aspects of the nation's experience

The activities of Chuck Norris and his elite commando unit, charged with rescuing POWs from behind enemy lines in the Vietnam War, serve as the starting point for Good Guys Wear Black (1978), an action film set for the most part in the years following the end of hostilities.

in Vietnam. But however many films are ultimately produced, they will not be able to show the armed forces winning glorious victories against an evil enemy as Hollywood was able to do when portraying earlier American conflicts. Vietnam simply does not lend itself to this type of characterization. Nor is it possible for filmmakers to produce the types of movies about the peacetime military that *Strategic Air Command* or *Gathering of Eagles* represent. Vietnam and Watergate have made Americans more skeptical of their institutions. No longer will they accept uncritical portrayals of the military, whether in peace or in war.

To Ron Kovic, the paralyzed Vietnam veteran and author of *Born on the Fourth of July*: "The war's not over. The war is between those who caught hell and those who give it out. Just 'cause it's not on TV doesn't mean they stopped giving it out. Ask someone who's fought one. They'll tell you a war isn't over until you don't have to live with it anymore."[31] But to those who have not known the horrors of combat and the pain of injury, to those who have fought yet retain memories only of the excitement and camaraderie created by their common confrontation with death, for all these the glamour symbolized by the uniform and the thrill of combat hold a special fascination.

The spectacular success of *Star Wars*, essentially a traditional war movie set in another time and place, undoubtedly resulted partly from the desire of the American people to re-experience the triumph of good over evil in glorious and honorable combat. If movies about Vietnam cannot delineate events in black and white or portray spectacular victories, they can still depict individual bravery, perseverance in the face of a determined enemy, and perhaps most important, the unique excitement of challenging death in personal combat. As long as war movies of whatever time and place do that, they will maintain their special place in American homes and theaters.

FILMS DISCUSSED

Above and Beyond, 1952. Air Froce, WWII, MGM. Directors, screenplay, and producers: Melvin Frank, Norman Panama. Stars: Robert Taylor, James Whitmore. Military cooperation.

Air Force, 1943. Air Force, WWII, Warner. Director: Howard Hawks. Screenplay: Dudley Nichols. Producer: Hal Wallis. Stars: John Garfield, Gig Young, Ward Bond. Military cooperation.

All Quiet on the Western Front, 1930. Army, WWI, Universal. Director: Lewis Milestone. Screenplay: Maxwell Anderson. Stars: Lew Ayres, Ben Alexander.

America, 1924. Army, Revolutionary, United Artists. Director: D. W. Griffith. Star: Lionel Barrymore. Military cooperation.

Americanization of Emily, 1964. Navy, WWI, MGM. Director: Arthur Hiller. Screenplay: Paddy Chayevsky. Producers: Martin Ransohoff, John Calley. Stars: James Garner, Melvyn Douglas, Julie Andrews, James Coburn.

Apocalypse Now, 1978. Army, Vietnam, United Artists. Director: Francis Coppola. Screenplay: John Milius, Francis Coppola. Producers: Fred Roos, Gray Frederickson. Stars: Martin Sheen, Marlon Brando, Robert Duvall, Dennis Hooper.

Attack!, 1956. Army, WWII, United Artists. Director and producer: Robert Aldrich. Screenplay: James Poe. Stars: Jack Palance, Eddie Albert, Lee Marvin.

Bataan, 1943. Army, WWII, MGM. Director: Tay Garnett. Screenplay: Robert Andrews. Producer: Dore Schary. Stars: Robert Taylor, George Murphy, Desi Arnaz, Lloyd Nolan.

Battle Cry, 1955. Marines, WWII, Warner. Director: Raoul Walsh. Screenplay: Leon Uris. Stars: Van Heflin, Aldo Ray, James Whitmore, Tab Hunter. Military cooperation.

Battleground, 1949. Army, WWII, MGM. Director: William Wellman. Screenplay: Robert Pirosh. Producer: Dore Schary. Stars: Van Johnson, George Murphy, Ricardo Montalban. Military cooperation.

Battle of San Pietro, 1945. Army, WWI, Army Signal Corps. Director and Screenplay: John Huston. Military cooperation.

Battle of the Bulge, 1965. Army, WWII, Warner. Director: Ken Annakin. Screenplay and Producer: Philip Yordan, Milton Sperling. Stars: Henry Fonda, Robert Shaw, Robert Ryan.

Beach Red, 1967. Marines, WWII, United Artists. Director and Producer: Cornel Wilde. Screenplay: Clint Johnston, Donald Peters. Stars: Cornel Wilde, Rip Torn. Military cooperation.

The Bedford Incident, 1965. Navy, Cold War, Columbia. Director and Producer: James Harris. Screenplay: James Poe. Stars: Richard Widmark, Sidney Poitier, Martin Balsam.

The Big Parade, 1925. Army, WWI, MGM. Director: King Vidor. Screenplay: Harry Behn. Stars: John Gilbert, Rene Adoree. Military cooperation.

Birth of a Nation, 1915. Army, Civil War, Epoch Producing Corp. Director: D. W. Griffith. Stars: Lillian Gish, Raoul Walsh. Military cooperation.

Bridge at Remagen, 1969. Army, WWII, United Artists. Director: John Guillermin. Screenplay: William Roberts, Richard Yates. Producer: David Wolper. Stars: Robert Vaughn, Ben Gazzara, George Segal.

A Bridge Too Far, 1977. WWII, Joseph E. Levine Productions. Director: Richard Attenborough. Screenplay: William Goldman. Producer: Joseph E. Levine. Stars: Robert Redford, Eliot Gould, Ryan O'Neal, Gene Hackman. Military cooperation.

Bridges at Toko-Ri, 1954. Navy, Korea, Paramount. Director: Mark Robson. Screenplay: Valentine Davies. Producers: William Perlberg, George Seaton. Stars: William Holden, Fredric March, Grace Kelley. Military cooperation.

The Caine Mutiny, 1954. Navy, WWII, Columbia. Director: Edward Dmytryk. Screenplay: Stanley Roberts, Michael Blankfort. Producer: Stanley Kramer. Stars: Humphrey Bogart, Jose Ferrer, Van Johnson, Fred MacMurray, Robert Francis. Military cooperation.

Catch-22, 1970. Air Force, WWII, Paramount. Director: Mike Nichols. Screenplay: Buck Henry. Producers: John Calley, Martin Ransohoff. Stars: Alan Arkin, Martin Balsam, Art Garfunkel, Buck Henry, Orson Welles, Richard Benjamin, Paula Prentiss.

Cinderella Liberty, 1973. Navy, Peacetime, 20th Century Fox. Director and Producer: Mark Rydell. Screenplay: Darryl Ponicsan. Stars: James Caan, Marsha Mason.

Command Decision, 1948. Air Force, WWII, MGM. Director: Sam Wood. Screenplay: William Laidlaw, George Froeschel. Producer: Sidney Franklin. Stars: Clark Gable, Walter Pidgeon, Edward Arnold, Van Johnson. Military cooperation.

Destination Tokyo, 1943. Air Force & Navy, WWII, Warner. Director and Screenplay: Delmer Daves. Producer: Jerry Wald. Stars: Cary Grant, John Garfield. Military cooperation.

Devil's Brigade, 1968. Army, WWII, United Artists. Director: Andrew McLaglen. Screenplay: William Roberts. Producer: David Wolper. Stars: William Holden, Cliff Robertson, Vince Edwards. Military cooperation.

Dive Bomber, 1941. Navy, Preparedness, Warner. Director: Michael Curtiz. Screenplay: Frank Wead. Producer: Hal Wallis. Stars: Fred MacMurray, Ralph Bellamy, Errol Flynn. Military cooperation.

Dr. Strangelove, 1964. Air Force, Cold War, Columbia. Director and Producer: Stanley Kubrick. Screenplay: Stanley Kubrick, Terry Southern. Stars: George C. Scott, Peter Sellers, Sterling Hayden, Slim Pickens.

Fail Safe, 1964. Air Force, Cold War, Columbia. Director: Sidney Lumet. Screenplay: Walter Brenstein. Producer: Max Youngstein. Stars: Henry Fonda, Walter Matthau.

Fighting Seabees, 1944. WWII, Republic. Director: Edward Ludwig. Screenplay: Borden Chase. Producer: Albert Cohen. Stars: John Wayne, Dennis O'Keefe. Military cooperation.

Flirtation Walk, 1934. Army, Peacetime, Warner. Director: Frank Borzage. Screenplay: Delmer Daves. Star: Dick Powell. Military cooperation.

From Here to Eternity, 1953. Army, Peacetime, Columbia. Director: Fred Zinnemann. Screenplay: Daniel Taradash. Producer: Buddy Adler. Military cooperation. Stars: Burt Lancaster, Montgomery Clift, Frank Sinatra, Deborah Kerr, Donna Reed.

Gathering of Eagles, 1963. Air Force, Cold War, Universal. Director: Delbert Mann. Screenplay: Robert Pirosh. Producer: Sy Bartlett. Stars: Rock Hudson, Rod Taylor. Military cooperation.

Go Tell the Spartans, 1978. Army, Vietnam, Mar Vista Productions. Director: Ted Post. Screenplay: Wendell Mayes. Producer: Allan Bodoh. Star: Burt Lancaster.

The Green Berets, 1968. Army, Vietnam, Warner. Directors: John Wayne, Ray Kellogg. Screenplay: James Lee Barrett. Producer: Michael Wayne. Stars: John Wayne, David Janssen, Aldo Ray, Jim Hutton. Military cooperation.

In Harm's Way, 1965. Navy, WWII, Paramount. Director and Producer: Otto Preminger. Screenplay: Wendell Mayes. Stars: John Wayne, Kirk Douglas, Henry Fonda. Military cooperation.

The Last Detail, 1974. Navy, Peacetime, Columbia. Director: Hal Ashby. Screenplay: Robert Towne. Producer: Gerald Ayres. Stars: Jack Nicholson, Otis Young, Randy Quaid.

Let There Be Light, 1945. Army, WWII, Army Signal Corps. Director: John Huston. Screenplay: Charles Kaufman.

Limbo, 1973. Air Force, Vietnam, Universal. Director: Mark Robson. Screenplay: Joan Silver, James Bridges. Producer: Linda Gottlieb. Star: Kate Jackson.

The Longest Day, 1962. Army, WWII, 20th Century Fox. Directors: Ken Annakin, Andrew Marton, Bernhard Wicki. Screenplay: Cornelius Ryan, James Jones. Producers: Darryl Zanuck, Elmo Williams. Stars: John Wayne, Henry Fonda, Robert Mitchum, Richard Burton, Red Buttons. Military cooperation.

MacArthur, 1977. Army & Marines, WWII/Korea, Universal. Director: Joseph Sargent. Screenplay: Hal Barwood, Matthew Robbins. Producer: Frank McCarthy. Stars: Gregory Peck, Ed Flanders, Dan O'Herlihy. Military cooperation.

M*A*S*H, 1970. Army, Korea, 20th Century Fox. Director: Robert Altman. Screenplay: Ring Lardner, Jr. Producer: Ingo Preminger. Stars: Elliot Gould, Donald Sutherland, Sally Kellerman.

Midway, 1976. Navy, WWII, Universal. Director: Jack Smight. Screenplay: Donald Sanford. Producer: Walter Mirisch. Stars: Charlton Heston, Henry Fonda, James Coburn, Glenn Ford, Hal Holbrook. Military cooperation.

The Men, 1950. Army, Peacetime, United Artists. Director: Fred Zinnemann. Screenplay: Carl Foreman. Producer: Stanley Kramer. Stars: Marlon Brando, Jack Webb. Military cooperation.

Men Without Women, 1930. Navy, Peacetime, Fox Film Studio. Director: John Ford. Screenplay: Dudley Nichols. Star: John Wayne. Military cooperation.

On the Beach, 1959. Navy, Cold War, United Artists. Director and Producer: Stanley Kramer. Screenplay: John Paxton. Stars: Gregory Peck, Ava Gardner, Fred Astaire, Anthony Perkins.

One Minute to Zero, 1952. Army, Korea, RKO. Director: Tay Garnett. Screenplay, William Haines, Milton Krims. Producer: Edmund Grainger. Star: Robert Mitchum. Military cooperation.

The Outsider, 1962. Marines, WWII/Peacetime, Universal. Director: Delbert Mann. Screenplay: Steward Stern. Producer: Sy Bartlett. Star: Tony Curtis. Military cooperation.

Paths of Glory, 1957. Army, WWI, United Artists. Director: Stanley Kubrick. Screenplay: Stanley Kramer, Calder Willingham. Producer: James Harris. Star: Kirk Douglas.

Patton, 1970. Army, WWII, 20th Century Fox. Director: Franklin Schaffner. Screenplay: Edmund North, Francis Coppola. Producer: Frank McCarthy. Stars: George C. Scott, Karl Malden. Military cooperation.

Pork Chop Hill, 1959. Army, Korea, United Artists. Director: Lewis Milestone. Screenplay: James Webb. Producer: Sy Bartlett. Star: Gregory Peck. Military cooperation.

PT-109, 1963. Navy, WWII, Warner. Director: Leslie Martinson. Screenplay: Richard Breen. Producer: Brian Foy, Jr. Stars: Cliff Robertson, Robert Culp. Military cooperation.

Pride of the Marines, 1945. Marines, WWII/Peacetime, Warner. Director: Delmer Daves. Screenplay: Albert Maltz. Producer: Jerry Wald. Star: John Garfield. Military cooperation.

Retreat, Hell!, 1952. Marines, Korea, Warner. Director: Joseph Lewis. Screenplay and Producer: Milton Sperling. Stars: Frank Lovejoy, Richard Carlson. Military cooperation.

Run Silent, Run Deep, 1958. Navy, WWII, United Artists. Director: Robert Wise. Screenplay: John Gay. Producer: Harold Hect. Stars: Clark Gable, Burt Lancaster, Jack Warden. Military cooperation.

Sahara, 1943. Army, WWII, Columbia. Director: Zolton Korda. Screenplay: John Howard Lawson. Stars: Humphrey Bogart, Lloyd Bridges, Dan Duryea. Military cooperation.

Sands of Iwo Jima, 1949. Marines, WWII, Republic. Director: Allan Dwan. Screenplay: Harry Brown, James Grant. Producer: Edmund Grainger. Stars: John Wayne, John Agar. Military cooperation.

Seven Days in May, 1964. Cold War, Paramount. Director: John Frankenheimer. Screenplay: Rod Serling. Producer: Edward Lewis. Stars: Burt Lancaster, Kirk Douglas, Fredric March, Ava Gardner.

Shipmates, 1932. Navy, Peacetime, MGM. Director: Harry Pollard. Screenplay, Delmer Daves. Producer: Paul Burn. Star: Robert Montgomery. Military cooperation.

Shipmates Forever, 1935. Navy, Peacetime, First National. Director: Frank Borzage. Screenplay: Delmer Daves. Star: Dick Powell. Military cooperation.

So Proudly We Hail, 1943. Army, WWII, Paramount. Director and Producer: Mark Sandrich. Screenplay: Allan Scott. Stars: Claudette Colbert, Paulette Goddard, Veronica Lake.

The Story of G.I. Joe, 1945. Army, WWII, United Artists. Director: William Wellman. Screenplay: Leopold Atlas, Guy Endore. Producer: Lester Cowan. Stars: Burgess Meredith, Robert Mitchum. Military cooperation.

Task Force, 1949. Navy, WWII, Warner. Director, Screenplay, and Producer: Delmer Daves. Star: Gary Cooper. Military cooperation.

Thirty Seconds Over Tokyo, 1944. Navy & Air Force, WWII, MGM. Director: Mervyn LeRoy. Screenplay: Dalton Trumbo. Producer: Sam Zimbalist. Stars: Van Johnson, Spencer Tracy. Military cooperation.

Tora! Tora! Tora!, 1970. Navy, WWII, 20th Century Fox. Director: Richard Fleischer. Screenplay: Larry Forrester, Michell Lindemann. Producer: Elmo Williams. Stars: Jason Robards, Martin Balsam, Joseph Cotten, James Whitmore. Military cooperation.

Twelve O'Clock High, 1950. Air Force, WWII, 20th Century Fox. Director: Henry King. Screenplay: Sy Bartlett. Producer: Darryl Zanuck. Stars: Gregory Peck, Gary Merrill, Dean Jagger. Military cooperation.

The Victors, 1963. Army, WWII, Columbia. Director, Screenplay, and Producer: Carl Foreman. Stars: Vincent Edwards, George Hamilton, George Peppard.

Wake Island, 1942. Marines, WWII, Paramount. Director: John Farrow. Screenplay: W. R. Brunett, Frank Butler. Producer: Joseph Sistrom. Stars: Robert Preston, William Bendix.

War Hunt, 1962. Army, Korea, United Artists. Director: Denis Sanders. Screenplay: Stanford Whitmore. Producer: Terry Sanders. Stars: Robert Redford, John Saxon, Charles Aidman.

What Price Glory?, 1926. Marines, WWI, Fox Studio. Director: Raoul Walsh. Screenplay: J. T. Donahue. Stars: Victor McLaglen, Edmund Lowe. Military cooperation.

Wings, 1927. WWI, Paramount. Director: William Wellman. Screenplay: Hope Loring, Louis Lighton. Stars: Clara Bow, Charles Rogers, Richard Arlen. Military cooperation.

Wings of Eagles, 1957. Peacetime, WWII, MGM. Director: John Ford. Screenplay: Frank Fenton, William Haines. Producer: Charles Schnee. Stars: John Wayne, Ward Bond. Military cooperation.

APPENDIX B

INTERVIEWS

★

Here is a list of those interviewed by Lawrence Suid as part of his research for this book. The number code accompanying each entry refers to the repository for the tape and/or transcript, as follows:

1) Georgetown University Special Collections Library
2) American Film Institute Oral History Collection
3) John F. Kennedy Library
4) George C. Marshall Library
5) University of Wyoming Special Collections Library
6) Stanford University Special Collections Library
7) Wisconsin Historical Society Film Archives

FILMMAKERS
(Actors, Directors, Producers, Screenwriters, Technicians)

Robert Aldrich, March 14, 1974 (1). Robert Andrews, September 19, 1975 (1). Sy Bartlett, February 9, 1974 (2). Michael Blankfort, July 19, 1975 (1). Julian Blaustein, June 28, 1974 (2). Bill Brown, January 1976 (1). John Calley, August 21, 1975 (2). Paddy Chayefsky, May 28, 1974 (1). Delmer Daves, January 31, 1974 and February 2, 1974 (1, 6). Melvyn Douglas, October 27, 1975 (2). Richard Fleischer, June 26, 1975 (2). Brian Foy, Jr., August 5, 1975 (1). Tay Garnett, July 13, 1975 (1). Buddy Gillespie, July 14, 1975 (1). Linda Gottlieb, June 15, 1973 (2). Edmund Grainger, July 30, 1975 (2). James Harris, February 25, 1974 (1). Arthur Hiller, March 14, 1974 (1). Stan Hough, July 1, 1975 (1). John Huston, March 27, 1974 (1). Ray Kellogg, July 3, 1975 (1, 2). Henry King, July 2, 1975 (1, 5). Stanley Kramer, February 8, 1974 (1). Beirne Lay, Jr., August 5, 1975 (1). Mervyn LeRoy, July 22, 1975 (2). Joseph Lewis, April 6, 1974 (1). Frank McCarthy, March 4, 1974 and July 31, 1975 (1, 2, 4). Karl Malden, August 9, 1975 (2). Delbert Mann, March 13, 1974 (2). Leslie Martinson, July 10, 1975 (1). Andrew Marton, July 21, 1975 (1). Lewis Milestone, February 7, 1974 (2). George Murphy, July 14, 1977 (1). Lloyd Nolan, July 1, 1975 (1). Edmund North, March 10, 1974 (1). Robert Pirosh, March 5, 1974 (1, 5). James Poe, August 4, 1975 (1). Otto Preminger, August 16, 1973 (2). Martin Ransohoff, March 1, 1974 (1). Stanley Roberts, April 6, 1974 (1). Mark Robson, July 2, 1975 (1). Mark

Rydell, September 3, 1975 (1). Terry Sanders, August 17, 1975 (2). Russ Saunders, July 30, 1975 (1). Dore Schary, March 20, 1973 and March 25, 1975 (1, 2, 7). George Seaton, March 4, 1974 (1). Milton Sperling, March 25, 1974 (1). Steward Stern, March 14, 1974 (1). Frank Tallman, August 21, 1975 (1). Daniel Taradash, March 27, 1974 (2). Ted Taylor, March 15, 1974 (1). Dalton Trumbo, April 10, 1974 (2). King Vidor, July 28, 1975 (2). John Wayne, February 7, 1974 (2). Michael Wayne, August 5, 1975 (1). James Webb, February 5, 1974 (1). William Wellman, June 23, 1975 (2). Cornell Wilde, August 15, 1975 (2). Elmo Williams, March 18, 1974 and July 11, 1975 (2). Robert Wise, April 10, 1974 (1). David Wolper, July 21, 1975 (2). R. W. Young, August 18, 1975 (2). Max Youngstein, April 5, 1974 (1). Fred Zinnemann, March 5, 1974 (1).

ORIGINAL AUTHORS OF BOOKS INTO FILMS

Edward Beach, *Run Silent, Run Deep*, May 30, 1974 (2). Ken Hechler, *Bridge At Remagen*, May 30, 1975 (1). James Jones, *From Here to Eternity*, December 30, 1974 (1). Fletcher Knebel, *Seven Days in May*, August 28, 1974 (1). S. L. A. Marshall, *Pork Chop Hill*, January 26, 1974 (1). Robin Moore, *The Green Berets*, December 22, 1974 (1). Leon Uris, *Battle Cry*, June 18, 1975 (1).

FILM INDUSTRY EXECUTIVES, WASHINGTON REPRESENTATIVES

Raymond Bell, April 8, 1975 (2). Robert Benjamin, May 28, 1974 (1). David Brown, April 11, 1974 (2). Kenneth Clark, December 17, 1973 and April 3, 1975 (2). Bernard Donnenfeld, March 13, 1974 (1). Oscar Doob, January 23, 1974 (1). Bill Hendricks, March 25 and 29, 1974 (1). John Horton, December 18, 1973 and April 8, 1975 (2). Jack Warner, Jr., April 4, 1974 (1). Jack Valenti, November 11, 1977 (1).

WRITERS, CRITICS, ACADEMICIANS

Josiah Bunting, December 23, 1974 (2). Vincent Canby, January 12, 1976 (1). David Halberstam, March 29, 1975 (1). Phil Jones, September 1976 (1). Ward Just, August 12, 1974 (1). Robert J. Lifton, June 8, 1976 (1). Bob Schieffer, August 1977 (1). Hugh Sidey, November 29, 1976 (1).

GOVERNMENT OFFICIALS

Donald Baruch, March 22, 1973 through publication of this book (1, 2). Clayton Fritchey, December 18, 1974 (1). Phil Goulding, April 4, 1975 (1). Norm Hatch,

December 17, 1974 through publication of this book (1, 2). Taylor Mills, August Interviews 15, 1973 (1). Paul Nitze, April 8, 1975 (1). Cong. Benjamin Rosenthal, December 18, 1974 (1). Arthur Sylvester, August 16, 1973 and December 23, 1974 (3). Walter Pforzheimer, October 24, 1977 (1).

MILITARY PERSONNEL
(Technical Advisors, Public Relations Officers, Administrators)

Bruce Arnold, Col. USA, March 13, 1977 (1). Marshall Beebe, Capt. USN, March 20, 1974 (1). Robert Berry, Adm. USN, August 17, 1975 (1). Charles Bialka, Col. USAF, June 17, 1975 (1). Blake Booth, Capt. USN, August 16, 1975 (1). Alan Brown, Capt. USN, March 27, 1974 (1). William Byrnes, Col. USA, June 25, 1975 (1). William Call, Col. USA, January 13, 1976 (2). William Collier, USA, January 18, 1977 (1). Slade Cutter, Capt. USN, June 21, 1975 (1). James Crowe, Col. USMC, December 11, 1977 (1). James H. Doolittle, Gen. USAF, June 30, 1975 (2). Frank Dorn, Gen. USA, January 7, 1976 (1). John Eisenhower, Col. USA, January 8, 1976 (1). J. D. Ferguson, Capt. USN, April 5, 1975 (2). Raymond Findley, Col. USMC, March 8, 1976 (1). Leonard Fribourg, Gen. USMC, August 17, 1975 (1). James Gavin, Gen. USA, March 2, 1977 (1). Dan Gilmer, Col. USA, August 9, 1975 (1). Ron Gruchey, USAF, July 25, 1975 (1). William Harding, USN, April 11, 1974 (1). Herb Hetu, Capt. USN, April 3, 1975 (1). Robert Hickey, Adm. USN, March 19, 1974 (1). H. Gordon Hill, Gen. USA, May 19, 1977 (1). Clarence Irvine, Gen. USAF, July 1, 1975 (1). H. W. O. Kinnard, Gen. USA, June 15, 1974 (1). Fred Ladd, Col. USA, April 2, 1975 (1). Curtis LeMay, Gen. USAF, August 17, 1975 (1). Arno Leuhman, Gen. USAF, July 1, 1975 (1). Anthony McAuliffe, Gen. USA, May 31, 1974 (1). Rob Roy McGregor, Adm. USN, August 15, 1975 (2). S. G. Mitchell, Capt. USN, April 5, 1975 (1). Lauris Norstad, Gen. USAF, June 11, 1977 (1). William Nuckles, Gen. USAF, October 6, 1976 (1). Barney Oldfield, Col. USAF, June 25, 1975 (1). Ben Ostlind, Col. USAF, August 21, 1975 (1). Lewis Parks, Adm. USN, December 31, 1974 (1). James Shaw, Adm. USN, August 17, 1974 (1). David Shoup, Gen. USMC, April 2, 1975 (1). Edwin Simmons, Gen. USMC, April 22, 1977 (1). Clement Stadler, Col. USMC, July 7, 1975 (1). Edward Stafford, Capt. USN, April 7, 1975 (2). Paul Tibbets, Gen. USAF, July 7, 1976 (1). Clair Towne, Col. USA, August 15, 1975 (1). Sam Triffy, Col. USAF, January 5, 1976 (1). John Will, Adm. USN, May 22, 1974 (2). Sam Wilson, Gen. USA, January 5, 1976 (1). John L. Winston, Gen. USMC, September 20, 1977 (1). George Watkins, Capt. USN, December 10, 1977 (1).

REFERENCES

★

Author's note. Research for this book has included approximately 300 interviews, which I have conducted with military officials, filmmakers, journalists, authors, and actors. (See Appendix B for a complete list of interviews.) In addition, many people have generously allowed me to quote from personal correspondence and other documents in their possession. I retain copies of these documents, which are designated in the references by: Author's File. Library sources include the following:

National Archives, Washington, D.C.: The Navy and Old Army Branch contains pre-1941 material; the Modern Military Records Division contains War Department records from 1941–1947 and material from the Department of Defense, Public Affairs Office for the period 1949–1953.

Department of Defense, Public Affairs Office, Washington, D.C.: Contains records on major productions of the 1960s and early 1970s as well as documents pertaining to all films produced from 1975 onward. This source is designated in the references by: DoD Files.

Academy of Motion Picture Arts and Sciences Library, Beverly Hills, California.

Library of Congress, Washington, D.C.: Contains prints of a large number of films produced before 1945 and virtually all films produced after 1945.

Dwight D. Eisenhower Library, Abilene, Kansas: Contains correspondence between General Eisenhower and Frank McCarthy.

Lyndon Johnson Library, Austin, Texas: Contains correspondence between President Lyndon Johnson and John Wayne.

John F. Kennedy Library, Boston, Massachusetts: Contains material on *PT-109*.

George C. Marshall Library, Lexington, Virginia: Frank McCarthy Papers.

Museum of Modern Art, Film Study Center, New York, New York. Designated as MOMA in the references.

Stanford University Special Collections Library, Stanford, California: Delmer Daves Papers.

Harry Truman Library, Independence, Missouri: Lyman Munson Papers.

UCLA Special Collections Library, Los Angeles, California: James Poe Papers.

University of Wisconsin, University Center for Film and Theater Research, Madison, Wisconsin: Contains scripts and other material on Warner Brothers films.

University of Wyoming Library, Division of Rare Books and Special Collections, Laramie, Wyoming: Robert Pirosh Papers.

References

CHAPTER ONE

1. This and subsequent quotations are from the script of *Patton*, Twentieth Century Fox, 1970. The speech is a synthesis of several that General Patton gave in the weeks before the Normandy Invasion. **2.** Interview with Otto Preminger, August 16, 1970. **3.** Interview with Joseph Heller, *Playboy*, June 1975, p. 6. **4.** Interview with Peter Hamill, Washington television station WJLA, November 23, 1977. **5.** Leon Trotsky, *My Life* (New York: Grosset & Dunlop, Universal Library, 1960), p. 233. **6.** Interview with David Halberstam, March 29, 1975. **7.** Navy memorandum, April 14, 1933, National Archives, Record Group 80, Box 80. **8.** James Jones, "Phoney War Films," *Saturday Evening Post*, March 30, 1963, p. 67. **9.** Interview with Tay Garnett, July 13, 1975. **10.** Letter from Maxwell Taylor to author, March 8, 1975. **11.** Interview with David Shoup, April 2, 1975. **12.** Interview with Paul Tibbets, July 7, 1976. **13.** Michael Herr, *Dispatches* (New York: Alfred A. Knopf, 1977), pp. 135–136.

CHAPTER TWO

1. Interview with King Vidor, File "The Big Parade," MOMA (cited hereafter as MOMA interview); this interview was summarized in the *New York Times*, November 8, 1925, sec. 8, p. 5. See also, King Vidor, *A Tree Is a Tree* (New York: Harcourt Brace, 1952), p. 111. **2.** Interview with King Vidor, July 28, 1975. Vidor, *A Tree Is a Tree*, p. 111. *New York Times*, September 3, 1974, sec. II, p. 1. **3.** MOMA interview. Vidor interview. Vidor, *A Tree Is a Tree*, pp. 111–112. **4.** "Notes on *The Big Parade*," (MOMA, 1941). Vidor interview. Vidor, *A Tree Is a Tree*, pp. 112–114. **5.** Ibid. **6.** Ibid. **7.** General H. H. Arnold, *Global Mission* (New York: Harper & Brothers, 1949), pp. 34–35. Lillian Gish, *The Movies, Mr. Griffith and Me* (Englewood Cliffs, N.J.: Prentice Hall, 1969), p. 47. Letter from Lillian Gish to author, June 12, 1975. **8.** Robert M. Henderson, *D. W. Griffith: His Life and Work* (New York: Oxford University Press, 1972), pp. 246–247. *New York Times*, September 30, 1923, sec. II, p. 3. "Chicago Industrial Solidarity, November 24, 1923," File "America," MOMA. **9.** Vidor, *A Tree Is a Tree*, pp. 120–121. Vidor interview. *New York Times*, October 4, 1925, sec. IX, p. 5. **11.** Ibid. Vidor, *A Tree Is a Tree*, p. 117. **12.** Vidor interview. *New York Times*, February 21, 1926, sec. II, p. 6. **13.** Vidor interview. *New York Times*, September 3, 1974, sec. II, p. 1. **14.** MOMA interview. **15.** Ibid. Vidor interview. **16.** Vidor interview. **17.** *Literary Digest*, March 6, 1926, p. 38. **18.** Ibid. **19.** *New York Times*, November 20, 1925, p. 18. **20.** Vidor, *A Tree Is a Tree*, pp. 114–115. MOMA interview. **21.** *New York Times*, February 21, 1926, sec. II, p. 4. *Outlook*, January 6, 1926, pp. 18–19. **22.** Ibid. **23.** Vidor, *A Tree Is a Tree*, pp. 124–125. **24.** "Films from the Archives," (MOMA, 1975). *New York Times*, April 14, 1974, sec. II, p. 13. **25.** Ibid. **26.** John Monk Saunders, "The Government Cooperated to Make *Wings* Thrilling and True," *New York Times*, July 31, 1927, sec. VII, p. 3. **27.** Ibid. John Monk Saunders, "Filming of an Epic," *Wings Theater Program*, reprinted in *Los Angeles Herald-Examiner*, April 9, 1972. This is a longer version of the *New York Times* story. **28.** Interview with William Wellman, June 23, 1975. **29.** William Wellman, *A Short Time for Insanity* (New York: Hawthorn Books, 1974), pp. 163–165. Wellman interview. **30.** Interview with General Bill Irvine, July 1, 1975. **31.** *New York Times*, July 10, 1927, sec. VII, p. 3. **32.** Wellman, *Short Time for Insanity*, pp. 170–174. Kevin Brownlow, *The Parade's Gone By . . .* (New York: Alfred A. Knopf, 1969), p. 202. **33.** *Motion Picture World*, quoted in "Films from the Archives," (MOMA, 1975). *Exceptional Photoplays*, September, 1972. *New York Times*, August 21, 1972, sec. VII, p. 3. **34.** *New Yorker*, September 25, 1971, p. 106. **35.** Irvine interview.

CHAPTER THREE References

1. Interview with Admiral John Will, May 22, 1974. **2.** Memo from Navy Department Motion Picture Board to Chief of Naval Operations, April 14, 1933, National Archives, Record Group 80, Box 432. **3.** Letter from Chief of Naval Operations to RKO Studios, December 21, 1932, National Archives, Record Group 80, Box 431. Orville Goldner and George E. Turner, *The Making of King Kong* (New York: Ballantine Books, 1976), pp. 167–169. Interview with General John L. Winston, September 20, 1977. (General Winston was a young Marine flier and one of the four pilots in the formation.) **4.** Letter from Arthur Keil to Frank Knox, December 1, 1941. Letter from Alan Brown to E. C. Roworth, August 26, 1941. National Archives, Record Group 80, Box 94. **5.** U.S. Congress. Senate. Committee on Interstate Commerce, *Propaganda in Motion Pictures,* Hearings before a subcommittee of the Senate Committee on Interstate Commerce, 77th Cong., September 1941, pp. 338–341. Interview with Jack Warner, Jr., April 4, 1974. **6.** *New York Times,* September 2, 1942, p. 19. **7.** Interview with Samuel Triffy, January 5, 1976. **8.** Ibid. **9.** War Department Memorandums, May 18 and 19, 1942, National Archives, Record Group 165, Box 6. **10.** Letter from War Department to Jack Warner, May 22, 1942. War Department Memo, June 6, 1942. National Archives, Record Group 165, Box 6. **11.** Triffy interview. **12.** Ibid. **13.** Ibid. Letter from General Hewitt Wheless to author, June 23, 1977. **14.** *New York Times,* February 4, 1943, p. 17. **15.** Interview with Dore Schary, December 20, 1973. **16.** Ibid. **17.** Ibid. War Department Memo, October 23, 1942, National Archives, Record Group 165, Box 7. **18.** Letter from War Department to Metro-Goldwyn-Mayer, October 26, 1942, National Archives, Record Group 165, Box 7. **19.** Tay Garnett, *Light Your Torches* (New Rochelle, N.Y.: Arlington House, 1973), pp. 248, 256–257. **20.** Ibid. Interview with Tay Garnett, July 13, 1975. **21.** *New York Times,* June 4, 1943, p. 17. *Time,* June 7, 1943, p. 94. **22.** Garnett, *Light Your Torches,* p. 248. Garnett interview. **23.** *New York Times,* November 12, 1943, p. 25. **24.** Ibid. **25.** Interview with General William Collier, January 18, 1977.

CHAPTER FOUR

1. Script of May 13, 1943, Delmer Daves papers. **2.** Interview with Robert Wise, April 10, 1974. Interview with Captain Edward Beach, May 30, 1974. Interview with Captain Slade Cutter, June 21, 1975. **3.** Daves Memo, May 20, 1943, Delmer Daves Papers. Interview with Delmer Daves, January 31, 1974. **4.** *New York Times,* January 1, 1944, p. 9. **5.** Preface to script of *Thirty Seconds Over Tokyo,* June 18, 1943, National Archives, Record Group 165, Box 41. Letter from War Department to Metro-Goldwyn-Mayer, August 25, 1943, National Archives, Record Group 165, Box 41. **6.** Ibid. **7.** Interview with Dalton Trumbo, April 10, 1974. **8.** Ibid. **9.** Ibid. **10.** Letter from War Department to Metro-Goldwyn-Mayer, August 25, 1943, National Archives, Record Group 165, Box 41. **11.** Ibid. Interview with Mervyn LeRoy, July 22, 1975. MGM Production Notes, File "Thirty Seconds Over Tokyo," Academy of Motion Picture Arts and Sciences Library. **12.** LeRoy interview. Interview with Buddy Gillespie, July 14, 1975. **13.** *New York Times,* November 16, 1944, p. 19. **14.** Trumbo interview. **15.** Ibid. **16.** LeRoy interview. **17.** *New York Times,* November 16, 1944, p. 19. **18.** Interview with William Wellman, June 23, 1975. **19.** William Wellman, *A Short Time for Insanity* (New York: Hawthorn Books, 1974). p. 81. **20.** War Department Telegram, September 6, 1943. Letter from Lester Cowan to War Department, September 13, 1943. War Department Memo, September 22, 1943. National Archives, Record Group 165, Box 15. **21.** Since United Artists had no studio facilities, it simply provided financial backing to independent filmmakers, who then rented facilities at a major studio. Letter from United Artists to War Department, October 8, 1943. Letters

References

from Lester Cowan to War Department, October 19 and November 17, 1943. War Department Letter, November 27, 1943. National Archives, Record Group 165, Box 15. **22.** Letter from Lester Cowan to War Department, June 28, 1944, National Archives, Record Group 165, Box 15. **23.** Ibid. **24.** Telegram from Lester Cowan to War Department, July 6, 1944, National Archives, Record Group 165, Box 15. **25.** War Department Memo, October 6, 1944, National Archives, Record Group 165, Box 15. **26.** Dudley Nichols, "Men in Battle: A Review of Three Current Pictures," *Hollywood Quarterly,* October 1945, p. 35. **27.** Wellman, *Short Time for Insanity,* pp. 81–82. Wellman interview. **28.** Ibid. **29.** Ibid., pp. 83–89. **30.** Ibid. War Department Memo, November 13, 1944, National Archives, Record Group 165, Box 15. Wellman interview. **31.** Ibid. **32.** Wellman, *Short Time for Insanity,* pp. 233–234. **33.** Ibid. Wellman interview. **34.** *Time,* July 23, 1945, p. 96. *New York Times,* October 6, 1945, p. 9. **35.** Nichols, "Men in Battle," p. 35. **26.** Ibid, pp. 35–36. **37.** Wellman, *Short Time for Insanity,* p. 235.

CHAPTER FIVE

1. Navy Department Memo, May 14, 1945, Delmer Daves Papers. **2.** Early script of *Task Force* (circa 1945), Delmer Daves Papers. **3.** Final script of *Task Force,* October 22, 1948, p. 110, Delmer Daves Papers. **4.** *New York Times,* September 4, 1949, p. 32. *Daily Variety,* September 28, 1949, p. 3. Scripts in Delmer Daves Papers and in Warner Brothers Collection at the University of Wisconsin Center for Film and Theater Research. **5.** Interview with Dore Schary, March 25, 1975. **6.** Ibid. **7.** Ibid. Letter from Dore Schary to author, April 21, 1977. Robert Pirosh, "Memo From a Man Who Never Had It So Good," *New York Times,* October 23, 1949, sec. II, p. 5. **8.** Pirosh, "Memo From a Man". Interview with General Anthony McAuliffe, May 31, 1974. **9.** Schary interview. Letter from Schary to author. **10.** Ibid. Robert Pirosh Papers, Box 1. Dore Schary, "I Remember Hughes," *New York Times Magazine,* May 2, 1977, pp. 42–43. **11.** Interview with Dore Schary, March 3, 1975. Letter from Schary to author. **12.** Schary, "I Remember Hughes," p. 43. Schary interview, March 25, 1975. McAuliffe interview. *Daily Variety,* October 6, 1948, p. 4. *Daily Variety,* December 28, 1948, p. 1. **13.** Schary, "I Remember Hughes," p. 43. Interview with William Wellman, June 23, 1975. Interview with Oscar Doob, January 23, 1974. **14.** Wellman interview. **15.** Interview with Dore Schary, December 20, 1973. Interview with George Murphy, July 14, 1977. Interview with Jack Dunning, March 12, 1974. **16.** Interview with Robert Pirosh, March 5, 1974. McAuliffe interview. Interview with General H. W. O. Kinnard, June 15, 1974. Wellman interview. **17.** From script of *Battleground,* Metro-Goldwyn-Mayer, 1949. **18.** Wellman interview. **19.** Memo from Robert Pirosh to Dore Schary (n.d.), File "MGM Publicity Book," Robert Pirosh Papers. **20.** Twentieth Century Fox Memo, April 16, 1947, Lyman Munson Papers. **21.** Twentieth Century Fox Memo, July 21, 1947, Lyman Munson Papers. **22.** Twentieth Century Fox Memos, September 10 and 11, 1947. Letter from Lyman Munson to Louis Lighton, September 19, 1947. Lyman Munson Papers. **23.** Twentieth Century Fox Memo, October 14, 1947, Lyman Munson Papers. **24.** Ibid. Letter from Air Force to Twentieth Century Fox, November 17, 1947, National Archives, Record Group 330, Box 677. Letter from Lyman Munson to Louis Lighton, October 28, 1947. Twentieth Century Fox Memo, January 22, 1948. Letter from Louis Lighton to Lyman Munson, July 29, 1948. Lyman Munson Papers. **25.** Letter from Darryl Zanuck to General Hoyt Vandenberg, September 17, 1948, National Archives, Record Group 330, Box 677. **26.** Ibid. Letter from General Hoyt Vandenberg to Darryl Zanuck, October 2, 1948. Letter from Stephen Leo to Darryl Zanuck, October 13, 1948. National Archives, Record Group 330, Box 677. **27.** Letter from Air Force to Twentieth Century Fox, November 17, 1948, National Archives, Record Group 330, Box 677. **28.** Interview with Sy Bartlett, February 9, 1974. **29.** Colonel Frank Armstrong, whom Bartlett and Lay used as the model for General Frank Savage, suffered no mental breakdown. However, according to Bartlett, individual fliers in the Eighth Air **References** Force did on occasion go through the type of collapse portrayed in *Twelve O'Clock High*. See also, Thomas Coffey, *Decision Over Schweinfurt* (New York: David McKay, 1977). **30.** Letter from Air Force to Twentieth Century Fox, November 17, 1948, National Archives, Record Group 330, Box 677. **31.** Ibid. **32.** *Twelve O'Clock High Exhibitors Campaign Book*, MOMA. Interview with Henry King, July 2, 1975. **33.** King interview. Don Dwiggins, *Hollywood Pilot* (Garden City, N.Y.: Doubleday, 1967), pp. 172–174; the author describes the crash as including a slide along the ground into the tents. In fact, the plane does not touch the ground until it hits the first tent. **34.** Ibid. Interview with Frank Tallman, August 21, 1975.

CHAPTER SIX

1. See, for example, Josiah Bunting, *The Lionheads* (New York: George Braziller, 1972); Robert Lifton, *Home from the War* (New York, Simon & Schuster, 1973); Phillip Caputo, *Rumor of War* (New York: Holt, Rinehart & Winston, 1977); Ron Kovic, *Born on the Fourth of July* (New York: McGraw-Hill, 1976); and Michael Herr, *Dispatches* (New York: Alfred A. Knopf, 1977). **2.** The first episode of "Baa, Baa Blacksheep" was broadcast on September 23, 1976. **3.** Quigley Publication Annual Poll of Exhibitors, which lists the Top Ten Money-Making Stars of each year, included John Wayne a record twenty-four times up to 1974. *Family Weekly*, a popular newspaper magazine in "middle America," rated Wayne as the most popular actor among its readers for three years in a row as recently as the early 1970s (*Product Digest*, May 22, 1974, pp. 101, 104). *Photoplay* announced that Wayne was its choice as its all-time movie star on NBC television special, June 17, 1977. **4.** Both films are in the Library of Congress, George Kleine Collection, along with documentary material on their production and promotion during wartime. **5.** Interview with Edmund Grainger, July 30, 1975. Republic Pictures, "Production Notes on Sands of Iwo Jima," (n.d.); *New York Times*, August 7, 1949, sec. II, p. 3. **5.** Grainger interview. Interview with General David Shoup, April 2, 1975. **6.** Shoup interview. **7.** Grainger interview. **8.** Interview with General Leonard Fribourg, August 17, 1975. **9.** Ibid. Grainger interview. **10.** Interview with John Wayne, February 7, 1974. **11.** Grainger interview. Letter from John Wayne to author, June 15, 1977. Letter from Edmund Grainger to author, July 12, 1977. In his letter, Wayne questioned the judgment that his career was "on the downgrade" during the period. In answer to a question about Wayne's reaction, Grainger wrote, "With reference to your inquiry about Mr. Yates' statement, that was his opinion, right or wrong. I quoted the facts." **12.** Fribourg interview. **13.** Ibid. **14.** Ibid. Letter from John Wayne to author. **15.** Letter from John Wayne to author. John Wayne interview. **16.** Shoup interview. Interview with Colonel James Crowe, December 11, 1977. **17.** Ibid. Grainger interview. **18.** *New York Times*, December 21, 1949, p. 9; *New Yorker*, January 14, 1950, p. 75. **19.** Shoup interview. Interview with Colonel Raymond Findley, March 8, 1976. Grainger interview. *Variety Annual*, January 3, 1951, p. 55. **20.** Interview with General Edwin Simmons, April 22, 1977. Interviews with Norm Hatch. Interview with Leon Uris, June 18, 1975. Crowe interview. **21.** *Newsweek*, January 16, 1950, p. 78. Interview with John Wayne, *Playboy*, May 1971, p. 80. *New York Times*, December 31, 1951, p. 9. **22.** Grainger interview. Shoup interview. **23.** Kovic, *Born on the Fourth of July*, p. 43. **24.** "Richard Pryor, King of the Scene-Stealers," *New York Times*, January 9, 1977, sec. II, p. 11. **25.** Script of *The Alamo*, United Artists, 1960. **26.** *New York Times Magazine*, January 27, 1974, p. 9. Author's personal inquiry, April 15, 1976. **27.** Interview with Michael Wayne, August 5, 1975. **28.** Interview with Dore Schary, March 25, 1975. **29.** Interview with Delbert Mann, March 13, 1975. **30.** "Owen Marshall" episode, March 30, 1975. Letter from R. W. Young to author, May 11, 1974. **31.** Bunting, *The Lionheads*, p. 162. **32.** Alther, *Kinflicks*, p. 447. **33.** Ronald Glasser, *365 Days* (New York: George

References

Braziller, 1971), p. 60. **34.** Kovic, *Born on the Fourth of July*, p. 61. Caputo, *Rumor of War*, p. 6. **35.** Interview with Bob Schieffer, August 6, 1977. Interview with Ward Just, August 12, 1974. *New York Times*, June 20, 1968, p. 49. Interview with David Halberstam, March 29, 1975. **36.** Interview with General Samuel Wilson, January 5, 1976. Interview with Josiah Bunting, December 23, 1974. **37.** Wayne interview. **38.** Bunting interview. **39.** Interview with R. W. Young, August 18, 1975. **40.** Halberstam interview. **41.** John Wayne, *Playboy*, p. 92. Interview with William Wellman, June 23, 1975. *Time*, May 10, 1976, p. 58. **42.** *Cleveland Plain Dealer*, January 21, 1976. *New York Times*, January 27, 1976, p. 33. **43.** Interview with Frank McCarthy, March 4, 1974. Wayne interview. **44.** Lifton, *Home from the War*, Chapter 8. Interview with Robert Lifton, June 8, 1976. Kovic, *Born on the Fourth of July*, p. 98. **45.** *Life*, January 28, 1972, p. 44. **46.** Lifton interview. **47.** John Wayne interview. **48.** Ibid.

CHAPTER SEVEN

1. Interviews with Donald Baruch, Chief Motion Picture Production Office, Directorate for Defense Information, Department of Defense, March 1973 onward. Interview with Clayton Fritchey, December 18, 1974. Interview with Admiral Robert Berry, August 17, 1975. **2.** Interview with Samuel Fuller, July 12, 1975. **3.** Interview with Tay Garnett, July 13, 1975. Interview with Edmund Grainger, July 13, 1975. Baruch interviews. Tay Garnett, *Light Your Torches* (New Rochelle, N.Y.: Arlington House, 1973), pp. 280–285. **4.** Interview with General Edwin Simmons, April 22, 1977. General Oliver P. Smith, quoted in *Time*, January 9, 1978, p. 72. **5.** Interview with George Seaton, March 4, 1974. Interview with Henry Bumstead, April 3, 1974. **6.** Dialogue from *Bridges at Toko-Ri*, Paramount Pictures, 1955. **7.** Interview with Julian Blaustein, March 28, 1974. **8.** Letter from Clair Towne to George Dorsey of Warner Brothers, August 25, 1951, DoD Files. **9.** Interview with Raymond Bell, April 8, 1975. **10.** Interview with Daniel Taradash, March 27, 1974. **11.** Bell interview. **12.** Letter from Daniel Taradash to author, June 10, 1976. **13.** Bell interview. **14.** Ibid. **15.** Letter from Clair Towne to Raymond Bell, April 3, 1951, DoD Files. **16.** Interview with James Jones, December 30, 1974. **17.** Taradash interview. *New York Times*, June 14, 1953, sec. II, p. 5. **18.** Ibid. **19.** Ibid. **20.** Ibid. *New York Times*, June 14, 1953, p. 5. Interview with Fred Zinnemann, March 8, 1974. **21.** Taradash interview. Letter from Taradash to author. **22.** Ibid. **23.** Donald Baruch Memorandum for the Record, February 11, 1952. Memorandum to Clayton Fritchey, February 14, 1952. DoD Files. Baruch interview, March 22, 1975. Interview with General Frank Dorn, January 7, 1976. Interview with Clair Towne, August 15, 1975. **24.** Letter from Clayton Fritchey to General Floyd Parks, February 19, 1952, DoD Files. **25.** Donald Baruch, Memorandum for the Record, February 19, 1952, DoD Files. **26.** Taradash interview. Donald Baruch, Memorandum for the Record, February 20, 1952, DoD Files. **27.** Taradash interview. Zinnemann interview. Letter from Fred Zinnemann to author, February 24, 1977. **28.** Donald Baruch, Memorandums for the Record, September 9, 10, 11, 1952, DoD Files. **29.** Baruch interview, March 22, 1973. **30.** Taradash interview. Letter from Taradash to author, May 5, 1976. **31.** Ibid. **32.** Zinnemann interview. Letter from Zinnemann to author, February 24, 1977. **33.** Diana S. Dreiman, "A Critical Analysis of the Films of Fred Zinnemann," (Unpublished Masters Thesis, UCLA, 1971), pp. 146–147. **34.** Zinnemann quoted in "Films of Fred Zinnemann." Taradash interview. **35.** Taradash interview. **36.** Zinnemann interview. Letter from Zinnemann to author. **37.** Taradash interview. Letter from Ray Bell with attachment to Clair Towne, January 28, 1953, DoD Files. **38.** Army Memo, July 10, 1953. Letter from Clair Towne to Ray Bell, July 10, 1953. DoD Files. **39.** Zinnemann interview. **40.** Ibid. **41.** *New York Times*, August 6, 1953, p. 16. **42.** Jones Interview. **43.** *Los Angeles Times*, October 1, 1953. **44.** Letter from Clair Towne to David Brigham, December 11, 1953. Letter from Clair Towne to Russ

McFarland, September 10, 1953. DoD Files. **45.** *Daily Variety*, August 31, 1953, p. 3. Letter from **References** Clair Towne to author, September 1975. Letter from Raymond Bell to author, January 13, 1976. **46.** Zinnemann interview. **47.** Letter from Admiral Lewis Parks to Raymond Bell (n.d., after September 8, 1953), DoD Files. **48.** Herman Wouk, Preface to *The Caine Mutiny* (Garden City, N.Y.: Doubleday, 1951). **49.** Consensus of Navy officers interviewed for this project. **50.** Letter from James Shaw to author, March 28, 1977. **51.** Interview with Admiral Robert Hickey, March 19, 1974. **52.** Interview with Colonel Bill Call, January 13, 1976. **53.** Hickey interview. **54.** Interview with Stanley Kramer, February 8, 1974, as amended March 1977. **55.** Ibid. **56.** Letter from Slade Cutter to author, June 13, 1974. Interview with Slade Cutter, June 21, 1975. **57.** Ibid. **58.** Letter from Raymond Bell to author, January 13, 1976. **59.** Kramer interview. **60.** Letter from Herman Wouk to author, undated (replies to questions submitted December 20, 1975). **61.** Kramer interview. **62.** Letter from Slade Cutter to author, June 13, 1974. **63.** Kramer interview. **64.** Bell interview. **65.** *Variety*, November 25, 1953, p. 17. **66.** *Christian Science Monitor*, July 21, 1953, p. 4. *Daily Variety*, November 26, 1952, pp. 1, 11. Letter from Cutter to author. Cutter interview. Interview with Admiral James Shaw, August 17, 1974. **67.** Parks interview. Kramer interview. *Daily Variety*, December 2, 1952, pp. 1, 4, and *Daily Variety*, December 19, 1952, pp. 1, 8. Interview with Michael Blankfort, July 19, 1975. Interview with Admiral James Shaw, August 17, 1974. Although Admiral Parks does not recall the meeting with Secretary Kimball and Kramer, the producer remembers it in vivid detail and believes it was responsible for his obtaining cooperation. **68.** Kramer interview. **69.** Letter from Admiral Lewis Parks to Raymond Bell (undated, after September 1953). **70.** Quoted in *Daily Variety*, January 21, 1954, p. 4. **71.** Letter from Herman Wouk to author (undated). **72.** Interview with Josiah Bunting, December 23, 1974. **73.** Dialogue from *The Caine Mutiny*, Columbia Pictures, 1954. **74.** Kramer interview. **75.** *Newsweek*, October 17, 1960, p. 117. **76.** Jones interview.

CHAPTER EIGHT

1. Mel Gussow, *Don't Say Yes Until I Finish Talking* (New York: Doubleday, 1971), pp. 198–199. **2.** *Variety*, December 7, 1960, p. 5. *New York Times*, December 3, 1960, p. 19. **3.** Interview with Elmo Williams, July 11, 1975. Interview with Andrew Marton, July 21, 1975. Interview with Henry Koster, July 17, 1975. Interview with Colonel Dan Gilmer, August 9, 1975. Interview with Arthur Hiller, March 14, 1974. **4.** Leonard Mosley, *Battle of Britain* (New York: Ballantine Books, 1969), pp. 51–62. **5.** *Variety*, December 7, 1960, p. 5. *New York Times*, December 3, 1960, p. 19. Letter from Ken Annakin to author, June 4, 1976. **6.** *New York Times*, September 30, 1962, sec. II, p. 7. **7.** James Jones, "Phoney War Films," *Saturday Evening Post*, March 30, 1963, p. 67. **8.** *Variety*, December 7, 1960, p. 5. *Los Angeles Times Calendar*, April 1, 1962, p. 6. *Film Daily*, December 5, 1960, p. 4. **9.** *Los Angeles Times Calendar*, April 1, 1962, p. 6. **10.** Interview with General Lauris Norstad, June 11, 1975. Letter from Darryl Zanuck to Eric Johnson, October 5, 1962, Author's File. *New York Times*, October 2, 1962, p. 45. Richard Oulahan, Jr., "The Longest Day," *Life*, October 12, 1962, p. 114. **11.** Ibid. **12.** *Los Angeles Times Calendar*, April 1, 1962, p. 6. **13.** Ibid. Darryl Zanuck to Eric Johnston, October 5, 1962, Author's File. Department of Defense Chronology for *The Longest Day* (n.d.), DoD Files. **14.** Letter from General Norstad to Arthur Sylvester, February 1, 1961, DoD Files. **15.** Letter from Arthur Sylvester to General Norstad, February 8, 1961, DoD Files. Interview with Arthur Sylvester, August 16, 1973. **16.** Letter from Darryl Zanuck to Burke Wilkinson, Public Affairs Advisor to General Norstad, February 20, 1961. Chronology for *The Longest Day*. Letter from Donald Baruch to Twentieth Century Fox, May 5, 1961. DoD Files. **17.** Interview with Elmo Williams, March 18, 1974. Gussow, *Don't Say Yes*, pp. 217–218. **18.** *Time*, December 9, 1974, p.

References

107. **19.** Gussow, *Don't Say Yes*, pp. 224-225. **20.** Ibid., p. 225. **21.** Ibid., p. 221. **22.** Williams interview. Marton interview. **23.** Gussow, *Don't Say Yes*, p. 224. **24.** *New York Times*, May 21, 1961, sec. II, p. 7. *New York Times*, September 30, 1962, sec. II, p. 7. Oulahan, "The Longest Day," p. 114. *Newsweek*, September 18, 1961, p. 104. *Time*, September 8, 1961, p. 74. **25.** *Los Angeles Times Calendar*, April 1, 1962, p. 6. *New York Times*, September 30, 1962, sec. II, p. 7. *New York Times*, May 21, 1961, sec. II, p. 7. Oulahan, "The Longest Day," pp. 116-117. **26.** *New York Times*, May 21, 1961, sec. II, p. 7. **27.** Oulahan, "The Longest Day," pp. 116-117. **28.** Gussow, *Don't Say Yes*, p. 229. Marton interview. Williams interview. **29.** Oulahan, "The Longest Day," p. 117. *Newsweek*, September 18, 1961, p. 104. **30.** Ibid. Marton interview. **31.** Ibid. *New York Times*, September 30, 1962, sec. II, p. 7. **32.** *New York Times*, September 17, 1961, sec. II, p. 9. *New York Times*, September 30, 1962, p. 7. Marton interview. **33.** Marton interview. Letter from Ken Annakin to author, June 4, 1976. *Newsweek*, September 18, 1961, p. 104. *New York Times*, September 17, 1961, sec. II, p. 9. **34.** Ibid. **35.** *New York Times*, September 30, 1962, sec. II, p. 7. Marton interview. **36.** Ibid. **37.** *Variety*, September 20, 1961, p. 7. **38.** Congressional Record, September 8, 1961, pp. 18733-18735. **39.** Ibid., pp. 18733-18736. **40.** *Variety*, September 20, 1961, p. 7. **41.** *Variety*, September 13, 1961, pp. 3, 30. Letter from Congressman Bob Wilson to Arthur Sylvester, September 13, 1961, San Diego State University, Bob Wilson Papers. Letter from Arthur Sylvester to Congressman Bob Wilson, September 25, 1961, DoD Files. **42.** *Los Angeles Times Calendar*, April 1, 1962, p. 6. **43.** *Variety*, October 4, 1961, pp. 5, 19, and October 18, 1961, p. 18. *New York Times*, October 17, 1961, p. 3. Norstad interview. **44.** *Variety*, October 18, 1961, p. 18. *New York Times*, October 21, 1961, p. 8. *Daily Variety*, October 24, 1961, pp. 1, 4. Norstad interview. **45.** Letter from Darryl Zanuck to Eric Johnston, October 5, 1962, Author's File. *Los Angeles Times Calendar*, April 1, 1962, p. 3. **46.** Department of the Army Message, November 1961, DoD Files. *New York Sunday News*, November 12, 1961, p. 6. **47.** *Variety*, January 3, 1962, p. 18. **48.** Letter from Donald Baruch to Twentieth Century Fox, September 24, 1962, DoD Files. **49.** Letter from Darryl Zanuck to Department of Defense, October 1, 1962, DoD Files. **50.** Letter from Donald Baruch to Darryl Zanuck, October 11, 1962, DoD Files. **51.** *New York Times*, October 7, 1962, sec. II, p. 1.

CHAPTER NINE

1. Interviews with Arthur Sylvester, August 16, 1973 and December 23, 1974. Interviews with Donald Baruch. Department of Defense file on *No Man is an Island*. *Daily Variety*, January 30, 1962, pp. 1, 4, 15. **2.** *Congressional Record*, February 22, 1962, pp. 2817-2818. **3.** Letter from Senator Hubert Humphrey to Arthur Sylvester, June 14, 1962. Letter from Arthur Sylvester to Hubert Humphrey, June 30, 1962, Author's File. **4.** Interview with Sy Bartlett, February 9, 1974. Baruch interviews. Interview with General Arno Leuhman, July 1, 1975. Requirements List for *A Gathering of Eagles*, DoD Files. **5.** Interview with General Curtis LeMay, August 17, 1975. Bartlett interview. **6.** LeMay interview. Air Force Memo from Curtis LeMay to Arthur Sylvester, June 7, 1962, DoD Files. **7.** Bartlett interview. Mann interview. LeMay interview. **8.** Interview with Leslie Martinson, July 10, 1975. Interview with Brian Foy, Jr., August 5, 1975. *Newsweek*, July 23, 1962, p. 72; Lewis Milestone was replaced as director shortly after he made these remarks. **9.** Letter from Pierre Salinger to Secretary of the Navy Fred Korth, January 6, 1962, Kennedy Papers. Interview with Jack Warner, Jr., April 4, 1974. **10.** *Wall Street Journal*, July 12, 1962, p. 1. *Time*, July 13, 1962, p. 54. **11.** Letter from Pierre Salinger to Fred Korth, January 6, 1962, Kennedy Papers. Bill Davidson, "President Kennedy Casts a Movie," *Look*, September 8, 1962, pp. 26-27. **12.** Letter from Arthur Sylvester to Hubert Humphrey, June 30, 1962, Kennedy Papers. **13.** Letter from Kenneth Clark to Charles Boren, August 8, 1962, Author's File. **14.** *New York Times*, October 2, 1962, p. 45.

15. Letter from Eric Johnson to Darryl Zanuck, October 11, 1962, Author's File. **16.** Sylvester interviews. **17.** Interview with Stan Hough, July 1, 1975. Memo from Stan Hough to Richard Zanuck, February 4, 1964, Author's File. **18.** Hough memo. **19.** Interview with John Horton, December 18, 1973. **20.** Interview with Kenneth Clark, December 17, 1973. **21.** Interview with Robert Aldrich, March 14, 1974. **22.** Marton caption to photograph of unused scene (n.d.). Mel Gussow, *Don't Say Yes Until I Finish Talking* (New York: Doubleday, 1971), p. 234. **23.** *Los Angeles Times Calendar,* August 17, 1975, p. 32. **24.** Bartlett interview. **25.** Interview with Cornel Wilde, August 15, 1975. **26.** Ibid. Department of Defense file on *Beach Red.* **27.** Letter from Cornel Wilde to author, November 17, 1977. **28.** *Chicago Daily News,* October 9, 1967. *Boston Globe,* August 31, 1967, p. 34. **29.** Interview with John Huston, March 27, 1974. John Huston interview with Robert Hughes in Robert Hughes, ed., *Film: Book 2, Films of Peace and War,* (New York: Grove Press, 1962). Barach interviews. **30.** Interview with Fred Zinnemann, March 5, 1974. Interview with Stanley Kramer, February 8, 1974. **31.** Interview with Linda Gottlieb, June 15, 1973. **32.** Interview with Terry Sanders, August 17, 1975. Undated Sanders memo with list of Army objections, Author's File.

CHAPTER TEN

1. Interview with Sy Bartlett, February 9, 1974. Letter from Navy Department to Columbia Pictures, September 10, 1941. Letter from Navy Department to Will Hays, Motion Picture Association, September 11, 1941. National Archives, Record Group 95, Box 80. **2.** Department of Defense file on *Close Encounters of the Third Kind.* Baruch interviews. **3.** *New York Times,* April 21, 1963, sec. II, p. 7. *Newsweek,* February 3, 1964, pp. 79–80. *Variety,* February 27, 1963, p. 11. **4.** Ibid. **5.** Arthur Ragen, *Image of the Military as Portrayed in Three Novels Made into Screenplays since 1958* (Unpublished Masters Thesis, Boston University, 1964). **6.** Interview with Max Youngstein, April 5, 1974. **7.** Ibid. **8.** Eugene Burdick and Harvey Wheeler, *Fail Safe* (New York: McGraw Hill, 1962). **9.** Youngstein interview. **10.** Ibid. Sidney Hook, *The Fail Safe Fallacy* (New York: Stein & Day, 1963). In this short book, Hook refutes the basis of Burdick's novel. **11.** Youngstein interview. **12.** Interview with Robert Aldrich, March 14, 1974. **13.** Youngstein interview. **14.** Ibid. **15.** Ibid. **16.** Ibid. **17.** *New York Times,* September 16, 1964, p. 36. **18.** Letter from Hubert Humphrey to Bill Moyers, September 28, 1964, Johnson Library. **19.** Letter from Bill Moyers to Lyndon Johnson, September 29, 1964, Johnson Library. **20.** *New York Times,* September 16, 1964, p. 36. **21.** Youngstein interview. **22.** Interview with Raymond Bell, April 8, 1975. **23.** Ibid. **24.** Ibid. **25.** Ibid. **26.** *Variety,* October 17, 1962, p. 5. **27.** Ted Sorenson, *Kennedy* (New York: Harper & Row, 1965), pp. 606–607. **28.** Gerald Pratley, *The Cinema of John Frankenheimer* (New York: A. S. Barnes, 1969), p. 114. **29.** Ibid. **30.** Ibid. **31.** Letter from Donald Baruch to the Motion Picture Association of America, August 16, 1963, Author's File. **32.** Ibid. **33.** Letter from Edward Lewis to author, October 25, 1976. **34.** Fletcher Knebel, "The White House Was Pleased, The Pentagon Was Irritated," *Look,* November 19, 1963, p. 95. **35.** Interview with James Harris, February 25, 1974. Interview with James Poe, August 4, 1975. **36.** Department of Defense Memo, June 14, 1964, James Poe Papers. **37.** Ibid. *Daily Variety,* August 3, 1964, p. 4. **38.** Ibid. **39.** Harris interview. Interview with Captain J. D. Ferguson, April 5, 1975. **40.** Ferguson interview. **41.** Letter from Richard Widmark to author, December 7, 1977. **42.** Ferguson interview. **43.** Ibid. **44.** Ibid. **45.** Bell interview. Ferguson interview. Letter from James Harris to author, October 13, 1977. **46.** *Hollywood Citizen-News,* December 30, 1964. **47.** Arthur Hiller, *Los Angeles Times Calendar,* January 3, 1965. **48.** *Newsweek,* November 2, 1964, p. 96. Chayefsky interview. Heller interview. **49.** Hiller, *Los Angeles Times Calendar.* **50.** Ibid. **51.** Arthur Knight, *Saturday Review,* October 24, 1964, p. 29. James Altieri, *Los Angeles Times Calendar,* January 10, 1965. **52.** Interview with Melvyn Douglas, October 27, 1975. **53.** Ibid. **54.** Interview with Martin Ransohoff, March 1, 1974. Drew Pearson Column,

References

Washington Post, January 27, 1965, p. D-15. **55.** Douglas interview. **56.** *New York Times*, October 28, 1964, p. 51.

CHAPTER ELEVEN

1. Interview with Paul Tibbets, July 7, 1976. **2.** Interview with John Wayne, February 7, 1974. **3.** Letter from Jack Valenti to Lyndon Johnson, January 6, 1966, Johnson Library. **4.** Letter from Herbert Hirschman to Los Angeles Branch, Office of Chief of Information, Department of the Army, January 24, 1963, DoD Files. **5.** Interoffice Memo, Public Information Division, Department of the Army, February 4, 1963. Memo from Chief, Public Information Division, Department of the Army to Assistant Secretary of Defense for Public Affairs, Production Branch, Audio-Visual Division, February 14, 1963. Letters from Donald Baruch to Raymond Bell, December 20, 1965 and June 23, 1966. DoD Files. **6.** Interview with Robin Moore, December 22, 1974. *Daily Variety*, May 10, 1967. p. 7. Interview with David Wolper, July 21, 1975. **7.** Letter from John Wayne to Lyndon Johnson, December 26, 1965, Johnson Library. **8.** Interview with Norman Hatch, June 4, 1976. **9.** Memo from Michael Wayne to "Green Beret" File, March 1, 1966, DoD Files. Interview with Michael Wayne, August 5, 1975. **10.** Letter from John Wayne to Bill Moyers, February 18, 1966, Johnson Library. **11.** Letter from John Wayne to Donald Baruch, April 18, 1966, DoD Files. **12.** Letter from John Wayne to Bill Moyers, April 18, 1966. Letter from John Wayne to Senators, April 15, 1966, Johnson Library. **13.** *Time*, June 9, 1967, p. 67. **14.** Letter from Michael Wayne to Donald Baruch, May 27 and June 30, 1966, DoD Files. **15.** Letter from Michael Wayne to Donald Baruch, August 19, 1966, DoD Files. **16.** Ibid. Memo from Donald Baruch to "Green Beret" File, September 1, 1966, DoD Files. **17.** Memorandum to Directorate for Information Services OASD (PA) from the Department of the Army, September 14, 1966, DoD Files. **18.** Letter from James Barrett to Donald Baruch, September 24, 1966, DoD Files. **19.** Michael Wayne interview. Donald Baruch to "Green Beret" File, September 29, 1966, DoD Files. **20.** Michael Wayne interview. **21.** Michael Wayne to "Green Beret" File, November 8, 1966. Letter from James Barrett to Army Office of Information, December 30, 1966, DoD Files. **22.** Letter from Michael Wayne to Donald Baruch, February 2, 1967. Army Comments on "Special Forces Movie Script" (n.d.), forwarded on February 15, 1967, DoD Files. **23.** Michael Wayne's copy with handwritten approval of changes, Author's File. Letter from Michael Wayne to Donald Baruch, March 1, 1967. Letter from Daniel Henkin to Michael Wayne, March 30, 1967, DoD Files. **24.** Enclosure to Henkin Letter, "Requested Changes for Screenplay" *The Green Berets* (n.d.). Henkin letter, March 30, 1967, DoD Files. **25.** Michael Wayne interview. *New York Times*, September 27, 1967, p. 41. **26.** Baruch interviews. *Daily Variety*, June 23, 1967, p. 1. **27.** Interview with Ray Kellogg, July 3, 1975. *Time*, June 9, 1967, p. 67. **28.** Kellogg interview. Letter from Michael Wayne to Donald Baruch, June 1, 1967, DoD Files. **29.** Memorandum from Office of Chief of Public Information, Department of the Army to Directorate for Defense Information, OASD (PA), June 8, 1967, DoD Files. Kellogg interview. Michael Wayne interview. Interview with Colonel William Byrnes, June 25, 1975. **30.** Baruch interviews. **31.** Michael Wayne interview. Kellogg interview. Byrnes interview. Joan Barthel, "John Wayne, Superhawk," *New York Times Magazine*, December 24, 1967, pp. 4, 22. **32.** *The Hollywood Reporter*, June 26, 1969, p. 1. Ibid., June 27, 1969, pp. 1, 4. *Motion Picture and Television Daily*, June 30, 1969, pp. 1–2. Michael Wayne interview. **33.** Interview with David Halberstam, March 29, 1975. **34.** Michael Wayne interview. **35.** Interview with John Wayne, *Playboy*, May 1971, p. 88. **36.** *New York Times*, June 20, 1968, p. 49. **37.** *Hollywood Reporter*, June 17, 1968, p. 3. **38.** *Congressional Record*, June 26, 1968, pp. 18856–18857. **39.** *New Yorker*, June 29, 1968, pp. 24–27. **40.** Interview with General Edwin Simmons, April 22, 1977. **41.** Michael Wayne interview. **42.** Letter from Warner Brothers to author, April 7, 1977. **43.** John Wayne, *Playboy*, p. 88.

CHAPTER TWELVE

1. Interview with David Wolper, July 21, 1975. United Artists, Trailer for *The Devil's Brigade*, 1968. **2.** Interview with Ken Hechler, May 30, 1975. **3.** Letter from Colonel Cecil Roberts to author, September 30, 1976. **4.** Hechler interview. **5.** Wolper interview. **6.** Ibid. *Los Angeles Times*, April 10, 1968, part V, p. 20. *Congressional Record*, June 30, 1969, pp. 17897-98. **7.** Ibid. **8.** Letter from General James Gavin to author, November 9, 1977. **9.** Interview with Frank McCarthy, March 4, 1974. *Film and Television Daily*, October 8, 1968, pp. 1-2. **10.** Donald Baruch, Memos for the Record, November 16, 18, 21, 1960, DoD Files. **11.** McCarthy interview. **12.** Ibid. **13.** Letter from law firm of Luce, Forward, Hamilton and Scripps to Twentieth Century Fox, September 11, 1961, DoD Files. **14.** Letter from Arthur Sylvester to Army Chief of Information, September 14, 1961, DoD Files. **15.** Letter from firm of Bingham, Dana, and Gould to Arthur Sylvester, December 13, 1961. Ibid., February 26, 1962. Letter from Frank McCarthy to Donald Baruch, February 5, 1962. Letter from Donald Baruch to Twentieth Century Fox, June 18, 1963. Letter from Public Affairs Office to Twentieth Century Fox, July 30, 1963. DoD Files. **16.** *Hollywood Reporter*, March 12, 1965, p. 1. *Daily Variety*, March 12, 1965, p. 1. **17.** Dwight Eisenhower, *At Ease*. (Garden City, N.Y.: Doubleday, 1967), p. 261. **18.** McCarthy interview. **19.** Letter from General Eisenhower to Frank McCarthy, January 6, 1966, Eisenhower Library. **20.** Letter from Frank McCarthy to Dwight Eisenhower, January 18, 1966, Eisenhower Library. **21.** Letter from Donald Baruch to Twentieth Century Fox, July 2, 1965, DoD Files. **22.** Letter from firm of Bingham, Dana, and Gould to Secretary of Defense Robert McNamara, August 10, 1965, DoD Files. **23.** Letter from Office of General Counsel, Department of Defense to firm of Bingham, Dana, and Gould, August 23, 1965, DoD Files. **24.** *Daily Variety*, July 26, 1965, p. 1. *New York Times*, April 21, 1971, p. 47. Letters from Twentieth Century Fox to Donald Baruch, June 1, 1966 and November 23, 1966, DoD Files. **25.** McCarthy interview. Letter from Twentieth Century Fox to Donald Baruch, August 7, 1967, DoD Files. **26.** *New York Times*, March 29, 1970, sec. II, p. 15, and April 21, 1971, p. 47. **27.** *New York Times*, April 21, 1971, p. 47. **28.** Interview with Fred Zinnemann, March 5, 1974. **29.** *New York Times*, April 21, 1971, p. 47. McCarthy interview. **30.** Letters from Edmund North to author, September 27 and October 10, 1977. **31.** Letter from Edmund North to author, September 27, 1977. Letter from Twentieth Century Fox to DoD Public Affairs Office, December 23, 1968. Letter from General Paul Harkins to author (n.d.). McCarthy interview. **32.** Interview with Edmund North, March 10, 1974. Letters from Edmund North to author. **33.** McCarthy interview. **34.** *New York Times*, April 21, 1971, p. 47. McCarthy interview. **35.** Letter from George C. Scott to author, December 21, 1977. **36.** *Variety*, March 10, 1971, pp. 1, 47. *New York Times*, March 29, 1970, sec. II, p. 15. George C. Scott, *Playboy*, April 1971, p. 140. **37.** Ibid. **38.** *Sunday London Times*, April 13, 1969, p. 11. **39.** Letter from Scott to author. **40.** Ibid. **41.** Ibid. **42.** Letter from Harkins to author (n.d.). **43.** *Film and Television Daily*, October 8, 1968, p. 2. **44.** McCarthy interview. **45.** *Patton* Press Book (n.d.). *Variety*, July 9, 1969, p. 19. *Dallas Morning News*, August 31, 1969. **46.** Ibid. McCarthy interview. **47.** *Los Angeles Herald Examiner*, June 18, 1969. McCarthy interview. Interview with Karl Malden, August 9, 1975. **48.** McCarthy interview. **49.** *Los Angeles Times Calendar*, May 18, 1969, p. 18. *Patton* Production Notes (n.d.). **50.** North interview. Letter from North to author, September 27, 1977. **51.** Letter from Scott to author. **52.** Letter from North to author, September 27, 1977. **53.** Ibid. **54.** Ruth Patton Totten, "All I Could Hear was Georgie Patton's Body Lies a-Moulderin," *San Francisco Sunday Examiner & Chronicle*, April 11, 1970. **55.** *New York Times*, February 8, 1970, pp. 1, 26. **56.** *New Yorker*, January 31, 1970. pp. 73-74. **57.** Ibid. *New York Times*, February 5, 1970, p. 33. **58.** David Frost interview with Richard Nixon, November 20, 1977. **59.** Hugh Sidey, "The Presidency," *Life*, June 19, 1970, p. 23. Interview with Hugh Sidey, November 29, 1976. **60.** Quoted in Sidey, "The Presidency."

References   **CHAPTER THIRTEEN**

1. *Commentary*, September 1970, p. 20. *New York Times*, March 22, 1970, sec. II, p. 19.
2. *Hollywood Citizen News*, February 20, 1970, p. 20. **3.** Interview with George C. Scott, *Playboy*,
April 1971, p. 192. **4.** Baruch interviews. **5.** Richard Corliss, ed., *The Hollywood
Screenwriters* (New York: Avon Books, 1970), pp. 142–143. **6.** Interview with Robert Altman, *Playboy*, August
1976, p. 62. **7.** *New York Times Magazine*, June 20, 1971, p. 47. "Sixty Minutes," January 22, 1977.
8. Interview with Joseph Heller, *Playboy*, June 1975, p. 60. **9.** Interview with Frank Tallman,
August 21, 1975. Interview with John Calley, August 21, 1975. **10.** *Time*, June 15, 1970, p. 66.
11. Interview with Mike Nichols, in Joseph Gelmis, ed., *The Film Director as Superstar* (New York:
Doubleday, 1970), pp. 268–269. Interview with Andrew Marton, July 21, 1975. **12.** *Time*, June 15,
1970. Joseph Heller, *Playboy*, pp. 60–61. **13.** Joseph Heller, *Catch-22* (New York: Simon & Schuster,
1961), p. 440. **14.** Joseph Heller, *Playboy*, p. 72. **15.** Ibid. **16.** *New York Times*, June 25, 1970, p. 54.
The New Republic, July 4, 1970, p. 22. **17.** Nichols, *Director as Superstar*, p. 268. **18.** *Time*, June 15,
1970, p. 66. **19.** *New York Times*, October 4, 1970, sec. II, p. 1. **20.** Vincent Canby, "The Last
Tycoon," *New York Times Magazine*, March 17, 1968, p. 33. **21.** *New York Times*, June 16, 1969, p.
A-24. *Washington Post*, June 16, 1969, p. 10. **22.** *Los Angeles Times Calendar*, June 15, 1969, p. 22.
23. Interview with Elmo Williams, March 18, 1974. **24.** Ibid. **25.** Williams interview. **26.** Ibid.
"Final Information Guide," Twentieth Century Fox, (n.d.). **27.** Ibid. **28.** *Air Classics*, February
1969, pp. 15, 20, 62, 66. Interview with George Watkins, December 10, 1977. **29.** Williams interview. "Department of Defense Assistance to Twentieth Century Fox Corporation in the Production
of *Tora! Tora! Tora!*," 1969. **30.** Williams interview. **31.** Interview with Richard Fleischer, June 26,
1975. **32.** Navy Memo, August 9, 1967, DoD Files. **33.** Confidential Navy Memo, October 15, 1968,
DoD Files. **34.** Fleischer interview. **35.** Navy Memo, August 9, 1967, DoD Files. **36.** "Review of
Support Provided By the Department of Defense to the Twentieth Century Fox Film Corporation for
the Film *Tora! Tora! Tora!*" by the Comptroller General of the United States, February 17, 1970.
37. Letter from Daniel Henkin to Twentieth Century Fox, February 2, 1968, DoD Files. **38.** Letter
from Twentieth Century Fox to Department of Defense, August 1, 1968. Letter from Department of
Defense to Twentieth Century Fox, August 27, 1968. DoD Files. **39.** Watkins interview. Interview
with Phil Goulding, April 4, 1975. **40.** Navy Memo to Phil Goulding, October 11, 1968, DoD Files.
41. Goulding interview. **42.** Interoffice Memorandum to Phil Goulding, October 8, 1968, DoD Files.
43. Confidential Navy Memo, October 15, 1968, DoD Files. **44.** Letters from Jack Valenti to Phil
Goulding and to Clark Clifford, October 3, 1968, DoD Files. **45.** Letter from Jack Valenti to Clark
Clifford, October 23, 1968, DoD Files. Interview with Jack Valenti, November 11, 1977. **46.** Letter
from Phil Goulding to Clark Clifford, October 24, 1968, DoD Files. **47.** Interview with Paul Nitze,
April 8, 1975. "Sixty Minutes," May 13, 1969. **48.** Department of Defense Project Officer's Final
Report, July 1969, DoD Files. **49.** Watkins interview. Stafford interview. Fleischer interview.
Williams interview. **50.** Stafford interview. Fleischer interview. **51.** "Sixty Minutes," May 13,
1969. **52.** Ibid. **53.** Letter from Phil Goulding to Department of the Navy, November 27, 1968. Letter
from Twentieth Century Fox to Department of Defense, November 29, 1968, DoD Files. As part of its
response to Bill Brown's request for research information in preparing his program (Bill Brown to
Navy Department, March 24, 1969), the Department of Defense Office of General Counsel ruled on
April 2, 1969 that the correspondence between Twentieth Century Fox and the military could be
made available to CBS under the Freedom of Information Act. A CBS-TV van containing television
equipment to cover the Apollo landing was also aboard the *Yorktown*. *Navy Times*, October 7, 1970,
p. 29. *Honolulu Star-Bulletin*, December 13, 1968, p. B-1. *Navy Times*, December 13, 1968.
54. Stafford interview. Baruch interviews. Department of Defense file on *Tora! Tora! Tora!*.
55. GAO Report of February 17, 1970. Military Operations Subcommittee Staff Memorandum of
Committee on Government Operations, House of Representatives, December 1969.

CHAPTER FOURTEEN

1. Letter from Gerald Ayres to Donald Baruch, August 17, 1972, DoD Files. **2.** Baruch Memo for the Record, August 24, 1972. Defense Department Memo to Navy, August 25, 1972. Gerald Ayres to Don Baruch (n.d.), before August 28, 1972, DoD Files. **3.** Navy Memo to DoD Public Affairs Office, September 7, 1972, DoD Files. **4.** Letter from Gerald Ayres to Navy Department, October 2, 1972, DoD Files. **5.** Ibid. **6.** Letter from Navy Department to Gerald Ayres, October 19, 1972, DoD Files. **7.** Interview with Admiral John Will, May 22, 1974. **8.** *New York Times*, September 5, 1976, sec. II, p. 9. **9.** Interview with Lieutenant William Harding, April 11, 1974. Interview with Mark Rydell, September 3, 1975. Interview with Don Baruch, August 16, 1976. **10.** Baruch interview. **11.** Ibid. Interview with Jack Valenti, November 11, 1976. **12.** Rydell interview. **13.** Interview with Major Ron Gruchey, July 25, 1975. **14.** Baruch interview. **15.** Interview with Mark Robson, July 2, 1975. **16.** Interview with Frank McCarthy, March 4, 1974. **17.** Ibid. **18.** *Hollywood Reporter*, September 7, 1972, p. 3. McCarthy interview. **19.** Navy Memo, December 19, 1974, DoD Files. **20.** Navy Memo, December 30, 1974, DoD Files. **21.** *Cleveland Plain Dealer*, January 25, 1976, sec. 4, p. 2. **22.** Ibid. **23.** *New York Times*, June 19, 1976, p. 11. **24.** *Time*, July 12, 1976, p. 49. **25.** Letter from Taylor Mills to author, November 11, 1977. **26.** *Pacific Stars and Stripes*, September 4, 1974, p. 14. **27.** Robert Sherrod, Memo to self, August 13, 1977, Author's File. **28.** *Time*, July 4, 1977, p. 54. **29.** Sherrod Memo to self. **30.** *Time*, June 13, 1977, p. 92. **31.** Letter from James Gavin to author, November 9, 1977. **32.** Interview with General Edwin Simmons, November 11, 1977 (General Simmons is a Marine historian and author). Interview with Walter Pforzheimer, October 24, 1977. (Mr. Pforzheimer was an intelligence officer during World War II, worked as an intelligence officer for the Central Intelligence Agency, knew Cornelius Ryan, had read *A Bridge Too Far*, and was personally familiar with the battlefields in the Netherlands.) **33.** *Los Angeles Times Calendar*, September 19, 1976, p. 40. *New York Times*, June 13, 1976, sec. II, p. 1.

CHAPTER FIFTEEN

1. Interview with Francis Ford Coppola, *Playboy*, July 1975, p. 65. **2.** *Los Angeles Times Calendar*, June 6, 1975, pp. 37, 39. **3.** Baruch interviews. Defense Department Memo to Department of the Army, June 2, 1975, DoD Files. **4.** Baruch interviews. **5.** Department of Defense Memo, June 2, 1975, DoD Files. **6.** Interview with General H. Gordon Hill, May 19, 1977. Army Memo to DoD Public Affairs Office, June 16, 1975, DoD Files. **7.** Ibid. Baruch interviews. **8.** Ibid. **9.** Department of Defense Memo for the Record, July 9, 1975, DoD Files. **10.** Ibid. Baruch interviews. **11.** *Variety*, September 3, 1975, p. 27. *Washington Star*, September 13, 1975, p. A-2. Letter from Fred Roos to the Pentagon, December 30, 1975, DoD Files. **12.** "Background of DoD Association with Francis Ford Coppola and *Apocalypse Now*," (n.d.). DoD letter to Francis Ford Coppola, November 18, 1975. DoD Files. **13.** Letter from Fred Roos to Department of Defense, December 30, 1975. "Coppola and Apocalypse Now." **14.** Letter from Fred Roos to William Greener, April 9, 1975. Telegram from Francis Ford Coppola to Donald Rumsfeld, April 22, 1976. DoD Files. **15.** Telegram from Donald Rumsfeld to Francis Ford Coppola, April 29, 1976, DoD Files. **16.** Mailgram from Coppola to Rumsfeld May 3, 1976. Telegram from Greener to Coppola, May 11, 1976. Telegram from Roos to DoD, May 17, 1976. Telegram from DoD to Roos, May 25, 1976. Telex from Roos to Greener, June 1, 1976. DoD Files. **17.** Telegram from William Greener to Fred Roos, June 9, 1976, DoD Files. **18.** Telegram from Coppola to President Jimmy Carter, February 12, 1977, DoD Files. **19.** DoD Memos, May 10 and 20, 1977, DoD Files. **20.** Letter from William Hoffman to DoD, June 3, 1977. Letter from Donald Baruch to William Hoffman, June 21, 1977. Letter from William Hoffman to Donald Baruch, June 24, 1977. DoD Files. **21.** *Cleveland Plain Dealer*, July 9, 1976. **22.** *Wall Street*

References   *Journal*, May 25, 1977, p. 1. **23.** *Los Angeles Times Calendar*, October 23, 1977, p. 32. **24.** *Newsweek*, June 13, 1977, p. 63. **25.** Francis Ford Coppola, Memorandum to his staff, April 30, 1976, published in *Esquire*, November 1977, p. 196. **26.** *Wisconsin State Journal*, June 27, 1976, sec. 4, p. 12. **27.** DoD Memo to Lawrence Gordon Productions, August 22, 1975, DoD Files. **28.** *Wall Street Journal*, November 1, 1977, p. 1. **29.** Ibid. **30.** Production Notes for *Go Tell The Spartans*, Mar Vista Productions, 1977. **31.** *Rolling Stone*, Tenth Anniversary Issue, December 15, 1977, p. 87.

PHOTO CREDITS

★

Cover photo
Cornel Wilde. Also appears on page 179.

Chapter 1

Page xxii, copyright © 1977 United Artists Corporation. **Page 3**, Air Force Still Photo Archives. **Pages 3 and 4**, The Museum of Modern Art/Film Stills Archive. **Page 5 (top)**, J. P. Willcox Collection, Marine Corps Museum. **Page 5 (bottom)**, copyright 1927 Paramount Famous Lasky Corporation. **Page 6**, Twentieth Century Fox and The Museum of Modern Art/Film Stills Archive. **Page 7**, L. E. Fribourg. **Page 11**, Andrew Marton. **Page 12 (left)**, Paul Harkins. **Page 12 (right)**, Edward Stafford.

Chapter 2

Pages 14, 18, 21, 22 and 23, The Museum of Modern Art/Film Stills Archive. **Page 17**, Bruce Arnold. **Pages 27, 28, 31 and 32**, copyright 1927 Paramount Famous Lasky Corporation

Chapter 3

Pages 34 and 49, William Collier. **Page 39**, National Archives Still Photo Collection.

Chapter 4

Page 52, National Archives Still Photo Collection. **Pages 57 and 60**, Air Force Still Photo Archives.

Chapter 5

Pages 70, 75, 77 and 78, Western Historical Research Center, University of Wyoming. **Page 79**, Air Force Still Photo Archives. **Page 83**, Twentieth Century Fox and The Museum of Modern Art/Film Stills Archive. **Page 86**, The Museum of Modern Art/Film Stills Archive. **Page 89**, Twentieth Century Fox.

Chapter 6

Page 90, George Kleine Collection/Library of Congress Motion Picture Section. **Page 93 (top left)**, Still Photo Archives/Marine Corps Historical Center. **Page 93 (top right)**, J. P. Willcox Collection/Marine Corps Museum. **Page 93 (bottom)**, L. E. Fribourg. **Pages 96, 99 and 100**, Leatherneck Magazine. **Page 105**, Delbert Mann.

Chapter 7

Pages 110, 121 and 124, Fred Zinnemann. **Page 115**, M. U. Beebe. **Pages 131 and 134**, James C. Shaw. **Page 138**, official U.S. Navy photograph.

Chapter 8

Pages 140, 146, 151 (left), 155, 156, 159 and 160, Andrew Marton. **Page 143,** Dan Gilmer. **Page 148 and 151 (right),** Ken Annakin.

Chapter 9

Pages 164 and 168, Delbert Mann. **Page 167,** Oscar Porter/U.S. Army photograph. **Page 169,** official U.S. Navy photograph. **Pages 173 and 177,** Andrew Marton. **Page 178,** National Archives Still Photo Collection. **Pages 181 and 182,** Cornel Wilde. **Pages 184 and 185,** Terry B. Sanders.

Chapter 10

Page 193, Delbert Mann. **Page 199,** Meryl Rosen. **Page 206,** copyright © 1965 Columbia Pictures Corporation, all rights reserved. **Pages 209 and 210,** James Harris.

Chapter 11

Page 212, The Museum of Modern Art/Film Stills Archive. **Page 219,** official Marine Corps photograph. **Page 220,** copyright 1927 Paramount Famous Lasky Corporation. **Page 225,** Herbert Hetu. **Page 227,** Delbert Mann. **Page 228,** *Insight,* alumni magazine of Case Western Reserve University.

Chapter 12

Pages 236 and 250, Paul Harkins. **Page 238,** David Wolper. **Pages 239 and 240,** Cecil E. Roberts. **Page 247,** Frank McCarthy Papers/George C. Marshall Research Foundation. **Pages 253, 258 and 261,** Twentieth Century Fox. **Page 263,** Twentieth Century Fox and The Museum of Modern Art/Film Stills Archive.

Chapter 13

Pages 266, 274, 279, 283 and 286, Edward Stafford.

Chapter 14

Pages 288 and 301, Edward Stafford. **Page 295,** George Watkins.

Chapter 15

Page 308, Newsweek/Maureen Orth. **Page 313,** Francis Ford Coppola. **Page 318,** Mar Vista Productions. **Page 320,** copyright © 1977 Action One Film Partners, Ltd.

INDEX

Boldface numerals indicate illustrations.

Guildford College
Learning Resource Centre

Please return on or before the last date shown
This item may be renewed by telephone unless overdue